Amsterdam: Sovereignty and Legal Agency of a 17th-Century Commercial City

Legal History Library

VOLUME 87

The titles published in this series are listed at *brill.com/lhl*

Amsterdam: Sovereignty and Legal Agency of a 17th-Century Commercial City

Edited by

Dave De ruysscher and Janne E. Nijman

BRILL | NIJHOFF

The open access publication of this book was funded by the Swiss National Science Foundation.

Project CaPANES (ERC Consolidator Grant 101044356, Dave De ruysscher) and Gieskes-Strijbis Foundation (Janne Nijman).

ISSN 1874-1793
ISBN 978-90-04-76110-0
ISBN 978-90-04-76153-7 (PDF)
DOI https://doi.org/10.1163/9789004761537

Library of Congress Control Number: 2026939990

Brill and Koninklijke Brill BV are part of De Gruyter Brill.
www.degruyterbrill.com

Questions about General Product Safety Regulation: productsafety@degruyterbrill.com

Cover illustration: View of the city of Amsterdam with Neptune and Artemis, the latter referring to the image of the Capitoline Wolf with Romulus and Remus (c. 1700) – Municipal Archives Amsterdam, *Tekeningen en prenten*, 010097005158.

Contents

Acknowledgments

The idea for this volume was conceived before the Covid pandemic, during conversations in the context of the workshop series "*Recht in Amsterdam en in de Republiek, 17e eeuw*". These inspiring sessions, which brought together legal historians and lawyers from Dutch and Belgian universities, made us realize once more how seventeenth-century Amsterdam is neglected as an object of research in (international) legal history. We issued a call for papers "Law and Governance of a Global City: 17th-Century Amsterdam" and selected papers for a first seminar. Covid delayed the process. We have been fortunate to have gathered together a group of dedicated authors, and we are all the more thankful that they pulled through with us. Ultimately, we managed to discuss our papers at a workshop held in Amsterdam on 24 and 25 September 2020, and at a follow-up workshop, organized in Amsterdam on 9 and 10 December 2022. We are grateful to the teams of the T.M.C. Asser Instituut and the Amsterdam Center for International Law – Ellyssia van der Werf – for their work to organize and facilitate these workshops. The discussions contributed to the quality of the chapters in this volume, and we are indebted to all the researchers who took the time to participate. John Eyck checked the language of this volume.

We are furthermore grateful to Brill-de Gruyter for recognizing that the urban lens in legal history, while still not commonly used, has great potential.

The work on this volume also benefitted from external funding. The presentations and papers of Dave De ruysscher and Maurits den Hollander were supported by the ERC-funded projects CLLS (Starting Grant 714759) and CaPANES (Consolidator Grant 101044356). Janne thanks the Gieskes-Strijbis Foundation for supporting her contribution to this volume and the workshops. This volume is one of the results of the research project *The Global City: Challenges, Trust and the Role of Law, Then and Now*.

We hope that this volume will spark more research on the legal history of seventeenth-century Amsterdam.

Dave De ruysscher/Janne E. Nijman
Tilburg-Brussels/Amsterdam-Geneva

Figures and Tables

Figures

Tables

Notes on Contributors

Tessa de Boer
(Leiden University) obtained a PhD in economic history at Leiden University in 2025. Her dissertation, entitled "A Truth Universally Acknowledged: Dutch Investment in French Colonial Resources in the Eighteenth Century" discussed the commercial and financial interests of Dutch merchants in the French West Indian colonies. She currently works as a program and policy officer at the NWO (Dutch organization for scientific research). Alongside this, she has held the position of Data Curator at the Amsterdam Municipal Archives. In addition, she is editor and secretary of the *Tijdschrift voor Zeegeschiedenis*, the journal of the Dutch Association for Maritime History.

Arjan de Koomen
(University of Amsterdam) is a lecturer of Southern European Art of the 14th–18th Century (Italian, French, Spanish) and European sculpture 14th–19th Century, a position he has held since 2006. His teaching area also covers Historiography of Art of the Early Modern Period and Technical Art History. He previously worked as a curator at the Rijksmuseum, as an inspector at the Dutch Ministry of Culture and as a research fellow in Florence, alongside various teaching appointments in art history. He has published multiple articles in art-history journals such as *Kunstschrift* and *Simiolus*.

Dave De ruysscher
(Tilburg University, Vrije Universiteit Brussels) is a professor of legal history. He obtained a PhD-degree at Leuven University in 2009, on the commercial legislation and legal practice in the Antwerp law court in the late sixteenth and in the seventeenth century. In 2016, he was awarded an ERC Starting Grant for the project "Analyzing Coherence in Law through Legal Scholarship". In 2022, he obtained an ERC Consolidator Grant for the project "Causal Patterns of Economic Sovereignty", which analyzes the economic sovereignty of early modern cities and what this can learn us looking at present-day sovereignty issues.

Marc de Wilde
(University of Amsterdam) is a professor of jurisprudence with a focus on legal history and the history of legal thought. His research interests include Hugo Grotius, the relation between natural law and empire and the regulation of religious diversity in the seventeenth century. He is a lecturer in

European Legal History, Legal Philosophy and History of Legal Theory. He is also chairman of the board of the Grotiana Foundation. His research has been published in multiple journals such as the *Journal of the History of International Law* and *History of European Ideas.*

Maurits den Hollander
(Tilburg University) is an assistant professor of Legal History, specializing in legal, institutional and socio-economic developments of medieval and early modern Europe. He published *Court, Credit, and Capital Amsterdam's Insolvency Legislation in the Dutch Golden Age* (CUP, 2025) and co-authored the book *Palace of Commerce* with Bob Wessels (Verloren, 2025). He is currently leading the Starter Grant project *Professionals and the People* which analyzes the influence of urban officials on law- and policymaking and good governance and accountability in late medieval and early modern Dutch cities.

Johannes W. Flume
(Paris Lodron University of Salzburg) is a professor of Private Law. His research is focused on civil and corporate law, capital markets and comparative legal history, with a strong emphasis on economic history. He obtained his doctorate in law in 2008 at the Universities of Regensburg in Cologne and Bonn. His research has been published in leading journals in Germany, France, Austria and the UK. His recently published book, *HGB Synopse* (de Gruyter, 2025, co-authored with Matthias Lüdeking), examines the development of German-Austrian commercial law over the past 200 years, alongside a synoptic presentation of the codification texts.

Victor Le Breton-Blon
(University of Bretagne Sud) is an assistant professor (*maîte de conférences*) of legal history. He wrote a dissertation on bills of exchange in eighteenth-century Bordeaux. His research interests focus on European Legal History, business law and social and economic history. He recently started as a post-doctoral researcher at the University of Paris Nanterre. He previously worked as a lecturer and researcher at the University of Bretagne Sud. His teaching area covered the History of Institutions, Banking Law and the History of the Law of Obligations. Prior to that he has held positions as lecturer and research assistant at the universities of Bordeaux and Lille-II.

Janne E. Nijman
(University of Amsterdam, Geneva Graduate Institute of International and Development Studies) is a professor of History and Theory of International

Law at the University of Amsterdam and a professor of International Law at the Geneva Graduate Institute. She is affiliated as a fellow with the Amsterdam Center for International Law (ACIL). Formerly, she served as Chair and Academic Director of the Executive Board of the T.M.C Asser Institute for International and European Law in The Hague. In 2021, together with Helmut Aust (Freie Universität Berlin), she co-edited the *Research Handbook on International Law and Cities*, which received the ESIL Collaborative Book Prize in 2022.

Vincent van Hoof
(University of Nijmegen) is Associate Professor of Legal History at Radboud University and a researcher at the Business and Law Research Centre. He teaches and publishes on (the legal history of) property law, the law of secured credit, and insolvency in Europe. He obtained his PhD in 2015 with a dissertation entitled "General Security Rights in Historical Perspective". In 2016 he completed the Grotius specialization program in Financing and Securities. He has held the position of Vice-Dean of Education at the Radboud University at the faculty of Law since February 2022.

Bart Wallet
(University of Amsterdam) is a full professor of Jewish studies: early modern and modern Jewish history. He obtained his PhD with a dissertation on eighteenth-century Yiddish historiography from Amsterdam. His research interests include Jewish urban cultures, Jewish diasporic practices and policies of belonging. He also teaches in Hebrew, Jewish Studies and Middle Eastern Studies at the University of Amsterdam. In addition, he lectures at the liberal rabbinical seminary Levisson Institute and at the Jewish Educational Center Crescas. He has published several books on Jewish history and the history of religion, as well as numerous articles in national and international journals. He co-edited and -authored *Reappraising the History of the Jews in the Netherlands* (Liverpool, 2021).

Introduction

Dave De ruysscher and Janne E. Nijman

From 1500 to 1700 Amsterdam grew from 12,000 to 200,000 inhabitants. Urbanization and globalization went hand in hand. During the seventeenth century, the Dutch Republic (and in particular its province of Holland) was the most urbanized region in Europe. The influx of Jewish newcomers, *Conversos* and Protestant refugees from the Southern Netherlands brought international commerce to Amsterdam. Amsterdam became a city of arrival, a city of immigrants, with implications both for urban life and for the city's economy. As Maarten Prak observed, "economic prosperity […] acted as both a cause and a consequence of immigration".[1] With the diversity of new Amsterdammers came widespread commercial relations and interests, and Amsterdam developed further as one of the main hubs of the global economy. These developments required the city's authorities to find the right balance between their legislation and innovations in the context of global trade.

This volume addresses the legal and institutional history of the city of Amsterdam against these changing backgrounds. It focuses on the agency and autonomy of the city, in connection to its political economy, from a combined local, regional and international perspective.

The economic history of Amsterdam has received ample interest, but less attention has been paid to the city's governance and legal institutions. In the eighteenth, nineteenth and early twentieth centuries, legal and institutional historians wrote about the development of Amsterdam's governing bodies and institutions.[2] Many of the source editions published in these eras are still valuable.[3] However, this is less the case for the narratives and analysis in

1 M. Prak, "Urbanization" in H.J. Helmers and G.H. Janssen (eds.) *The Cambridge Companion to the Dutch Golden Age*, Cambridge, 2018, 15–31, at 17.

2 A. Bredius, *Amsterdam in de zeventiende eeuw*, The Hague, 1897–1904, 3 vols.; J. Gouw, *Geschiedenis van Amsterdam*, Amsterdam, 1879–1894; P.H.J. van der Laan, "De autonomie van Amsterdam in de middeleeuwen", *Holland* 1 (1969), 147–164; J. Wagenaar, *Amsterdam, in zyne opkomst, aanwas, geschiedenissen, voorregten …*, Amsterdam, 1762–1768, 13 vols.

3 J.C. Breen, *Rechtsbronnen der stad Amsterdam, The Hague*, 1902; C. Pijnacker Hordijk, "De oudste willekeuren van Amsterdam", *Nieuwe Bijdragen voor Rechtsgeschiedenis en Wetgeving* (1879), 1–57. More recently, important source publications saw the light of day as well: P.H.J. van der Laan (ed.), *Oorkondenboek van Amsterdam tot 1400*, Amsterdam, 1975; P.D.J. van Itterson and P.H.J. van der Laan, *Resoluties van de vroedschap van Amsterdam, 1490–1550*, Amsterdam, 1986; also P.H.J. van der Laan, and R. Bessem, *Resoluties van de vroedschap van Amsterdam, 1551–1565*, Hilversum, 2008.

the older literature. How the municipal institutions contributed to the city's economic expansion has only been studied partially. Recently, economic and legal historians have reconsidered the importance of law and institutions, as underpinning the economic growth of Amsterdam.[4] However, it remains largely unclear whether Amsterdam's administrators were always pursuing economic goals. Many institutions that had existed before Amsterdam's growth were maintained. Policies towards newcomers could touch upon other issues than economic ones, such as religion, for example. Moreover, it is evident that Amsterdam's commercial rise resulted in challenges for its government. The rights of different groups of immigrants had to be combined with a goal of urban peace. The efforts of legislating the communities within the city were upon closer inspection not always inspired by equality. Some groups received more rights than others.[5]

Merchants made use of the city's legal infrastructure, which supported their practices, as is detailed in the recent literature mentioned. However, the complex institutional landscape of the Dutch Republic has not often been connected with Amsterdam's political economy. Economic and political historians have studied the institutions of the county of Holland,[6] in which Amsterdam was located, though less frequently in connection to the city or its

4 M. den Hollander, "Restoring trust and credit through innovative governance in 17th-century Amsterdam", *Tijdschrift voor rechtsgeschiedenis* 89 (2021), 481–499; O. Gelderblom, *Cities of Commerce. The Institutional Foundation of International Trade in the Low Countries, 1250–1650*, Princeton, 2013; S. Go, "The Amsterdam Chamber of Insurance and Average: A New Phase in Formal Contract Enforcement (Late Sixteenth and Seventeenth Centuries)", *Enterprise & Society* 14/3 (2013), 511–543; C.M. In't Veld, "Was there a rule of law in early modern Amsterdam? Mercantile customary law as a test", *Hague journal on the rule of law*, 15(2) (2023), 263–282.

5 Slavery was not institutionalized in the city but could exist in the private sphere. See K. Fatah-Black and M. van Rossum, "Slavery in a "Slave-Free Enclave". Historical Links between the Dutch Republic, Empire, and Slavery, 1580s-1860s", *WerkstattGeschichte* 66 (2015), 55–74, at 58–59; M. Ponte, "'*Al de swarten die hier ter stede comen*'. Een Afro-Atlantische gemeenschap in zeventiende-eeuws Amsterdam", *TSEG-The Low Countries Journal of Social and Economic History* 15/4 (2018), 33–62; B. Wallet, "Rembrandt's Other Jews: The Amsterdam Ashkenazim in the Seventeenth Century" in M. Knotter and G. Schwartz (eds.), *Rembrandt Seen through Jewish Eyes*, Amsterdam, 2024, 71–88. See also the chapters by Marc de Wilde and Bart Wallet in this volume.

6 Th. de Nijs and E. Breukers, *Geschiedenis van Holland tot 1572*, Hilversum, 2002, 2 vols.; M. Prak, "The Dutch Republic City-State Culture (17th–18th Centuries)" in *A Comparative Study of Thirty City-State Cultures: An Investigation Conducted by the Copenhagen Policy Centre*, Copenhagen, 2000, 343–358; J.L. Price, *Holland and the Dutch Republic in the Seventeenth Century. The Politics of Particularism*, Oxford, 1994; M. 't Hart, "Cities and State-Making in the Dutch Republic, 1580–1680", *Theory and Society* 18/5 (1989), 663–687; J.D. Tracy, *Holland under Habsburg Rule 1506–1566: The Formation of a Body Politic*, Berkeley,

commercial importance. As for any European city in the early modern era, Amsterdam's institutional constellation in the seventeenth century had largely been created in the Middle Ages, when the city was small. Therefore, the city's governance structures were strongly embedded in the institutions of Holland. The city was represented in the States-Provincial of Holland, the consulting body in which most cities of the province had a seat. Moreover, the jurisdiction of the municipal court of Amsterdam was subjected to the Court of Holland in The Hague, which heard appeals brought against its verdicts.[7] And yet, whether the economic transformations of the city impacted its institutional networks in the province and Republic has for all intents and purposes not been studied.[8] Therefore, it remains largely an open question to what extent the city had the agency often attributed to it, and with regard to how decision-making processes developed in the pluralist context of both the province and the Republic.

Furthermore, it is largely unknown which discourse on governance prevailed in the city of Amsterdam in the seventeenth century, in relation to the economy and the city's international aura. Merchants flocked to the city, which made it a central node in European and Atlantic business networks.[9] Investments were made in the Amsterdam-dominated Dutch East India Company (1602), which controlled territories overseas. The globalization in which the city and its inhabitants took part had no doubt effects on the city's governance and self-portrayal, but these consequences have not been analyzed thus far. Did Amsterdam consider itself as the 'capital' of the Republic, which officially would be the case only from 1808? Did Amsterdam's leaders make use of the city's economic weight to change the institutional equilibriums that existed within Holland and the Republic? Did the new *ius naturae et gentium* doctrine of the seventeenth century, which was closely connected to the creation of a Dutch colonial empire, have an impact on how the urban leaders presented the city?

1990; J.P. Ward, *The cities and States of Holland (1506–1515): a participative system of government under strain*, unpublished PhD thesis Leiden University 2001.

7 On the Court of Holland, see M.-Ch. Le Bailly, *Procesgids Hof van Holland, Zeeland en West-Friesland*, Hilversum, 2008.

8 For some notions, see M. van Tielhof, "Een open economie, in voor- en tegenspoed. De economische ontwikkeling van Holland" in *Geschiedenis van Holland, 1572–1795*, vol. 2, Hilversum, 2002, 135–179, at 162–168.

9 See e.g. in this context, C. Antunes, "On Cosmopolitanism and Cross-Culturalism: An Enquiry into the Business Practices and Multiple Identities of the Portuguese Merchants of Amsterdam" in F. Bethencourt (ed.), *Cosmopolitanism in the Portuguese-Speaking World*, Leiden, 2017, 23–39.

This volume aims to provide initial answers to the issues mentioned. It is inspired by recent developments in the disciplines of economic history, legal history, international law, and the history of international relations. Over the past two decades, economic historians have put more effort into the analysis of institutional frameworks and governance.[10] Legal historians have rediscovered the history of commercial law and its supporting institutions. There is new attention for the local law of mercantile cities as well.[11] In international legal scholarship, the turn to critical history came with a focus on how international law developed in service of the expansion of global trade, (commercial) empire, and colonization.[12] Within the history of international law, cities have gained in interest.[13] There is a clear shift away from the state as sole entity of importance towards other institutional entities and bodies.[14] In addition, diplomatic practices originating in cities are highlighted more, including

10 New Institutional Economics was begun in the 1970s. Noble Prize laureates Douglas North (1993), Daron Acemoglu (2024) and James Robinson (2024) have used historical arguments in their scholarship regarding the relationship between law, institutions and economic growth. See, for example, D. North, *Institutions, Institutional Change and Economic Growth*, Cambridge, 1990; D. Acemoglu and J.A. Robinson, *Why Nations Fail*, New York, 2012. For the influence of NIE on economic history and a critical assessment, see G.D. Libecap, "The New Institutional Economics and Economic History", *The Journal of Economic History* 57 (2002), 718–721; S. Ogilvie, "'Whatever is, is right'? Economic institutions in pre-industrial Europe", *The Economic History Review* 60 (2007), 649–684.

11 One can refer to the ERC Grant project CaPANES, which studies economic sovereignty of commercial cities in the period of c. 1450–c. 1620 (ERC Consolidator Grant 101044356, 2023–2027), and ERC Grant project MICOLL, which analyzes the dispersal of merchant terminology in networks between the commercial cities of Genoa, Venice, Nuremberg and Lübeck (ERC Consolidator Grant 101002084, 2021–2025).

12 See e.g. B. Kingsbury and B. Straumann, "The State of Nature and Commercial Sociability in Early Modern International Legal Thought", *Grotiana* 31 (2010), 22–43; M. Koskenniemi e.a. (eds.), *International law and empire: historical explorations*, Oxford, 2017; M. Koskenniemi, *To the Uttermost Parts of the Earth, Legal Imagination and International Power, 1300–1870*, Cambridge, 2021; A. Orford, *International law and the politics of history*, Cambridge, 2021.

13 See e.g. Part I "International legal Histories and cities" of the *Research Handbook on International Law and Cities*, H.P. Aust and J.E. Nijman (eds.), Cheltenham, 2021, with contributions by V. Hansen, "Chapter 2: Silk Road cities and their co-existing legal traditions"; T. Boestad, "Chapter 3: Legitimizing interurban cooperation in the Middle Ages: the legal system of the Hanse"; S. Lepsius, "Chapter 4: The legal system among Italian city republics"; L. Nuzzo, "Chapter 5: Cities and international law: an imperial perspective". Also, e.g. Luigi Nuzzo on Tianjin: L. Nuzzo, "The Birth of an Imperial Location: Comparative Perspectives on Western Colonialism in China", *Leiden journal of international law* 31 (2018), 569–596.

14 For example, Ph. Stern, *The Company-State: Corporate Sovereignty and the Early Modern Foundations of the British Empire in India*, Oxford, 2012.

when these municipalities were not city-states.[15] Among urban historians, too, alliances and agreements between cities are currently studied more than before.[16]

The chapters that follow thus zoom in on aspects of the legal and political-economic settings of seventeenth-century Amsterdam. In the first three chapters – by Dave De ruysscher, Arjan de Koomen and Janne Nijman, and Tessa de Boer, respectively – the focus is mostly on the legal agency of the city. The chapter by Dave De ruysscher highlights the medieval origins of Amsterdam's institutions and urban institutional culture. Amsterdam was de facto independent from the county of Holland, even though the city's institutions had always been embedded within the comital structures. In the sixteenth century, urban republicanism gained ground, but it did not result in separatism or stark affirmations of urban sovereignty. Also in the 1600s, the leaders of Amsterdam made sure that their actions respected the institutions of the county and the Republic. De ruysscher's chapter argues – rather counterintuitively – that the cautious urban attitudes in Amsterdam's 'Golden Age' can be explained by economic superiority. The city's administrators could play along with the institutional tradition and dominate in the facts. As a result, there was no need for the city to claim more jurisdiction or formal sovereignty.

Arjan de Koomen and Janne Nijman offer an interpretation of the cosmological iconography of Amsterdam City Hall and its sculptures by situating it in the development of the legal-political ideas of its times. The building, which was designed by Jacob van Campen (d. 1657) and inaugurated in 1655, is analyzed for its symbolic meaning and in reference to humanist and legal thought. De Koomen and Nijman argue that many parts of the city hall reflect the new science of *ius naturae et gentium*, for which Hugo Grotius (d. 1645) was so important, as well as humanist ideas that considered cities as being part of as well as in touch with the cosmic order. Their account maintains that the city of Amsterdam accepted rule by the universal laws of nature (directly), and that guidance by these laws would serve urban harmony and universal peace. While some have argued that Amsterdam City Hall was all about visualizing

15 H. Leira and B. de Carvalho, "The Intercity Origins of Diplomacy: Consuls, Empires, and the Sea", *Diplomatica* 3 (2021), 147–156; R. Marchetti, *City Diplomacy: From City-States to Global Cities*, Ann Arbor, 2021.

16 J.P. Huffmann, "Urban Diplomacy: Cologne, the Rhenish League (1254–1257) and the Rhenish Urban League (1381–1389)", *Anales de la Universidad de Alicante. Historia Medieval* 19 (2015–2016), 193–219; R. Mordekai Makleff, "Inter-Urban Alliances and the Archives of Legitimacy in the Southern Low Countries, 1250–1450", *Past & Present*, 268/1 (2025), 3–44. See also, supra in footnote 13, Boestad, "Chapter 3".

an Amsterdam-centric world in which its local government boasted of its global reach and riches, De Koomen and Nijman contend that Van Campen's emphasis on the importance of law and justice for the good government of the city is extended through the cosmological iconography beyond the limits of local law. The city hall depicts Amsterdam's subjection to the universal law of nature and nations, which should guide and constrain the government, judiciary, and citizenry of Amsterdam – a powerful seafaring and trading global city nonetheless.

Tessa de Boer explores the theme of diplomats in seventeenth- and eighteenth-century Amsterdam. She argues that the city had agency in several regards, even though diplomacy was considered a matter that resorted under the States General in The Hague. The implementation of immunities regarding diplomatic agents was carried out at the local level, for instance, meaning that the Amsterdam administrators could decide practical matters on their own. Moreover, due to Amsterdam's economic importance, the city did in fact host diplomatic agents (albeit of lower rank, with ambassadors concentrated in The Hague). De Boer therefore stresses that the status and rights of diplomatic actors in Amsterdam was ambiguous and contested, and that rules referring to them developed in interaction between on the one hand cities – and the city of Amsterdam in particular – and the central level of government on the other.

The next four chapters delve into municipal policies and institutions and how they developed in relation to the economic activities and scenes of the burgeoning city. Maurits den Hollander explains how the *Desolate Boedelskamer* (Insolvency Chamber) was established in the middle of the seventeenth century as a municipal institution. The decision of the Amsterdam administrators to institute this chamber was meant to stimulate accords between insolvent debtors and their creditors. The strategy of concentrating negotiations in a municipal body was an example of the restrictive attitudes towards property rights; in addition, the backing by the municipal authorities, as well as the professionalization of the Chamber and its protocols, helped to foster trust among economic actors, along with the enforcement of these accords. As a result, the institutional innovation of the Insolvency Chamber counterbalanced reticence regarding accords, which in the seventeenth century were not accepted in many countries.

Victor Le Breton-Blon demonstrates the attractiveness of Amsterdam's financial market in the seventeenth and eighteenth centuries. The development of the Amsterdam Exchange and its Exchange Bank soon supported a vibrant ecosystem of bills of exchange, one in which older practices and rules were adjusted. The Amsterdam financial procedures helped to turn the bill of exchange into a more abstracted instrument. There was no direct intervention from the city's rulers; rather, practices condoned by the municipal leaders developed spontaneously.

Johannes Flume analyzes the emergence of *rescontre* at the Amsterdam Bourse. This practice entailed the settlement of derivatives, which developed from the practice of existing contracts on future deliveries before their due date. As a result, contracts received a sale price, which fluctuated. The technique of *rescontre* was highly sophisticated and helped to optimize contractual performance. As was the case for practices surrounding bills of exchange, these developments were created in the Bourse and not with active assistance from the city's leaders.

Vincent van Hoof investigates the municipal leaders' reservations towards renewal in rules on security interests. No priority was granted to later special hypothecs, even when the *prior tempore* rule changed in the county of Holland. The city actively sought to protect its traditional approach against the new rules that were introduced in Holland. It was felt that priority of subsequent special hypothecs was fraud-sensitive, and therefore the city's administrators discouraged legal change that would favour contractual flexibility in security interests. General hypothecs were considered as effective hypothecs, even though they encompassed all goods of the debtor, even future ones. This condition confirms what can be derived from the chapters of Den Hollander and Le Breton-Blon. Property rights were approached more strictly than contractual rights (*in personam* rights). The Insolvency Chamber was set up to prevent forced sales of assets, which inevitably would result in – at least partial – losses for the creditors. The administrators of the city stated that mercantile papers only encompassed claims *in personam* and, as a result, the rules relating to these papers could develop more freely. Active interventions on the part of the Amsterdam leaders mainly served to protect property rights against contractualization, less to facilitate financial instruments. Conservatism clearly existed in this regard: the rules on property and collateral were not amended but maintained.

From the four chapters mentioned, it is evident that the policies of the Amsterdam authorities did not always directly facilitate trade and finance. Their approaches show they condoned emerging mercantile practices and techniques, but at the same time resisted any hollowing out of the existing system of property rights and security interests. Implicit approval of innovations was common (for bills of exchange and forward contracts, for example, a minimum of municipal rules applied). While the city's commerce globalized, grew in volume and sparked innovation, the city authorities were required to maintain control.

Similar concerns of oversight existed with regard to immigration and the co-existence of communities in the city. Thousands migrated to Amsterdam; by the mid-1600s, one third of the city's population was born elsewhere. Many having Jewish roots came from Eastern Europe and the Iberian peninsula, often with a stopover in the Southern Netherlands, and they sought refuge in a city having a reputation for tolerance. This welcoming approach was indispensable to Amsterdam's economic growth and the development of its global trade relations. At the same time, the influx and growth of population also created social tensions that challenged the municipal government. The city's administrators needed to address the city's rapid expansion and the changes that came with it. The attitude of the "*gevestigden*",[17] the native Dutch Amsterdammers, was rather ambivalent. On the one hand, they embraced the economic opportunities and networks that came with the newly arriving traders and merchants. On the other hand, they often opposed equal rights of the new Amsterdammers to participate in city life, the guilds or the municipal government.[18] However, even with a distinction of "we and them" in play, Amsterdam was a multicultural city in which Amsterdammers lived relatively peacefully together.[19] Differentiations between *gevestigden* and foreigners, but also between the richer classes and the poorer immigrants, lasted throughout the seventeenth and eighteenth centuries. The city's government at times stipulated regulations but there was not a city policy on immigration and integration.

In this volume, two chapters examine the regulations on Jews in Amsterdam. Marc de Wilde demonstrates that the 1616 municipal regulations on Jews in the city were not as severe as has often been thought, even though Amsterdam in this regard was stricter than other cities. The city supported the private practice of Jewish religion, and strict rules were not always implemented. The Amsterdam administrators refrained from fierce interpretations when drafting these regulations, only condemning specific behaviour, while allowing other practices.

Bart Wallet shows how the Ashkenazi community in Amsterdam gradually emerged as a distinct Jewish entity, known as the High-German Jewish Nation. It developed between 1635 and 1642, alongside the established Portuguese congregation. Although the founders of the Ashkenazi community brought

17 See e.g. E. Kuijpers and M. Prak, "Gevestigden en buitenstaanders" in W. Frijhoff & M. Prak (Eds.), Geschiedenis van Amsterdam 1578–1650. Centrum van de wereld. Amsterdam, 2004, 189–240.

18 Ibid.

19 Ibid., 223.

governance models and practices from German-speaking regions, the Portuguese congregation – along with the political frameworks of early modern Amsterdam – significantly influenced the development of the Amsterdam Ashkenazi congregation's own governance structures. The chapter contends that the community's governance and membership policies closely mirrored the practices of the city itself. In addition, it shows how the communal autonomy of the High-German Jewish Nation developed in the seventeenth century and how its own forms of jurisdiction functioned.

When setting all the above off against the problem of the city's autonomy, it is evident that Amsterdam's powers were in fact quite considerable, even though they formally existed within the institutional trappings of the Dutch Republic. In the sixteenth and seventeenth centuries, sovereignty as a concept was debated and in flux. In the context of the Dutch Republic, it has commonly been understood as distributed between the States General and the States of the provinces.[20] In Grotius' work we find a discussion of divided (or relative) sovereignty.[21] And it is generally acknowledged that within the Republic, urban autonomy was high.[22] However, all this did not translate into any formal recognition of urban sovereignty; the city of Amsterdam remained loyal to the States General and the States-Provincial of Holland. Yet Amsterdam also made these institutional structures work for that loyalty.

In economic matters, the agency of the Amsterdam administrators was most self-evident. Practices at the Amsterdam Bourse were monitored by the city's government; they could be condoned or prohibited, but there was no resorting to the States General in this respect. Moreover, decisions taken at the higher, central level of government in the Dutch Republic were not merely implemented but rather interpreted and brought in line with practice in the city of Amsterdam. This coordination marked the city's de facto authority to decide even on matters that legally were under the jurisdiction of the States General. All this invites further analysis of the practical normative culture of jurisdiction and sovereignty, in particular with reference to mercantile cities, and of the development of the law of nations through the engagement of a city such as Amsterdam. The chapters in this volume subscribe to the understanding that sovereignty in the Republic was layered, fluid and pragmatic. They add considerable nuance to the common understanding of sovereignty as a

20 G. de Bruin, "De soevereiniteit in de republiek: een machtsprobleem", *Bijdragen en Mededelingen betreffende de Geschiedenis der Nederlanden*, 94 (1979), 27–40, at 28–33.

21 H. Grotius, *De Jure Belli ac Pacis* (1625), J. Brown Scott and F.W. Kelsey (eds.), Washington, 1995, 123 and following. (book I.III.XVII).

22 J. Israel, *The Dutch Republic: Its Rise, Greatness, and Fall, 1477–1803*, New York, 1995, 278–279.

monolithic representation of clearly delineated levels of government. City governments were not merely filling in gaps left by 'higher' authorities but stood in a reciprocal relation to these authorities. This connection was also translated into unwritten norms on jurisdiction, as pertained to administrative culture, and which allowed for leeway for cities.[23] They were as important as doctrinal rules of *potestas* and *imperium*. Analysis of the normative approaches towards jurisdiction in practice is an open field, but it will undoubtedly see detailed analysis in the future. Similarly, further research into how exactly the local Amsterdam legal developments related to the interests of the city in global commerce and to extra-European expansion is highly promising and called for, as is research into how these interests shaped the development of international law.

23 See, for example, D. De ruysscher, *The city as networked agent: towards a new legal history*, Tilburg, 2023, which argues for a broader understanding of sovereignty of cities, as encompassing symbolic and mirrored sovereignty.

CHAPTER 1

Hiding in Plain Sight: Sovereignty and the City of Amsterdam (Sixteenth–Seventeenth Centuries)

Dave De ruysscher

1 Introduction[1]

This chapter analyzes the legal self-image of Amsterdam. Amsterdam was part of the county of Holland but had franchise rights as a city as well. Yet the city of Amsterdam was not a city-state. This status invites the question as to what extent in the seventeenth century the legal and economic powers of Amsterdam were reconciled when the city was at its commercial zenith. Did the city boast authority in reference to its mercantile importance? If that was the case, was the sovereignty of Amsterdam factual rather than legal? Or did the municipal administrators increase the autonomy of the city in legal terms as well?

It will be argued that the Amsterdam administrators were relatively modest, for they did not often portray Amsterdam as an independent city. Even though there were some instances in which the Amsterdam leaders attempted to extend their jurisdiction, for the most part cooperation was sought with the other cities of the county and the institutions of Holland, which was a deliberate and functional strategy, serving the city's interests. The institutional complexity of the county of Holland and of the Dutch Republic allowed the leaders of the city to wield the power that came with the affluence of trade, silently but surely. Presenting an image of Amsterdam as one of the cities of Holland served its leaders well in playing out its factual prominence.

2 The Oldest Components in the Legal 'City-Ness' of Amsterdam

The oldest mention of *Amestelledamme* dates from 27 October 1275. In a charter on that date, Count of Holland Floris V (d. 1296) granted the inhabitants of Amsterdam (*homines manentes apud Amestelledamme*) toll freedom in the

1 I'd like to thank Maurits den Hollander, Femke Gordijn and Janne Nijman for their comments on an earlier version of this chapter.

entire county.[2] This charter came five years after Floris V separated Amstelland, the region to which Amsterdam belonged, from the Land of Utrecht (the so-called *Sticht*). This latter area was the territory under the rule of the bishop of Utrecht. By then, Amsterdam was already a fairly large settlement, located on the east bank of the Amstel river. Amsterdam had come into existence over the course of the twelfth century and derived its name from a dam built for protection against floods.[3] The charter mentioned above did not formally establish any rights of franchise but went strongly in that direction. Elsewhere in Holland, too, the count tolerated jurisdiction for towns and communities, even without a formal charter of liberty.[4]

In spite of its size, in the thirteenth century Amsterdam was not an important city. Utrecht, Dordrecht and Haarlem had more weight in economic terms. Slowly, however, the city grew. Its strategic location, near the mouth of the Vecht and along the Zuiderzee, meant that ships carrying goods from the Baltic increasingly concentrated on Amsterdam.

In tandem with this economic attraction, the city received more rights, privileges that also accrued in response to dynastic disputes. Amsterdam was initially dominated by the Van Amstel family. This family leased tolls on the Vecht and came into conflict with the bishop of Utrecht, the lessor of the tolls. Floris V removed the Van Amstels from power. However, the lords of Amstel resisted after their subjugation and eventually succeeded in killing the count. In 1296, Amsterdam again became part of the *Sticht* of Utrecht.[5]

A few years later, Holland and Utrecht ended up in the same family, of the Avesnes. On 21 May 1300, John II of Hainault (d. 1304), count of Holland, pledged to his brother Guy of Avesnes the property of the perpetrators of Floris V's death, which included Amstelland and thus also Amsterdam.[6] Quite soon after that date Guy, who was also bishop of Utrecht, was inaugurated as city lord in Amsterdam. On that occasion he handed out an official charter, stipu-

2 Municipal Archives of Amsterdam, *Archief van de Burgemeesters* (inv. 5054), 70.

3 G. Mak, *Amsterdam: A Brief Life of the City*, London, 2010, 26.

4 C.M. Cappon and H. van Engen, "Stad door stadsrecht? De betekenis van de stadsrechtverlening voor de stadjes Goedereede (1312), Brielle (1330 en 1343), Geervliet (1381) en Brouwershaven (1403)", *Jaarboek voor Middeleeuwse Geschiedenis* 4 (2001), 168–188; P. Henderickx, "Graaf en stad in Holland en Zeeland in de twaalfde en vroege dertiende eeuw" in R. Rutte and H. van Engen (eds.), *Stadswording in de Nederlanden: op zoek naar overzicht*, Hilversum, 2008, 47–62.

5 For these episodes, see Th.A.A.M. Amstel, *De heren van Amstel, 1105–1378. Hun opkomst in het Nedersticht van Utrecht in de twaalfde en dertiende eeuw en hun vestiging in het hertogdom Brabant na 1296*, Hilversum, 1999, 135–152.

6 Amstel, *De heren van Amstel*, 167–168; P.H.J. van der Laan, "De autonomie van Amsterdam in de middeleeuwen", *Holland* 1 (1969), 147–164, here 149–150.

lating the jurisdiction of Amsterdam.[7] The charter was the first tangible symbol of the franchised rights of the city.

After the death of Guy of Avesnes on 29 May 1317, Amstelland and Amsterdam passed from the *Sticht* of Utrecht to the county of Holland. Count William III of Holland (d. 1337) had made an end to the reign of Guy as bishop. William had quarreled with Guy ever since the latter had reversed the rights of the Utrecht guilds, which had been obtained following an uprising in 1304.[8] The integration of Amsterdam into Holland now proved definitive. On 9 December 1342, William IV (d. 1345), count of Holland, granted a new, more extensive charter,[9] which came about at the initiative of the people of Amsterdam themselves. Indeed, in the early fourteenth century, the city gained more leverage, due to its growing trade. The city's strategic location provided the backdrop for economic prosperity. This had been the case before, but Amsterdam only really rose to prominence when the Hanseatic League began to orient its trade towards the North Sea coasts. Thus, Amsterdam became the main port in the county of Holland and along the Zuiderzee. At the Hanseatic Diet of 1367, Amsterdam formally became a member of the Hanse.[10]

Economic power translated into considerable clout in negotiations. The increased importance of Amsterdam impacted the relation between the count of Holland and the city. In the later Middle Ages, cities guarded their privileges and traditions. However, at the same time, municipal institutions could change. The aforementioned charters of 1300–1301 and 1342 left jurisdiction to the city of Amsterdam, but always in combination with criminal jurisdiction for the lord. Moreover, it was common for the count to have representatives on the council of city administrators (*scabini* or aldermen). Ordinances of the city (so-called *willekeuren*) were voted on by the *scabini*. However, they were promulgated by the count's pro-bailiff (*schout*), who also chaired the meetings of the city council. The pro-bailiff's superior, the bailiff of Amstelland, had the highest authority in criminal matters.[11] And this came together with control over the *scabini*, who were in office for one year only. In the 1342 charter, it was stipulated that municipal bylaws were valid for the term of one year, unless a longer application was explicitly granted.[12] In this

7 F. Ketner, *Oorkondenboek van het Sticht Utrecht tot 1301*, vol. 5, The Hague, 1959, no. 2961. For an analysis of its content, see Van der Laan, "De autonomie van Amsterdam", 149.

8 Mak, *Amsterdam*, 30.

9 P.H.J. van der Laan (ed.), *Oorkondenboek van Amsterdam tot 1400*, Amsterdam, 1975, no. 49.

10 *Hanserecesse*, C. Koppmann (ed.), vol. 1, Leipzig, 1870, 373–376 (no. 413, 19 Nov. 1367).

11 Van der Laan, "De autonomie van Amsterdam", 152.

12 Ibid., 154.

way, municipal law was connected to the legal order of the count. However, the confirmation required for prolongations also meant that the urban administrators could receive support from their lord regarding the measures they wanted to implement further.

In the decades following the 1342 charter, Amsterdam began to present itself increasingly as a free city. However, Amsterdam did not cast itself as an autonomous city, but rather as the first of the cities in the county of Holland. Since 1345, in dynastic conflicts, the aldermen of Amsterdam had tried to steer a course allowing them to strengthen their privileges. Amsterdam chose the side of the subsequent Count William V (d. 1389) in the disputes at that time between the *Hoeken* and *Kabeljauwen*. In the course of the fifteenth century, the former, pertaining often to traditional gentry and noble classes, were increasingly outmaneuvered by the latter, who were more oriented towards the cities and trade.[13]

During the decades of our most recent past, the historiographical accounts of the 'democratization' of cities in the thirteenth and fourteenth centuries have changed considerably. Henri Pirenne (d. 1935) considered the uprisings of the 1280s, early 1300s and 1340s as indications of social unrest, viewing the outcomes as moves towards more democratic regimes. When councils of cities were changed and extended in the wake of revolts, historians for a long time viewed it as a development towards deliberative institutions, even to the point that the new councils were deemed precursors of parliaments. Participation was considered one of the goals of those who rose against the governing elites.[14] However, in the 1960s, Raymond van Uytven (d. 2018) broke with this view and labeled the institutional constellation of late medieval cities as "plutocracies". Van Uytven was one of the first to demonstrate that traditional elites still largely dominated the municipal institutions after the uprisings.[15]

Furthermore, the 'freedom' of cities, vis-à-vis their lord, has been exaggerated. Rhetoric on the rise of the 'commune' was only partially translated into institutional change. From the middle of the thirteenth century onwards, it became common to frame demands for institutional adaptations and control of cities' finances in terms of popular sovereignty. Leaders of protests referred

---

13 F. Ketner, *Handel en scheepvaart van Amsterdam in de vijftiende eeuw*, Leiden, 1946, 104–106.

14 H. Pirenne, *Les anciennes démocraties des Pays-Bas*, Paris, 1910.

15 R. Van Uytven, "Plutokratie in de "oude demokratieën der Nederlanden": Cijfers en beschouwingen omtrent de korporatieve organisatie en de sociale struktuur der gemeenten in de late middeleeuwen", *Handelingen van de Koninklijke Zuid-Nederlandse maatschappij voor taal- en letterkunde en geschiedenis* 16 (1962), 373–409.

to the *gemeen*, the people or the *communitas*.[16] Most probably Amsterdam fits this picture of cities where the uprisings were influenced by political strife both at the level of the city and the county. Cities in Holland had few craft and merchant guilds, which has been explained in reference to the late rise of these cities and the cooperative approach of the Holland counts.[17] Yet this phenomenon may instead have had more to do with permeable boundaries between the highest classes in the city. Amsterdam may have been a city where "patricians", who belonged to the oldest elite families in the city, remained in control of active trade longer than elsewhere. Pirenne famously considered the earliest *scabini* of cities to be merchants, and he emphasized their independence as representatives of the city's population vis-à-vis their overlords.[18] At the same time, he also stressed the gap, growing from the thirteenth century onwards, between municipal leaders who turned into aristocrats on the one hand side and active traders on the other.[19]

However, recent research for late medieval cities in the Italian peninsula and the Low Countries demonstrates that within the traditional elites political factions could exist, allying themselves to different guilds or social groups.[20] Therefore, civil unrest did not always follow from social differences. The confrontations between *Hoeken* and *Kabeljauwen* seem to illustrate this point. These parties were factions rather than socially homogeneous groups. The *Kabeljauwen* were more supportive of trade but had nobles in their ranks as well. They were not a party that favoured participatory government or resisted the nobility or elites as such.[21]

Amsterdam's institutional development was most probably the result of occasional clashes between such factions. However, compared to – for exa-

16 J. Haemers and J. Dumolyn, *Communes and Conflict: Urban Rebellion in Late Medieval Flanders*, Leiden, 2023, 50, 64, 146; E. Lecuppre-Desjardin, "Le bien commune en Flandre médiévale: une lutte discursive entre princes et sujets" in E. Lecuppre-Desjardin and A.-L. Van Bruaene (eds.), *De Bono Communi. The Discourse and Practice of the Common Good in the European City (13th-16th c.)*, Turnhout, 2010, 253–266.

17 J. Dijkman, *Shaping Medieval Markets: The Organisation of Commodity Markets in Holland, c. 1200–c. 1450*, Leiden, 2011, 349–351.

18 Pirenne, *Les anciennes démocraties*, 68, 90–91.

19 Ibid., 143–148.

20 Apart from the literature on the county of Flanders in footnote 16, see for an overview of the debates and new insights, also J. Braekevelt, F. Buylaert, J. Dumolyn and J. Haemers, "The Politics of Factional Conflict in Late-Medieval Flanders", *Historical Research* 85 (227), 13–31. With regard to the Italian peninsula, see Ph. Jones, *The Italian City-State: From Commune to Signoria*, Oxford, 1997; Ch. Wickham, *Sleepwalking into a New World. The Emergence of Italian City Communes in the Twelfth Century*, Princeton, 2015.

21 For this nuanced, largely revisionist appraisal, see M.J. van Gent, *"Pertijelike saken": Hoeken en Kabeljauwen in het Oostenrijks-Bourgondische tijdperk*, The Hague, 1994.

mple – cities in Flanders, institutional change was not often considered as an adequate response to unrest. And it seems that friction within the city of Amsterdam was less common than in other cities. One consequence of these factors was the late appearance of the *vroedschap* (the *consilium sapientorum*). The *vroedschap* of Amsterdam was active only in the 1400s, and there are not many traces of earlier 'councillors'.[22] It was typical for cities in Holland that councillors advised the aldermen and could be integrated into a body of council (*raden*, later called *vroedschap*). Councillors were prominent citizens.[23] Alongside the *vroedschap* emerged the Amsterdam *Oud Raad* (Old Council), the members of which were former aldermen. In the fifteenth century, the Amsterdam *vroedschap* participated in the passing of legislation and in rendering judgements on important matters together with the *scabini*.[24] However, as an institution, the most important task of the *vroedschap* was its ceremonial role in the installation of a new city council. After 1477, the sovereign or their representative (typically, the governor-general) picked the names of the new aldermen from a list that had been drafted by the *vroedschap*.[25]

Another indication of modest institutional change as connected to social strife is the late appearance of burgomasters in Amsterdam. These officials did not emerge until the end of the fourteenth century.[26] In many cities, they were installed following revolts, and they supervised the city's council of aldermen since they were deemed to represent the 'commune'. The concept of *communitas* had become particularly strong starting with the end of the thirteenth century. Slowly, it was felt that the body politic of the city was no longer exclusively represented by the council of aldermen. The Amsterdam burgomasters were chosen by the governor-general from a list proposed by the *Oud*

22 Some authors identify two institutional bodies, the so-called *gemeente* and the *vroedschap*. The *gemeente* was probably a general category, not pointing to a specific group or institution. See P.D.J. van Itterson and P.H.J. van der Laan, *Resoluties van de vroedschap van Amsterdam, 1490–1550*, Amsterdam, 1986, 9–10.

23 Research on the *vroedschappen* for cities in Holland is rather limited. A main, yet outdated study is E.A.M. Eibrink Jansen, *De Opkomst van de Vroedschap in enkele Hollandsche Steden*, Haarlem 1927. Recent literature typically covers the period after 1500. See for example also S.A. Lamett, "The *Vroedschap* of Leiden, 1550–1600: The Impact of Tradition and Change on the Governing Elite of a Dutch City", *The Sixteenth Century Journal* 12/2 (1981), 15–42.

24 For examples of judgements, see Van Itterson and Van der Laan, *Resoluties*, 41–42 (1 Sept. 1500). This is one of the latest examples; in the sixteenth century, the *vroedschap* no longer participated in verdicts of the *scabini*. See also P.H.J. van der Laan, and R. Bessem, *Resoluties van de vroedschap van Amsterdam, 1551–1565*, Hilversum, 2008.

25 J.E. Elias, "Geschiedkundige inleiding" in *De vroedschap van Amsterdam*, vol. 1, Amsterdam, 1892, xxxiii–liii.

26 Van der Laan, "De autonomie van Amsterdam", 157.

Raad.[27] The late arrival of burgomasters, as well as the limited access to the *vroedschap* and *Oud Raad*, suggest that the municipal governance structures of Amsterdam were conservative. The continuity and the oligarchic features of the municipal government may reflect lasting dominance and openness of the elites who had controlled the city early on.

3 The City's Growth in the Sixteenth Century

The medieval institutions mentioned above continued to exist in the sixteenth century. However, because of a rise of centralism under the Habsburg monarchs, there was a trend to again increase supervision over the Amsterdam *scabini*.

A bylaw of 1508 regulated the functioning of the city's council of aldermen. It stipulated that proposals of bylaws be made by the *scabini* and sent to the burgomasters for first approval. The pro-bailiff (*schout*) opened the meeting at which the proposals were discussed, after which commissioned aldermen brought a report on the matter. Thereafter, when the vote on the measure was organized, the pro-bailiff voted as well. Upon request of the burgomasters, the pro-bailiff had to cast his vote first, even before the burgomasters gave their opinion on the proposal at hand.[28] The bylaw of 1508 shows that the pro-bailiff could not veto legislation or take the initiative to draft a bylaw. However, he participated in the deliberations and his voice was considered important.

It seems that this vote by the *schout* had emerged slowly. At first, in the fourteenth century, the pro-bailiff had been appointed by the count and most probably – as was the case in other cities – did not have many ties to Amsterdam. The pro-bailiff monitored the aldermen. However, in the middle of the fourteenth century, the pro-baillif's position became weaker and de facto could not veto the legislative initiatives of the *scabini*. The rule in the 1342 charter that *willekeuren* were valid for only one year referred to the autonomy of the aldermen to determine their contents.[29] From the late fourteenth century, the *schout* more commonly was a citizen of Amsterdam.[30] In the

27 Van der Laan and Bessem, *Resoluties*, 10–11.

28 J. Wagenaar, *Amsterdam, in zyne opkomst, aanwas, geschiedenissen, ...*, vol. 12, Amsterdam, 1768, 204–205.

29 See also a charter of 15 March 1388, which explicitly reserved the *scabini* the right of judgement and stipulates that the *schout* only executes the decisions. See van der Laan, "De autonomie van Amsterdam", 152.

30 Van der Laan, "De autonomie van Amsterdam", 152.

1400s, the powers of the *scabini* and burgomasters were considerable. As had been the case before, the pro-bailiff chaired the city council but could not block the approval of proposals. This institutional set-up reveals a growing municipal autonomy of the city of Amsterdam. However, in comparison to other principalities of the Low Countries (in particular, Flanders and Brabant), strife between the cities and their prince, the count, was exceptional in Holland. This situation changed in the later fifteenth century, though. From 1477 onwards, the grip of the sovereign became stronger. The Burgundian dynasty changed the status-quo. The *scabini* were formally appointed and the pro-bailiff was deemed merely an official of the count. The *schout* had to serve the prince's agenda. It was in this context that his participation in deliberations came about. Moreover, in the early sixteenth century, the role of the *vroedschap* decreased as well.[31]

Slowly the earlier institutional *entente* that had existed between the lord and the ruling classes of the city came under pressure. In the 1520s, Amsterdam strongly pushed back against the growing pressure to prosecute Lutherans. The pro-bailiffs of this period were born and raised in Amsterdam. For that reason, they also sided with the burgomasters and *scabini* in their attempts to preserve tolerance in the city.[32] In 1535–1538, all this culminated in Charles V's subjugation of the city council. New aldermen were appointed that stood under close princely control, and for the first time convictions for heresy were pronounced by the Amsterdam *scabini*.[33] One of the outcomes of the process of centralization was a growing portrayal of the city as being de facto autonomous. In the disputes with the central government, the city often referred to its privilege *de non evocando*. This medieval privilege ensured that citizens of cities in Holland had to be tried before the city council of their hometown. The argument was regularly raised against intrusions from the monarch.[34]

The argument of the city's immunity had connections to humanism as well. In the period between *c.* 1520 and *c.* 1580, cities throughout the Low Countries presented themselves as *civitates* or *respublicae*. Moreover, in the course of the 1500s, in the county of Flanders and the duchy of Brabant, the medieval notion

31 Elias, "Geschiedkundige inleiding", xxxiii–liii.

32 A.F. Mellink, *Amsterdam en de wederdopers*, Nijmegen, 1978, 41–42, 56.

33 H.F.K. van Nierop, "De eenheid verbroken, 1522–1566" in *Geschiedenis van Amsterdam: een stad uit het niets (tot 1578)*, Amsterdam, 2004, 313–363, here 337–350. With more detail about the 1530s, is J.J. Woltjer, "Het conflict tussen Willem Bardes en Hendrick Dirckszoon", *Bijdragen en mededelingen betreffende de geschiedenis der Nederlanden* 86/2 (1971), 178–199.

34 For the use of the argument by the States of Holland, see J.D. Tracy, *Holland under Habsburg Rule, 1506–1566. The Formation of a Body Politic*, Berkeley, 1990, 153–154.

of *libertas* acquired new connotations. These had originated in the Italian Renaissance, where the medieval meanings of liberty were supplemented with new ones, many of which were derived from antiquity. In the Middle Ages, *libertas* referred to *immunitas*. It was an immunity granted by a lord, and it implied protection against usurpers. At the same time, the 'immunity' was an exemption from lordly dues; charters stipulating the 'liberty' of communities often provided a special tax regime.[35] In the 1520s, Cornelius Aurelius of Gouda (d. 1531) wrote a tract on *Prosopopoeia Phrisiae* in which he mingled the above-mentioned medieval notion with *libertas* in the sense of freedom. Holland had intervened in Friesland in the war against Guelders. According to Aurelius, Holland had had immunity from taxes since Charlemagne and aimed to protect this 'freedom' when rising against the tyranny of the duke of Guelders.[36]

In the 1420s, Leonardo Bruni (d. 1444) had used *libertas* as a central concept in his *History of the Florentine People*.[37] Bruni referred to the self-control of Florence as a power to defend itself legally and factually against threats from outside. However, Bruni not only mentioned the de facto autonomy of the city or its "freedom" of self-control. *Libertas*, in Bruni's view, was an attribute of the polity. It was the freedom to take part in political life and the city's legal system supported this freedom. Well-known citizens were free to express their opinions and chose who administered the city. *Libertas*, thus, also represented the virtue of the politically engaged citizen in Bruni's writing.[38] Similar concepts had been presented by Bruni in a previous work, a *Laudatio* of the city of Florence, in which he also connected them to the medieval concept of *libertates*. The 'freedoms' of the city were those privileges which citizens could invoke. The emperor recognized these as the city's customs. The city's chartered immunities guaranteed the customs' continued existence.[39]

---

35 In the 1200s, the term *libertas* was clearly resonating with *libertas ecclesiae*-ideas (i.e., the protection of the Church against intrusion from the state), and it referred to shielding against impositions of force and taxations. See, on this concept, K. Pennington, "Libertas Ecclesiae on the Eve of the Reformation", *Bulletin of Medieval Canon Law* 33 (2016), 185–207.

36 K. Tilmans, *Historiography and Humanism in the Holland in the Age of Erasmus. Aurelius and the Divisiekroniek of 1517*, Hilversum, 1988, 58–60.

37 L. Bruni, *Historiarum Florentini populi libri XII e Rerum suo tempore gestarum commentaries*, Florence, 1926. See also L. Bruni, *History of the Florentine People*, ed. and transl. J. Hankins, Cambridge (MA), 2001–2007.

38 For further analysis, see N. Rubinstein, "Florentina libertas", *Rinascimento*, 26/2 (1986), 3–26.

39 L. Bruni, "*Laudatio Florentinae Urbis*" in H. Baron (ed.), *From Petrarch to Leonardo Bruni*, Chicago, 1986, 232–263.

One can find several examples of comparable ideas, connected to *libertas*, in sixteenth-century texts written by legal practitioners in the Low Countries. When such authors described the jurisdiction and political regimes of cities in the Low Countries, they resonated with Italian Renaissance ideas. In 1567, for example, Frans Goethals (d. 1616) wrote a treatise on the "republic" of Bruges,[40] in which he referred to Venice when arguing in favour of autonomy for the city of Bruges. Bruges did not have full legal autonomy. As a city, it had received municipal rights from the count of Flanders; this grant entailed the right to pass bylaws on matters relating to the security, health and economy of the city.

The late fifteenth century saw the introduction of the notion of *emporium* to the Low Countries. The term *emporium* was coined by ancient authors such as Strabo (d. *c.* 25 AD) and Ptolemy (d. *c.* 170 AD). The word (*emporion*, a Greek term meaning market or commercial settlement) suggested a centre for trade. It articulated how specific geographic elements, such as being close to the ocean, drew traders to a port or city. Thucydides (d. *c.* 400 BC) used the concept in these contexts. Moreover, his *History of the Peloponnesian War* describes Corinth as an emporium with a "commercial network" that linked many people and was intimately related to a centrality in shipping routes.[41] Strabo's fascination with emporia is widely recognized. He saw harbours with flourishing markets as natural phenomena, and their economic prosperity was explained by their geographic location – that is, by being close to the sea. Emporium was also used by Strabo to refer to a *Hinterland*, since it was common knowledge that a people's emporium was a certain city or harbour. Consequently, emporium also acquired the connotation of power derived from a centre's economic allure. Successful markets drew customers from a wide radius.[42]

The new terms also found their way to Holland. In 1556, an unknown author published *De situ orbis* by Pomponius Mela (d. *c.* 45 AD) and included commentary. In some of the latter, he referred to Amsterdam as the "*maximum Hollandiae emporium mercatorum*".[43] Around the same time, Roverus Pontanus (d. 1567), a cleric who wrote a chronicle of the first half of the sixteenth century, referred to Amsterdam as an emporium.[44] Other comparable descrip-

40 F. Goethals, *De foelici et infoelici republica, ad senatum Brugensem*, Leuven, 1566.

41 D. Pettigrew, *The Isthmus of Corinth: Crossroads of the Mediterranean World*, Ann Arbor, 2016, 44–46.

42 On these meanings, see M. Gárcia Morcillo, "Patterns of Trade and Economy in Strabo" in D. Dueck (ed.), *The Routledge Companion to Strabo*, London, 2017, 137–149.

43 *Pomponii Melae De situ orbis libri tres*, Paris, 1557, 96.

44 R. Pontanus, *Rerum memorabilium, iam inde ab anno Domini MD ad annum fere LX in rep. christiana gestarum libri quinque*, Cologne, 1559, 253.

tions can be found in Olof Månsson's *Historia de gentibus septentrionalibus* (1555)[45] and in Lodovico Guicciardini's *Descrittione di tutti i Paesi Bassi* (1567).[46] The term *emporium*, in reference to Amsterdam, was typically combined with the observation that the city was frequented by foreign merchants coming from all parts of Europe. Moreover, in an implicit allusion to Thucydides, it emphasized Amsterdam's closeness to the sea. In the *Satisfactie* of 1578, which was the agreement drafted by Stadtholder William of Orange (d. 1581), detailing the rights of Protestants in the city, it was stressed that "navigation and commerce will be exercised freely".[47] This phrase clearly stood in the tradition of urban liberty as it had become defined in the decades before.

In the course of the 1540s and 1550s, the city council of Amsterdam made more frequent use of the city's coat of arms. One example is the famous city landscape drawn by Cornelis Antonisz in 1541, which in the upper right-hand corner describes Amsterdam as a "famous merchant city" (*vermaerde koopstadt*) (Figure 1.1). The drawing pictures the god Neptune holding the city's coat of arms. This was a clear reference to the city's connection to the sea, as pertaining to its commercial attractiveness and power. The above-mentioned notion of *emporium* no doubt was behind linking the city to Neptune. From the 1520s, Amsterdam printers were given a license to add the city's arms to their books.[48] The municipal coat of arms was prominent during the Joyous Entry of Philip, the future Philip II (d. 1598), in 1549.[49] From the 1560s, printers obtained contracts to publish bylaws of the city, featuring the city's arms.[50] The prominent use of the city's coat of arms in publications covering Amsterdam's history or institutions continued into the eighteenth century.[51]

The ideology of city republicanism often went hand in hand with cities' attempts to act autonomously or in symbolic concordance with the sovereign. Cities could consider their actions as representing their overlord, which thus

45 O. Magnus, *Historia de gentibus septentrionalibus*, Rome, 1555, 439.

46 L. Guicciardini, *Description de tous le Pais-Bas*, Antwerp, 1568, 252–253.

47 Art. 14, *Poincten ende articulen vanden Satisfactie* ..., Amsterdam, 1578.

48 One of the first examples dates from 1523; see E.W. Moes, *De Amsterdamsche boekdrukkers en uitgevers in de zestiende eeuw*, Amsterdam, 1896, vol. 1, 247.

49 N. De Roever, "Amsterdamsche boekdrukkers en boekverkoopers in de zestiende eeuw (tot omstreeks 1580)", *Oud Holland* 2 (1884), 68–79, 170–208, at 158.

50 For example, *Ordonnantien ende Willekeuren mitter Clocke binnen der Steede van Aemstelredammen ghepubliceert* (3 March 1568 ns), Amsterdam, widow Jan Ewoutsz.

51 For example, I. Le Long, *Historische beschryvinge van de reformatie der stadt Amsterdam* ..., Amsterdam, 1729; Noordkerk, *Handvesten; ofte Privilegien ende octroyen: mitsgaders willekeuren, costuimen, ordonnantien en handelingen der stad Amstelredam* ..., Amsterdam, 1748.

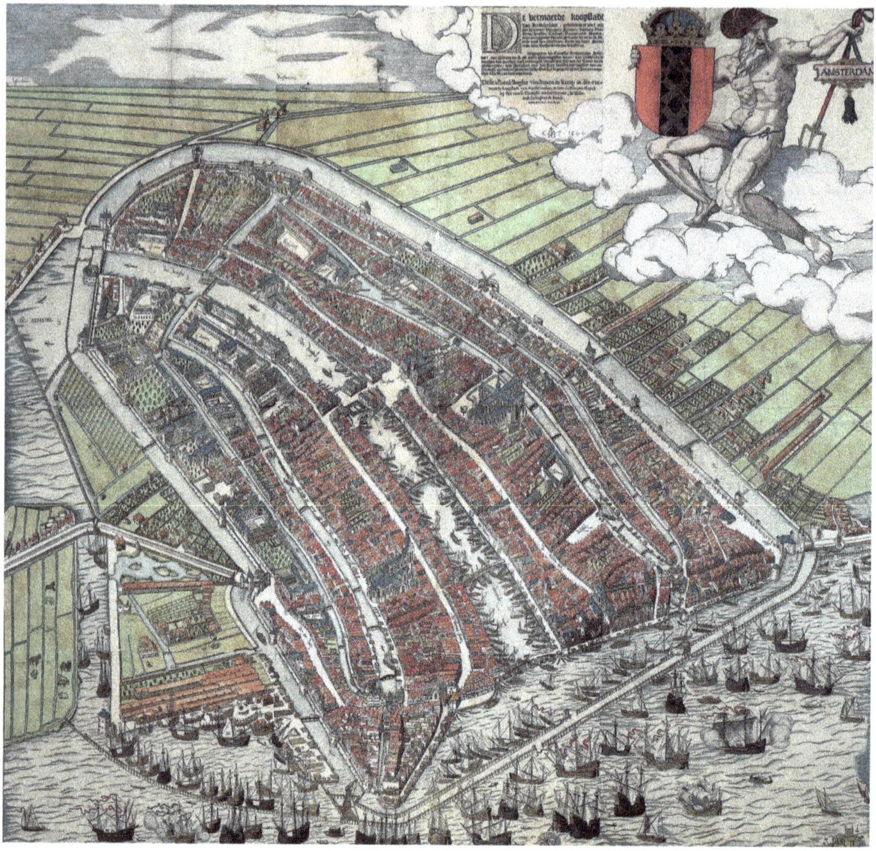

FIGURE 1.1 Cornelis Anthonisz., map of Amsterdam, 1541 – Rijksmuseum Amsterdam, KOG 2684

allowed for some agency. Also, for some topics, in particular with regard to riverine traffic, contacts between cities could take the form of agreements without express confirmation from a 'higher' level of authority.[52] Amsterdam is interesting in this regard because in the seventeenth and eighteenth centuries its administrators refrained from establishing deals with cities outside the Dutch Republic. Correspondence with cities abroad mostly concerned the recognition of citizen rights of foreigners or court cases pending in which a foreigner was defendant.[53] This was a marked difference with, for example,

52 D. De ruysscher, *The City as Networked Agent: Towards a New Legal History*, inaugural address Tilburg University, 2023, 40–49.

53 See the examples in Municipal Archives of Amsterdam, *Archief van de Burgemeesters* (inv. 5054), 41–42 (1594–1794).

sixteenth-century Antwerp. Indeed, Amsterdam typically self-restricted its powers, even though there had been a modest tradition to extend the scope of municipal jurisdiction.[54]

4 Amsterdam's as Holland's Proxy: Navigating a Complex Institutional Landscape

In interactions with the sovereign in the sixteenth century, Amsterdam duly referred to its urban privileges. Before the Revolt, however, instances of strife over infringements on municipal rights, as in the 1520s and 1535–1538, were relatively exceptional. The newly emerging tradition of urban republicanism could coincide with political antagonism but was largely non-political. The new discourses served to augment older notions of municipal rights and government but did not fundamentally change what had existed before. The city sought to protect its rights, but it did not seek to extend its liberties in any direct confrontation with the prince. In a similar vein, the city did not break with the institutions of the county of Holland.

The States-Provincial of Holland had originated in the fourteenth century. By the early 1500s, it was an institution with seven representatives, one being the nobility of the county and the other six delegates from the cities of Dordrecht, Haarlem, Delft, Leiden, Gouda and Amsterdam. The seven members each had one vote. As a result, cities had to negotiate and cooperate in order to reach decisions. The competences of the States of Holland were restricted to consultation, mostly in matters of taxation.[55] Before the Dutch Revolt, the States of Holland were not very powerful. The sovereign or their agent summoned the delegates to convene. As a result, the representative of the Spanish king, the stadtholder, was more prominent and had more authority than the States. The office of stadtholder had been created under the Burgundians in the 1430s. The stadtholder was typically a member of the highest nobility and

54 On this tradition, see D. De ruysscher, "Changes in sovereignty concepts of cities of trade and the impact on diplomatic relations (Low Countries, 15th–16th centuries)" in L. Brunori (ed.), *La dynamique juridique des réseaux marchands: hanses, nations, agences, filiales et comptoirs*, Toulouse, 2023, 83–98.

55 On the States-Provincial of Holland, see Tracy, *Holland under Habsburg Rule*; J.L. Price, *Holland and the Dutch Republic in the Seventeenth Century. The Politics of Particularism*, Oxford, 1994, 122–133; J.P. Ward, *The cities and States of Holland (1506–1515): a participative system of government under strain,* unpublished PhD thesis Leiden University 2001.

had a seat in the council of the Burgundian dukes, and from 1531, in the Council of State. Usually, the stadtholder of Holland was also stadtholder of Zeeland, sometimes combining these positions with that of admiral.[56]

During the Revolt, Amsterdam after a while became one of the cities to join the forces of the States General against the Spanish king. In 1578, the *Alteratie* brought Amsterdam in the anti-Spanish alliance. During the Revolt, the States-Provincial of Holland were one of the leading institutions. In 1572, they accepted that William of Orange, who had been stadtholder until 1567, took up this title again, this time as de facto representative of Holland.[57] The States-Provincial and the stadtholder held each other in check. Besides them, the States General emerged as the assembly of representatives of all provincial states that had joined the Revolt. In 1581, when King Philip II was deposed, the States General represented the sovereignty of the newly established Republic of the Seven Provinces. Even though the seven principalities of the Republic were represented equally, within the States General the delegates of Holland were in fact very important. Each province had one vote. However, the advocate-pensionary (*landsadvocaat*) of the States of Holland became the leader for the delegation of Holland and acquired powers on behalf of the States General in their entirety. The advocate-pensionary became the de facto leader in the external and international affairs of the Republic.

This figure of the *landsadvocaat* had become firmly connected to the cities of Holland in the later fifteenth and early sixteenth centuries. At first, the advocate-pensionary had been the spokesman for the nobility in the States of Holland. Starting with the second half of the 1400s, this picture changed. Since the middle of the fifteenth century, several cities in Holland had allied themselves with the Burgundians, in their conflict with factions of the nobility.[58] In 1444, a coup was instigated by a group of *Hoeken* in Amsterdam. In 1445, Philip the Good (d. 1467) ended this episode, thereby ensuring himself the support of the *Kabeljauwen*. As a result, when in the 1480s cities in Flanders and also Zeeland rose up against Maximilian, Amsterdam was the latter's

56 M. Damen, *De staat van dienst. De gewestelijke ambtenaren van Holland en Zeeland in de Bourgondische periode (1425–1482)*, Hilversum, 2000, 50–61; Price, *Holland and the Dutch Republic*, 134–135; R. Stein, *Magnanimous Dukes and Rising States. The Unification of the Burgundian Netherlands*, Oxford, 2017, 127–130.

57 Price, *Holland and the Dutch Republic*, 135.

58 J.W. Koopmans, *De Staten van Holland en de Opstand. De ontwikkeling van hun functies en organisatie in de periode 1544–1588*, The Hague, 1990, 87–93; H. Kokken, *Steden en staten. Dagvaarten van steden en Staten van Holland onder Maria van Bourgondië en het eerste regentschap van Maximiliaan van Oostenrijk (1477–1494)*, The Hague, 1991, 71–90.

FIGURE 1.2 Imperial crown and the coat of arms of the city of Amsterdam – G. Commelin, *Beschryvinge van Amsterdam* ..., Amsterdam, 1694, 183.

ally. This affiliation resulted in the adornment of the city's coat of arms with imperial insignia, such as the crown (Figure 1.2). Of course, economic growth contributed to Amsterdam's prominence as well. Commerce with the Baltic regions contributed highly to Amsterdam's rise to importance. Leiden, which had been Holland's most prominent economic centre in the thirteenth century, was in serious decline, due to the collapse of its textile industry. Also Haarlem, Delft and Gouda suffered because of setbacks in the dwindling textiles trade.[59]

Not only did Amsterdam have a dominant position, the city also navigated the complex institutional landscape in a clever way. When in the second half of the 1400s it was one of the most important cities of Holland, it nonetheless forged coalitions with the other cities. When the States of Holland were confronted with new demands from the sovereign for taxes, the cities coordinated their resistance. Trade contacts mattered greatly. Therefore Dordrecht, a natural commercial hub at the conflux of several rivers, and Amsterdam joined forces. Also, there are examples of cooperation between the cities along the Zuiderzee in their contacts with foreign powers. In October 1493, Amsterdam and other cities of the "*Waterland*" joined forces and sent letters to France, England and Gelre in order to maintain peace and secure trade.[60] Of course,

59 Tracy, *Holland under Habsburg Rule*, 21–32.
60 Van Itterson and Van der Laan, *Resoluties*, 39–40 (25 Oct. 1493).

every city gained from forming a united front. Amsterdam could obtain concessions or regulation to its favour in exchange for cooperation.[61]

After 1581, Amsterdam pursued a similar tactic with regard to the States General. In the new Republic the city had to seek its position in an even more complex institutional constellation. As had been done before, Amsterdam's administrators did not seize more sovereignty, and they accepted that the *plenitudo potestas* had moved from the Spanish monarch to the States General. There are several examples of new regulations, imposed by the States General, that went against Amsterdam's interests and which were nevertheless accepted. In other instances, exceptions to generalizing laws or new negotiations of treaties were demanded and obtained.[62]

It is indeed striking that after the Revolt, when the city's economic importance reached new heights in the early 1600s, Amsterdam's administrators did not use the opportunity to bolster more independence in legal terms. The city did not portray itself as a city republic, at least not in stronger terms than had been the case since the 1520s.[63] The *scabini* and burgomasters continued to consider the province of Holland, and increasingly also the States General, as the leading entities. Among historians the argument has been made that since the early sixteenth century the county of Holland acted as one entity and that its cities were remarkably unanimous. Most have attributed this unity to the rising pressure of the Habsburg rulers and the external threat of the Gelre duke since the late fifteenth century.[64] However, the rise of Amsterdam was most probably important in this development, as well. When one city thrived, and most of the others suffered economic decline, this situation could have contributed to unity. From the perspective of Amsterdam, a certain generosity

61 On the 1525 prohibition of certain trades in surrounding villages, which was granted to Amsterdam as compensation for its acceptance of a new tax, see P. Knevel, "Vijfde stad in Holland" in M. Carasso-Kok (ed.), *Geschiedenis van Amsterdam. Een stad uit het niets*, vol. 1, Amsterdam, 2004, 388.

62 One example of a demand to negotiate with a foreign power was Amsterdam's petition to the States General regarding tax policies of Bremen in 1612. See *Resoluties der Staten-Generaal*, New Series, vol. 1, The Hague, 1971, 635 (4 May 1612).

63 For example, J.I. Pontanus, *Beschrijvinghe der seer wijt beroemde coop-stadt Amsterdam* ..., Amsterdam, 1614.

64 J. Israel, *The Dutch Republic. Its rise, greatness and fall, 1477–1806*, Oxford, 1995, 170; L. Sicking, "De integratie van Holland. Politiek en bestuur in de Bourgondisch-Habsburgse tijd" in T. de Nijs e.a. (ed.), *Geschiedenis van Holland, deel 1: Tot 1572*, Hilversum, 2001, 259–290, at 273–275. For a critical analysis of this argument, see J. Burgers, "De steden van Holland in oorlog (1506–1515)", *Historisch Tijdschrift Holland* 41/4 (2009), 273–290, here 288–290.

towards its counterpart cities in the county may have been a deliberate strategy to further inflate its importance.

Even so, the Amsterdam leaders did not hesitate to impose their will in the political arena. In the period 1601–1611, Amsterdam's administrators protested against reforms of the tolls on the River Scheldt. This river was sealed off with a fiscal barrier. However, Amsterdam merchants could continue to trade with the Baltic, and they had ample opportunities to circumvent the regulations. Initiatives by the province of Zeeland to replace the *licenten* with a contribution spread over other states was opposed by Amsterdam.[65] The episode was also at the roots of a friction with the *landsadvocaat* Van Oldenbarnevelt (d. 1617), who had negotiated a truce with the Spanish, thus ending the privateering expeditions that had successfully been waged from Holland and Zeeland. In the 1640s, when Amsterdam had become more moderate again and had shifted from the stricter to a more lenient variety of Protestantism, its leaders advocated for the end of the war with Spain. However, this resulted in a breach with the stadtholder, Frederick Henry of Orange (d. 1647). Amsterdam's power further contributed to the decision not to accept Frederick Henry's grandson William III as stadtholder.[66]

These conflicts could come together with arguments on the jurisdiction or sovereignty of the city, but only inasmuch as there were infringements on older charters. In the 1520s, for example, Amsterdam's administrators had regularly clashed when it came to prosecutions for heresy, not only with the stadtholder, but also with the Court of Holland. This provincial court was a princely institution, which heard cases in *casus reservati* and which checked judgements of municipal courts in appeal. The Amsterdam *scabini* and burgomasters refused to bring alleged heretics before the court, and in doing so contested the Court of Holland's jurisdiction in what the former categorized as municipal matters.[67] Such disputes also occurred after the Revolt and independence of the Republic. For example, in January 1662, the Amsterdam merchant Isaac Cooimans was convicted of a breach of the monopoly of the West India Company (1622). Cooimans had cooperated with the Amsterdam patrician Nicolaas Pancras to trade on the coast of Guinea, under the license of the

65 M. Hell, "De Oude Geuzen en de Opstand. Politiek en lokaal bestuur in tijd van oorlog en expansie, 1578–1650" in M. Carasso-Kok (ed.), *Geschiedenis van Amsterdam. Een stad uit het niets*, vol. 2, Amsterdam, 2004, 241–297, here 264.

66 Israel, *The Dutch Republic*, 595–609.

67 J.E.A. Boomgaard, *Misdaad en straf. Een onderzoek naar de strafrechtspleging van de Amsterdamse schepenbank 1490–1552*, Zwolle, 1992, 109–112; M. Vrolijk, *Recht door gratie. Gratie bij doodslagen en andere delicten in Vlaanderen, Holland en Zeeland (1531–1567)*, Hilversum, 2017, 280.

Danish king. Cooimans was convicted by the Amsterdam court of *scabini*. By contrast, Pancras managed to stay outside the reach of the court. However, the proctor-general of the Court of Holland appealed against the verdict. In consequence, the Amsterdam aldermen engaged in a heated dispute with the Court, stating that criminal jurisdiction had been granted to the city in 1409, and that appeal against criminal sentences was not possible.[68]

This case is not very different from a dispute that emerged in 1567. In February of that year, Governor-General Margaret of Parma (d. 1586) wrote a letter to the city of Amsterdam about a case that the *scabini* had tried against Antonis van Oudenburgh. Since the latter was a count, this went against the *privilegium fori* of nobles, who had the right to be tried directly before a princely court. It was mentioned in the letter that the *privilegium* applied when proceedings were started that were not concerned with real rights (*actiones reales*).[69]

The position of Amsterdam within Holland was de facto dominant. This status was also acknowledged in external contacts. As mentioned above, the *landsadvocaat* took on the largest role in the external affairs of the Republic.[70] It was no surprise that the city became a pole of attraction for envoys and diplomats. After 1648, several countries had special delegates and consuls for the city of Amsterdam, even with colleagues stationed in The Hague or other cities as well. Tessa de Boer has emphasized that Amsterdam continued to advocate for city diplomacy, *inter alia* through these connections, in the seventeenth century. Even though independent diplomacy on behalf of cities had been forbidden since the early Republic, this culture continued to simmer long afterwards.[71]

The connections between the foreign relations of the Republic, the centrality of the city of Amsterdam and urban republicanism are prominent in the new city hall, which was designed from 1648 onwards. The new building sought to celebrate the end of the Eighty Years' War and the Republic's status as an internationally recognized state, which only had happened with the

68 J.C.E. Bartelds, "Coymans, Isaac" in *Nieuw Nederlandsch Biografisch Woordenboek*, vol. 8, The Hague, 1930, 331–333; H. Bontemantel, *De regeeringe van Amsterdam, soo in't civiel als crimineel en militaire (1653–1672)*, vol. 1, The Hague, 1897, 264–272.

69 Municipal Archives of Amsterdam, *Archief van de Burgemeesters* (inv. 5026), 102 (letter, 15 Febr. 1567 ns).

70 J. de Haan, *De eerste minister van de Republiek. De Hollandse raadpensionaris in de zeventiende eeuw*, Hilversum, 2024, 20.

71 T. de Boer, ""*Ma coustume ne soit de m'addresser aux villes*"; Early Modern Amsterdam's Dealings in City Diplomacy", *Diplomatica* 3 (2021), 167–179. See also the chapter by Tessa de Boer in this volume.

Peace of Westphalia in 1648. The building, which was inaugurated in 1655, combines elements of sixteenth-century urban republicanism with the more baroque discourse of *ius gentium*.[72] In the *Burgerzaal* (Citizen's Hall), which depicts a map of the world and which is surrounded by Roman deities, the maid of Amsterdam takes a central place.

In 1650, no stadtholder had been appointed, meaning that the position of the States General, the States of Holland, and the city of Amsterdam had markedly increased. A poem of praise by Joost van den Vondel (d. 1679), a leading man of letters, emphasized the parallels between Rome and Amsterdam. Both cities had been vanguards of their time, profiting from their access to the sea and rivers. Vondel echoed the ideas of sixteenth-century humanists when referring to both "the citadel of the commonwealth" and the city as a "mountain of gold".[73] One can consider the new city hall as an emblem of the identification of Amsterdam with the Republic. This connection was indeed new in the middle of the seventeenth century. Through the figure of the state pensionary, Amsterdam could directly have an impact in the States General. Amsterdam's central position in the Republic's finances had contributed to further dominance. Therefore, the 'Amsterdam Palace' did not contain references to the States of Holland, but only hinted at the city as focal point of the Republic, being itself the new commercial *umbilicus mundi*.[74]

5 Conclusion

The leaders of Amsterdam presented the city as a chartered city. In their connections to the count of Holland, they watched over the respect for their municipal rights. However, it was only from the 1520s that urban republicanism became more common. At Amsterdam, this new trend did not serve political purposes but could coincide with disputes over jurisdiction and privileges. Also after the Revolt, Amsterdam respected the institutional set-ups of both the county of Holland and the Republic. The administrators of the city

72 See the chapter by J. Nijman and A. de Koomen in this volume.

73 J. Van den Vondel, *Inwydinge van 't stadthuis t'Amsterdam*, Amsterdam, 1982. On this poem, see F.-W. Korsten, "What Roman Paradigm for the Dutch Republic? Baroque Tragedies and Ambiguities Concerning Dominium and Torture" in J. Bloemendal and N. Smith (eds.), *Politics and Aesthetics in European Baroque and Classicist Tragedy*, Leiden, 2016, 43–74, here 57–60.

74 For further reading on the symbolism underlying the architecture of Amsterdam City Hall, see S. Bussels, C. van Eck and B. van Oostveldt, *The Amsterdam Town Hall in Words and Images: Constructing Wonders*, London, 2021.

acknowledged that sovereignty was located at the level of the States General. In this regard, Amsterdam was different from other cities in the Low Countries, in particular Antwerp, which had sought to extend the borders of its jurisdiction in tandem with its economic clout. However, in political practice, the growing importance of Amsterdam was a clear consequence of its rise as commercial and financial centre. Institutional pluralism did not frustrate the Amsterdam leaders. On the contrary, the complex landscape of institutions and jurisdictions proved interesting for the skilled Amsterdam administrators who sought to impose the natural weight of their city. This situation explains why Amsterdam had a huge influence at crucial moments in the history of the Republic, such as, for example, in the demise of Oldenbarnevelt and the *Seclusie* of 1650, when no stadtholder was appointed. The new city hall, inaugurated in 1655, bears testimony to these ideas. Amsterdam is depicted as a central place both in the Republic and the world at large. Therefore, all in all, the history of Amsterdam in the sixteenth and seventeenth centuries demonstrates interesting differences between legal and economic sovereignty, both of which were reconciled in political practice. Even though Amsterdam's legal autonomy was restricted, its power transpired in what resulted from political negotiations, which is what mattered. In that regard, institutional pluralism served as a façade for pretended modesty. On paper the power of Amsterdam was much more reduced than it was in actual fact. Still, the institutions mattered, and making using of their intricacies could contribute to factual dominance.

CHAPTER 2

Amsterdam's Seventeenth-Century City Hall: A Cosmological Iconography of Local Government, Global Trade and Universal Law

Arjan de Koomen and Janne E. Nijman

1 General Introduction

In 1648 – the year of the Peace Treaty of Münster that brought an end to the Eighty Years' War between the Dutch Republic and Spain – Amsterdam started building its city hall on Dam Square. Seven years later, the new city hall was inaugurated – that is to say, the first offices went into use, although the building was far from finished. The event was celebrated by *Inwydinge van't stadthuis t'Amsterdam* (1655) (Inauguration of Amsterdam's City Hall),[1] a long descriptive and didactic poem by Joost van den Vondel. Further construction and decorations went on for about another decade, ultimately resulting in one of the most impressive artistic achievements of the seventeenth century. The classicist architecture of Jacob van Campen, the baroque sculptures of Artus Quellinus (d. 1668) and the many paintings by several Dutch artists form an impressive artistic ensemble. All these elements fit into an extensive iconographical programme, designed by the architect, which is exceptional in its scope and intellectual inventiveness. It aims to teach lessons of good government, presented in the guise of allegories and narratives drawn from the world of classical mythology as well as ancient history and philosophy.

Many aspects of this iconography, especially those envisioned in the paintings, have been studied and explained very well, above all by Katherine Fremantle and Eymert-Jan Goossens.[2] The general reading of the city hall is one

1 J. Van den Vondel, *Inwydinge van't stadthuis t'Amsterdam*, Amsterdam, 1982.

2 B.J. Buchbinder-Green, *The painted decorations of the Town Hall of Amsterdam*, PhD dissertation Northwestern University 1974; K. Fremantle, *The Baroque Town Hall of Amsterdam*, Utrecht, 1959; E.-J. Goossens, *Het Amsterdamse paleis: Schat van beitel en penseel*, Zwolle/Amsterdam, 2010, and his dissertation *Heel en al: Het iconografische programma van het Stadhuis van Amsterdam 1647–1665*, defended at Utrecht University in 2022; E.-J. Goossens, *Schat van beitel en penseel: het Amsterdamse stadhuis uit de Gouden Eeuw*, Zwolle/Amsterdam, 1996. Among the other studies that have contributed, the following deserve mentioning: S. Bussels, "Meer te verwonderen, als immer te doorgronden. Het Amsterdamse stad-

HTTPS://DOI.ORG/10.1163/9789004761537-004

of showing the world "the greatness of Amsterdam", its power as the centre of global commerce, and its virtue as the successor of Republican Rome. As Van Campen's plans for the iconographical programme have not come down to us, it takes a vast body of knowledge to arrive at a convincing interpretation of the whole of the building's decorative features. Some elements remain particularly hard to understand, above all the messages contained in sculpture. It is not that the work of Artus Quellinus – the sculptor called from Antwerp for lack of a suitable Dutch master for this job – has not been studied.[3] Yet the sculptural visualizations in this decorative scheme generally tend to embody a higher degree of abstraction than the episodes from ancient history painted elsewhere in the building, the intentions of which are easier to grasp.

While decoration in marble and bronze is dominant in several sections of the building, we are particularly fascinated by the use of sculpture on the exterior, that is, the two central gables of the building's eastern and western façades, which are both surrounded by sculptures of virtues and surmounted by Pax, the goddess of Peace, and by Atlas, the mythological Titan with the heavens on his shoulders. In the interior, the central *Burgerzaal* is also fully adorned with sculpture. Another striking feature in marble is the series of Olympic gods personifying the seven planets and the earth in the galleries of the building.

Together with other cosmological decorative elements, the expensive marble and bronze sculptures adorning the interior and exterior of the building seem to allude to the higher principles of justice, good government and civic or republican virtue. In a recently published study with which we will engage hereinafter, Goossens also understands Van Campen's decorative plan as a

huis, een overweldigende burgerspiegel", *Tijdschrift voor Geschiedenis* 126/2 (2013), 234–248; S. Bussels, C. van Eck, B. van Oostveldt (eds.), *The Amsterdam Town Hall in Words and Images: Constructing Wonders*, London, 2021; Q. Buvelot, "Ontwerpen voor geschilderde decoratieprogramma's" in J. Huysken, K. Ottenheym and G. Schwarz (eds.), *Jacob van Campen: het klassieke ideaal in de Gouden Eeuw*, Amsterdam, 1995, 121–153; R. Cohen Tervaert e.a. in *Verborgen Verhalen. Wijze lessen in de decoratie van het voormalige Stadhuis van Amsterdam*, Amsterdam, 2015; P. Vlaardingerbroek, *Geschiedenis van het stadhuis van Amsterdam*, Zwolle, 2011; *Van heeren, die hunn' stoel en kussen niet beschaemen: Het stadsbestuur van Amsterdam in de 17e en 18e eeuw = Of lords, who seat nor cushion do ashame : The government of Amsterdam in the 17th and 18th centuries*, Amsterdam, 1987.

3 For literature with specific attention paid to the sculpture of the city hall: Exhibition catalogue *Beelden kijken: De kunst van Quellien in het Paleis op de Dam / Focus on Sculpture: Quellien's art in the Palace on the Dam*, text by K. Fremantle, Amsterdam, 1977 (reprint 1983); E.J. Goossens, "De rol van de beeldhouwkunst" in J. Huysken, J. Ottenheym and G. Schwarz (eds.), *Jacob van Campen: het klassieke ideaal in de Gouden Eeuw*, Amsterdam, 1995, 201–226; F. Scholten, *Artus Quellinus: beeldhouwer van Amsterdam*, Amsterdam, 2010; and also Goossens, *Heel en al*.

"cosmological programme".[4] While we subscribe to this reading, we would like to add a piece to this iconographic puzzle and, doing so, to our understanding of the building's message.

This interdisciplinary chapter comes from a coincidental meeting between the authors about 18 years ago. We discovered that neither of us was fully satisfied with the existing interpretations of Amsterdam's City Hall's decorative programme and that we shared a fascination for what the overarching cosmological decorative programme meant to communicate: a recognition of a higher normative order guiding while also constraining Amsterdam as seafaring and trading global city? A universal order in which Amsterdam inscribed itself? Since our first meeting in 2006, methodological discussions have developed in both our fields.[5] Coming from very different academic disciplines, we will first note how we situate this study methodologically and then explicate how we go about bringing our disciplines together.

Iconology, the deciphering of the meaning of visual imagery, has for a long time been one of the central tasks of art history. Uncovering the ideas and moral messages in works of art was mostly done by the intense study of textual sources that might be key to the meaning of an artwork. It made the field of art history 'interdisciplinary' long before this became a general practice in academia. This article belongs to the tradition of iconology, as it is foremost an attempt to relate images to the history of ideas. A specific category with iconological studies is the issue of coherence between a series of images that belong together, called a 'programme'. In the case of Amsterdam's City Hall we can certainly speak of a programme, as the decorations were designed as a conceptional unity. A coherent explanation of the ideological content of a programme requires familiarity with a vast body of knowledge that goes from the reality of building to philosophical ideas, from literary sources in several languages to the historical understanding of political reality. Almost everything under the heading of context can be relevant – or perhaps not: many discussions in the field are about the relevance of 'the context' for the understanding of art. With Amsterdam's City Hall, most of the imagery can be identified and placed in a visual and humanist tradition, yet the primary motivation for putting together the city hall programme is harder to grasp.

In order to enhance understanding of the iconography of Amsterdam's City Hall and in particular the sculptures on the exterior and interior, we argue that

4 Goossens, *Heel en al*, 246–250.

5 Part of the 'material turn' in international law is an interest in objects, including buildings, as part of the archives of international law. One of the authors of this chapter aims to write a future paper to situate the building and to examine the place it occupies in this body of literature.

familiarity with an additional body of knowledge is required. That is, seventeenth-century legal and political thought and in particular the theory of the law of nature and nations (*ius naturae et gentium*). It is what we, as an art historian and an international law scholar, aspire to do in this chapter: to merge two academic traditions that usually do not join forces. While there are quite a few studies on the iconography of the city hall, it has never been studied in the context of the history of *ius naturae et gentium* – the emerging body of law applicable to questions of war and peace, trade and navigation, good government and extra-European expansion. We argue that elating iconology to the history of international law – a field normally too specialized to access for art historians – allows us to understand building and sculptures better.

In section 2, we present the building and its sculptures. After a brief discussion in section 3 as to why we find the standard iconographic reading of the decorative programme of Amsterdam's seventeenth-century city hall still somewhat unsatisfactory (section 3.1), we push the interpretation of its cosmological imagery further (section 3.2). Here, for the purpose of interpretation, we discuss a few important ideas dominant in Dutch intellectual and political debates[6] at the time and familiar to the Amsterdam political and commercial elite who were in charge of the design and construction of the new city hall. We mobilize seventeenth-century moral, legal and political thought – most notably, the new ideas on *ius naturae et gentium* brought forward so influentially by the Northern humanist Hugo de Groot (Grotius), and to a lesser extent Dutch republicanism – common in the Dutch Republic, the city of Amsterdam and discussed at its Athenaeum Illustre.[7] In section 4 we present our conclusions and reflect upon how the iconography relates to the political position of Amsterdam and its global commercial enterprise. As we will show, the theme of this book – the dynamics between the local and the global in seventeenth-century Amsterdam as well as the relation to the development of legal thought and practice – provides a solid background for the study both of the sculptures in this highly ambitious municipal palace and of the legal and political ideology embodied in the programme.

6 See e.g. A. Weststeijn, "Dutch Republicanism" in F. Lovett and M. Sellers (eds.), *The Oxford Handbook of Republicanism*, Oxford, forthcoming.

7 D. van Miert. *Humanism in an Age of Science: The Amsterdam Athenaeum in the Golden Age, 1632–1704*, Leiden, 2009, see e.g. 221 and following.

2 Building a New City Hall with Richly Sculpted Decorations

2.1 Getting Started

The decision to build a new city hall was taken in 1639.[8] Burgomasters informed the *vroedschap* of their plans on 28 January 1639.[9] A year later, a commission of four – Cornelis de Graeff, Anthony Oetgens van Waveren, Joan Huydecoper and Jan Cornelisz. Geelvinck – was appointed to implement the plan.[10] They were responsible for the construction of a new city hall, one fitting for a city with global (trade and seafaring) interests and aspirations. Together, the committee chose the architect Jacob van Campen to design the building. Van Campen and the burgomaster Cornelis de Graeff (d. 1664) moved among the 'humanist circles' of Amsterdam and the Republic at large, where they met scholars like Barlaeus (d. 1648), Hugo Grotius, P.C. Hooft (d. 1647), Constantijn Huygens (d. 1687), Joost van den Vondel and Vossius (d. 1649), among others.[11] While Erasmus was the pivotal figure of early Dutch humanism in the late fifteenth to early sixteenth centuries,[12] humanism remained a prominent intellectual approach in the Dutch Republic in the sixteenth century and early seventeenth centuries.[13] Van Campen is credited with the 'classicist' shift in architectural style, as can be seen in Amsterdam's City Hall.[14] He was intellectually well equipped to conceptualize a programme with references to classical history and philosophical ideas.[15] The rectangular building came to speak the timeless language of order and harmony. The *Burgerzaal* – the main central hall where citizens and governmental officials entered – served as an interior forum and was adorned with imagery showing once

8 Municipal Archives Amsterdam, Notaries (inv. 5025), 18, fol. 198r–198v.

9 W. Frijhoff and M. Prak (eds.), *De Geschiedenis van Amsterdam: Centrum van de wereld 1578–1650*, Amsterdam, 2004, 295.

10 Fremantle, *The Baroque Town Hall*, 24, footnote 8.

11 Ibid., 54; see more extensively on humanism in the Dutch Republic: J. Israel, *The Dutch Republic: Its Rise, Greatness, and Fall, 1477–1803*, New York, 1995.

12 Israel, *The Dutch Republic*, ch. 3 "Humanism and the Origins of the Reformation, 1470–1520", in particular at 41–54; also B. Bradshaw, "Transalpine humanism" in J.H. Burns (ed.), *The Cambridge History of Political Thought 1450–1700*, Cambridge, 1991, 95–131.

13 Israel, *The Dutch Republic*, in particular at 565–591 (ch. 24 "Intellectual Life, 1572–1650").

14 On Van Campen and his contacts, A.M. Hammacher, "De relatie van Jacob van Campen tot de gemeenschap van zijn tijd", *De Gids* 120 (1957), 297–308, at 297, and M.J. Bok, "Familie, vrienden en opdrachtgevers" in J. Huysken, K. Ottenheym and G. Schwarz (eds.), *Jacob van Campen: het klassieke ideaal in de Gouden Eeuw*, Amsterdam, 1995, 27–52.

15 Hammacher, "De relatie", 307.

again classical ideas on the order of the universe and the relationship between earth and heaven. Van Campen designed and initially also oversaw the making of the rich sculptural and painted decoration, which not only served to enhance the monumental effect of the building, but also emphasized the moral character of the city hall, teaching lessons of good government, justice, and republican virtue to all entering the building.

What do we see when our eyes wonder at the sculptures of the building's interior and exterior? The imagery in the building often refers to the stories of classical antiquity to provide meaningful analogies between Amsterdam and the capitals of the ancient world, Athens and Rome.[16] Especially Rome's republican period provided many *exempla* for political instruction. The erudite iconography of these sculpted and painted stories is usually, if identified, quite easy to relate to the ideals of justice and good government supposedly upheld by the Amsterdam burgomasters and *schepenen*. With his *Inwydinge van't stadthuis t'Amsterdam*, Joost van den Vondel helps us read the imagery and its meaning of many elements in this iconographical programme. Generally, he celebrated the city hall as a symbol of peace.[17] His fellow poet Reyer Anslo did the same in "*Aan de Vreede, Op de grondtbouw van't Stadthuis*" (To Peace, on the foundaments of the City Hall).[18] After all, the actual construction had started in October 1648, a few months after Spain and the United Provinces had signed the Peace of Münster (30 January 1648), which had been under negotiation since 1646. It ended the Eighty Years' War against Spain, a war waged inside and outside Europe. The Amsterdam regents' Bicker-de Graeff faction had pushed forcefully for these peace negotiations.[19] They belonged to the republican political movement of the so-called *Staatsgezinden* that, contrary to the adherents of the stadtholder, wanted to arrive at peace in order to stimulate the further development of trade in which they were heavily invested, rather than winning more territory from the Spanish Netherlands as the *Prinsgezinden* aspired. With this peace, the king of Spain recognized the "sovereignty" of the Republic of the United Provinces and of its ruling body of the States General (Art. 1).[20] The treaty not only recognized the Dutch Republic's formal independence, it

16 For example in the literature of the times, see e.g. Grotius *Parallelon* and *De Antiquitate Reipublicae Batavicae* (1610).

17 Fremantle, *The Baroque Town Hall*, 30 and following.

18 R. Anslo, *Aan de Vreede, Op de grondtbouw van't Stadthuis*, in *Klioos Kraam, vol verscheyden gedichten*, vol. 2, Leeuwarden, 1657, 18–19.

19 This regent families' faction included the aforementioned Cornelis de Graeff, his brother Andries de Graeff, Andries Bicker and his brother Bicker. See more below.

20 Peace of Münster, art. 1.

also settled overseas issues of trade, property and colonial rule, basically by a *grosso modo* recognition of the status quo in the Far East and the West.[21]

2.2 The Sculptural Decorations

Vondel's *Inwydinge* may guide our view – when standing at Dam Square, a square so central to the city's affairs that he compares it to Rome's Capitol – over the eastern façade, from the entrances, along the columns, up the tympanum with at the centre the city maiden of Amsterdam. Above the tympanum, *Pax* crowns the top accompanied by the virtues *Prudentia* and *Justitia* at either end (Figure 2.1). These two cardinal virtues are often seen in the decoration of governmental buildings.[22] Peace, on the other hand, is a very rare iconography.[23]

This front tympanum relief, a flat triangle of more than 20 meters wide, shows a multitude of figures and animals that bend toward the city maiden of Amsterdam in the centre (Figure 2.2).[24] She is identified by the shield adorned with city's crest of the three crosses held in one hand, while the other holds an olive branch, a sign of peace of biblical origin. The sea gods revere and praise "Amsterdam":[25] Neptune with his trident, Nereids and Tri-

21 E.g. Peace of Münster, art. 5: "*De navigatien ende traffiquen opte Oost ende West Indien sullen worden gemainteneert* [...]"; also articles 6 and 7 deal with overseas colonial territories and the WIC and VOC. With art. 75 the parties reaffirm their protection of free navigation on sea and rivers. See also, C. Martínez Shaw, "The overseas Spanish Empire and the Dutch Republic before and after the Peace of Münster", *De Zeventiende Eeuw* 13 (1997), 131–138; also, J. Israel, *Dutch Primacy in World Trade, 1585–1740*, Oxford, 1989, 197: "The conclusion of the Dutch-Spanish conflict was the most important factor in determining the conditions in which the Dutch world-trade system reached its zenith, the peak of its sway over the markets of the globe, during the quarter of a century down to 1672".

22 Goossens (*Heel en al*, 95) points out that in Van Campen's first sketch for the tympanum (kept in the Rijksmuseum), the right figure was to represent Wealth as indicated by the word "Rijkdom". She has been replaced by the traditional Justice. Pax was already envisioned in the drawing, identified with "Vreede". The left figure is drawn but not identified with any inscription or attributes.

23 Only the city hall of Leiden shows a sculpture of Peace too.

24 Fremantle, *The Baroque Town Hall* gives an extensive description of the gable reliefs in chapter 7 "Argo sails Home" (169–181) followed by an overview of classical and Italian sources for the sculpted tympanum reliefs (182–185).

25 Vondel's *Inwydinge*: "*De Watergoden slaen een ongelijck geluit, En blazen haeren lof op alle watren uit. | De Zeegodinnen, nu geweckt door zulcke galmen, Vereeren haer met wier, en krans, en mosch, en palmen.*" (The water gods utter an uneven sound and tout their praise over all waters. The Sea Godesses, now raised by such reverb, honour her with weed, and crown, and mos and palms).

FIGURE 2.1 Hubert Quellinus after Artus Quellinus, *Virtues on the eastern façade of Amsterdam City Hall: Prudentia, Pax and Justitia*, etching, in: *Secunda pars praecipuarum effigierum ac ornamentorum amplissimae curiae Amstelrodamensis* ..., 1663.

FIGURE 2.2 Hubert Quellinus after Artus Quellinus, *The relief of the eastern pediment of Amsterdam City Hall*, etching, in: *Secunda pars* ..., 1663.

tons, some of them riding the Hippocampus. They all seem to rejoice in the leading role of peaceful Amsterdam. The Nereids around her even offer her laurel wreaths, symbols of victory and glory. This mythological gathering is easy to understand: it celebrates the importance of Amsterdam as a seafaring city.

Above Pax is a bell tower with a cupola. In the original design, Van Campen had envisioned sculptural decoration all-around with personifications of the Eight Winds and on top a compass rose in the shape of the medieval cog ship (*koggeschip*), an old symbol of the city of Amsterdam (Figure 2.3). Goossens helps us see how the design and specific location of the cupola right on the

FIGURE 2.3 Hubert Quellinus after Artus Quellinus, *The relief of the western pediment of Amsterdam City Hall, etching, in: Secunda pars…*, 1663.

east-west axis refer to universal harmony.[26] In his view, the message of the bell tower with cupola was: "Amsterdam puts itself at the service of the heavenly laws".[27] The cupola, which can be seen as a symbol of heaven and the heavenly laws of nature, is also a space of harmony as it provides a dome for the carillon located right underneath.[28] In his *Inwijdinge*, Vondel links the carillon to heavenly harmony and peace. The tower seems to be a reference to the Tower of the Winds in ancient Athens, described in Vitruvius's *Books on Architecture*. That ancient tower was also decorated by eight personifications of the winds, holding the building's clockwork.

Turning to the apex of the western façade at the rear, we see a large bronze Atlas, the Titan who carries the heavens on his shoulders. The celestial globe is a symbol of "universal laws" or "heavenly rules" (Figure 2.4).[29] He is accompanied by statues of *Vigilantia* and *Temperantia*. The latter belongs to the cardinal virtues. *Vigilantia* was a replacement of the conventional *Fortitudo* that was originally envisaged and described by Vondel. If the earlier plan had been executed, the front and rear together would have presented a complete set of the Four Cardinal Virtues, the moral qualities of statesmanship since the Greek *polis*. The reason for this replacement has, once again, not come down to us, and an obvious explanation is not easily found.[30] The tympanum relief below these statues shows the world's continents, exemplified by personifications,

26 Goossens, *Heel en al*, 246.
27 Ibid.
28 Ibid.
29 See A. de Koomen, "The Atlas on Amsterdam's Town Hall: the interpretation of a "meaningless bearer of heaven"', *Simiolus* 43 (2021), 287–318; and Goossens, *Heel en al*, 63.
30 See below.

FIGURE 2.4 Hubert Quellinus after Artus Quellinus, *Virtues on the western façade of Amsterdam City Hall: Temperantia, Atlas, Vigilantia, etching, in: Secunda pars …*, 1663.

characteristic animals and a few figures carrying merchandise (Figure 2.3). They form corteges that move from both sides to a personification of Trade in the centre. She is recognized as such by the *petasus*, Mercury's winged traveling hat. The globe at her feet typifies her as world trade. Nautical instruments near the globe – such as the Jacob's staff, compass and the astrolabe – refer to the scientific requirements for navigation on a global scale and thus also to the heavenly laws of nature on which Amsterdam seafarers depended for their navigation. Often the figure is called *Amsterdam*, in analogy with the central figure on the side of Dam Square. This designation is not correct, yet it is clear that this personification of world trade is positioned *in* Amsterdam, as the river gods of Amstel and IJ lie at her feet. The ship behind her, which is not a contemporary East Indiaman, is again a *koggeschip*, an emblem of the city dating from the Hanse period. Because of its classical ornamentation, the ship is far from a depiction of a real *koggeschip*. It figures here as a symbol of Amsterdam, also underlined by its flag bearing Amsterdam's three crosses.

What exactly is depicted in the western fronton? We have to be aware that again we are looking at allegory, not at an illustration of Amsterdam trade of the middle of the seventeenth century. The figure of Trade, residing in Amsterdam, receives the people of the world bringing their merchandise. Asia, being the oldest civilization, and Europe stand close together. The camel and ostrich (!) accompany Asia, while the mythological bull and horses do so for Europe. The attire of the personification of Asia, however, derives from the Ottoman Empire, as marked by the crescent moon on the headgear. He is not, as might be expected, a figure from the Far East, where the VOC was active. The children that accompany him carry tulips, which reached Europe from the Ottoman world (resulting in the "tulip mania" of the 1630s), an incense burner and an elegant casket, referring to the riches of this continent. These goods are also associated with the Levant. Most elements from this imagery derive from the *Iconologia* of Cesare Ripa, a handbook for composing personifications and allegories, translated from the Italian into Dutch in 1644.[31] It ignores, so to say, the mid-seventeenth century reality of the East Asian trade. Africa – with lion and elephant – and the "young" continent America – with crocodile and armadillo – are positioned further away from the centre and weighed down by the sloping triangle. On America's side we see the bent upper body of a mine-worker and two feathered Native Americans wearing loincloths, one of whom carries what seem to be sugar loafs on his back, referring to the major export products of South America: silver and sugar. The extreme corner provides space for two tiny monkeys. In the opposite corner, carriers crawl with ivory tusks and other bags and packages from African territory. In all this imagery, Amsterdam takes a central role as she is positioned within the arrangements of traditional Eurocentric notions of geographical hierarchy.[32]

The six sculptures that crown the exterior of the building have also been placed inside the *Burgerzaal*. This time not in bronze but in sandstone versions painted white. They were the full-scale models for the making of the bronzes. The reuse of the sculptures has been explained as an iconographical accident: a compromise to save money, necessitated by the costs of the First Anglo-Dutch War (1652–1654).[33] The statues, though, were erected much later, in 1665. The cost factor would not have been a permanent argument in view of

31 C. Ripa, *Iconologia*, translation Dirk Pers, Amsterdam, 1644, 603–605. Ripa states in it that the personification of Asia holds "*in de rechter hand eenige taxkens met blaederen en vruchten van Cassie, Peper, Nagelen, Muscaet-nooten &c. in de lincker heeftse een konstigh Wieroock-vat, waer uyt een seer groote roock opstijght.*" (in the right hand some branches with leaves and fruits of berries, pepper, cloves, nutmeg and others; in the left she has an artful censer, from which much smoke emerges). The goods in the right hand match the merchandise of the VOC, but despite Ripa's prescription, tulips have been chosen, symbols of the Ottoman Empire. Another element that does not derive from Ripa's handbook is the crescent moon. Ripa states that "*de Vrouwen, allerhande kostelijcke verciersełen draegen van goude keetens, braseletten, oorpeerlen, en ander cierlijcke opproncksełen*" (the women wear costly decorations of golden chains, bracelets, ear pearls and other graceful ornaments), but mentions no moon.

32 See for a colonial reading of art and architecture of the city hall, M. Pantjes (ed.), *Sporen van Slavernij in het Koninklijk Paleis Amsterdam*, Amsterdam, 2023.

33 Goossens, *Heel en al*, 127–130.

the other items of expenditure, the more so given the fact that the sculptures must have been more expensive than the planned paintings. Since the *Burgerzaal* was to be the glorious centre of the new city hall, it is hard to imagine that anything that would have distracted from the programme would have been permitted on the grounds of thrift. Rather, what we see is the exact replication of the exterior's virtuous and cosmological imagery, now on the inside of the building in the public space where the citizens and civil servants deliberate and work.

Inside, this imagery is further supported by other sculptures and wall paintings. The *Burgerzaal* was reached from staircases at the eastern entrance (Figure 2.5). At the opposite side of the great hall, a portal opened to the *Schepenzaal*, the court room. In the four corners, gates with rounded arches open to the galleries that lead to the municipal offices. All these entrances are decorated with marble: the spandrels above the gates of the galleries with female personifications of the Four Elements (Earth, Water, Fire, and Air), resulting in four pairs on each gate making two cycles of the Four Elements. Elements were believed to be the primal materials of Nature, and their reciprocal equilibrium was, according to classical learning, the key to the stability of the physical world.

FIGURE 2.5 View of the *Burgerzaal* looking to the *Schepenzaal* – photo Wim Ruijgrok

The entrance to the *Schepenzaal* shows an allegory of Justice and Punishment. The opposite portal leading to the exit – to the city – was crowned by the Maiden of Amsterdam, flanked by – this time – *Fortitudo* and *Sapientia*.

Amsterdam and her adjutants preside over various cycles of time ruling the physical world. On the architrave, the sun and the moon represent day and night, and signs of the zodiac refer to the cycle of the year. Other symbols of time are the hourglass and the ouroboros, an emblem of eternity, seen in the centre of the lintel (Figure 2.6).

Another dazzling decorative element is the rendering of heaven and earth, each in two flat hemispheres, on the floor of the *Burgerzaal*. The earth was to be found in two large-scale halves inlaid at both ends of the floor with trading posts marked-in (Figure 2.7). The heavenly halves are to be found on the vertical axis: in the middle of the floor and in the vault above it. Together with the spandrels depicting the Elements, they stood for the physical world of the earth. The cardinal directions of the world were supposed to be adorned through mythological paintings in the superstructure of the hall: the Fall of Phaethon from the heat of the sun in the south; the abduction of Oreithyia by the northern wind Boreas; Apollo's chariot at sunrise in the east; and Diana riding out for moonrise on the western side. These were not executed, however, and large sculptural models took their place: Atlas, Vigilance and Temperance on the west side; Peace, Justice and Prudence on the other side.

FIGURE 2.6 Artus Quellinus, eastern portal of the *Burgerzaal*: the crowned city maiden of Amsterdam between *Fortitudo* and *Sapientia*, above allegories of Time on the lintel, marble, 1655–1660, Paleis op de Dam / formerly Amsterdam City Hall – photo Andrew Michael Bergman

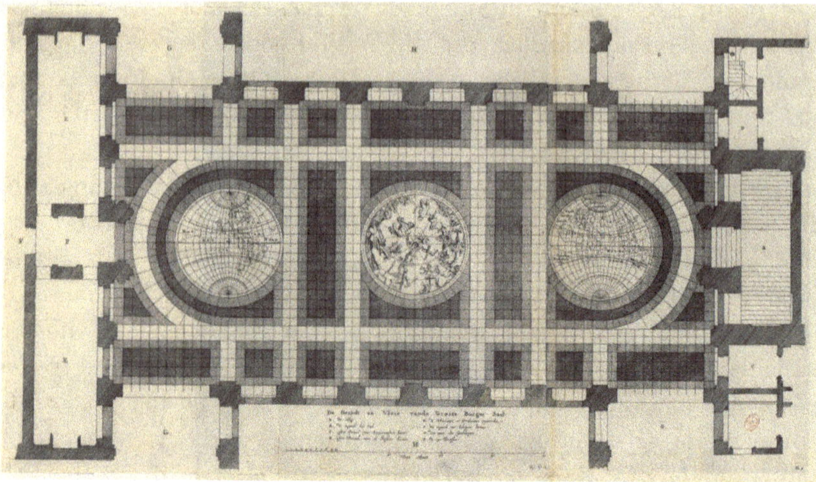

FIGURE 2.7 Floorplan of the *Burgerzaal* in Amsterdam City Hall, etching and engraving in: *Afbeelding van't stadt huys van Amsterdam, In dartigh Coopere Plaaten, geordineert door Jacob van Campen; en Geteeckent door Iacob Vennekool.* Amsterdam: Dancker Danckerts, 1661.

These six virtues are again situated between the heavenly and earthly spheres. Initially, as we know from prints, the large lunettes were reserved for two painted scenes illustrating the battle between order and chaos: Jupiter and the Battle of the Titans; and Neptune calming the storm at sea caused by the rebellious gods of the winds, the so-called *Quos ego* from Vergil's *Aeneid.* Together with Phaethon's ride across the sky and Boreas's abduction of the maiden, these are the depictions of the threat, insubordination, and defiance of disorder. Despite the fact that their placement was not foreseen, gigantic Atlas and Peace fit well as they both individually and jointly play a role in guarding order and harmony.

In the *Burgerzaal*, next to the entrances to the rooms of the burgomasters and the city council, there are two reliefs with mythological scenes referring to the virtues of good governance. One is showing the Greek mythical figure of Amphion playing his harp to inspire the construction of the ancient city of Thebes (Figure 2.8). We have to understand this rather obscure figure as a political metaphor. As Vondel says, "As this harpist has taught us: keeping to the measure is the best government." This exemplum of harmony and measure – elsewhere personified as the virtue *Temperantia* – has its companion in the relief of the story of Argus, Io and Mercury. Argus, the cyclops of the hundred eyes does not allow himself to be lulled to sleep by Mercury's flute, as he has to watch over Io, who had been changed into a white cow in order to keep

FIGURE 2.8 Hubert Quellinus after Artus Quellinus, *Relief of Amphion and Zethos in the* Burgerzaal *of Amsterdam City Hall:*, etching, in: *Secunda pars* ..., 1663.

Jupiter at a distance. This depiction can be understood as exemplification of the virtue *Vigilantia*, represented as a large figure on the opposite wall.

Inside the building, the most conspicuous sculptures are the classical gods placed in pairs in the four corners of the galleries. They are depicted as full-length figures, surrounded by attributes and objects associated with the specific god. They are not in their role of Olympic deities, yet personify the seven planets of the Ptolemaic system as seen from the earth, which was within this system believed to be the centre of the universe. We see Diana (Moon), Mercury, Venus, Apollo (Sun), Mars, Jupiter and Saturn. As another one was needed to make eight – Earth was added in the guise of Rhea Cybele. Traditionally not considered a planet, she fits well in the cycle, for Rhea was the wife (as well as the sister) of Saturn and, therefore, they are suited to form a couple. Together within the Ptolemaic system they form the centre – earth – and the end of the universe – Saturn. The placing of the eight figures follows the cosmological order, yet with one remarkable exception: Venus and Jupiter have traded places. This must have happened deliberately, as the Seven Planets had their well-known immutable place in the design of the world. The exact reason for this change has, once again, not come down to us. One of the better modern explanations is that the pairing of Mars and Venus – the result of the substitution – works as an emblem of peace, as in this company Mars is distracted from war to love (Figure 2.9).[34] The number and selection of classical gods, as well as the addition of the goddess of Earth, leave no doubt that they are here to form a planetary series. Modern viewers might be puzzled, however, that the Copernican system is not rendered, while already known for more than a century – even more so, because there were plenty of adherents of the heliocentric system in the Dutch Republic.[35] The fact that it has been ignored, speaks to the fact that the iconography did not aspire to reflect the latest insights of the Scientific Revolution, but rather allegorically the cosmological learning from a classical tradition.

For long, this planet-figures configuration has been "one of the least understood aspects of the decoration of the city hall".[36] The planetary world was considered so remote from the reality of law and government, as well as from the commercial inclinations of Amsterdam policy, that these sculptures have been approached as being somewhat lost in the galleries of the city hall. Vondel interestingly enough ignores the planetary role of the Olympic gods, just as he did not 'discuss' the role of Atlas in his poem. Apparently, the poet

34 As was suggested by J. Bedaux, "In search for simplicity: Interpreting the Amsterdam Town Hall" in K.L. Selig (ed.), *Polyanthea. Essays on art and literature in honour of William Sebastian Heckscher*, The Hague, 1993, 37–43. An earlier explanation is found in Fremantle, *The Baroque Town Hall*: she believed the gods refer to specific offices behind the doors next to them, but her attempt to relate this couple to *Huwelijkse Zaecken* has been considered far-fetched and unconvincing. Goossens (2010, 66; repeated in 2020, 156) also refutes Bedaux's explanation. He proposes the change comes from the aspiration to distribute the Four Elements, associated with the planets, symmetrically over the east-west axis of the building. Yet the two planets that changed places, Venus and Jupiter, are both associated with Air. Therefore, the original order did not show a lack of symmetry to be restored. Coupling Mars and Venus in service of peace is a better explanation. We might wonder why Apollo and Mars (both Fire) were not exchanged. Then the order would have been less rigorously disturbed. The answer might be in the coupling: As Mars and Venus were to be represented as a couple, the man had to be on the dexter side. We see the same arrangement between Saturn and Cybele, but not with Diana and Mercury (they were not a couple).

35 See e.g. H. Nellen, *Hugo Grotius. A Lifelong Struggle for Peace in Church and State 1583–1645*, Leiden, 2007, 358; here, he discusses a 1634 letter to Vossius in which Grotius elaborated on the contemporary cosmological discussions on the geocentric position of the Earth. Nellen points to a 1621 poem within which "Grotius challenged the old Ptolemaic system and suggested that the Earth revolved around the Sun."

36 Goossens, *Het Amsterdamse paleis*, 66.

FIGURE 2.9 Hubert Quellinus, *The sculptures of Venus and Mars in the northwestern corner of the galleries of Amsterdam City Hall*, in: *Secunda pars* ..., 1663.

missed the allegorical message, despite his knowledge of classical literary sources. Nor have other seventeenth-century commentators offered a satisfying explanation of these sculptures. It is only very recently that the "cosmopolitical coherence" of the decorations has been recognized.[37]

3 A Legal Interpretation of the Seventeenth-Century Amsterdam City Hall

In the iconological interpretation of Amsterdam's City Hall, as presented by Fremantle in 1959, Van Campen's programme is explained as an impressive body of learning belonging to a humanist tradition of classical studies. Yet this

37 See the article of one of the present authors on the significance of the Atlas, De Koomen, "The Atlas on Amsterdam's Town Hall"; and Goossens, *Heel en al*, for the interpretation of the whole of the programme from the cosmological perspective in his dissertation *Heel en Al*.

interpretation somewhat goes beyond the reality of the here and now. Nowadays we see the tendency to read the city hall differently: learning is put somewhat aside in favour of a propagandistic perspective emphasizing self-glorification: Amsterdam presenting itself as the centre of the world, claiming and legitimizing the idea of global dominance for the city.[38] There is in our view, however, more to Van Campen's design than self-congratulation and self-centredness – Amsterdam at the "centre of the cosmos".[39]

In recent years, Goossens has pushed the interpretation of the art and architecture of Amsterdam's seventeenth-century city hall further with his extensive cosmological reading of the programme.[40] For his reconstruction of the intellectual background of the design, he discusses architectural theory, the role of religion and the sciences as well as on the socio-political challenges with which the intellectual and political elite was 'struggling'. All these defined the world of ideas Van Campen and the commissioning committee lived in.[41] We agree with many of Goossens interpretations, but he overlooks a new and upcoming science, that is, the universal law of nature and nations, so relevant for a city of global trade and navigation as Amsterdam at the time.

In the early decades of the seventeenth century, Europe was in need of a new body of morality and law to deal with questions of war and peace. Within Europe, the Holy Roman Empire or *Respublica Christiana* fragmented further, nation-states started to develop while religious wars continued. Outside Europe, merchants and trade companies maintained and expanded relations with peoples overseas leading to colonization of land and to warfare to protect the mercantile interests. The city hall was a monument to peace in Europe and, in particular, to peace with Spain, which now recognized the Dutch Republic as an independent state. Yet it was also the new building for a rather confident local government that ruled a city that led the world in global trade and navigation. In Holland, the argument that peace was good for trade and navigation had been made many times, most notably by Amsterdam's heavily invested

38 See Cohen Tervaert, *Verborgen verhalen*; Scholten, *Artus Quellinus*; A. Taatgen, *The Universe of Amsterdam: Treasures from the Golden Age of Cartography*, exhibition catalogue Paleis op de Dam, 2020; Bussels, Van Eck and Van Oostveld, *The Amsterdam Town Hall in Words and Images* (2021), 2: "With the Town Hall, the Burgomasters wanted to visually represent their leading position in the city and the Republic, as well as their aspirations to world domination"; E. Kolfin, *De Kunst van de Macht: Jordaens, Lievens en Rembrandt in het Paleis op de Dam*, Zwolle, 2023.

39 *The Amsterdam Town Hall in Words and Images* (2021), 46.

40 Goossens, *Heel en al*, 61 and following.

41 Ibid.

political and mercantile elite.[42] The city flourished during the Twelve Years' Truce, and the States-Provincial of Holland and the city of Amsterdam called for permanent peace ever since its end in 1621. In other words, questions of war and peace in Europe and overseas were highly relevant for Amsterdam. All over Europe, the "new science of morality"[43] or the rising moral-legal language to discuss these questions was natural jurisprudence and in particular the new domain of *ius naturae et gentium*, the law of nature and nations. Importantly, it was moreover the law that established the universal rights to trade and navigation, which were so vital to Amsterdam. Hugo Grotius's *Mare Liberum* (1609) had been instrumental in that debate.

Grotius was the leading Dutch scholar in this new domain. For his ideas, Grotius drew heavily on Roman law;[44] ancient legal and political thought, in particular, (neo-)stoicism; and Erasmian humanism.[45] He was moreover intensively connected, both professionally and privately, with the Amsterdam ruling elite. He knew first-hand many of the Amsterdam regents, including the Bicker-de Graeff faction, already mentioned above. Personal relations continued also when he lived in exile – e.g. with Cornelis de Graeff, who visited him in Paris in the 1620s. The book he wrote to develop domestic Dutch law, the *Inleydinghe tot de Hollandsche rechts-gheleerdheydt* (first edition 1631), must have been well known to all involved in government. In its first sections, it also explains the relationship with natural law and the law of nations. In these early years of Grotius's career, the VOC was a client, and Grotius wrote his *Mare Liberum* – a chapter of *De Jure Praedae*, which he never published – in service of this trading company and its many (Amsterdam) shareholders to provide them with legal justifications for their trade and seafaring activities in the Indies.[46] In other words, Grotius's writings are a relevant and important source to consult so as to grasp fully the world of ideas that Van Campen, the

42 See supra, text to footnote 19–21.

43 R. Tuck, *The Rights of War and Peace: Political Thought and the International Order from Grotius to Kant*, Oxford, 2001, 78.

44 In Roman law, *ius gentium* was the body of natural law that ruled relations among Roman citizens and non-Roman people. In the sixteenth century, the Spanish scholastic theologians had developed the Roman law notion of *ius gentium* into a natural law that ruled relations among all peoples, European and non-European. See also e.g. Richard Tuck, *The Rights of War and Peace*.

45 J.E. Nijman, "Images of Grotius, or the International Rule of Law beyond Historiographical Oscillation", *Journal of the history of international law = Revue d'histoire du droit international* 17/1 (2015), 83–137.

46 See the Preface to the *Defense of Chapter V of Mare Liberum* (1614).

local government, and its Building Committee lived in.[47] In addition, the humanist Grotius was one of the leading thinkers in Dutch republicanism, another set of ideas relevant in the context of this chapter.[48] The Amsterdam regents of the powerful Bicker-de Graeff fraction belonged to the *Staatsgezinde* republicans as mentioned above. They led Amsterdam's republicanism vis-à-vis the princes of Orange, who held the position of stadtholder and as such accumulated political and military power in one hand.[49]

Republicanism was debated widely, intensely and transnationally in early seventeenth-century Europe. Evidently, republicanism in the Dutch Republic repudiated monarchy as the form of government,[50] but for the purpose of this chapter it is important to stress their love for the classics,[51] their emphasis on (civic) virtues and good government, and profound thinking on liberty and the location of sovereignty in a *respublica mixta*.[52] Here, Grotius's thinking, for example, about the natural rights of self-preservation, free trade and free navigation, in addition to natural rights and responsibilities of those in office, are a case in point of how republicanism and natural law jurisprudence was intertwined in Dutch political thought.[53] Ernst Kossmann wrote about Dutch political theory of the first half of the seventeenth century: "The respectable and civilized Dutchman of those days was an Aristotelian, a Humanist, a Calvinist

---

47 See for Hugo Grotius as a Northern humanist, e.g. J.E Nijman, "Images of Grotius, or the International Rule of Law beyond Historiographical Oscillation", *Journal of the history of international law = Revue d'histoire du droit international* 17/1 (2015), 83–137.

48 H. Grotius, *The Antiquity of the Batavian Republic* [*Liber de antiquitate reipublicae batavicae* (1610)], ed. and transl. by J. Waszink e.a., Assen, 2000; also, H. Grotius, [*Apology of the Lawful Government of Holland*] (1622). Grotius also contributed much thought to the government model of the *respublica mixta*. See M. van Gelderen in M. van Gelderen and Q. Skinner (eds.), *Republicanism: A Shared European Heritage. Vol. I: Republicanism and Constitutionalism in Early Modern Europe,* Cambridge, 2002, 199 and following. Also e.g. Weststeijn, "Dutch Republicanism".

49 W.R.E. Velema, "That a Republic is Better than a Monarchy": Anti-monarchism in Early Modern Dutch Political Thought", in Van Gelderen and Skinner (eds.), *Republicanism,* vol. I, 9-25, at 11. This position led to a conflict in 1650, upon which William II had to step down and the office of stadtholder was abolished.

50 See e.g. Van Gelderen and Skinner (eds.), *Republicanism,* vol. I, 2. Therein, the chapter by Velema, "That a Republic".

51 With this view came a way of thinking about liberty and citizenship that put the concept in contrast with slavery.

52 M. Van Gelderen, "Aristotelians, Monarchomachs, and Republicans: Sovereignty and *respublica mixta* in Dutch and German Political Thought, 1580–1650" in Van Gelderen and Skinner (eds.), *Republicanism,* vol. 1, 195–217, at 199 and following.

53 Van Gelderen, „Aristotelians, Monarchomachs, and Republicans", 201 and following. See also Weststeijn,"Dutch Republicanism".

and an advocate of natural law".[54] When Van Gelderen discusses Grotius's legal and political theory in the context of Dutch republicanism, he too emphasizes the notion of *ratio naturae* or 'the ordered plan of nature' that should guide government in order to attain peace and social order and harmony. Since 1960, the image has become diversified and nuanced thanks to the work of Martin van Gelderen and Arthur Weststeijn, among others, in revisiting the topic. One of the political issues at stake at the time in Europe, as well as in the Dutch Republic and Amsterdam specifically, was the triangle of natural law, liberty, and (popular) sovereignty, which in the Republic allowed for the cities to participate in (the administration of) sovereignty. Over the course of the seventeenth century, the *ius naturae et gentium* became fully integrated in the Dutch political debates.[55] It came together with, as Arthur Weststeijn explains, a culture of strong local urban autonomy: "The fundamental unit of Dutch republican politics was the city or *civitas*, the urban community".[56] Dutch republicanism was according to Weststeijn in the first place an "urban republicanism", that is, an urban practices-based political philosophy. He articulates moreover the link of republican practices and theories in the Dutch Republic with the polity's development into a colonial empire.[57] Insightfully, he explains how also "the institutions of [...] colonial rule" – with the government-directed companies VOC and WIC as a case in point – were organized on the basis of shared government and urban autonomy.[58] To specify further: Dutch republicanism, in short, "prioritized the local over the national and the collective [the urban community and the province] over the individual".[59] Consequently, the Dutch Republic was also an "oligarchy", a republic "ruled by familial coalitions."[60] For Amsterdam and its ruling elites, this set of ideas – local urban autonomy, shared government and sovereignty, and universal law (*ius naturae et gentium*) – served their global commercial activities and interests well.[61] Grotius's work reflects this political and eco-

54 As cited in Van Gelderen, 196.

55 H.E. Bödeker, "Debating the respublica mixta: German and Dutch Political Discourses Around 1700" in Van Gelderen and Skinner (eds), *Republicanism*, vol. 1, 219–245, at 221.

56 Weststeijn, "Dutch Republicanism". Here he follows e.g. Maarten Prak.

57 Weststeijn, "Dutch Republicanism": "into an aggressive colonial power that imposed its rule over peoples and places in Asia, Africa, and the Americas."

58 Ibid.

59 Ibid.

60 Ibid.,: "a republic ruled by familial coalitions of male officeholders who monopolized through co-option the seats of local, provincial, central, and colonial government."

61 Also, Weststeijn on how "[t]he rationalization of the Dutch republican order [...] went hand in hand with the rationalization of Dutch colonial expansion."

nomic reality. In his view, social concord or harmony was essential to a *civitas*, its "cohesion [...] the ultimate expression of human nature".[62] As such, human nature was the source of the *ius naturae et gentium*.

Guided by the sculptures themselves – that is, individually and in the relationships between them – we argue for an interpretative scheme in which they position the city within a cosmic order and under the rule of universal natural law (a), that is, an idea that comes with the support of universal virtues, as cosmology and ethics were tightly interwoven (b). Moreover, we note that the iconography does not visualize Amsterdam's position within the political reality of the Dutch Republic as a confederation of provinces. It ignores, so to say, a worldly superior, the political implications of which suggest a certain urban autonomy, as the programme only recognizes the cosmic order and universal natural law as its governing body of law (c). It is exactly the power of the cities within the provinces that fits this visualization. For our discussion of the intellectual background of the design, we focus first on the relationship between cosmology and the universal law of nature and nations.

4 The Cosmos as the Visualization of Universal Law of Nature and Nations (*Ius Naturae Et Gentium*)

For a long time, in both ancient and Christian European thought, representations of the cosmos or the heavens were a reference to the divine order of the universe as created by God.[63] The cosmos was a law-governed order, and this idea did not merely refer to the laws of physics, but also to a metaphysical understanding that it was a divine, natural law order providing moral and legal guidance for all humanity on earth.[64] By the middle of the seventeenth century, the cosmos was still conceived of as a universal natural order created by God. It was also subject to debate, though, and Grotius for example suggested controversially that God himself was also bound to it.[65] Natural reason implanted by God in humans was central to the new science or language of morality, politics and law.

62 Ibid., this applied to the cities in the Republic; the (urban) communities overseas were subjected to colonial domination. The primacy of the urban and urban concord in republican thought continued in the following decades, even with authors who rejected Grotius's aristocratic perspective.

63 See e.g. "Thomism" in Tuck, *The Rights of War and Peace*, 68 *and following*.

64 See e.g. Tuck, *The Rights of War and Peace*.

65 See "*etiamsi daremus*" in the *Prolegomena*, par. 11 of the *De Jure Belli ac Pacis*.

For the purpose of this chapter, it is important to note that this understanding of the cosmos, arguably in different versions, was widespread. In Europe, since the days of the ancient Greeks, the cosmos featured as a normative notion in political thought. It referred more specifically to the idea of a universal human society governed by right reason: the world as a *polis*, a universal city, ruled by natural law. Eric Brown has explained how the Greek Stoics came to the *cosmopolis* metaphor: "if the natural law is right reason organizing the whole cosmos as law should organize a city, then the cosmos is like a city. This is the Stoic metaphor of the cosmopolis."[66]

Seventeenth-century humanists rediscovered Stoic cosmology and philosophy with its ideas of natural order and a universal human society.[67] The realization that humanity was inhabiting one "terrestrial globe" fuelled moreover the idea of a universal human society ruled by natural law. It is crucial to realize that the core idea of Stoic cosmology continued in seventeenth-century neo-Stoic thinking, not least of all because of Cicero's reception by Dutch humanist political thinkers. They used the Stoic cosmological idea that inherent in nature, inherent in the cosmos, is universal intelligence (*logos*) or reason (*ratio*) to write about world's universal human society and its law.

As a Christian humanist, Hugo Grotius was among the Northern humanists who reconciled ancient and Christian thought.[68] The cosmological language and imagery of both antiquity – most notably, of ancient Rome – and Christianity are present in his writings on the universal law of nature and nations. Stoic philosophers were referenced frequently when he developed the idea of a universal human society ruled by natural law.[69] This idea of the world as a

66 E. Brown, "The Emergence of Natural Law and the Cosmopolis" in S. Salkever (ed.), *The Cambridge Companion to Ancient Greek Political Thought*, Cambridge, 2009, 331–366, at 355. Also, he elaborates "later Stoics assume that all human beings are citizens of the cosmos by virtue merely of being subjects of the natural law". Ibid., 356.

67 Neo-Stoic scholar Justus Lipsius was one of the driving forces of the revival of Stoic thinking on ethics, law, and politics in the Netherlands and Europe at large. In his political theory of the state, Roman stoicism and Christian thought were reconciled through conceptions of providence, order, virtues, self-preservation, right reason and nature. Grotius, a student of Lipsius in Leiden, engaged with Lipsius's work actively. J. Papy, "Lipsius' (Neo-)Stoicism: constancy between Christian faith and Stoic virtue", *Grotiana* (New Series) 22/23 (2001–2002), 47–72. Gerhard Oestreich famously wrote about the Stoic "Netherlands Movement" in terms of practical morality and political prudence as traits of good governance.

68 Bradshaw, "Transalpine humanism".

69 See e.g. the special issue on Grotius and the Stoa: *Grotiana* (New Series) 22/23 (2001–2002).

universal society – already at the time called a *cosmopolis* by some – was foundational to Grotian thought.[70]

We find the *cosmopolis* idea used explicitly by Grotius in his response to the attacks by the Scottish Protestant jurist William Welwod (d. 1622) in his arguments on free trade and free navigation in *Mare Liberum*. To establish the universally binding law of nature and nations and the natural rights to free trade and free navigation, Grotius had developed the concept of a universal human law-governed society. It allowed him, to develop the understanding of "common" or "public" goods of humanity and a theory of punishment regarding violations of these rights to free trade and free navigation. The natural law of nature and nations then was the basis for the duty to fight against pirates and – as the consequence of a just war about the violations of these rights – the legitimacy of prize and booty.[71] In *Defense of Chapter V of Mare Liberum* (1614) he explained his use of the word "public" to counter arguments that the sea, the air or water could be appropriated and made "private" goods:[72] the "sea [...] no less than the air, it can be added to the goods of no nation."[73] Here, he explicated the idea of the world as a *cosmopolis* that underpins his theory:

> sometimes the word [public] is properly taken for that which belongs to the people and sometimes in a broader sense to include also those things which belong to the entire human race, by a metaphorical use of the word which is not obscure; because the human race is like a great people, and hence some philosophers call this world a city and themselves "cosmopolitans." Nor is this transferred use of the word "public" found only among the jurists. We have cited that noble passage of Ovid:
>
> ... The use of water is *common*:
>
> *Nature* hath made nor sun nor air nor billowing waters
>
> Proper to one alone: I have come for gifts that are *public*.[74]

---

70 See e.g. H. Blom, "Hugo Grotius (1583–1645) Kosmopolis en autarkie: het moderne individu in de grensoverschrijdende samenleving" in E. de Bom (ed.), *Een nieuwe wereld: denkers uit de Nederlanden over politiek en maatschappij (1500–1700)*, Antwerp, 2015, 217–257.

71 Remember the Santa Catarina, Grotius was the VOC's lawyer and wrote *Mare Liberum* and *De Jure Praedae* to defend the legitimacy of the exceptional booty against complaints of the Portuguese that the capture was illegal. Prize is the acquisition of enemy property through war.

72 *The Free Sea* [*Mare Liberum*], trans. R. Hakluyt, with William Welwod's *Critique* and Grotius's *Reply*, ed. by D. Armitage, Indianapolis, 2004, 25.

73 H. Grotius, *The Free Sea*, 34.

74 H. Grotius, "Defense of Chapter V of the *Mare Liberum*" *Which had been attacked by William Welwod, Professor of Civil Law, in Chapter XXVII of that book written in English to*

The seas comprise a public or common good that belongs to humanity. The world as a *polis* of the entire human race, the idea of humanity living in a universal law-governed society,[75] is the foundational idea of *Mare Liberum* as well as his later work *De Jure Belli ac Pacis*. In *Mare Liberum* itself the idea is discussed in somewhat more indirect terms. Grotius's reference to the "ordered plan of nature" has cosmological overtones – all the more so, when read in conjunction to a description of natural law, where he drew on Cicero and Sophocles and defined it as "not written law, but the law sprung from nature" and as "the immutable laws of Heaven".[76] When he argued in *Mare Liberum* that "[b]y the law of nations navigation is free for any to whomsoever", and so is trade,[77] he indicated how the primary law of nations is found in nature:

> Our purpose is shortly and clearly to demonstrate that it is lawful for the Hollanders, that is the subjects of the confederate states of the Low Countries, to sail to the Indians as they do and entertain traffic with them. We will lay this certain rule of the law of nations (which they call primary) as the foundation, the reason whereof is clear and immutable: that it is lawful for any nation to go to any other and to trade with it. God himself speaketh this in nature ...[78]

Elsewhere in *De Jure Praedae*, the work of which only its Chapter XII was published as *Mare Liberum*, Grotius draws just as often on Cicero to reconcile ancient and Christian thought on natural law:

> The Will of God is revealed, not only through oracles and supernatural portents, but above all in the very design of the Creator; for it is from this last source that the law of nature is derived. Thus Cicero very wisely maintains that the study of celestial phenomena is beneficial in relation to justice, as well as in other ways, because the student "becomes acquainted with the will, plan and purpose of the Supreme Ruler and Lord, to whose nature (so say the philosophers) that true rational principle and sovereign law conform."[79]

---

which he gave the title "An Abridgement of All Sea-Lawes", published in H. Grotius, *Mare Liberum*, 93.

75 See e.g. "the law of nations regulates those which look to the common association of the human race": Ibid., 107.

76 H. Grotius, *De Jure Praedae*, ch. 1. *Commentary on the Law of Prize and Booty*, edited by and with an Introduction by M.J. van Ittersum, Indianapolis, 2006, 16.

77 H. Grotius, *The Free Sea*, chapters 1 and 8.

78 Ibid., 10.

79 *De Jure Praedae*, Chapter 2, the *Prolegomena*, 20.

Since his earliest writings on the law of nature and nations, the Stoic idea of a universal human society governed by rational principles is foundational to Grotian thought. It is further developed in Grotius's famous magnum opus *De Jure Belli ac Pacis* (1625). Again, we find instances of the cosmological and Stoic understanding foundational to Grotius's thought. In the dedication of this treatise to Louis XIII, Grotius uses cosmological imagery and compares the French king to a star in the universe.[80] When he discusses popular sovereignty, Grotius used cosmological language to indicate that the sovereign rulers have to account for their actions to God or the "celestial courts".[81] Ultimately, Grotius ended the third book with a paragraph in which he called on the rulers to be "the ministers of Heaven" when they govern and to make sure they take the law of nature and nations as their guidance:

> VIII. May the *ALMIGHTY* then (who alone can do it) impress these Maxims [of the law of nature and nations] on the Hearts of Christian Powers; may he enlighten their Minds with the Knowledge of every *Right,* Divine and Human, and inspire them with the constant and dutiful *Sense* of their being the *Ministers of Heaven,* ordained to govern *Men; Men,* for whom, of all his Creatures, *GOD* has the greatest *Regard* and *Affection.*[82]

Apart from some explicit references to the cosmos as a normative order, cosmopolitical thought is continued through a profound engagement with Cicero[83] and the Stoics.[84] Cicero adopted the Stoic understanding of natural law as right reason in agreement with Nature and God: "It is a true Law of universal application, unchanging and everlasting, valid for all nations and

80 "For just as the heavenly bodies not only flood the vast expanses of the universe but suffer their force to descend to each living thing, so you, a most beneficent star upon the earth, not content to lift up princes and to succour peoples, willed to become a protection and solace also to me, who had been badly treated in my native country."

81 H. Grotius, *De Jure Belli ac Pacis Libri Tres,* The Classics of International Law edition, Book I, J. Brown Scott (ed.), Oxford, 1925, 110.

82 Grotius, *De Jure Belli ac Pacis,* 3.25.8.1. as cited from this edition: Hugo Grotius, *The Rights of War and Peace* (3 volumes), edited and with an introduction by Richard Tuck from the edition by Jean Barbeyrac in the Natural Law and Enlightenment Classics series, Knud Haakonssen, general editor, Indianapolis, 2005.

83 Constantijn Huygens, a prominent member of the humanist intellectual circles in Holland, called Grotius at some point the "Cicero of Delft". See e.g. H.J.M. Nellen, "Een Haags dichter over 'de Delftse Cicero'. Hugo Grotius in de brieven en gedichten van Constantijn Huygens", *De Zeventiende Eeuw* 3–2 (1987), 125–134, at 132.

84 Papy, "Lipsius' (Neo-)Stoicism".

all times."[85] This statement was for centuries the classical formulation of natural law: universal, unchanging and eternal. In *De Jure Belli ac Pacis*, Grotius stated: "The law of nature is a dictate of right reason"[86] and earlier (in the *Prolegomena*) that human nature is "the mother of natural law".[87] As explained elsewhere, Grotius's *imago Dei* anthropology reconciled Christian and Stoic thought in a humanist approach to human nature and the law of nature and nations.[88] In the *Prolegomena* of *De Jure Belli ac Pacis*, he takes on board explicitly the Stoic theory of sociability and defines human nature by the capacity of reason and the desire to live in harmony with society (*oikeiosis*).[89] Sociability is thus constitutive of human societies, including the universal human society, and thus in Stoic thought of world citizenship (*cosmopolites*). In other words, in this understanding of human nature, shared by all members of humanity, Grotius grounded the idea of the universal human society and the law of nature and nations. At the time, the image of the cosmos was part of the normative language of this early modern tradition in natural law. The imagery established a world view and a normative approach to good government and to issues of war and peace, along with trade and navigation. It called upon all its subjects – (relatively) sovereign rulers, peoples, merchants, military officers, and citizens generally – to live by the rules of natural law and justice to contribute to peace in the city and beyond. In view of the discussion of the role of human virtues in the city hall's cosmological iconography, it is helpful to present the basis for Grotius's argument in full:

> Among the things which are unique to man is the desire for society [*appetitus societatis*], that is, for community with those who belong to his species – though not a community of any kind, but one at peace, and with a rational order [*pro sui intellectus modo ordinatae*]. [...] we should understand that it is appropriate to human nature rationally [*pro humani intellectus modo*] to follow good judgment in these matters, and not be disturbed by fear or the lure of immediate pleasure, and that whatever is plainly contrary to good judgment is also contrary to the law of nature (that is, of human nature).[90]

---

85 F.H. Llano Alonso, "Cicero and Natural Law", *ARSP: Archiv Für Rechts- Und Sozialphilosophie / Archives for Philosophy of Law and Social Philosophy* 98(2) (2012), 157–168.

86 H. Grotius, *De Jure Belli ac Pacis*, 1.1.

87 Ibid., *Prolegomena*, par. 16.

88 J.E. Nijman, "Grotius' *Imago Dei* Anthropology: Grounding *Ius Naturae et Gentium*" in M. Koskenniemi, M. García-Salmones Rovira and P. Amorosa (eds.), *International Law and Religion: Historical and Contemporary Perspectives*, Oxford, 2017, 87–110.

89 H. Grotius, *De Jure Belli ac Pacis*, *Prolegomena*, 6.

90 Ibid.

Thanks to these features of human nature, humans are able to understand what natural law prescribes and, so doing, to come to good judgement, thus producing harmony, peace and justice, in line with the universal natural legal order.[91]

These concepts cannot be illustrated directly in the visual language of the building but are so to say translated in the iconographical programme. On the exterior, Peace and Atlas are the messengers of harmony and connect it to the whole of the world: to the oceans and continents on the tympanums. These further illustrate the fruits brought by harmony: flourishing trade and navigation. The decoration of the cupola with Music and the Winds, as so planned, also intended to express the idea of universal harmony as the highest principle of this government building.

In the interior, the statues of the planets in the galleries are key. In the annular form with which they unite the layout of the building, they embody the overall idea of the heavenly origin of order. So does Atlas with the celestial sphere, inside and outside, as cosmos signifies since the days of the Greeks natural and rational 'order'. In the *Burgerzaal*, as we have seen, the earthly and heavenly worlds are also connected, under the aegis of the virtues of good governance, as are themes of order and chaos. The visual language deriving from the classical world might be abstract and hard to grasp, but ultimately the message cannot be misunderstood: government and jurisdiction, international trade and navigation should all be exercised in conformity with the cosmic order, with natural law and justice.

5 The Role of Virtues in the Observance of the Universal Law of Nature and Nations

As described in section 3, the virtues Prudence, Justice, Vigilance, and Temperance take up a prominent place within the cosmological iconography, for both the exterior and the interior of the building. For centuries, virtues abounded in town hall decoration. In the seventeenth-century Dutch Republic, they were still very much part of the moral, legal and political language and imagery,[92] as

91 Ibid.

92 P.J.E. Kail, "Virtue and Vice" in Clarke and Wilson (eds.), *The Oxford Handbook of Philosophy in Early Modern Europe*, at 363, with reference to the work by Jerome Schneewind; also, M. Somos, "Virtue" in R. Lesaffer and J.E. Nijman (eds.) *The Cambridge Companion to Hugo Grotius*, Cambridge, 2021, 91–117.

well as part of the early modern reconciliation of ancient thought – most prominently, Stoic moral philosophy – with Christian ethics and philosophy.[93] At the public building of Amsterdam's mayors, magistrates and judges, political or civic virtues, such as the four depicted, were there to inspire good government and judgement. Being the city hall of Amsterdam, it is also important to keep in mind that (republican) citizenship, government and politics were shaped to serve the urban, commercial society. It suffices here to build on this bigger vision when we ask what role and function these virtues had within the thought regarding the law of nature and nations.

The classical republican language of virtue was clearly put to use in Amsterdam. One source that testifies to contemporary thought on the government of the city of Amsterdam as concerned cosmic order and virtues is the first and was for some time the only historiographical work on Amsterdam, namely, the *Historische beschrijvinghe der seer wijt beroemde coop-stad Amsterdam*, published in 1611/1614 by Johannes Isacius Pontanus (1571–1639). Pontanus was well versed in classical political thought and corresponded, for example, with Barlaeus, Vossius and Grotius. His writings show familiarity with the latter's *De Antiquitate Republicae Batavicae* (1610) and with Grotius's legal ideas about the natural rights of free trade and free navigation.[94] With his foreword to the *Historische beschrijvinghe*, Pontanus addressed the magistrates of the city. He praised Amsterdam's local government for its policies contributing to Amsterdam's prosperity. Here, too, we find an outlook that related the state of the city to "God as the creator of everything" ("*God selve den auteur van alles*"), who had given the magistrates "prudence and other virtues" ("*voorsichticheyt en andere deuchden*") to govern well and contribute to the "happy state of the Republic" ("*soo gheluckighen state der Republijcke*") – that is, Amsterdam.[95] Placing the virtues at the top level of the city hall and in a relationship with Peace and the Universe brings this idea home to the Amsterdam local government. Acting virtuously meant acting in harmony with the universal rational order, to abide by the laws of nature.

This body of law included natural rights that derive from strict, expletive justice and imperfect natural rights that derive from attributive justice.[96] Politics and the administration of justice have to be guided by both. That is, by

---

93 See again Lipsius.

94 J.I. Pontanus, *Discussionum historicarum libri II, quibus praecipue quatenus et quodnam mare liberum vel non liberum clausumque accipiendum, discipitur expenditurque* 1637.

95 See also Dave De ruysscher, in this volume, chapter 1.

96 Nijman, "Images of Grotius". Also, J.E. Nijman, "Grotius' 'Rule of Law' and the Human Sense of Justice: An Afterword to Martti Koskenniemi's Foreword", *European Journal of International Law* 30/4 (2019), 1105–1114.

what is obligatory (natural law and justice *in stricto sensu*) and by what is called for by attributive or governmental justice. In other words, the universal order of natural law and justice demands Amsterdam's local governors and judges to act on the basis of natural law and justice, but also and additionally to act virtuously – to be guided by Prudence, Justice, Vigilance and Temperance – for example, in case of punishment or in case of (political) decision-making; the public good had to be served.[97]

As became clear already with Pontanus's work, the virtue of prudence was of the highest importance in the context of government. In Book II of *De Jure Belli ac Pacis*, Grotius observes that "Prudence [...] is indeed a Virtue peculiar to the Prince [i.e. the ruler], but Justice belongs to every Man as he is a Man" (*De Jure Belli ac Pacis* 2.26.4). For Grotius, as for many, prudence is a virtue that should belong to those in government. They should govern with prudence and wisdom.

Indeed, Grotius's work can be an exemplary source for contemporary virtues theory in humanist Amsterdam. While Grotius's discussions of virtue are "scattered over multiple works" (as Mark Somos rightly observes), his philosophy of virtues is foundational to his theory of the law of nature and nations.[98] Natural law is virtue-driven; without virtues it is an unattainable standard of morality and law. Virtues are crucial for bringing Amsterdam or any society closer to the ideal of natural harmony and peace. As Somos shows, virtues are understood to be useful for peace and profit also in the context of overseas relations and trade.[99]

In Grotius's theory virtues are foundational to law, but also reach beyond law in the sense that virtue can correct actions pursuant to strict, corrective justice.[100] Somos explains, "Natural law respects not only strict, expletive just-

---

97 As also John Pocock has shown, the relationship between virtue and right was one of the much-discussed topics in early modern political thought. In Dutch republicanism, virtue is a central notion that is in a relationship with natural right or law but not to be identified with it. It refers to the common or public good that government should serve. See J. Pocock, *Virtue, commerce, and history: Essays on political thought and history, chiefly in the eighteenth century*, Cambridge, 1985.

98 Somos, "Virtue".

99 Ibid.

100 H. Grotius, *De Jure Belli Ac Pacis*, 2.22.16 as cited by Somos: "[I]f a Man owes another any Thing, not in Strictness of Justice but by some other Virtue, suppose Liberality, Gratitude, Compassion, or Charity, he cannot be sued for it in any Court of Judicature, neither can War be made upon on that Account; for to either of these it is not sufficient, that that which is demanded ought for some moral Reason to be performed, but besides it is requisite we should have some Right to it, such a Right as both divine and human Laws do sometimes give us to those Things which are due by other Virtues (...)."

ice, but also the virtues of temperance, prudence and fortitude."[101] The latter go to distributive justice, that is, to the idea that justice may require duties that go beyond strict justice. For the maintenance of the universal normative order, the support of the four political virtues is necessary. Interestingly, the classical fourth virtue, *fortitudo*, which was envisaged at the right end of the Western tympanum, was replaced by *vigilantia*, which also has a long history as a political virtue (see below).[102]

Grotius's biographer Henk Nellen has explained the relationship between virtues and peace in Grotius's work too: "By cultivating the virtues that were rooted in man's natural appetite for a steady community life, violence could be avoided or limited to a minimum."[103] It is indeed in the context of the use of force that *Temperantia* (self-constraint or self-discipline) features prominently in Book III of *De Jure Belli ac Pacis*, which deals with what is permissible according to the law of nature and nations in warfare. Chapters XI-XVI all deal with moderation in warfare and thus argue that the virtue of moderation is also applicable in times of war. Moderation is however demanded by natural law and justice, that is, beyond expletive justice, by attributive justice. What then does moderation mean in the context of peace iconography? Moderation was the virtue that had to guide the interpretation and application of the law of nature and nations as well as its enforcement. In *De Jure Belli ac Pacis*, moderation features in the more general natural law theory of punishment,[104]

101 Ibid., 93. See also in another translation: "natural Right, considered as a Law, does not only respect what we call expletive Justice, but comprehends the Acts of other Virtues, as of Temperance, Fortitude, and Prudence" (*DJBP* 2.1.9.1).

102 In Grotius's works on the law of war and peace, fortitude as a virtue to endure danger plays a role in the context of warfare more than in times of peace. This may be relevant to the replacement. See also below.

103 H. Nellen, "Life and Intellectual Development: An Introductory Biographical Sketch" in R. Lesaffer and J.E. Nijman (eds.) *The Cambridge Companion to Hugo Grotius*, Cambridge, 2021, 17–44, at 29.

104 "XXVIII. *The Punishment is to be proportioned to the Crime.* From what has been already said, it appears, that in Punishments two things are to be considered, the Reason why and the End for which. The Reason why, is the Demerit; the End for which, is the Advantage of Punishment. No Body is to be punished above his Desert, according to those Passages of *Horace,* which we have before quoted, and that of *Cicero There is a Measure,* saith he, *and Moderation to be used in punishing, as well as in all other Things*". (Footnotes were omitted.)

along with human judgement too.[105] In the *Prolegomena*, moderation operates for example also in relation to the 'right reason' or *recta ratio* and "well-tempered[ness of] judgement".[106] Measurement or moderation and alertness are crucial capacities when making government decisions in service of the common good – that is, generally, the purpose of virtue in government. Alertness was also an important virtue beyond government, whether in navigation or trade.

Temperantia was one of the key virtues of neo-Stoicism and Northern humanism more generally. In the context of peace and commerce, a valuable source for the interpretation of *Temperantia* on the corner of the tympanum dedicated to trade is Barlaeus' inaugural lecture, *Mercator Sapiens*, which he held at the Amsterdam Athenaeum Illustre on 9 January 1632. Here we see how Stoic cosmopolitan thinking was brought to the worlds of trade and commerce. Barlaeus deliberately taught on the Stoics, among other ancient philosophers, to engage his merchant-class students in a moral philosophical discourse on how to be wise in trade and commerce – or so he wrote to his friend Huygens in late January 1632.[107] With Stoic thought, Barlaeus mobilized such concepts as – "*recta ratio*"[108] that "moderate[s]" the merchants' "love of money, glory and pleasures."[109] As for the idea of a global trade *community*? Central to Barlaeus' argument, Dirk van Miert explains, is "that although money is important, science and virtue are even more important." Barlaeus did not despise earthly riches: although his explicit allegiance was to the "manly and strict school of the Stoics", his own views were in fact closer to Aristotle's ideal of moderation than to the Stoic ideal of *apatheia*, freedom from desire.[110] Virtues are central to wise trade.[111] A widespread idea at the time was that wealth inspired the virtues, and with wealth came responsibility for the common good.[112] "[T]o trade *wisely*", Barlaeus argued, "[a]part from *tempering*

105 *"A Survey of our own Actions will make us more moderate in passing Judgment upon others, if we consult our own Breasts, and consider whether we have not been guilty of the like Crimes"*. (Footnotes were omitted.)

106 *DJBP*, *Prolegomena*, par. 9.

107 C. Barlaeus, *The Wise Merchant*, Anna-Luna Post (ed.) and critical text and translation by Corinna Vermeulen, Amsterdam, 2019, 38, 43.

108 Barlaeus, *The Wise Merchant*, 68–69.

109 Ibid.

110 D. van Miert. *Humanism in an Age of Science: The Amsterdam Athenaeum in the Golden Age, 1632–1704*, Leiden, 2009, 226.

111 "But I would like to consider the virtues of merchants more closely and demonstrate with some serious precepts borrowed from philosophy how wisdom can also remedy their shortcomings." Barlaeus, *The Wise Merchant*, 85, 8–10.

112 Anna-Luna Post in Barlaeus, *The Wise Merchant*, 49–50.

their desire for riches, merchants should use their wealth to serve the common good."[113] Here, too, commerce and trade should be done virtuously: "natural law has laid down that nothing should be done insidiously, dishonestly or deceitfully."[114] Barlaeus, too, finds the rules of trade in the law of nature and nations.

> Who gives rules for the entire trade, who distinguishes filthy from respectable trade, poor from abundant? Who brings order to the entire trade with *rules taken from natural, international and civil law*? [*quis depromtis ex jure naturali, gentium, civili praeceptis eam universam ordinat?*] The politician.[115]

Barlaeus then continues, citing the basic Roman law principles that featured as principles of natural law and justice in Grotius's work:

> Now he, according to Aristotle, is the prince and architect of the whole of philosophy. And who presents the merchants as well as the lawyers with his principles: that one should live honourably, should not harm another, should give everyone what he is entitled to? The moral philosopher.[116]

With "the moral philosopher", Barlaeus refers here to the new moral science of natural law. Natural jurisprudence thinking about trade reworked these private or Roman law principles into natural law principles foundational to the law of nations.[117] The emerging law of nature and nations was equally relevant to the merchants; the rights to travel and trade were part of the natural law of nations.

Though Grotius resided clandestinely in Amsterdam at the time of his friend's lecture, he did not attend, nor did he go to the inaugural lecture of his friend Vossius a day earlier.[118] Grotius and Vossius had been fellow students in Leiden, where they studied together with Josephus Justus Scaliger

---

113 Ibid., 49 italics added to tempering.

114 Barlaeus, *The Wise Merchant*, 99.

115 Ibid., 103. Italic added. Footnotes omitted.

116 Barlaeus, *The Wise Merchant*, 103, also "trade goes hand in hand with moral philosophy," for Barlaeus to then turn to natural philosophers, 105.

117 For profound insights on how Roman law structured the state of nature (in which sovereigns and rising states lived), B. Straumann, *Roman Law in the State of Nature. The Classical Foundations of Hugo Grotius' Natural Law. Ideas in context,* Cambridge, 2015.

118 Nellen, *Hugo Grotius*, 454–455.

(d. 1609). Barlaeus was also a friend of Burgomaster Cornelis de Graeff, for whom Barlaeus wrote a poem on the occasion of his marriage.[119]

In sum, Barlaeus also emphasized the importance of *Temperantia* in relation to trade and pursuit of profit and wealth. The virtue of moderation should prevent humans from succumbing to greed.[120] That said, Barlaeus message was "double-edged," as Post describes it;[121] while he condemned greed, he did not aim "to condemn the pursuit of wealth, but to keep it in check with the brake of reason".[122] The sculpture of *Temperantia* on the building is Reason with a bridle – that is, tempered reason or moderation. Interestingly, Barlaeus also emphasized the importance of *Vigilantia*, which – it goes without saying – is an essential quality for those operating in the commercial world. According to Barlaeus it is for that reason that the rooster, symbol of vigilance, is the attribute of Mercury, the classical god of commerce.

The same animal is also to be found at the feet of the statue of Vigilance on the city hall, together with book and torch. What do they siginify in this setting? Cesare Ripa's *Iconologia* from 1644 provides explicit explanations for these attributes.[123] Compared to Barlaeus's, they are less straightforward, but rather

119 Post in Barlaeus, *The Wise Merchant*, 22. The poem "Amor Sapiens" was written in 1633, and Post explains how it was part of Barlaeus's broader activities to "consolidat[e]" with the "powerful families" Bicker and De Graeff, who "formed a strong alliance in Amsterdam, and ensured a more lenient climate for the Remonstrants in the city." See for the text of the poem, the *Barlaeus Bibliografie* at https://www.let.leidenuniv.nl/Dutch/Latijn/BarlaeusBibliografie.html (last consulted 13 June 2025).

120 Barlaeus, *The Wise Merchant*, 87. "For the wise have revealed that wealth should be estimated not with a valuation, but by one's way of life and one's culture. Someone who needs many things to provide for himself and his family does not possess more than someone who needs very little. The masculine and strict school of the Stoics agrees with me: they proclaimed rich whoever could enjoy the sky and the earth, and claimed that nothing was so narrow-minded and silly as being unable to love those things less to which the masses are drawn, inflamed with greed. But the Aristotelians, our friends who are the summit of abundance, learning and earnest, although they certainly do not despise money or the other protections of this life, still limit the love of all that with *moderation*; and they rightly question whether it is convenient for someone to be the master of more goods than he could be the guardian of."

121 Post in Barlaeus, *The Wise Merchant*, 46.

122 Barlaeus, *The Wise Merchant*, 77.

123 Ripa, *Iconologia*, gives three variants for Vigilanza (*Wackerheyt*). The rooster is mentioned in the second: "*Een Vrouwe in 't wit gekleet, met eenen Haen, hebbende een Lantaerne in der hand, om dat ons de Haen des nachts door zijn gewoonlijck gekray opweckt, en nimmermeer naelaet de verborgene onderwijsinge van de natuyre, te gehoorsaemen, leerende alsoo den Mensche de Wackerheyt. De Lantaerne vertoont even het selve, om dat de duysternisse de loflijcke wercken niet hinderlijck soude zijn. Hier over leestmen, dat Demosthenes gevraeght zijnde, wat middel hy gebruyckt hadde, om een goed Reedenaer*

abstract philosophical properties. "The crowing rooster wakes us from the night and by doing so obeys to the teachings of nature." The book "expresses awakeness of mind and body as it is learning that makes people attentive and proficient in withstanding misfortunes and passions of the mind."[124] The lit torch is there "to avoid that darkness obscures learning." The implication is that the rooster voices the cycles of the cosmos, not unlike the virtuous man should do, guided by studying the higher principles of nature.

Does this help us to understand why Vigilance was to replace Fortitude? As we have said, the reason behind this alteration has not come down to us and is not easy to understand. As Fortitude was a standard element in the quadruplet of the Cardinal Virtues, there must have been a good reason to prefer Vigilance. In Ripa's explanation, Vigilance is a disposition of mind to open oneself to learning and to avoid the obscuring effects of inattentiveness and complacency. Usually, as with Barlaeus, its meaning was less sophisticated.

In order to put its position on the city hall in perspective, Vigilance as a motif in political allegory of the seventeenth century needs to be considered. Although not many, there are several instances in which Vigilance was propagated in word and image. The motto *Servat Vigilantia Concors* (united vigilance protects) is inscribed on commemorative medals and coins on several occasions – even as an admonition: there is a medal from 1606 coined on the occasion of the defeat of Admiral Willem de Zoete against the Spanish fleet at the Battle of Cap St Vincent. As the Dutch fleet was misled and driven apart by the Spanish, the motto calls for greater unity and alertness.

---

te worden, voor antwoorde gaf, dat hy meer Oly als Wijn gebruyckt hadde, verstaende by de Oly de Naerstigheyt, en by den Wijn de dertelheyt". (A woman dressed in white, with a rooster, holding a lantern in her hand, because the rooster awakens us at night with its usual crowing, and never fails to obey the hidden teachings of nature, thus teaching mankind about wakefulness. The lantern shows the same, so that the darkness does not hinder praiseworthy works. About this, one reads, that Demosthenes, being asked what means he had used to become a good rhetorician, answered that he had used more oil than wine, understanding by the oil the zeal, and by the wine the frivolity). See pp. 588–589.

124 The book is explained in Ripa's first variant (with the crane as the symbolic animal): "*wort soo wel de Wackerheyt des lichaems, als des geests, door dit beeld uytgedruckt, te weten, de Wackerheyt des Geests door 't Boeck, waer in men de wetenschap leerende, den Mensche wacker en vaerdigh maeckt, om de ongevallen der fortuyne tegen te staen, en de driften des gemoeds te beschouwen*" (the vigilance of the body as well as the mind is expressed by this image, namely, the power of the mind via the book, in which one learns science, which makes man awake and capable, so as to resist the accidents of fortune, and to consider the passions of one's nature), 588.

Vigilance was, on the other hand, also staged to underscore the military successes of the Dutch. A large allegorical print by Jan Saenredam in honour of the victory at Nieuwpoort in 1600 shows this virtue as a woman with a dog, symbol of watchfulness, centrally in the foreground. The Latin explanatory verse claims her to be "our companion". In her train follows a group of music-making young men inscribed *Feliciter patriae*. The other protagonist in this allegory is Concordia, who leads the chariot of victory pulled by Spanish prisoners of war.[125] Both qualities are indispensable for military victory and safety. Interestingly, the engraving was re-issued and adapted for later military successes of the Dutch Republic, such as those of Tromp and De Ruijter in the First Anglo-Dutch War in 1654.[126]

Might it be meaningful that Vigilance got its place on Amsterdam's city hall exactly during the years of the First Anglo-Dutch War? Was it added as a call for vigilance in the military sense?[127] Not directly, for it adorns a temple of peace, though obviously protecting it requires vigilance.[128] So does Fortitude, however, and therefore the military associations expressed in coins and prints cannot be the full explanation. It is rather its place in statesmanship and political stability that suits its place on a town hall. It recalls a specific disposition of mind required in politics: to be attentive to everything, even to that which is

125 J. Saenredam, *Elenchus rerum, deo auspice, a confoederatis Belgis praeclare gestarum* engraving 415 x 554 mm, 1600, Rijksmuseum, RP-P-OB-70.090, (Hollstein Dutch 120–2 (5)). The phrase on Vigilance from the six columns of Latin verses reads: "*His et adest alata pedes vigilantia, nostro que comiti semper comes est caepta secundat*" (Winged feet are watching over them, and our count, who is always the count, is captured and seconded).

126 For these later adaptions see sheets in the collection of the Rijksmuseum, RP-P-OB-81.824 (Hollstein Dutch 120–4(5)). The new inscription, in Dutch and French this time, written by Jan Zoet, does not refer to the central figure of Vigilance. Therefore, we do not know the importance attached to it. Another edition followed in 1666, this time to celebrate successes from the Four Day's Battle in June of that year during the Second Anglo-Dutch War, Rijksmuseum, RP-P-OB-77.987 (Hollstein Dutch 120–5(5)).

127 Goossens, *Heel en al*, 98 suggests a "possible political explanation" and refers to the Anglo-Dutch wars of 1652–1654 and 1664–1667.

128 There is another example in which Vigilance serves the world of Peace: the allegory etched by Michiel Serwouters after a design from 1608 by David Vinckboons on the Twelve Years' Truce (realized a year later). As an explanatory text states, vigilance is represented here by a dog that accompanies a guard, together with a porcupine (Steadfastness) and snake around his rod (Prudence). The guard and his animals protect a fenced garden with the personifications of the provinces of the Dutch Republic, together with Minerva holding a flag inscribed *viglia*. Rijksmuseum, RP-P-OB-80.746A (Hollstein Dutch 14).

still obscured and, moreover, to be open to the lessons of the highest learning. The fact that the book and illumination were added underlines that learning must lead us. Vigilance brings, so to say, wisdom, attentiveness and acting together. More than Fortitude it stresses the exigencies of intelligence and open-mindedness in matters of state. This bookish guise of Vigilance fits well, we can conclude, with the overarching message of the city hall connecting universal law and order with good governance.

Finally, though, the most prominent virtue of the republican canon of civic virtues is Justice. It is the chief virtue for government officials and citizens to live by and contribute to the common good. Above, the two conceptions of justice – attributive and distributive – as distinguished in Grotius's work were mentioned. Both conceptions were relevant for Amsterdam government officials working in the city hall and for the citizens and inhabitants living in the city's streets. Justice as the cardinal virtue has a long history, as Goossens also points out, of adorning town halls.[129] With respect to the role of virtue in relation to the universal legal order – spanning the virtues at the tympanums from Atlas's celestial globe to the clocktower cupola and Peace's olive branch – here, too, Nellen's observation applies. Cultivation of justice as a virtue rooted in human nature is crucial to the discernment of *ius naturae et gentium* and the service of peace.[130] The *ius naturae et gentium* relies on the virtue of justice – in fact, on all four virtues.[131] In other words, for Grotius as the leading legal scholar of the early seventeenth century, "virtues are essential in both assessing the justice of human laws and for guiding human action beyond the domain of such laws".[132] Their relevance is not restricted to the urban domain but extends globally to the natural society of humankind.

In sum, Amsterdam as the city maiden is positioned underneath Peace and Atlas's cosmos, connected through the universal, rational and eternal laws of nature visualized by Music (and the Winds) and supported by the virtues on the four corners of the tympanums. These four political virtues are placed here as authorities that should guide the city's government to govern well and justly. As the layer of sculptures placed one level beneath the span of the universal natural legal order, these virtues have to support the realization of the latter order. They call on rulers, magistrates and judges as well as mer-

129 Goossens, *Heel en al*, 96.

130 See for an elaboration on Grotius's understanding of justice, Nijman, "Images of Grotius".

131 In this context, it is interesting to note that *Vigilantia* is a virtue also used in the context of law and justice. See infra.

132 Somos, "Virtue", 92.

chants and sea captains – who were the Amsterdam representatives abroad in peace and war – to comply with universal natural law and justice.

6 A City Directly under Heaven: Urban Autonomy and Sovereignty

With the rise of cities in the later Middle Ages, the town hall became a category of its own: monumental buildings in stone expressing the town's political pride and position. In this period they were palaces in the gothic style, often lavishly decorated with sculpture on the outside, while paintings adorned the interior. Imagery related to justice was always to be found, as the courtrooms were housed in these buildings. In the larger halls local glories – mythical, historical or territorial – were depicted. The exterior of these buildings spoke another language. There, we hardly encounter narrative scenes, but just single figures (and coats of arms). Often, they stand in niches, or they crown portals or gables. With rows of statues, they can become very impressive, as can be seen in the large examples that have survived (or have been rebuilt), such as these of Bremen, Brussels or Bruges.

In general, those sculptures embody the authorities to which the city considered itself subjected. This could be a feudal or legal reality, but also a historical origin or even an aspirational claim. As a legal reality, these authorities were usually the overlord and his predecessors. Their presence is to be understood as an expression of the mutual relationship between a sovereign and the city. As this relationship was often complicated, the city strove for the maximum of independence from an overlord but needed at the same time the approval of the sovereign for the confirmation of the privileges that provided this freedom. A dynastic series on a town hall's façade confirmed the long endurance of such a political alliance. These contracts were celebrated with *Blijde Intochten* when a new lord visited the city. Such a procession would end at the town hall, where the ruler met his predecessors in stone: a reminder to opt for continuity. Examples, still visible today, are: the town hall of Middelburg, where 25 counts of Zeeland are displayed from the eleventh century till the sixteenth century when Charles V bore this title (replaced in the nineteenth century); and the smaller collection of six rulers (twentieth-century versions) of the county of Holland on the elegant fifteenth-century town hall of Gouda. The mid-sixteenth century town hall of Nijmegen included Roman emperors next to medieval rulers, as the city took pride in its Roman origin as *Ulpia Noviomagus Batavorum*.

In general, the town halls built during the Renaissance have the number of statues reduced. Series of rulers disappear and virtues are reduced in number. For Antwerp's famous municipal edifice, constructed in the 1560s, there were just three: Brabo (the legendary founder of the city) and the virtues *Justitia* and *Prudentia*. These two showed a particular iconographical tenacity and survived till deep in the seventeenth century.

Amsterdam City Hall shows virtues but no overlords or historical figures from the city's history. In the political reality of the seventeenth century, there were no ties anymore to such sovereigns, while the city's relation to the province of Holland and the States General was ignored in the decoration. The city hall's programme inscribes the city into the cosmic order governed directly by the universal law of nature and nations. The city government seems to recognize itself as a subject of that body of law. This presentation of Amsterdam fits the contemporary culture of strong local urban autonomy discussed above. As such, we can recognize a political self-conception with a relative autonomy from the States General and the Republic, one that is led by abstract concepts of harmony, virtues and universal natural law, fully in line with the urban republicanism present in Amsterdam at the time.

Previously, we mentioned Pontanus's history of Amsterdam. Pontanus approached Amsterdam not so much as a town but as a "very laudable republic" ["*seer loflijcke republijcke*"].[133] He positioned Amsterdam as a free and independent city, a state in itself. Like Grotius in *De Antiquitate Republicae Batavicae* (1610), the humanist Pontanus put his historiography of Amsterdam in the tradition of the history of Rome and in the historiographical tradition of Tacitus, Pliny and Varro. Amsterdam is described as a republic within a republic, a city of commerce and navigation with relations all over the world: "*Alwaer nu V.E. Stadt van Amsterdam met eenen wijden schoot haer tot den Coophandel der ganscher Werelt opent.*" (Where your City of Amsterdam with a wide embrace opens her to the trade of the whole world).[134] Pontanus wrote about the new routes Amsterdam seafarers opened to China, the East Indies and the Moluccas, and how the Amsterdam "*burghers*" concluded "contracts" ["*contracten*"] and maintained "relations" ["*verbanden*"] with peoples there, which also helped the *Coop-stadt* to resist the "very powerful Spanish Monarch" for decades. Amsterdam's involvement in global trade helped to finance the war against Spain.[135] This historical narrative of the republic of Amsterdam continued

133 J.I. Pontanus, *Beschrijvinghe der seer wijt beroemde coop-stadt Amsterdam* ..., Amsterdam, 1614, foreword.

134 Pontanus, foreword.

135 Pontanus, foreword, see also book 2, chapters 19 and 20.

through the century. It was not just any imagery, though: it was a firm political cause to write Amsterdam into the republican tradition. The de facto urban autonomy was also articulated in legal terms of sovereignty.[136]

It is rather unlikely that the sculptor Quellinus was unaware of the republican cause of the burgomasters.[137] The notion of sovereignty – what it meant and where it was invested – was still very much debated at the time. While in countries around the rebellious Republic, sovereignty became invested in a centralized state and ruler, in the Low Countries it was rather dispersed. In the Dutch Republic, provinces and cities were constitutive of the state and participated in its sovereignty:

> While sovereignty is an attribute of states alone, the state consists of parts such as provinces, cities, and corporations, which cannot be cut off from the state without their own consent – and the authority to grant or withhold such consent makes their sovereignty equal to the whole state's in the narrow but important respect of their self-determination. Conversely, in cases of extreme necessity, such parts may continue to be viable even when the state as a whole fails.[138]

In *De Jure Belli ac Pacis*, Grotius treats sovereignty as supreme power that can be limited or "divided".[139] A city hall that does not depict any other authority than virtues and the universal law of nature and nations suddenly makes perfect sense. Amsterdam placed itself as a (relatively) sovereign city republic directly within and underneath the universal legal order – neither on the exterior nor elsewhere in the building do we find other levels of governance or law placed in between.

136 See the chapter by Dave De ruysscher in this volume.

137 F. Scholten, "Quellinus's Burgomasters: A Portrait Gallery of Amsterdam Republicanism", *Simiolus: Netherlands Quarterly for the History of Art* 32/2-3 (2006), 87–125.

138 H. Blom and M. Somos, "Public-Private Concord through Divided Sovereignty: Reframing societas for International Law", *Journal of the History of International Law / Revue d'histoire du droit international* 22/4 (2021), 565–588. The omitted footnote refers to Grotius, *De Jure Belli Ac Pacis*, 2.6.4, 568–569.

139 Grotius, *DJBP*, 1.3.16–17, "*a Division of sovereign Power*".

7 Conclusion: Amsterdam Submits to the Emerging Universal Law of Nature and Nations

In this chapter, we have discussed key ideas for understanding the iconography of Amsterdam's city hall in relating the sculptural decoration to legal-political ideas of the times. Cosmopolitical thought in this period still aspired to be universal and timeless: the notion that the order of the universe should serve as the model for good governance and harmony for urban as well as global society. The repertoire of classical mythology and allegory was deployed to embody this thinking. In addition, virtues – also deriving from the classical (republican) tradition – were staged as the moral-juridical forces essential for the application of the universal natural legal order to social reality in times of peace.

Justice, prudence, vigilance and temperance are crucial to the art of governance and "well-tempered judgement", as well as to the support of peace and harmony. These virtues were thus visualized as relevant guides for reason in political decision-making, law-making and administering justice. Whether by political and legal government officials or judges (who had their offices and court rooms in the town hall too), as well as in commerce, trade and seafaring by merchants and maritime officers, these qualities may be seen as a call for conduct that would bring Amsterdam closer to universal natural order.

To be sure, these globe-and-cosmos references propagate Amsterdam's global commercial empire, thereby invoking the idea that the burgomasters of Amsterdam saw their city as the centre of the universe, bragging chauvinistically about its global reach and riches. Despite this conventional reading, however, we have argued that such a merely self-celebratory reading does not fully cover what we understand as a somewhat more complex, indirect – though no less self-serving – iconographical language. Van Campen's emphasis on the importance of law and justice for the good government of the city is extended through the cosmological iconography beyond the limits of local law. It visualizes Amsterdam's place in the universe and its subjection to the universal law of nature and nations, which should guide and constrain the government, judiciary and citizenry of Amsterdam – a powerful seafaring and trading global city.

Placing itself directly below the universal law of nature and nations, the city hall's programme enables Amsterdam to present itself as being directly governed by the universal law of nature and nations. With this cosmological idealism that ignores political reality, the city exalts its autonomy and authority vis-à-vis the Republic and the United Provinces. We can understand this selective framework as an *ex silentio* manifestation of the pride and the political sovereignty of Amsterdam. Yet the iconographical programme wisely does not render explicit these self-congratulatory claims. The city still recognizes that it is subject to the universal law of nature.

We have argued that for the interpretation of the Amsterdam City Hall programme the upcoming field of law of nature and nations is key, as it provided a new normative language used by legal and political philosophers of the times – among whom most prominently Hugo Grotius – for matters of societal organization, war and peace, and the foundation for the freedom of navigation and trade. Although we do not exactly know how these ideas reached the architect Jacob van Campen, nor do we have the written sources to reconstruct the creative origins of the building's decoration, the programme he devised shows that he was able to translate the thinking of law of nature and nations into a tangible iconography.

We hope that our collaborative effort is convincing as a deeper interpretation of the decorative programme of Amsterdam's City Hall. We believe that bringing our two disciplines together has for that reason been rewarding. It takes the practice of iconology further by way of a more substantiated understanding of the significance of ideas, rather than just features from the humanist tradition. For legal-political thinking, it has proven to be an excellent example of the 'material turn' in the history of law, as it shows how eloquently the history of legal ideas manifested themselves beyond the written word.

CHAPTER 3

Used and Abused: Diplomatic Immunity in Early Modern Amsterdam

Tessa de Boer

1 Introduction

> Request by Francisco Mollo, Agent of his Majesty of Poland, aspiring to enjoy liberties and exemptions on equal footing with other Residents – denied[1]

On 9 March 1679, the States-Provincial of Holland were confronted with a particularly tough dossier on a matter of diplomatic immunity.[2] Francisco Mollo, an envoy to the Dutch Republic on behalf of the king of Poland, had made the conspicuous decision to cold-shoulder the diplomatic capital, The Hague and take up his residence in Amsterdam.[3] Having settled there, he now requested the Dutch authorities to grant him the full set of diplomatic immunities that he, as a diplomatic envoy, would be entitled to. With him, he brought a letter of support from the king, which argued that the Dutch commissary in Poland enjoyed similar liberties and that reciprocity in this regard was certainly expected. The States of Holland, however, were not convinced. Bestowing the envoy Mollo with diplomatic immunity beyond The Hague was "against all custom and example";[4] diplomatic status was not to be abused this way. Yet this principle proved flexible: on 22 April 1692, seemingly without further comment, Mollo was awarded his prized immunities after all.[5]

The case of Francisco Mollo is emblematic of the paradox that was early modern diplomatic immunity. On the one hand, it was an established legal

1 *Resolutien van de Heeren Staten van Hollandt ende Westvrieslandt,* vol. 59, 311. Original text: "*Het versoek van Francisco Mollo, Resident van sijn Koninglyke Majesteit van Polen, tendeerende, om te moogen genieten vrydom en exemtie, gelyk andere Residenten, afgeslaagen*". All translations in this chapter are by the author.

2 *Resolutien,* vol. 59, 311.

3 O. Schutte, *Repertorium der buitenlandse vertegenwoordigers, residerende in Nederland 1584–1810*, The Hague, 1983, 543.

4 *Resolutien,* 311.

5 Municipal Archives Amsterdam, *Archief van de Burgemeesters: Groot Memoriaal* (inv. 5023), 8, fol. 24.

concept with roots reaching back to antiquity, and (for its time) it enjoyed an unusually high level of international political agreement on its implementation.[6] On the other, the case demonstrates that in practice a myriad of factors determined the actual, practical and potentially diverse face of diplomatic immunity. Multiple levels of political authority had a tangible role in implementing it; geography determined the spatial limits and intensity of its exercise; sociopolitical ideals on fairness and reciprocity were held over policymakers' heads; the passage of time turned decisions upside down. The potential, local manifestation of an abstract, international concept thus implied multiple levels of adaptive implementation. This chapter studies this process with regards to the implementation of diplomatic immunity in early modern Amsterdam – an atypical diplomatic centre – and assesses to what extent this implementation was effective, in the sense that immunity optimized the diplomatic process, and the risk of abuse was minimized.

Early modern cities such as Amsterdam were highly involved in these processes of implementation. They were often host to (groups of) individuals who, by virtue of their origin, religion, or profession, were not (completely) subject to the sovereignty or jurisdiction of the urban authorities, and/or the state.[7] Because immunities were principally *exercised* locally (for example, no liability for contracted debts), and therefore confronted local subjects and jurisdictions first,[8] municipal governments had a vested interest in their implementation – bestowing, denying, protecting or asserting the immunities of individuals or communities. Diplomatic envoys, along with their far-reaching, deep-rooted immunities, were prominent subjects of this implementation. Three concrete immunities, allocated to them in their host society, lay at the heart of this practice: tax exemption, full restitution of assets, and immunity from criminal persecution.[9]

---

6 E.R. Adair, *The Extraterritoriality of Ambassadors in the Sixteenth and Seventeenth Centuries*, London, 1929, 6–9; M. Ogdon, "The Growth of Purpose in the Law of Diplomatic Immunity", *The American Journal of International Law* 31/3 (1937), 449–465; R. van Alebeek, *The Immunity of States and Their Officials in International Criminal Law and International Human Rights Law*, Oxford, 2008, 159–164.

7 A famous example is the Sephardic/Jewish nation of Amsterdam. See the edited volume by J. Israel and R. Salverda, *Dutch Jewry: Its History and Secular Culture (1500–2000)*, Leiden, 2002.

8 Cl. Parry, *British International Law Cases. Volume 6: Diplomatic and Consular Agents – Treaties – Addendum*, London, 1967, 2; Van Alebeek, *The Immunity of States*, 159–164.

9 D. Fedele, "The Renewal of Early-Modern Scholarship on the Ambassador: Pierre Ayrault on Diplomatic Immunity", *Journal of the History of International Law* 18 (2016), 449–468, here 449–451.

Under the guise of New Diplomatic History, diplomats themselves (as opposed to the negotiations they conducted) and indeed their position in the host society has become the subject of intensified study.[10] However, a significant and persistent flaw in these current discourses is that they lean heavily towards the diplomats found in capital cities and/or (royal) courts.[11] These sites were populated by diplomats of the highest rank, such as ambassadors and envoys extraordinary. The implication in the literature is that the legal status of these diplomats is generalizable for the whole early modern diplomatic corps. However, this assertion is dubious and an all the more curious one considering the increased interest in lower-ranked or even pseudo-diplomatic agents which has also been a staple of New Diplomatic History.[12] These subsidiary agents, such as envoys or consuls, made up a considerable part of the diplomatic corps of the time. Their tasks proved crucial in the day-to-day maintenance of international relations and went far beyond the signing of a treaty in an audience chamber. They were mostly stationed in cities that were important centres of commercial, financial or industrial activity, as opposed to a political capital or court.[13] The degree to which these lower agents subsequently qualified for diplomatic immunities was contested. This controversy derived from the ancient historical *and* legal core of diplomatic immunity, with the status of 'ambassadors' (of foreign states) and *legati* (of other Roman provinces) finding distinction in the Roman law on immunity.[14]

In the early modern period, this controversy on the status of lower agents manifested along geopolitical patterns: often lower agents were established

10 A. Krischer and H. von Tiessen, "Diplomacy in a global early modernity: the ambiguity of sovereignty", *The International History Review* 40 (2018), 1100–1107, here 1101; L. Sicking and M. Ebben, "Nieuwe diplomatieke Geschiedenis van de premoderne tijd. Een inleiding", *Tijdschrift voor Geschiedenis* 127/4 (2014), 541–552; T. Sowerby, "Early modern diplomatic history", *History compass* 14/ 9 (2016), 441–456, here 444–445; T. Sowerby and J. Hennings (eds.), *Practices of Diplomacy in the Early Modern World, c. 1410–1800*, London, 2017.

11 This tendency is for example visible in H. Scott, "Diplomatic Culture in Old Regime Europe" in H. Scott and B. Simms (eds.), *Cultures of Power in Europe During the Long Eighteenth Century*, Cambridge, 2007, 58–85, here 59–61.

12 J. Black, *A History of Diplomacy*, London, 2010, 47; Sowerby, "Early modern diplomatic history", 444; B. Tremml-Werner and D. Goetze, "A multitude of actors in early modern diplomacy", *Journal of Early Modern History* 23 (2019) 407–422, at 411.

13 H. Leira and B. Neumann, "The Many Past Lives of The Consul", *Consular Affairs and Diplomacy* 7 (2011), 223–246, here 238.

14 J.E. Nijman, *The Concept of International Legal Personality. An Inquiry Into the History and Theory of International Law*, The Hague, 2004, 37; Ogdon, "The Growth of Purpose", 452, 458, 461; Parry, *British International Law Cases*, 1–2; van Alebeek, *The Immunity of States*, 159.

in 'secondary' cities, removed from the courts and capitals from whose perspective and (sovereign) prerogatives the existing playbooks on diplomatic immunity were written. The status of diplomats, therefore, was also determined by the diplomatic prerogatives of the host city itself: it was intricately tied up in extensive debates on the nature of sovereignty, as well as the relationship between diplomacy and sovereignty.[15] Although states in the early modern period made strides in centralizing authority and sovereignty, provincial, municipal, noble or religious assemblies often retained significant power. As observed by Christian Windler, these institutions continued to compete for diplomatic prerogatives and a tangible role in foreign relations.[16] The Dutch Republic was also marked by turbulence in this regard, with the central government in The Hague and the urban authorities in Amsterdam concurrently claiming diplomatic prerogatives, muddling the concept and practice of sovereignty. Through this lens, we will examine how debates about the exercise of diplomatic immunity (and by extension sovereignty) manifested in terms of space, again revealing the importance of the *local* context.

The implementation of diplomatic immunities presented a dual challenge to municipal authorities: a challenge in its complexity, in addition to a challenge in its importance in preventing abuse. A study of the mechanisms behind this implementation, using Amsterdam as a case study, provides insight into overarching political historical themes, such as the negotiation of privilege and power, (resistance to) premodern state centralization, or the conversion of prolific commercial activity into political influence. It similarly illustrates the constant interplay between the realms of law and politics, confirming the oft-cited premise that legal principles were inextricably tied up with political considerations.[17] This chapter argues that the implementation of diplomatic status was accomplished through different 'levels', each with their own emphasis, mechanisms, and documentary instruments. It asks the question of *who* determined what diplomatic status entailed in this specific context, and *who* subsequently took charge in implementing it. As we will see, international, domestic, local and internal/diplomatic regulations, informed by scholarly, political, social or cultural considerations, all had a part to play. Ultimately, the day-to-

15 Nijman, *The Concept of International Legal Personality*, 29–79.

16 Ch. Windler, "Afterword. From Social Status to Sovereignty – Practices of Foreign Relations from the Renaissance to the Sattelzeit" in T. Sowerby and J. Hennings (eds.), *Practices of Diplomacy in the Early Modern World, c. 1410–1800*, London, 2017, 254–265, here 258.

17 Adair, *The Extraterritoriality of Ambassadors*, 1; Nijman, *The Concept of International Legal Personality*, 4, 9, 30; Ogdon, "The Growth of Purpose", 454, 461; Van Alebeek, *The Immunity of States*, 158.

day regulation of diplomatic status in Amsterdam was configured in a web of top-down, internationally recognized, external regulations, cross-stitched with locally or internally concocted checks and balances.

2 Amsterdam as a Diplomatic City

The city of Amsterdam has nestled itself in many a historiography over the centuries, and the lustre of its 'Golden Age' has famously attracted the attention of economic historians, as well as historians of art. However, for a city so famed and nowadays critically questioned[18] for its exploitation of global resources and peoples in order to fuel its international economic and artistic ascendancy, there has been relatively little attention to the role of Amsterdam on the *diplomatic* stage.

When it came to determining and negotiating the state of international relations, diplomacy was (and is) the peaceful counterpart to warfare. Although war created plenty of opportunities for specific types of economic growth,[19] peace created even more. Diplomacy, therefore, was an essential tool in safeguarding sustained and increasingly global economic growth. In seventeenth-century Amsterdam, few things were of more importance to the regency of the city than ensuring its continued economic, commercial and financial ascendancy. It is therefore unsurprising that throughout the early modern period, diplomatic activity *in* and *with* Amsterdam was a regular occurrence.

Yet the diplomatic status of Amsterdam was controversial in the context of the 'constitutional' arrangements of the Dutch Republic. The Republic had a layered political structure, principally consisting of the statewide (States General), *gewestelijke* (provincial assemblies) and city/local authorities (regencies). Each had their own responsibilities and prerogatives. As will be discussed in more detail later on, foreign relations and diplomacy were one of the areas in which the States General were sovereign: it was there that decisions were made, and provincial or city authorities were to abstain from independently involving themselves in diplomatic relations with foreign powers. Nominally, the city of Amsterdam was thus politically disqualified from (independently) meddling in diplomatic relations – although this proscription did

18 P. Brandon e.a., *De slavernij in Oost en West. Het Amsterdam onderzoek*, Amsterdam, 2020.

19 Ph.-T. Hoffman and J.L. Rosenthal, "The Political Economy of Warfare and Taxation in Early Modern Europe: Historical Lessons for Economic Development" in J. Drobak and J. Nye (eds.), *The Frontiers of the New Institutional Economics*, San Diego, 1997, 31–55.

not always stop the city from involving itself in it, not to mention entering onto the international stage as a diplomatic *actor* in its own right.[20]

The political permissibility of the city as a *space* for diplomatic activity (diplomats visiting, residing in, or providing services within city limits) is less clear, however. It is somewhat ambiguous whether the physical presence of diplomats in Amsterdam was fully accepted from the point of view of The Hague. There are some indications that physical diplomatic presence in Amsterdam was (kept) restricted, and that full diplomatic status could only be claimed and exercised within the limits of The Hague (see, for example, the case of Francisco Mollo at the beginning of this chapter).[21]

A myriad of other indications, however, provides much stronger evidence that the physical presence of diplomats in Amsterdam was in fact widely accepted, and that the city of Amsterdam was certainly a *space* wherein diplomats, diplomatic activity and diplomatic immunity were common features of the urban fabric. To start, Amsterdam was host to a non-negligible diplomatic community throughout the early modern era. Entangled with Amsterdam's commercial and financial ascendancy from the late sixteenth century onwards was its attraction for foreign powers to establish a diplomatic presence in the city. The number of concurrent diplomatic establishments in Amsterdam roughly followed the rhythm of Amsterdam's economic conjectures: rising until the final quarter of the seventeenth century and subsequently stabilizing (or, put more negatively, stagnating) for much of the eighteenth century. On average, this pattern resulted in approximately two dozen diplomatic establishments concurrently existing in Amsterdam per decade, and about 200 verified individuals of diplomatic status in total over the course of the two centuries.[22] This diplomatic community was decisively smaller than that of diplomatic capital The Hague, but decisively larger than in any other city of note in the Dutch Republic: Amsterdam was the only other Dutch city that could even remotely approach The Hague in terms of diplomatic presence. In addition, the number of diplomats and diplomatic establishments in Amsterdam likely exceeded the aforementioned 200. Their numbers

20 T. de Boer, ""*Ma coustume ne soit de m'addresser aux villes*": Early Modern Amsterdam's Dealings in City Diplomacy", *Diplomatica* 3/1 (2021), 167–179.

21 See also National Archives The Hague, inv. 1.01.02, 12547.384: *Extract uit de resoluties van de Staten-Generaal waarbij de instructie wordt vastgesteld voor Frederick Hessel van Dinter als hofmeester van de Staten-Generaal.* See also J. Heringa, *De eer en hoogheid van de staat. Over de plaats der Verenigde Nederlanden in het diplomatieke leven van de zeventiende eeuw*, Groningen, 1961.

22 Based on data compiled from Schutte, *Repertorium der buitenlandse vertegenwoordigers*, and Municipal Archives Amsterdam, Notaries (inv. 5075).

and biographies are rather poorly sketched out in the only existing repertoire,[23] and further research into other archives in Amsterdam (principally the notarial records) as well as state collections abroad[24] continues to unearth previously unattested diplomats stationed in Amsterdam.

The diplomatic community in Amsterdam mostly consisted of envoys of lesser or subsidiary rank. Foreign powers sent their ambassadors or envoys (higher diplomatic ranks) to the official diplomatic forum The Hague, and generally stationed residents, agents, consuls or commissaries in Amsterdam.[25] Although the terminology certainly differs – and in the international context, court cases as well as political treatises insisting on the legal and political peculiarities of each of these ranks exist[26] – in Amsterdam their daily labours, roles and even exercised (or claimed) immunities were very much the same in practice. The terminologies of rank, in addition, were regularly mixed up by individuals and institutions alike. One of many such examples pertains to Pierre Balguerie, a Frenchman who represented Sweden in Amsterdam. In a notarial deed on his inheritance, he is identified as "late Agent and consul of the king and Crown of Sweden",[27] when in fact Balguerie was never consul, and the terms are thus seemingly used in a conflated fashion, even in a rather formal legal document such as a notarial deed.

The day-to-day labour of the Amsterdam-based diplomatic corps was mainly geared towards (diplomatic) assistance towards expatriate subjects and less focused on interstate negotiation. Diplomats in Amsterdam were

23 Schutte, *Repertorium der buitenlandse vertegenwoordigers.*

24 Preliminary reading into French state archives already reveals that the French state maintained more agents/operatives in early modern Amsterdam than those currently identified in the (Dutch) literature. See Archives Nationales Paris, inv. MAR B7, 77, 88, 96, 99.

25 Based on data compiled from Schutte, *Repertorium der buitenlandse vertegenwoordigers,* and Municipal Archives Amsterdam, inv. 5075. See also de Boer, ""*Ma coustume ne soit de m'addresser*"", 175–176.

26 See, for example, the debate on the consulate as a diplomatic posting (or not): A. Bartolomei, "Débats historiques et enjeux scientifiques autour de l'utilité commerciale des consuls" in S. Marzagalli and J. Ulbert (eds.), *Les études consulaires à l'épreuve de la Méditerranée,* Nice, 2016, 59–59, here 49–50; D. Fedele, "Plurality of Diplomatic Agents in Premodern Literature on the Ambassador" in M. Ebben and L. Sicking (eds.), *Beyond Ambassadors. Consuls, Missionaries, and Spies in Premodern Diplomacy,* Leiden, 2021, 38–62. For a primary source which dissects (lower) diplomatic ranks, see Fr. Callières, *The Art of Negotiating with Sovereign Princes. Of the Usefulness of Negotiations; of the Choice of Ambassadors and Envoys; and of the Qualifications necessary for succeeding in those Imployments*, London, 1738, 67–69, 72. For court cases related to this, see Parry, *British International Law,* particularly Barbuit's case (1737), 261–262.

27 Municipal Archives Amsterdam, Notaries (inv. 5075), 11393B, deed 159.

the first point of contact for general support or information for the expatriate nation – much like today. They assisted expatriates by issuing or ratifying transnationally valid documents (such as passports),[28] by offering judicial support, or by acting as an arbiter in conflicts involving compatriots.[29] In addition, they served as the default broker for all matters related to bonds, annuities or other securities issued by their home state.[30] Along with providing services to expatriates, diplomats in Amsterdam were above all expected to serve their home state. They were expected to consistently dispatch updates on the latest political, commercial and financial developments. Amsterdam was a major hub for news and intelligence, a function that went hand in hand with the buzzing commercial and financial traffic in the city.[31] They also represented their sovereign in said sovereign's legal or contractual conflicts with private parties in Amsterdam, again often with a financial element: for example, by recovering collateral from Amsterdam business entities who had promised to supply this sovereign with capital loans, but whose bankruptcy prevented them from meeting the payment terms of the contract.[32]

Although the tasks of these subsidiary diplomats in Amsterdam were multiple and varied, they rarely constituted full-time employment. Neither (or perhaps therefore) did foreign sovereigns always make the effort to send over one of their own subjects to reside in Amsterdam on their behalf. About half of individuals who were officially accredited as diplomats in Amsterdam verifiably had another occupation in the city.[33] A diplomatic assignment was most often combined with merchantry or banking, but civil service or law were also common careers that intertwined with the diplomatic corps. In addition, approximately half of the diplomatic community in Amsterdam consisted of Dutch subjects and/or Amsterdam burghers.[34] Whereas some diplomats were selected in their home state and sent over by their sovereign to take up residence in Amsterdam, others were born and raised in the city and asked by a foreign sovereign to act as said sovereign's representative. In most cases, the

---

28 Municipal Archives Amsterdam, *Personalia* (inv. 30579), 92; Archives Nationales Paris, inv. MAR B7, 402: 30 Sept. 1756.

29 Municipal Archives Amsterdam, Notaries (inv. 5075), 9348, deed 6893; 12366, deed 309.

30 *Oprechte Haerlemsche Courant,* 6 Febr. 1691, 29 Nov. 1698.

31 M. Van Groesen, *Amsterdam's Atlantic. Print Culture and the Making of Dutch Brazil,* Philadelphia, 2017, is a case study on news on Dutch Brazil, as well as a good illustration of how global commerce, trade, news and intelligence went hand in hand.

32 Municipal Archives Amsterdam, Notaries (inv. 5075), 14114, deed 6546; M. Buist, *At Spes Non Fracta. Hope & Co. 1770–1815,* The Hague, 1974, 21, 483.

33 Based on data compiled from Schutte and Municipal Archives Amsterdam, Notaries (inv. 5075).

34 Ibid.

Dutch subject already had established ties with the foreign state, for example by having trade interests there.[35] Therefore, although they were not subjects of the foreign sovereign, they were no strangers either.

Both professional occupation and subject status were potential complicating factors in obtaining diplomatic immunity and exercising it. This plurality of roles came with the risk of individuals invoking different legal personalities in order to avoid consequences for (potentially) controversial actions. Tamar Herzog has argued that this "wearing multiple hats" was to some degree accepted in the premodern period;[36] however, it occasionally provoked discussions in the context of the perceived abuse of diplomatic immunity in Amsterdam. As we will see, ancillary occupations held by diplomats were a potential source for abuse. Similarly, the *obligations* that came with being a Dutch subject actively competed with the *privileges* that accompanied diplomatic immunities. The diplomatic community in Amsterdam was thus partly composed of individuals whose diplomatic status needed strict assessment by various authorities in order to determine the boundaries between functional and personal immunity.[37]

3 The Impact of Early Modern Scholarship on Implementing Diplomatic Immunity

Before the authorities in Europe, the Dutch Republic, or Amsterdam could engineer appropriate policies applicable to the city's diplomatic community, what diplomatic immunity actually entailed as a legal and political concept first needed to be established. By the seventeenth century, diplomatic immunity had already undergone nearly two millennia of legal conceptualization and practical application.[38] However, in the early modern period and particularly the seventeenth century, this conceptualization again entered a phase of flux, urgency and innovation. On the one hand, this shift came in response to changing political circumstances: the reconceptualization and reconfiguration of both "sovereigns" and "states", increasingly tying the prerogative to define,

35 For an example, see the biography of Christoffel van Brants, merchant and agent of Russia in Amsterdam: Schutte, *Repertorium der buitenlandse vertegenwoordigers*, 560; Municipal Archives Amsterdam, *Archieven van Brants* (inv. 404), 183–191.

36 T. Herzog, *A short history of European law: the last two and a half millennia*, Cambridge, 2018, 190–191; Windler, "Afterword", 261.

37 Van Alebeek, *The Immunity of States*, 158–166.

38 Ibid.; Ogdon, "The Growth of Purpose", 449–454.

distribute and accommodate diplomatic immunity to "sovereign states".[39] Traditionally, the origin of this change has been pinpointed to the negotiations and treaties at Westphalia in 1648. In more recent assessments, the critical spark of these developments is subject to debate, with Westphalia instead considered as emblematic for a more *longue durée* development in premodern international relations and political thought.[40] On the other hand (and along with the above), diplomatic practices evolved, with resident embassies (as opposed to incidental missions) becoming not only commonplace, but the standard organizational form of diplomatic relations. Long-term residence abroad necessitated an arguably intensified understanding of diplomatic immunity in order to better protect the ambassadors' labour, assets and person.[41]

The principle of necessity had been at the core of the concept of diplomatic immunity since antiquity, having found a thorough basis in Roman law.[42] Diplomatic immunity was an asset in international relations. It upheld the dignity of those negotiating them and, more importantly, protected envoys from the risks to their person and properties that 'foreigners' were ordinarily exposed to outside of their home territory. The "unhampered and free exercise of the diplomatic function"[43] was thus its goal; this principle was so fundamental and so sacred that it was regarded as part of natural law.[44] This basis continued to lead medieval and eventually early modern legal thought. In discourses such as those of the influential lawyer Pierre Ayrault (1536–1601), diplomatic immunity was reiterated as consisting of three central components, all serving the principle of necessity.[45] First, the diplomat's person as well as his assets were immune from taxation in the host country. His person and assets remained taxable only by his own sovereign; this principle prevented an often-unbear-

39 Nijman, *The Concept of International Legal Personality*, 29–45.

40 Black, *A History of Diplomacy*, 27; J. Melissen, "Introduction. The Consular Dimension of Diplomacy" in J. Melissen and A. Mar Fernández (eds.), *Consular Affairs and Diplomacy*, Leiden, 2011, 1–17, here 2; Nijman, *The Concept of International Legal Personality*, 10–12, 32–33; M. Pal, *Jurisdictional Accumulation. An Early Modern History of Law, Empires, and Capital*, Cambridge, 2020, 36.

41 Adair, *The Extraterritoriality of Ambassadors*, 6–8; Nijman, *The Concept of International Legal Personality*, 35; Ogdon, "The Growth of Purpose", 453–545; Van Alebeek, *The Immunity of States*, 167.

42 H. Fox and Ph. Webb, *The Law of State Immunity*, Oxford, 2013, 566; Nijman, *The Concept of International Legal Personality*, 35; Ogdon, "The Growth of Purpose"; Parry, *British International Law Cases*, 261–262; Van Alebeek, *The Immunity of States*, 159–164.

43 Ogdon, "The Growth of Purpose", 449.

44 Ibid.

45 Fedele, "The Renewal of Early-Modern Scholarship", 449–451; Ogdon, "The Growth of Purpose", 455–456.

able double fiscal burden. Second, the diplomat could count on full restitution of assets (*restitutio in integrum*). Under Roman law, if a foreigner was deceased or bankrupt whilst on another sovereign's territory, said sovereign was entitled to claim the foreigner's assets. Diplomats – or heirs thereof – were exempted from this. Third and last, a diplomat was immune from (formal) accusations or punishments for crimes committed or debts incurred. Attitudes varied however on whether the severity of the infraction should be taken into account, as well as whether certain aggravated grievances – by definition committed against the receiving sovereign('s subjects) – would be able to override this immunity.[46]

The seventeenth-century context revealed some uneasiness in applying or interpreting the Roman law principles. The aforementioned political and diplomatic 'revolutions' of the seventeenth century impacted the way in which the triad of immunities (from taxation, seizure of assets, and criminal prosecution) should be implemented: *who* would have the right to said implementation, and *who* would be allowed to enjoy the immunities. With (resident) diplomacy increasingly conceptualized as the prerogative of sovereigns, what precisely was the status of diplomats sent by or residing in entities whose sovereign status was ambiguous, such as cities of commerce like Amsterdam?[47] Did they have the capacity to participate in international relations, maintain an international legal personality, or implement diplomatic immunity? Already on this abstract level, Amsterdam's position as a mere city within the statal whole of the Dutch Republic meant its role in implementation was not straightforwardly established.

Yet despite these intellectual disagreements, there is broad historiographical consensus that this period did witness the establishment of an international (Western European) common line of thought in the way diplomacy was understood in general terms, interrelatedly both as a concept (what should it *do*?) and as a practice (how should it be *done*?).[48] In order to make sure that this diplomatic system functioned as intended, all sovereigns partici-

46 Ibid.; M. Anderson, *The Rise of Modern Diplomacy 1450–1919*, Harlow, 1993, 53–54; G. Mattingly, *Renaissance Diplomacy*, New York, 1988, 233, 241–242; Parry, *British International Law Cases*, 2; N. Steensgaard, Consuls and nations in the Levant from 1570–1650", *The Scandinavian economic history review* 15 (1967), 13–55, here 18; Van Alebeek, *The Immunity of States*, 159–164.

47 Term coined by O. Gelderblom, *Cities of Commerce. The Institutional Foundation of International Trade in the Low Countries, 1250–1650*, Princeton, 2013.

48 Anderson, *The Rise of Modern Diplomacy, 1450–1919*; Black, *A History of Diplomacy*, 90; Fedele, "The Renewal of Early-Modern Scholarship"; Scott, "Diplomatic Culture in Old Regime Europe".

pating in the 'Westphalian system' needed to comply. The sending sovereign was responsible for properly accrediting the diplomat to qualify him for immunity; the receiving sovereign for making sure that the foreign diplomat's immunities were safeguarded. Dante Fedele outlines the two underlying principles on why this system of internationally recognized diplomatic immunity 'worked'. On the one hand, the diplomat represented (or in some cases, personified) the sovereign who sent him. Insulting the diplomat by disregarding his immunities equaled insulting his sovereign, spurring a potentially serious international conflict. On the other hand, based again on the principle of necessity, diplomat's activities were considered as being of universal benefit (*communis utilitas*). This notion justified any particular advantages that might be bestowed on a diplomat in order to successfully pursue said activities.[49] To ensure that it was properly accomplished and thus subjected to coherent implementation by various authorities, commonly accepted and up-to-date definitions were needed.

This is where bodies of early modern scholarship on diplomacy and diplomatic immunity continued to play a role. Published works on diplomacy rapidly grew in size as well as in scope from the late sixteenth century onwards, with some works going through multiple editions and demonstrably gaining a European-wide reputation.[50] Hugely influential in their day, they set the international legal and philosophical standard on what diplomatic status and privilege entailed. Scholars or professionals of different backgrounds participated in these discourses. Jurists such as Ayrault were central in defining the immunities diplomats should be entitled to; scholars such as Grotius or Leibniz attempted to further embed natural law immunities in international law and the law of nations.[51] Career diplomats or courtiers focused more on the correct behavioural norms (i.e. dignity) that the privilege of diplomatic immunity prescribed, as seen in the manuals for diplomatic agents which they authored; famous examples include François de Callières (1645–1717)[52] and Abraham de Wicquefort (1606–1682).[53] They reiterated the immunities at stake and elaborated on them by explaining how diplomats (and the sovereigns that

49 Fedele, "The Renewal of Early-Modern Scholarship", 453–454.

50 Mattingly, *Renaissance Diplomacy*, 183.

51 Fedele, "Plurality of Diplomatic Agents"; Fedele, "The Renewal of Early-Modern Scholarship"; Nijman, *The Concept of International Legal Personality*, 30, 46–48, 65, 76–80; Ogdon, "The Growth of Purpose", 454.

52 The edition used in this chapter is Callières, *The Art of Negotiating with Sovereign Princes*.

53 A.J. van der Aa e.a., *Biographisch woordenboek der Nederlanden, bevattende Levensbeschrijvingen van zoodanige Personen, die zich op eenigerlei wijze in ons Vaderland hebben vermaard gemaakt. Deel 20*, Haarlem, 1877, 178–181.

sent or received them) could optimally wield them. Callières, for example, reflected on the diplomatic tax exemption in his work *De la Manière de Négocier avec les Souverains*.[54] He warned readers that this privilege was under no circumstance to be abused in order to cheaply conduct private trade on the side – this was beneath the dignity of a diplomatic envoy, not to mention a disgrace to the sovereign he represented.[55] Callières' suspicion that this immunity lent itself to abuse was, as we will see in the case of diplomats in Amsterdam, not completely unfounded.

These scholarly discourses were highly influential in spreading notions on diplomatic immunity and how it should be wielded throughout Western Europe. Long after their initial publication they continued to be referenced as authoritative voices in these discussions.[56] For example, in passing verdicts on cases related to the abuse of diplomatic immunity, early modern British courts were known to reference and base themselves on Wicquefort's opinions.[57] This example demonstrates the interplay between abstract legal concepts, political and ceremonial norms of diplomacy, and the implementation of said norms on an everyday (local) basis. The international, general concept of diplomatic immunity was established by scholarly authorities; it was now up to political authorities who adopted their ideas to turn them into (legal) practice.

4 The Impact of Treaties on Implementing Diplomatic Immunity

The legal concept of diplomatic immunity enjoyed general, international acceptance among (Western) European political entities in the seventeenth century. However, the first steps towards implementing said concept were also taken in the international sphere. The respective status of diplomats in the receiving state was contingent on the specific relationship between the

54 Callières, *The Art of Negotiating*, 98.

55 Ibid.

56 Bartolomei, "Débats historiographiques", 50–51; S. Externbrink, "Abraham de Wicquefort et ses traités sur l'ambassadeur (1676–1682). Bilan et perspectives de recherche" in S. Andretta, S. Péquignot and J.-Cl. Waquet (eds.), *De l'Ambassadeur. Les écrits relatifs à l'ambassadeur et à l'art de négocier du Moyen Âge au début du XIXe siècle*, Rome, 2015, 405–430; Pal, *Jurisdictional Accumulation*, 242; Scott, "Diplomatic Culture in Old Regime Europe", 62–63.

57 Parry, *British International Law Cases*, 261–262.

sending and the receiving state.[58] The official status of this relationship was – as a result of diplomacy itself – codified in multilateral or bilateral treaties. Early modern treaties of friendship, peace or commerce could contain clauses on the respective immunities of diplomats which were mutually exchanged. These clauses could add to (or sometimes limit) the 'standard' set of diplomatic immunities that diplomats on the respective signatories' territories were endowed with, by mutual agreement: a strong element of reciprocity was usually present. In short, multi- or bilateral treaties regulated diplomatic immunity on an international level, though only specifically between two or more signatories.

The concrete impact that treaties could exercise on diplomats and their status in Amsterdam is exemplified by the Franco-Dutch ban on consulates from the late seventeenth century onwards.[59] As we will see, this treaty-originated ban posed a challenge to the day-to-day assertion and implementation of diplomatic status in the city – a challenge which reverberated through several levels of political authorities.

Throughout the seventeenth century, France and the Dutch Republic maintained embassies in Paris and The Hague, and a number of consulates in subsidiary cities. Amsterdam was one of the cities where (at least from 1649 onwards) a French consul-general was stationed.[60] However, perhaps fueled by decades of intermittent military and commercial conflict between the two countries, the consulates were abolished in 1697. That year, the Peace of Rijswijk put an end to the Nine Years' War (1689–1697). A Franco-Dutch commercial sub-treaty of Rijswijk, the *Traité de paix et de commerce, navigation et marine* of 21 September 1697, contained the following clause:

> In the future, no Consuls will be admitted on either side, & if it is deemed appropriate to send Residents, Agents, Commissioners or others, they will only be permitted to establish themselves in the places where the Court normally resides.[61]

58 Van Alebeek, *The Immunity of States*, 164.

59 *Traité de Commerce, Navigation et Marine, entre le Roy et les Estats Generaux des Provinces-Unies des Pays Bas* (21 Sept. 1697), art. 39.

60 Schutte, *Repertorium der buitenlandse vertegenwoordigers*, 48.

61 *Traité de Commerce, Navigation et Marine*, article 39: "*À l'avenir aucuns Consuls ne seront admis de part & d'autre, & si l'on jugeoit à propos d'envoyer des Residens, Agens, Commissaires, ou autres, ils ne pourront établir leurs demeures ordinaires que dans les lieux de la residence de la Cour*".

Reading between the lines of memos with instructions for the French plenipotentiaries in Rijswijk, France seems to have reasoned that having no consuls in the Dutch Republic was an acceptable sacrifice to make in order to be able to not tolerate the accreditation of Dutch consuls to France.[62] Both states stood by it for the following decades. The commercial sub-treaty of the Peace of Utrecht in 1713 reaffirmed the Rijswijk clause verbatim.[63] Then, when the Utrecht treaty was set to expire after 25 years, the renewed treaty (signed at Versailles on 21 December 1739) reiterated it for the third time.[64] The policy was finally abandoned in the 1770s.[65]

The Rijswijk clause did not only seek to ban a specific type of diplomatic establishment (i.e. the consulate). It also invalidated diplomatic establishments in certain locations. It was accepted for France to maintain a non-consular, subsidiary diplomatic envoy (such as an agent, resident or commissary), but only "in the places where the Court normally resides"; for the Dutch Republic, this was The Hague. Thus, the legitimacy of any and all French diplomatic establishments in Amsterdam was invalidated. French 'envoys' could not claim diplomatic immunity in Amsterdam. This is a clear example of how an international treaty could be the instrument that adapted (in this case, restricted) an internationally accepted legal concept to a distinct, bilateral setting.

These bilateral, international agreements, of which Amsterdam was not a signatory in its own right, subsequently directly impacted the situation in the city itself. The treaty-based ban on diplomatic presence in Amsterdam proved highly inconvenient on a day-to-day basis. Despite the seeming hostility of curtailing diplomatic presence, the treaties securitized the political, commercial and demographic exchange between France and the Dutch Republic into the eighteenth century.[66] This mobility of people and goods came with a sustained *need* and *demand* for typical consular or diplomatic services. However, the institutions that normally rendered these services were kept rather artifi-

62 Archives Nationales Paris, MAR B7 533: *Memoire concernant le commerce, la navigation et les colonies, pour servir d'Instruction aux* [...] *plenipotentiaires de sa Mate. pour la paix generale* (1697).

63 Archives Nationales Paris, MAR B7 533: *Traité de Commerce, Navigation et Marine entre la France et les Etats Generaux des Provinces Unies des Pays-Bas* (11 April 1713), art. 38.

64 Archives Nationales Paris, MAR B7 536: *Traité de Commerce, Navigation et Marine, entre le Roy et les Estats Generaux des Provinces-Unies des Pays Bas* (21 Dec. 1739), art. 40.

65 O. Schutte, *Repertorium der Nederlandse vertegenwoordigers, residerende in het buitenland 1584–1810*, The Hague, 1976, 58–73.

66 J. De Vries and A. van der Woude, *The First Modern Economy. Succes, Failure, and Perseverance of the Dutch Economy, 1500–1815*, Cambridge, 1997, 486–487.

cially repressed. In Amsterdam, a major centre for (French) trade, shipping and finance, this inconvenience was most acutely felt.

To circumvent their own imposed ban on consulates, the French state installed officials in the Dutch ports who – quite literally – were consuls in all but name. Officially, the posting in Amsterdam was a commissariat, manned by a *commissaire de la Marine*. The Amsterdam *commissaire* was widely regarded to have been a consul in all but name.[67] Even the French ministry of the Marine, under whose purview the consulates fell, were occasionally plagued by Freudian slips: on notes scribbled on correspondence received by the ministry from commissary Saint-Sauveur in Amsterdam, the letter is jotted to be from *"M. de St. Sauveur Consul"*.[68] Yet, while simply changing the official title of the French diplomat in Amsterdam circumvented the Rijswijk treaty's interdiction of *consulates* in the Dutch Republic, it did not circumvent the ban on *diplomatic presence* in Amsterdam, which was neither a capital nor a court. To complicate matters, the French state outfitted their commissaries with the full set of conventional consular duties, responsibilities, and jurisdictional powers. They were also instructed to apply for the regular diplomatic immunities granted to consuls, such as tax exemptions.[69] However, contrary to settings where consuls were bilaterally admitted, there was no guarantee that the relevant authorities in the receiving state (i.e. the States General and the burgomasters of Amsterdam) would go along with abrogating the existing treaties, thereby actually permitting these subsidiary French diplomats to claim these immunities on their territories. The outcome tended to vary, thus demonstrating how implementing diplomatic immunity was sometimes a balancing act between political conventions, practical benefits, and the assessment of several levels of government thereof.

67 Municipal Archives Amsterdam, Notaries (inv. 5075), 14281, deed 38: the commissary Jacques Astier's janitor, Carel Schrick, identifies his employer as *"consel"* of the king of France; W. Oldewelt (ed.), *Kohier van de Personeele Quotisatie te Amsterdam over het jaar 1742. Deel II*, Amsterdam, 1945, 297: in Amsterdam's tax register of 1742, commissary Laugier de Tassy's profession is noted as "consul of France"; In Archives Nationales Paris, MAR B7 294: 20 May 1728, it is recorded that the burgomasters of Rotterdam accuse the French agent of acting like a consul.

68 Archives Nationales Paris, MAR B7, 402: 12 Jan. 1756.

69 For examples of admission and (usually rejected) tax exemption requests by French commissaries in Amsterdam, see Municipal Archives Amsterdam, *Archief van de Burgemeester: Groot Memoriaal* (inv. 5023), 12, fol. 121; 13, fol. 62, 201.

5 The Impact of Domestic Political Structures on Implementing Diplomatic Immunity

International agreements between two or more states on the exercise of reciprocal diplomatic immunities within their territories were generally negotiated and signed between the highest[70] sovereign power of said states. In a treaty between France and the Dutch Republic, for example, the (envoys of) the king of France on the one hand, and the Dutch States General on the other, were the official signatories for the respective sovereigns. Yet, in order to properly apply the terms of treaties on the domestic level, it was essential to involve different layers of *internal* government and authority. To safeguard and implement the internationally agreed immunities, collaboration between different levels of (internal) government was a practical necessity. However, the practical responsibilities of these different levels of government potentially clashed with the formal prerogatives that these lower-level bodies were constitutionally assigned.[71] In the age of Westphalia, diplomacy and engagement with diplomats increasingly became the (nominal) monopoly of sovereigns, at the cost of lower-level authorities.[72]

The Dutch Republic was a composite state, and its layered power structure had deep historical roots as well as (comparatively) high levels of emancipation among its lower-level governments. However, the prerogative to directly engage with diplomats was one of the exclusive sovereign domains of the statewide assembly, the States General.[73] Although the Dutch Republic did not have a formal constitution, several treaties dating from the Eighty Years' War (1568–1648) outlined how power and sovereignty was to be divided in the

70 See Nijman, *The Concept of International Legal Personality*, 60–68 for an exploration of the concept of relative sovereignty.

71 Black, *A History of Diplomacy*, 89.

72 Anderson, *The Rise of Modern Diplomacy*, 42. 'Nominal' being a key term here; in addition, this centralization process of diplomatic power was by no means complete(d) by the end of the early modern period. For a more critical and up-to-date discussion of the topic, see J. Watkins, "Premodern Non-State Agency: The Theoretical, Historical, and Legal Challenge" in M. Ebben and L. Sicking (eds.), *Beyond Ambassadors. Consuls, Missionaries, and Spies in Premodern Diplomacy*, Leiden, 2021, 19–37.

73 de Boer, ""*Ma coustume ne soit de m'addresser*", 168–169; M. Franken, *Coenraad van Beuningen's politieke en diplomatieke aktiviteiten in de jaren 1667–1684*, Groningen, 1966, 23–24; R. Fruin, *Geschiedenis der staatsinstellingen in Nederland tot den val der Republiek*, The Hague, 1901, 184–185; S. Groenveld, "De institutionele en politieke context" in J. Smidt (ed.), *Van Tresorier tot Thesaurier-generaal: Zes eeuwen financieel beleid in handen van een hoge Nederlandse ambtsdrager*, Hilversum, 1997, 55–88, here 59; Th. Thomassen, *Instrumenten van de macht. De Staten-Generaal en hun archieven 1576–1796*, The Hague, 2015, 281.

nascent state. The tenth article of the Union of Utrecht (1579; a watershed treaty that formally unified the Northern Netherlands against Spain) forbade all other governmental bodies in the Dutch Republic to "enter into any sort of cooperation or treaty with neighbouring countries without the consent of the United Provinces and allies".[74] These quasi-constitutional documents were thus the instruments that determined that cities (as governmental entities) in the Dutch Republic could in principle not independently engage with diplomats and, therefore, were not able to exercise any formal role in the implementation of their immunities. What follows is that in the Dutch Republic, it was the *domestic* dimension upon which Amsterdam's position as a diplomatic city hinged and, therefore, its legal and political capacity to implement diplomatic immunities.

However, as previously established, it was highly convenient for foreign sovereigns to have a diplomatic presence in the city for reasons of commerce, finance and intelligence. Added to this external pressure for diplomatic presence in Amsterdam was internal/domestic convenience. Throwing the regents of Amsterdam a metaphorical bone by permitting them to occasionally involve themselves with diplomacy relieved some tension between the different layers of government. In addition, the practical 'national' benefits of continuous diplomatic presence in the economic capital of the Dutch Republic were evident: it facilitated all manner of profitable commercial and financial transactions, from support for small-scale private enterprise to negotiating comprehensive state loans.[75] This victory of pragmatism over domestic political arrangements in diplomatic affairs is evidenced in the way that the aforementioned Franco-Dutch ban on diplomatic establishments in secondary cities (barely) worked out. In the words of the French ambassador d'Havrincourt in 1764, French diplomats continued to reside in Amsterdam (and Rotterdam) because "it is at least as useful for Dutch commerce as for [French commerce]".[76] Neither a treaty nor domestic political arrangements in the Dutch Republic would stop it.

It seems that, for these pragmatic reasons, an equally pragmatic (domestic) resolution was engineered. If a diplomat was appointed by his foreign sovereign to a post in Amsterdam and desired to enjoy diplomatic immunity, the States General allowed this on condition that the diplomat would *first* present

74 Union of Utrecht, art. 10. Original text: "*Dat geen van dese voorz. provincien, steden ofte leden van dyen enyge confederatien ofte verbonden met enyge naerbuerheeren ofte landen sullen moegen maecken sonder consent van dese geunieerde provincien ende bontgenoten*".

75 De Boer, ""*Ma coustume ne soit de m'addresser*"". For examples, see Municipal Archives Amsterdam, Notaries (inv. 5075), 5917, fol. 844; 5857, deed 474.

76 Archives Nationales Paris, AE B.III 423: 17 Febr. 1764.

his accreditation for the Amsterdam posting to The Hague. The diplomat's accreditation would be affirmed by the States General first, and only then could the diplomat turn to Amsterdam as a place of residence, as well as an authority to apply to. Within this system, the States General retained the upper hand in the implementation of diplomatic status – even if only nominally. By obliging newly arrived diplomats who were bound for Amsterdam to go 'through' The Hague, all subsequent implementative power that Amsterdam could exercise was only by virtue of the sovereign authority of The Hague.

Numerous references to this practice survive in the records. See, for example, the admission documents of the French-consul general Pierre Chabert in 1679 (pre-consul ban):

> We, burgomasters and regents of the city of Amsterdam, affirm to all those to whom it pertains, [and] certify to be the truth, that we, having seen the attached act of the Lords of the States General of the United Netherlands, in which Messr. Pierre Chabert was admitted as Consul General of the French nation in this country, have consented upon his request that he, according to the aforementioned act of Their High Mightinesses, is allowed to reside here in this city with the aforementioned status, and serve and exercise the aforementioned consulate on the terms and conditions expressed in said act of T.H.M.[77]

In the wording of Chabert's admission to Amsterdam, the centrality of the States General's sanctioning is clear. The terms and conditions regarding the implementation of diplomatic immunity were set in The Hague, and in order to formally admit diplomats to the city, the regency of Amsterdam had to adopt these in their own affirmations. In all, this system of diplomatic admissions thus pays homage to domestic power structures. It places local authorities' ability to implement diplomatic immunity back under the umbrella of statewide authority, therefore realigning it with existing quasi-constitutional arrangements.

---

77 Municipal Archives Amsterdam, *Archief van de Burgemeester: Groot Memoriaal* (inv. 5023), 6, fol. 234. Original text: "*Wij Burgemeesteren en Regeerders der stad Amsterdamme doen cond eenen ijrgelyk dien 't behoord, certificierende voor de waerheyd, dat wij, gesien hebbende de geannexeerde acte van de heeren Staten Generael der Vereenigde Nederlanden, waerbij d'Hr. Pierre Chabert werd geadmitteert als Consul Generael van de France Natie hier te lande: den selven t zijnen versoeke, geconsenteert hebben, om, volgens de Voorsz Acte van Haer Ho: Mo: hier ter Stede in de voorsz. Qualiteit te mogen resideren ende het geseide Consulaetschap te bedienen ende te exerceren op de Voet en de conditien bij de voorsz acte van Haer Ho: Mo: naerder geëxpresseert*".

6 The Impact of Urban Authorities on Implementing Diplomatic Immunity

As a last step in formally claiming diplomatic immunity and, more importantly, in exercising it, the diplomat had to submit his application to the local authorities of the place where he was to take up his posting. Urban authorities thus bestowed, denied, and implemented diplomatic privileges on a local level, in accordance with existing domestic arrangements and international agreements.[78] The gatekeeping role of local authorities in the regulation of diplomatic status is unsurprising: the exercise of certain immunities – for example, immunity from taxation – was on an everyday level most keenly felt in a local context. Diplomatic immunities often first confronted the authority of local institutions, such as municipal courts or tax farms. At the same time, urban authorities were often in the best position to determine to what extent an individual qualified for diplomatic status in the first place, if, for example the applicant was native to the city. This was particularly the case in Amsterdam, where about half of the applicants were Dutch subjects and burghers of the city itself, which disqualified them from enjoying certain diplomatic immunities. The final implementation of diplomatic immunity in Amsterdam was thus the prerogative of the burgomasters.

This determination was accomplished by means of two separate declarations by the burgomasters: one that formally admitted the diplomat to his posting in Amsterdam and one that granted *or* denied the diplomat (certain) immunities while he resided in the city.[79] In its most extreme form, it was possible for an individual to be a fully accredited diplomat in Amsterdam *without* enjoying any kind of diplomatic immunity. This deviation from the 'norm' was possible because two other factors could supersede these widely established international norms of diplomatic immunity.

The first factor was the subject status of the applicant. Being a subject, a precursor to modern citizenship, equated subjection to a sovereign authority, and acceptance of the obligations that came with this.[80] If one was a Dutch subject, for example, one was obligated to pay taxes to the Dutch authorities, and subjected to Dutch law jurisdiction. A legal contradiction thus arose if a Dutch subject was named the diplomatic representative of a foreign sover-

78 For Amsterdam, the admission documents are found throughout Municipal Archives Amsterdam, *Archief van de Burgemeester: Groot Memoriaal* (inv. 5023).

79 Ibid.

80 T. Herzog, *Defining Nations: Immigrants and Citizens in Early Modern Spain and Spanish America*, New Haven, 2003, 3.

eign, and in this capacity applied for diplomatic privileges such as tax exemptions or immunity from persecution *in* the Dutch Republic. This situation frequently arose in Amsterdam, where many 'foreign' diplomats were Dutch subjects and residents of the city. Barring some exceptions, decisions made in these cases show that the obligations of being a subject usually trumped the granting of diplomatic and immunities. Dutch subjects were then denied diplomatic immunities, as the admission documents of the Dutchman Joseph van de Put as an agent of Sweden (1700) show:

> Supplicant shall be recognized and admitted as Agent of the King of Sweden in Amsterdam, under the express condition that he by means of such shall not be exempted from the duty which he, as a subject of the Province of Holland[81] [...] is submitted to, without any exemptions, especially regarding the payment of all ordinary and extraordinary taxes and impositions [...], or jurisdiction over his person or family, both criminal and civil.[82]

These decisions imply that, in the formal scope of diplomatic immunity for Dutch subjects, a distinction was made between functional and personal immunity, where in the exercise of their diplomatic duties they did enjoy functional, necessity-based exemptions, but in their personal acts (where these were subject to local jurisdiction) they did not.[83] This distinction was furthermore needed to reduce the potential for fiscal abuse of immunities by Dutch subjects: a Dutch merchant-diplomat, for example, could be tempted to abuse these tax advantages to gain a competitive edge. This disrupted free market mechanisms in Amsterdam and lessened the institutional equality that was one of the city's commercial strengths.[84]

---

81 'Dutch' subjecthood was interchangeably conceptualized by institutions and individuals alike as being a subject of the Dutch Republic, a Dutch province, or a Dutch city; evidently, all were considered sovereign sources of Dutch subjecthood identity.

82 Municipal Archives Amsterdam, *Archief van de Burgemeesters: dagelijkse notulen, resoluties en missivenboeken* (inv. 5024), 8, fol. 204. Original text: "*den Suppl., als Agent van de Coningh van Sweden tot Amsterdam, zal werden erkent, ende geadmitteert, onder expresse conditie nogtans, dat hij daer door niet zal wesen geëximeert van de pligten van onderdanigheid, die hij als een onderdaen van de Provincie van Holland en Westvriesland, onderworpen is, zonder eenige exeptie, ende onder anderen mede specialijken ten aensien van de betalinge van alle ordinaris en extraordinaris schattingen, ende impositien, zo wel personele als reële, mitsgaders ten reguarde van de jurisdictie over zijn persoon en familie, zoo in het crimineel, als in het civil*".

83 G. McClanahan, *Diplomatic Immunity. Principles, Practices, Problems*, London, 1989, 58; Van Alebeek, *The Immunity of States*, 159–166.

84 Gelderblom, *Cities of Commerce*, 38–40.

The second factor that could supersede the standard arrangement vis-à-vis diplomatic immunity in local admissions were preexisting agreements between states on the matter. The aforementioned 1697 Franco-Dutch ban on diplomatic establishments in subsidiary cities is an example. Amsterdam, recognizing the benefit of a sustained French diplomatic presence in the city, engineered a solution, which was to admit the commissaries to the city under a specific set of conditions to be followed, as seen in the admission documents of *commissaire* Maillet du Clairon in 1766:

> Mr. Maillet du Clairon, having addressed himself to the lords Burgomasters with the adjacent deed, in which he is appointed as *commissaire de la Marine* by His Majesty the King of France [...], has been judged as follows: that [following the existing Franco-Dutch treaties] those who have since maintained their residence here [in Amsterdam] have not been publicly recognized, but have been tacitly tolerated by virtue of their utility to the inhabitants. Whereupon the lords Burgomasters have approved that said Mr. Maillet du Clairon is admitted to the city *bij oogluiking* [i.e. they will turn a blind eye], without receiving any of the privileges or immunities that are granted to Ministers of Foreign Powers.[85]

Thus, the commissaries were allowed to reside and perform their duties in Amsterdam, on the condition that they would not draw too much attention, and that they would not claim any of the special perks that diplomats enjoyed in the Dutch Republic and Amsterdam.

Regulating the diplomatic immunity of (local) tax exemption caused the most issues for urban authorities in Amsterdam. Diplomats who were denied this privilege for reasons of subject status or preexisting treaties did not always agree with this decision. Some continuously fought the urban authorities over

85 Municipal Archives Amsterdam, *Archief van de Burgemeester: Groot Memoriaal* (inv. 5023), 12, fol. 121. Original text: "*De Heer Maillet du Clairon zig aan haar Ed: Gr: Agtb: hebbende geaddresseerd met de hier onder gestelde acte, maer bij dezelve door zijn Majestijt de Koning van Vrankrijk weird aangesteld als commissaire de la Marine* [...] *zijnde nagezien is bevonden, dat ingevolge de Tractaaten van Commercie* [...] *die gene die zig zeedert die tijd hier hebben opgehouden niet publicq erkend, maar om het nut dat de Ingezeetene er van trekken tacite gedoogd Zijn. Waar op haar Ed: Groot Agtb: dan ook hebben goedgevonden dat de gemelde Heer Maillet du Clairon hier bij oogluijking toe te laaten, zonder denzelven te doen Jouisseren van eenige privilegien of immunitijten aan de Ministers van Vreemde Mogendheeden*". See also Municipal Archives Amsterdam, *Archief van de Burgemeester: Groot Memoriaal* (inv. 5023), 13, fol. 62 and Archives Nationales Paris, AE B.III 423: 7 Jan. 1763 for (references to) similar terms of admission for successors Astier and de Lironcourt.

this decision, or they attempted to exercise the privilege despite not formally possessing it. The authorities frequently had to call diplomats to order regarding irregularities in their handling of taxes. Some of these incidents were caused by honest mistakes or unclear conditions on either the part of the authorities or the diplomat. The English agent William Davidson, for example, politely requested the burgomasters in 1665 that they waive a recent tax bill he had been served, as he "judged himself to be exempt and free from all such payments".[86] Other diplomats, however, were more prone to abuse it. The French commissaries Astier and de Lironcourt submitted similar petitions to Davidson's, but these were denied by the burgomasters on grounds that the French commissaries knew perfectly well that the terms of their admission to the city did not exempt them from local taxes.[87] Still, in their regulation of de Lironcourt's attempt at illicit tax avoidance, the burgomasters remained nothing but diplomatic: "as much as they wished to please him", it was simply inappropriate to grant the French diplomat this diplomatic immunity.[88]

These examples are also indicative of the fact that diplomats in Amsterdam were not passive scions. Rather, they actively asserted and defended their (perceived) diplomatic status when they felt that local authorities had infringed on it. Implementation on a local level was thus a two-way street. Local authorities attempted to implement the immunities of diplomats, and – if said implementation was perceived as lackluster or as abrogating what one believed to be entitled to – diplomats themselves did not hesitate to actively negotiate said implementation. In a 1752 example, the Swedish agent Pierre Balguerie turned to the Amsterdam notary Jan Ardinois to file a complaint against civil servants Jaques Rijswijk and Hendrik Coeymans.[89] The duo had solicited him for several years that he had to fulfil his burgherly duties in the city watch and had now turned to actively fining Balguerie for supposedly forsaking this duty. Balguerie insisted that he considered himself free from any such impositions, "as is usual amongst the Crown's ministers",[90] despite being a permanent resident of the city of Amsterdam. In this miscommunication, we again observe the

86 Municipal Archives Amsterdam, *Archief van de Burgemeesters: missiven aan de burgemeesters* (inv. 5026), 42: 30 June 1665.

87 Archives Nationales Paris, AE B.III, 423: 7 Jan. 1763; Municipal Archives Amsterdam, *Archief van de Burgemeesters: missiven aan de burgemeesters* (inv. 5026), 42: 31 July 1792.

88 Municipal Archives Amsterdam, *Archief van de Burgemeester: Groot Memoriaal* (inv. 5023), 13, fol. 201.

89 Municipal Archives Amsterdam, *Archief van de Burgemeester: Groot Memoriaal* (inv. 5023), 9222, deed 291.

90 Ibid.

difference between functional and personal immunity arising in the interpretation of 'diplomatic immunity' by the agent Balguerie on the one hand, and the local authorities in Amsterdam on the other.[91] Balguerie clearly considered himself to be in possession of 'full' diplomatic immunity, including for his personal acts, thus exempting him from local duties (in this case, not a tax but the obligation to serve on the city watch). Rijswijk and Coeymans, representing the local authorities, evidently did not share this view and considered that, as a permanent resident of the city of Amsterdam, Balguerie was only entitled to functional immunity as directly related to his diplomatic activities. Therefore, he was still obligated to perform local duties and was considered a finable individual. This miscommunication, as well as the divergent decisions that were made in similar cases (other 'permanent residents', burghers or subjects of Amsterdam *did* receive diplomatic exemptions in the realm of personal immunity[92]), demonstrates that in practice, the 'correct' implementation of diplomatic immunity was often an ambiguous dossier.

Despite his active insistence on his diplomatic immunities, Balguerie was one of the diplomats in Amsterdam who took the conditions that came with them less seriously. Aside from his diplomatic career, he was also a prominent merchant and owned several plantations in Suriname.[93] In his business dealings, he leveraged his diplomatic title in otherwise unrelated business transactions with partners who were more prominent – in a sense, using a publicly bestowed dignity in a private transaction.[94] While this did not constitute outright abuse, it is indicative of how practices vehemently condemned by the diplomatic manuals of the time could arise, particularly in mercantile environments. Gerbrand Barthout de Hollande, the Spanish consul in Amsterdam in the late seventeenth century, was also a merchant, and frequently desired to enjoy the diplomatic exemption from local excise duties for his mercantile imports.[95] This type of abuse was widely bemoaned in the aforementioned diplomatic manuals,[96] yet to no avail. Not only in Amsterdam, but throughout

91 McClanahan, *Diplomatic Immunity,* 58; Van Alebeek, *The Immunity of States,* 159–166.

92 See, for example, Municipal Archives Amsterdam, *Archief van de Burgemeesters: Groot Memoriaal* (inv. 5023), 8, fol. 24; Schutte, *Repertorium der buitenlandse vertegenwoordigers,* 543.

93 See, for example, Municipal Archives Amsterdam, Notaries (inv. 5075), 9218, deed 564; 9209, deed 216.

94 National Archives The Hague, inv. 1.05.11.14, 689, scans 375–386.

95 Municipal Archives Amsterdam, *Archief van de Burgemeesters: missiven aan de burgemeesters* (inv. 5026), 42.

96 Callières, *The Art of Negotiating,* 98.

the early modern diplomatic world diplomats exploited their fiscal advantages not only for their functional benefit, but also their personal enrichment.[97]

7 The Impact of Intra-Diplomatic Dynamics on Implementing Diplomatic Immunity

Abuses such as these did not befit polite diplomatic society. In exchange for the perks that came with diplomatic immunity, a certain degree of behavioural dignity was expected for several reasons. First, the (natural) legal basis of diplomatic immunity departed from the premise that the diplomatic function was 'sacred' and that this condition justified the extensive immunities attached to it.[98] Second, due to the representative character of diplomats (in its most extreme form, the personification of the sovereign itself), undignified behaviour reflected badly not only on the diplomat's person but also on the sovereign itself.[99] Third, abusing immunities in local society was disrespectful to the receiving sovereign by whose virtue the diplomat could exercise these immunities in the first place. In all, the abuse of diplomatic immunity was an affront to all it represented in its legal, political and societal core. Acutely aware of this status, diplomatic missions sought to internally correct their members whose behaviour did not comply with the carefully agreed upon implementation of their immunities. In this sense, intra-diplomatic dynamics also tangibly influenced the 'face' of diplomatic immunity in local society.

Historiographically, the dynamic between embassies and subsidiary diplomatic establishments (as part of a singular diplomatic network in a specific setting) has not been studied in detail. However, the few existing case studies that do touch in-depth upon this dynamic reveal that the interaction between embassies and consulates was very much part and parcel of their daily functioning.[100] Cooperation was essential: it optimized the efficiency of both the

97 Black, *A History of Diplomacy,* 62.

98 Adair, *The Extraterritoriality of Ambassadors,* 6; Ogdon, "The Growth of Purpose", 449–452; Van Alebeek, *The Immunity of States,* 159.

99 Fl. Kühnel, "The Ambassador is Dead – Long Live the Ambassadress: Gender, Rank and Proxy Representation in Early Modern Diplomacy", *The International History Review* 44/5 (2022), 1004–1020; Parry, *British International Law Cases,* 2; Van Alebeek, *The Immunity of States,* 159–164.

100 For some existing examples/case studies, see Pal, *Jurisdictional Accumulation,* 227–235; C. Antunes, "Dutch-Portuguese diplomatic encounters, 1640–1703: exchanges, sovereignty, and "world peace", *Journal of Early Modern History* 23 (2019) 458–474; M. Ebben, "Uwer Hoog Moogenden onderdaenigsten dienaers. Nederlandse consuls en staatse diplomatie in Spanje, 1648–1661", *Tijdschrift voor Geschiedenis* 127/4 (2014), 649–672.

embassy and the subsidiary establishments' ability to render services to the state and expatriate nations alike. It is therefore unsurprising that diplomatic missions had a vested interest in ensuring that all branches remained free of (allegations of) abuse and corruption, while taking concrete action when signs of it emerged.

As a general rule, the embassy and ambassador in The Hague were the heads of foreign diplomatic missions in the Dutch Republic, and the subsidiary establishment in Amsterdam answered to The Hague. In some missions this arrangement was more informal, arising naturally from the political structure of the Dutch Republic, while in others this hierarchical relation was formally and explicitly acknowledged by both sovereigns as well as the diplomats themselves. For example, the Spanish diplomatic mission in the Dutch Republic was structured this way. The Spanish ambassador in The Hague had a formal role in the nomination, appointment, salary payout, and supervision of the Spanish agent in Amsterdam, and for this reason was regularly in touch with the burgomasters to discuss affairs related to Spanish diplomacy in the city.[101] Agent Manuel de Belmonte was tellingly referred to by Ambassador de Lira y Castillo as "agent de *l'ambassade*" (as opposed to agent of the king or the state).[102] Spanish agents or delegates in Amsterdam are also frequently reported upon as travelling to The Hague to assist the ambassador with affairs of state.[103] What follows is that within this hierarchical relationship, it was up to the ambassador to call to order and discipline 'his' diplomat in Amsterdam if required.

A clear example of this kind of internal diplomatic mandate is found within the French mission. This mission was similarly structured in a hierarchical manner and also marked by close collaboration between the branches in The Hague and Amsterdam. In 1749, after the death of the Amsterdam commissary Jacques Philippe Laugier de Tassy, his seventeen-year-old son Jacques Gabriel acceded as the (temporary) successor.[104] The acting ambassador Chiquet in The Hague was alarmed by the adolescent commissary's undignified

101 See the correspondence by ambassador Gamarra in Municipal Archives Amsterdam, *Archief van de Burgemeesters: missiven aan de burgemeesters* (inv. 5026), 42.

102 Municipal Archives Amsterdam, *Archief van de Burgemeesters: dagelijkse notulen, resoluties en missivenboeken* (inv. 5024), 65, fol. 160.

103 *Oprechte Haerlemsche courant,* 15 Jan. 1688, 16 June 1689; Municipal Archives Amsterdam, *Archief van de Burgemeesters: dagelijkse notulen, resoluties en missivenboeken* (inv. 5024), 58, fol.180.

104 Municipal Archives Amsterdam, Notaries (inv. 5075), 10248, deed 396.

behaviour.[105] Jacques Gabriel was openly Protestant (an impermissible attribute for French civil servants),[106] surrounded himself with unsuitable company, dishonoured and threatened his mother, acted spoiled by demanding a larger house, and spent the salary he earned as a diplomat on frivolous affairs. The acting ambassador Chiquet realized that Jacques Gabriel's behaviour did not comply with the dignities that possessing diplomatic immunity demanded and that this situation was harmful for the reputation of France and French diplomacy in Amsterdam and the Dutch Republic. In addition, the matter was especially delicate because French diplomats in Amsterdam were, per the Franco-Dutch treaties, only tolerated in the city on the condition that they did not attract too much attention. Even the limited diplomatic immunity that had been granted to them by the Dutch/Amsterdam authorities had been charitable; abusing it would therefore be a highly sensitive matter. Chiquet thus repeatedly invited Jacques Gabriel to The Hague and sat down with the adolescent diplomat for multiple tutoring sessions. These included lectures on how the sociopolitical perks, privileges and immunities of the commissariat also came with certain expectations in terms of duty, responsibility and outward adherence to the correct religion. He also assigned Pierre Balguerie, the Swedish delegate in Amsterdam, as a mentor of sorts to Jacques Gabriel – Balguerie, a French subject, was held in high esteem by the French state for his perceived dignity and loyal service. However, these attempts at regulating behaviour within the diplomatic sphere were seemingly fruitless. In a report to the minister in France, Chiquet wrote:

> [Perhaps] orders given to him by you, Monsieur, to return to his duty, accompanied by threats to deprive him of an Employment whose advantages he enjoys if he does not submit, would maybe make a healthy impression on him.[107]

Chiquet reasoned that the threat of *losing* the diplomatic immunities that Jacques Gabriel possessed might be the only way to resolve the issue – and the most efficient way of removing said privileges would be to remove Jacques Gabriel from the diplomatic post. The next year, this replacement was indeed

105 Archives Nationales Paris, AE B.III 423: 3 June 1749, 20 June 1749.

106 J. Ulbert, ""A History of the French Consular Services" in J. Melissen and A. Mar Fernández (eds.), *Consular Affairs and Diplomacy*, Leiden, 2011, 303–324, here 316.

107 Archives Nationales Paris, AE B.III 423: 3 June 1749. Original text: "*Des ordres qui luy seroient donnés de votre part, Monseigneur, de rentrer dans le devoir, accompagnés de menacer de le priver d'un Employ dont il connoit les avantages, s'il ne se soumet, feroient peut être une impression salutaire sur luy.*"

what happened: in 1750, Jean-Baptiste Décury de Saint-Sauveur, a perfectly qualified, straight-laced and dignified Catholic adult landed in Amsterdam to take up the position.[108]

The regulatory role of the diplomatic mission was not only internally corrective. It could also be mobilized to combat infractions on diplomatic immunities from an external source. Ambassadors in The Hague were to safeguard the diplomatic immunities of 'their' agents if these were threatened or disrespected, for example by the local authorities. Because of the pervasive adherence to the principle of necessity, diplomatic missions had a vested interest in making sure that immunities were protected. On some occasions, the Amsterdam diplomat had to stand their ground, as we have seen; on others, however, bringing in the ambassador to plead on their behalf would give a more powerful push, because the sociopolitical sway of ambassadors was generally greater. Such interventions by ambassadors are usually found in correspondence between said ambassadors and the burgomasters of Amsterdam. Again, perceived infractions on the fiscal immunities of diplomats were a source of frequent complaints. In 1686, for example, Fredrik Kragh, the Danish envoy in The Hague, petitioned the burgomasters of Amsterdam on behalf of the Danish consul Joan Nicolas Abo.[109] Abo had been served a tax bill pertaining to his use of a carriage and horses in the city. Riding a carriage in the inner city was heavily taxed in Amsterdam, with the goal of not only reserving it for the upper classes, but also to discourage it, given that the vibration of heavy vehicles caused damage to the buildings.[110] Kragh was of the opinion that Consul Abo was exempt from paying carriage tax in Amsterdam. He constructed his plea on various grounds:

> The Dutch consul in Elsinore [also] enjoys full Exemption of all Taxes; because His Majesty on all occasions maintains a particular Affinity for the City of Amsterdam and its subjects, it would please Your Lords [burgomasters] to grant His Majesty's Consul this consideration, and bestow your Protection upon him, that he may possess carriages and Horses without taxation; principally, because they are used in service of said Consul as well as myself, when I happen to be in Amsterdam.[111]

---

108 A. Mézin, *Les consuls de France au siècle des lumières (1715–1792)*, Paris, 1998, 229–230, 661; *Leydse Courant*, 29 Oct. 1749.

109 Municipal Archives Amsterdam, *Archief van de Burgemeesters: missiven aan de burgemeesters* (inv. 5026), 42, scan 4.

110 Anonymous, *The present state of Holland, or a Description of the United Provinces*, 159.

111 Municipal Archives Amsterdam, *Archief van de Burgemeesters: missiven aan de burgemeesters* (inv. 5026), 42, scan 4. Original text: "*dat naerdemaelen aen haer Ho. Mo. Consul*

The Amsterdam authorities, according to Kragh, disrespected Abo's general tax exemption. Kragh even (more or less implicitly) counters any arguments contesting that, as a consul, Abo would qualify for this particular immunity. He does so by presenting Abo as part of a singular diplomatic network or ambassadorial suite, whose members (according to most conceptualizations of diplomatic immunity) qualified for this immunity by virtue of their membership.[112] Taxing the carriage disregarded the principle of necessity in diplomatic immunity, because it harmed the efficiency of the Danish diplomatic mission in the Dutch Republic. On top of that, reciprocity factored once more into the discussion: in Denmark, these immunities were in face properly implemented and respected for Dutch consuls, as was to be expected between befriended political entities. Kragh's request, however, was refused by the Amsterdam burgomasters. They argued that the matters were simply "outside of their power".[113] The tax was supposedly levied at the state level, meaning that a city government was not authorized to distribute exemptions. Amsterdam also disagreed that the diplomatic status of the consular rank – or, possibly, membership in an ambassadorial suite – merited the carriage tax exemption.[114]

This case demonstrates that, in spite of large-scale convergence on the concept of diplomatic immunity in the early modern period, on a day-to-day basis certain ambiguities as to what it entailed and who should assume responsibility for its implementation remained.

8 Conclusion

Under the auspices of the 'Westphalian' re-configuration of political sovereignty, as well as the emergence of resident embassies as the standard organ-

---

tot Elseneur in de Zond noch nieuwelycks vollencomene Exemptie van alle Oplagen ende belastingen is toegestaen ende vergunt, Ende daerenboven hoogstgede. Syne Cone. Majesteyt by alle occasien, eene particuliere Genegentheyt voor de Stadt Amsterdam ende derselver ingezetenen betuyght, het U.E.G.A. gelieven mogen voor hoogstgeme. Syne Majesteyts Consul die consideratie te hebben, ende met haere Protectie in diervoegen te begunstigen, dat gy sonder belastinge magh koetse en Paerden houden, voornaementlyck naerdemaelen deselve meer tot mynen als tot de Hr. Consul syn eygen gebruyck en dienste staen, om mijn soo wel onder wegens als oock tot Amsterdam daervan te bedienen".

112 Adair, *The Extraterritoriality of Ambassadors*, 13; see also the cases discussed in Parry, *British International Law Cases*, 201–209; McClanahan, *Diplomatic Immunity*, 57–58.

113 Municipal Archives Amsterdam, *Archief van de Burgemeesters: dagelijkse notulen, resoluties en missivenboeken* (inv. 5024), 71, fol. 177.

114 Ibid.

izational mode of diplomatic relations, the 'correct' implementation of diplomatic immunity gained renewed priority in the dynamism of seventeenth-century Europe. Having inherited a strong commitment to the principle of necessity in its (natural) Roman law basis, diplomatic immunity – from taxation, seizure of assets, and criminal prosecution – was universally considered essential for early modern diplomatic relations to be conducted efficiently and for diplomatic services to be rendered optimally. For this reason, it was similarly pivotal that irregularities in the implementation or exercise of diplomatic immunity (i.e. abuse) were to be prevented and corrected.

For all the international agreement on the basis, content and function of diplomatic immunity, its practical manifestation on the ground was eclectic, contested and ambiguous. A locally situated case study of early modern Amsterdam – an atypical diplomatic centre of dubious sovereignty with an economic (as opposed to political) foundation for its diplomatic power – reveals the layered nature of diplomatic immunity as it was eventually implemented and exercised in the urban space. The face of diplomatic immunity in Amsterdam was composed (and the result) of several levels of intersecting implementation. International scholarly discourses established what diplomatic immunity in this seventeenth-century society should entail; treaties prescribed these principles in bi- or multilateral sovereign settings; these principles were translated across domestic power structures; applied by local authorities; propagated, corrected and defended internally by the diplomatic missions themselves. Across these different levels and authorities involved in them, a wide range of legal or political instruments emerge that formalized crucial ideas, arrangements or practices. From legal-philosophical treatises to bilateral treaties, constitutions, municipal declarations, or diplomatic correspondence: all of these instruments were implicitly or explicitly connected, ultimately tying them and the authorities who produced them together in a large and complex web of implementation. At times, this complexity was overwhelming: the lived, historical experience was a contested one, and disagreements or misunderstandings continued to arise.

Early modern Amsterdam is a compelling laboratory to trace these processes. Its case also reminds us of the continuing impact that cities were able to exercise – formally and informally – on diplomatic relations in an era where these relations were increasingly monopolized by sovereign entities or 'states'. This situation invites us to further question the way sovereignty was conceptualized and operationalized, both internally (by the cities themselves) and externally (as viewed by others, sovereign as well as non-sovereign): after all, as the case of Amsterdam demonstrates, diplomacy beyond the sovereign monopoly was a delightfully rich, complex and colorful affair.

CHAPTER 4

Law as Resource? Debt Adjustment Schemes and the Amsterdam Economy (Seventeenth Century)

Maurits den Hollander

1 Introduction

On Sunday, 7 July 1652, in the middle of the night, an unexpected disaster hit the city of Amsterdam in its political and economic core. Even though over the seventeenth century, the main streets of the flourishing city of commerce started to display its inhabitants' increasing wealth and grandeur, the old city hall on the central Dam Square (Figure 4.1) remained a messy assemblage of various late medieval buildings. At two o'clock in the morning, the derelict and primarily wooden structure caught fire. The burgomasters' tower burnt so fiercely, one of the fire masters remarked, that it was a miracle that not more damage was done to surrounding properties. According to Jan Wagenaar, "at this occasion many old registers and [archival] pieces were burned".[1] At the same time, thanks to heroic acts of a number of brave citizens many other documents were rescued from the inferno:

> A number of brave zealots managed to reach the Secretariat through the flames, returning with their arms full of books and paperwork. One of them even entered the Orphan Chamber, which was entirely ablaze, throwing all books and registers on which he could lay his hands out of a window onto the street, from where they could be salvaged. Thereafter, he had to escape using a rope lowered from the tower, as the stairway by which he had entered had already burned down.[2]

1 J. Wagenaar, *Amsterdam in zijne Opkomst, Aanwas, Geschiedenissen, Voorregten, Koophandel, Gebouwen, Kerkenstaat, Schoolen, Schutterije, Gilden en Regeeringe*, vol. 2, Amsterdam, 1765, 583–584.

2 "*Eenige ijveraars voor Stads dienst streefden, midden door de vlammen, naar de Secreterije, en keerden, met armen vol boeken en papieren, te rug. Een was 'er, die naar de Weeskamer liep, toen zij in vollen brand stond, en de boeken en registers, welken hij magtig worden kon, ten vensteren uit, op straat smeet, daar zij waargenomen en gebergd werden: waarna hij zig, bij*

© 2026 THE AUTHOR(S) | HTTPS://DOI.ORG/10.1163/9789004761537-006

Even though it shows some burn marks, it is thanks to these brave citizens that Amsterdam's oldest register of the appointment of curators in cases of insolvency has survived to the present date.[3] This is important, because the register allows to shed light on a crucial legal transition in seventeenth-century Amsterdam. Whereas before 1643, citizens who could not make ends meet were placed into the care of the aldermen through the procedure of *curatele*, after this date a special Chamber of Insolvent and Abandoned Estates (the *Desolate Boedelskamer*) was established to take over this task.[4]

As will be argued further below, the establishment of the Desolate Boedelskamer represents an intriguing mix of continuity and change. Even though the management of insolvent estates was professionalized, many existing laws on, for instance, the pooling of assets or the application of *cessio bonorum* were kept. More radical innovations, such as the introduction of majority compositions between 1647 and 1659, were rooted in legal and commercial practice rather than pre-existing black-letter law. In a way, the Amsterdam insolvency procedure reflects the patchwork character of the old medieval town hall rather than the 'eighth wonder of the world' that replaced it in the form of Jacob van Campen's citizen-palace. Studying the evolution of debt adjustment schemes in seventeenth-century Amsterdam makes it possible to shed light on how law functioned as an institutional resource for its flourishing commerce in this period.

In recent decades, both legal and economic historians have devoted attention to the interactions between urban law and commerce in late medieval and early modern Europe. Adherents of the 'new institutional economics' clearly link explanations for economic growth to (private) law, more specifically to the protection of property rights and contract enforcement by governmental authorities who would thereby guarantee transactional security.[5] Unlike Douglass North, who argued that the creation of state-sponsored central courts obviated older (local) legal solutions for third-party enforcement, Oscar Gelderblom has shown that supreme courts – such as the *Grote Raad* in Meche-

---

een touw, langs den tooren, nederliet, alzo de trap, die hij opgekomen was, reeds was afgebrand."

3 Municipal Archives Amsterdam, *Archief van de Commissarissen van de Desolate Boedelkamer* (inv. 5072) (hereinafter DB), 469.

4 For the *Desolate Boedelskamer*'s founding ordinance, see: Rooseboom, *Recueil*, 304–309. On its functioning in the seventeenth century: M. den Hollander, *Court, Credit, and Capital. Amsterdam's Insolvency Legislation in the Dutch Golden Age*. Cambridge, 2025.

5 D.C. North and R.P. Thomas, *The Rise of the Western World. A New Economic History*, Cambridge, 1973; D.C. North, *Institutions, Institutional Change, and Economic Performance*. Cambridge 1990.

FIGURE 4.1 The old city hall of Amsterdam by Pieter Jansz. Saenredam, 1657 – Rijksmuseum Amsterdam, SK-C-1409

len – were generally irrelevant for commercial dispute resolution. The intervention of local courts – such as the Amsterdam aldermen's bench – remained a crucial complement to the private settlement of early modern business disputes. The security provided by municipal bylaws and courts would have created a fertile environment for commerce and economic growth.[6]

In his analysis of long-term economic and social change in the medieval Low Countries, however, Bas van Bavel points out that "the relationship between market exchange, economic growth, and modal standards of living is not unilinear". To be truly successful in the long run, efficient systems of exchange need to be coupled with social equilibrium. All regions in the Low Countries that successively experienced phases of rapid economic growth had, in these

6 O. Gelderblom, "The Resolution of Commercial Conflicts in Bruges, Antwerp, and Amsterdam (1250–1650)" in D. Ma and J. Luiten Van Zanden (eds.), *Law and Long-Term Economic Change: A Eurasian Perspective*, 244–276. See also: O. Gelderblom, *Cities of Commerce. The Institutional Foundation of International Trade in the Low Countries, 1250–1650*, Princeton, 2013.

same periods, a fairly even distribution of power and property. Stagnation usually seems to have occurred once an optimum was reached for main interest groups, after which path dependencies led the socio-institutional framework to become increasingly incapable of flexibly adapting to changing circumstances.[7]

A well-functioning and broadly accessible legal treatment of insolvencies is generally seen as a good example of an institution that has a positive effect on economic growth by providing additional security to property rights. The increasing study of Roman law in the Dutch Republic would have helped to justify a new commercial morality in seventeenth-century Holland, which became, among other things, visible in an ever more lenient treatment of insolvents.[8] Nevertheless, due to its many doctrinal restrictions, James Whitman argues, "It is just nonsense to suppose that Roman law 'caused' the rise of western commercial society."[9] Furthermore, Jérôme Sgard points out that even though insolvency legislation helps private contracting to recover after a breach of trust, it does so not by protecting or restoring past property rights, but rather by *intervening* in private contracts and reallocating wealth for the common good.[10]

The rise of majority compositions made possible by the introduction of the Amsterdam Desolate Boedelskamer in the mid-seventeenth century is a clear example of such a restructuring of property rights. Minorities of creditors were forced to accept a restructuring of debts, which subsequently allowed insolvent citizens to rebuild their businesses in order to be able to once more contribute to civil society as a whole. This chapter argues that good insolvency legislation could serve as a resource for economic growth by helping to maintain social equilibrium for at least half a century after the absolute economic high point of the Dutch 'Golden Age' around 1650. This position will also help to illustrate that positive law was impacted by the social, cultural and economic environment in which it was embedded rather than being a driver of economic growth purely in and of itself. The remainder of this chapter will

---

7 B. Van Bavel, *Manors and Markets. Economy and Society in the Low Countries, 500–1600*, Oxford, 2010, 403–408. On the point of stagnation caused by elite rent-seeking, see also: S. Ogilvie, *Institutions and European Trade: Merchant Guilds, 1000–1800*, Cambridge, 2011; S. Ogilvie, *The European Guilds: An Economic Analysis*, Princeton, 2019.

8 J. Whitman, "The Moral Menace of Roman Law and the Making of Commerce: Some Dutch Evidence." *The Yale Law Journal* 105/7 (1995), 1841–1889.

9 J. Whitman, "Long Live the Hatred of Roman Law!", *Rechtsgeschichte – Legal History* 2 (2003), 40–57.

10 J. Sgard, "Bankruptcy Laws: East versus West" in D. Ma and J. Luiten van Zanden (eds.), *Law and Long-Term Economic Change: A Eurasian Perspective*, Stanford, 2011, 198–220, at 207–209.

focus on the decades surrounding the establishment of the Desolate Boedelskamer in 1643, discussing both continuities and discontinuities in the organization of insolvency procedures in preceding decades as well as in the period after its new 1659 ordinance. Utilizing empirical evidence based upon archival research demonstrates how the Desolate Boedelskamer could build upon earlier innovations to open up new legal and economic prospects for both individual insolvents and society in general.

2 Continuity

When Amsterdam residents were unable to repay their debts and became insolvent, "of old, the aldermen took over the management of their estates and, to the benefit of the creditors, appointed curators, who had to account to the [aldermen's] bench".[11] After joining the Dutch Revolt in 1578 (an event known as its *Alteratie*), Amsterdam went through a phase of explosive demographic growth. This resulted in such increased workloads for the aldermen that they delegated their old responsibilities related to the management of insolvent estates to the commissioners of the newly created Desolate Boedelskamer in 1643.[12] There are obvious signs of continuity in the Amsterdam procedure of *curatele* before and after 1643. If we want to fully appreciate the effect of the changes in Amsterdam's insolvency legislation throughout the seventeenth century on its economic growth, it is necessary to understand the important legal innovations that already took place before the establishment of the Desolate Boedelskamer.

The Amsterdam procedure for the management of insolvent estates was partially based on Antwerp precedents, but innovated on this example in two important ways. First, it unified the enforcement of debts, conducted by a judge, with the management of the insolvent estate. This synthesis constituted a solution for the problematic information asymmetries that used to hamper the work of judges and curators. Second, facts gained the upper hand over rumours. While in late sixteenth-century Antwerp, the *failliet* of a debtor who had not run away from his creditors was based upon rumours – such as gossip about his failure to attend the stock exchange – in seventeenth-century Amsterdam the factual establishment of over-indebtedness became the formal starting point of the insolvency procedure. Through the investigation of a debtor's books and papers which started every curatele procedure, it

11 Wagenaar, *Amsterdam in zijne Opkomst*, vol. 3, Amsterdam, 1767, 461.

12 The 1643 founding ordinance was printed in: Rooseboom, *Recueil*, 304–309.

was possible to take decisions based upon facts and figures rather than hearsay and rough estimates. Furthermore, it is also important to note that the Amsterdam insolvency procedures were collectivized, uniting the claims of all creditors.[13]

In the partial copy of the oldest register of curatele, compiled after the fire mentioned in the introduction above, we find evidence of interesting links between the involvement of the aldermen with curatele in the 1630s and the direct continuity in the treatment of the same cases by the commissioners of the new Desolate Boedelskamer after 1643. This register will now be discussed in some detail, which will help to illustrate the most important components of the Amsterdam curatele procedure. Generally, administrative entries about the appointment of curators are placed on the left pages (verso) of the register. On the right pages (recto), in some cases one can find additional comments about the management of the insolvent estates and/or the resolution of the insolvency. After an alphabetical index, the register contains three main parts.[14]

Firstly, between fols 1v-66r we find entries about the appointment of curators to insolvent estates by the aldermen from, roughly, the mid-1630s until 1643. Secondly, there is a chronological continuation of these entries between fol. 66r-132v. As noted in the register, however, the entries in this part of the record were made on orders of "the lords commissioners of *desolate boedels* from the creation of their honourable college onwards". Whereas the first part of the register only contains sixteen entries on the recto pages, in the second part these become both more frequent and of a different nature. This part of the register will be analyzed further in the next section of this chapter. Thirdly, after a white space on fol. 132v-133r, between fol. 133v and the end of the register on fol. 150r, we find a series of older insolvent estates that chronologically range from the 1610s until the early 1640s without any clear sort of order. What separates these cases from the first parts of the register is that every entry is accompanied by a recto entry "*actum et presentibus* commissarissen", as well as a marginal reference to one of the Chamber's other series of administrative ledgers, such as a book of repartitions. Interestingly, all recto entries in the first and third part of the register refer to the actions of the commissioners between 19 February 1644 and 8 March 1644. Those found in the second part,

13 D. De ruysscher, "Antwerp Commercial Legislation in Amsterdam in the 17th Century: Legal Transplant or Jumping Board?", *Tijdschrift voor Rechtsgeschiedenis* 77 (2009), 459–479; D. De ruysscher, "Designing the Limits of Creditworthiness. Insolvency in Antwerp Bankruptcy Legislation and Practice (16th–17th Centuries)," *Tijdschrift voor Rechtsgeschiedenis* 76 (2008), 307–327. See Den Hollander, *Court, Credit, and Capital*, 113–140.

14 Municipal Archives Amsterdam, DB, 470.

however, are dated up to 1649, apart from a single outlier that was only resolved in 1657. This suggests that parts one and three of the register might represent the new commissioners' initial inventory and audit of the estates and active curators previously appointed by the aldermen.

How can we explain the difference between especially these first and third parts of the register, which both concern cases in which curators had been appointed by the aldermen? One possible explanation might be fire damage, resulting in a loss or illegibility of information for the entries copied into the first part, whereas 'complete' entries were copied into the separate third part of the register. This seems unlikely, however, because in some of the former cases, actions taken under the auspices of the commissioners *were* noted on the recto pages, even if these are relatively rare. A more likely explanation would be the difference between cases that had already been resolved and those in which the curatele had not ended yet at the moment of the creation of the Desolate Boedelskamer. The entries in the first part would in this scenario simply be leftovers from the old register related to the time in which insolvencies were still treated by the aldermen themselves. The entries in the third part would be 'open cases' that were quickly wrapped up by the commissioners. It is interesting to note that almost all its recto entries concern a sum of money that had been collected and repartitioned to the creditors after a public auction organized by the city's clerk. This was also the case for seven out of sixteen recto entries in the first part of the register.

The actions of the commissioners clearly demonstrate the fact-based nature of the Amsterdam curatele procedure. On 9 September 1644, the estate of carpenter Thomas Jacobsz. was placed in the hands of curator Zebert Huijbertsz. Kruck. However, because Thomas and his wife "re-appeared" ("*weder tevoorschijn zijn gecomen*") and this event had subsequently been reported to the commissioners, the curatele order was withdrawn.[15] Similarly, even though the commissioners had ordered city clerk Thomas Jacobsz. Haringh to initiate the auction of the goods of Claes Abrahamsz. Tapper on 8 May 1646, presumably on request of his creditors, this order was subsequently cancelled when his wife "presented her person" on 30 May. It was discovered that Claes had switched careers, sailing to the East Indies on board a VOC ship. The barkeeper and his wife had been "missing" because she had shortly "accompanied him to say goodbye" ("*hem uytgeley gedaen hebbende*"), perhaps even as far as the Marsdiep, from where the East Indiamen departed. It is not unlikely that Claes had been forced to sign up for this hazardous job by dire financial conditions. When the commissioners learned about these facts, they ordered that

15 Municipal Archives Amsterdam, DB, 470, fol. 83v-84r.

the estate should be given back to his wife.[16] Once more, this finding shows how the commissioners preferred to act based upon factual evidence and, if necessary, were prepared to overturn earlier decisions to ensure a just treatment of all parties involved.

One of the most important tasks of the commissioners, and the aldermen before them, was the supervision of the curators they appointed. Once a curator's management of an insolvent estate had ended, he was required to present his account to a commissioner delegated for that purpose. The latter would check the curator's acts and discharged him from his responsibilities if all was found to be in order. Only after this formal discharge, were the salary and further statements paid out.[17] At various places in the first register of curatele, we already encounter such entries referring to curators who had to present the accounts detailing their actions before a case could be closed. On 20 February 1644, for instance, the curator Salomon de la Voije had to pay back fl. 5 – 14 to the commissioners after they had audited his account of the curatele of Jan Clerck's estate.[18] One day earlier, Aldrich Stipel and Nicolaes Cocquin, who had received the 'books' of Arent Pietersz. Brughman on 16 August 1636, after having been appointed as curators of his estate, were relieved of their duty to account in this case by the commissioners. The reason for this breach of normal procedures was that Brughman's estate had become entangled in a legal procedure before the High Court of Holland and Zeeland in The Hague. The curators were allowed to charge fl. 6 – 2 as compensation for their actions up to that moment.[19]

In general, the entries found in this register indicate clear continuities between the work of the aldermen and the commissioners of the Desolate Boedelskamer, before and after 6 November 1643, respectively. At the same time, however, these careful decisions are clear indications of the attention to detail given in the commissioners' supervision of curators, which likely would have been much improved compared to what would previously have been possible for the aldermen, in addition to the numerous other matters they had to attend to. The basic procedures for curatele of insolvent or abandoned estates, the pooling of assets, as well as disputes about preference between creditors show continuities before and after 1643. The quality and accessibility

16 Municipal Archives Amsterdam, DB, 470, fol. 111v-112r. The Amsterdam regents were generally lenient towards impoverished (relatives of) sailors, who were structurally in high demand to fulfill the needs of its enormous trading fleet: M. van Leeuwen, "Amsterdam en de armenzorg tijdens de Republiek", *NEHA-Jaarboek* 59 (1996), 132–161, at 152–154.

17 Den Hollander, *Court, Credit, and Capital*, 152–155.

18 Municipal Archives Amsterdam, DB, 470, fol. 53v–54r.

19 Municipal Archives Amsterdam, DB, 470, fol. 69v–70r.

of legal services provided, however, will surely have been improved by the introduction of the Desolate Boedelskamer. As will be explained further below, these changes were mainly related to the substitution of the notaries' services with those of a professional public institution, one firmly grounded in transparent rules and procedures.

3 Change

Whereas in large parts of Europe in the later Middle Ages public notaries came to occupy a crucial role in the production of commercial instruments such as contracts, in the Low Countries their role remained more limited. This can be explained by the fact that here they had to compete with reliable alternatives that were already well established by the end of the twelfth century: local, public courts that produced simple written deeds at a competitive rate. These courts were used for all kinds of legal matters and produced huge quantities of written documents, a position that was strengthened by their early switch from Latin to the vernacular. According to Bas van Bavel, this trend came from below. Local bylaws in Zeeland, for instance, were already written in Dutch from the late twelfth century, whereas the chancery of the count of Holland and Zeeland only changed to the vernacular around 1285.[20] One of the most important discontinuities in the management of insolvencies in seventeenth-century Amsterdam is the substitution of notaries by the Desolate Boedelskamer. Whereas before the 1640s, they had often functioned as supporting agents to curators – for instance, by drawing up inventories of the goods found in an insolvent estate or registering a composition or *akkoord* concluded between an insolvent and his creditors – in the first decade after the establishment of the Desolate Boedelskamer their role was increasingly diminished. This important development can already be seen in the first register of curatele.

In the second part of this register, we find clear innovation in the acts of the commissioners of the Desolate Boedelskamer when compared to the insolvency procedure before 1643. The very first recto entry of this part of the register concerns an *akkoord* (accord) or composition between Jan Beuningh Coeckebacker and his creditors. On 27 January 1644, the insolvent baker had been placed under curatele of Franck van den Does, Jacques de Wint, and Jan van

20 J. Dijkman, "Debt Litigation in Medieval Holland, 1200–1350" in D. Ma and J. Luiten van Zanden (eds.), *Law and Long-Term Economic Change: A Eurasian Perspective*, Stanford, 2011, 221–243; Van Bavel, *Manors and Markets*, 315.

den Bergh. This assignation eventually resulted in an agreement with all his creditors effectuated on 23 March of that same year.[21] In total, the second part of the register contains thirty-three entries referring to such accords between insolvents and their creditors. This sets it apart from parts one and three, in which all entries refer to simple executions of insolvent estates organized by the city's clerk, after which proceeds were repartitioned among the creditors. It is in this type of case that we can most clearly observe how the more professionalized treatment of insolvencies by the Amsterdam Desolate Boedelskamer innovated on prior legal arrangements. Hereinafter, the case of Jan Beuningh is examined in further detail.

Interestingly, the original accord to which this entry refers has also been preserved in the archives of the Desolate Boedelskamer, not just once but in two copies: one signed by Beuningh himself; one written in a different hand, signed by his creditors. From the first lines of this document, we learn that the direct cause of Beuningh's insolvency was "a very considerable sum of money" owed to him by the Rouen merchant Hendrick Kindt, who had become insolvent himself. When Beuningh failed to restructure his debts through credit from other sources, Kindt's insolvency dragged the Amsterdam baker along into the financial abyss.[22]

The accord as originally drafted differs from the document preserved in the Amsterdam archives. Before all parties had signed the agreement, Beuningh and his curators had second thoughts about its provisions, which would have led to his "substantial damage and prejudice" ("*merckelijcke schaeden ende prejuditie*"). They visited the commissioners various times to discuss these issues. In response, the latter summoned Beuningh's creditors to the Desolate Boedelskamer in order to inform themselves of these creditors' positions. Thanks to the arbitrating efforts of the commissioners, it was possible to arrive at a modified accord, which was eventually signed by Beuningh and all of his creditors. The insolvent would be allowed to keep his furniture, jewellery, silverwork, and clothing (including woollen and linen fabrics). Furthermore, Beuningh would be allowed to retain half of the thirty percent that Kindt promised to pay his creditors in four instalments of six months each. Beuningh's creditors received the other half of these instalments, as well as the twenty percent that Kindt would pay out immediately, in cash. All other goods, outstanding claims, and possessions found in Beuningh's estate would be liquidated to repay his creditors as much as possible of their debts, *pro rata*. If his creditors agreed to these conditions and signed the accord, they would not be allowed to

21 Municipal Archives Amsterdam, DB, 470, fol. 68r–69v.

22 Municipal Archives Amsterdam, DB, 1234.

engage in any further litigation about their remaining debts, given that Beuningh lived up to its provisions. The insolvent baker promised, however, that if "through God's blessing he might arrive at better fortune" at some point in future, he would strive to repay all remaining arrears of his former creditors.[23]

However interesting this accord may be in and of itself, it does not teach us everything we might wish to know about the precise functioning of the Desolate Boedelskamer. Fortunately, we can supplement its contents with information found in other series of registers produced by this same institution. From the first book of minutes of the commissioners, we learn that on Tuesday morning, 26 January 1644, Jan Beuningh as well as his three curators (who had yet to be appointed at the time) were summoned to appear before the court.[24] They convened with the commissioners that same afternoon. Interestingly, the curators Van der Does, Van den Bergh, and De Wint are described here as Beuningh's *assistenten* or "assistants".[25] It appears that the proceedings could not be finished that afternoon, as the commissioners' first act on the morning of 27 January was the appointment of these three "assistants" to be curators of Beuningh's estate. Furthermore, the commissioners note that they would discuss the documents provided to them with the aldermen, before they would continue to proceed in this case. It is possible that one or more of the aldermen had already been involved in this case before the Desolate Boedelskamer was established. That might explain such a consultation, of which we do not usually find evidence in later years, when the institution was more firmly established. This hypothesis is strengthened by the fact that Beuningh asked for a prolongation of his *seureté de corps* (usually granted for six months) soon afterwards (see below).[26]

In the weeks after these initial meetings, the curators managed the estate, until an accord could be reached or the commissioners issued an order for the estate's execution. During the negotiations with the creditors, the curators would already start to sell (trade) goods from the estate and try to liquidate outstanding debts. Even though the curators must have had some discretionary leeway when fulfilling such tasks, important decisions always needed to be confirmed by the commissioners. On 12 February 1644, for instance, the curators Jacques de Wint and Jan van den Bergh appeared in the Desolate Boedelskamer to receive permission to let the debt in Rouen run its course for a

23 Municipal Archives Amsterdam, DB, 1234.
24 Municipal Archives Amsterdam, DB, 1, fol. 46r.
25 Municipal Archives Amsterdam, DB, 1, fol. 47v.
26 Municipal Archives Amsterdam, DB, 1, fol. 48r.

while (*"vooreerst op haer beloop te laeten"*).[27] The curators were probably awaiting the results of negotiations with the representatives of Hendrick Kindt. On Friday 18 March, at half past twelve in the afternoon, Beuningh and his curators arrived at the Boedelskamer to sign the accord proposed by Kindt, which eventually resulted in the repayment scheme noted in Beuningh's own accord.[28]

That same afternoon, Jan Beuningh also requested the commissioners to support a request for prolongation of his *seureté de corps* for six months. This legal benefice, granted by the High Court of Holland and Zeeland, could only be obtained with the assent of the local court that treated the insolvency. It temporarily protected the insolvent from incarceration by his creditors, while trying to arrive at a legal solution for his financial problems.[29]

In the meantime, other officials and institutions had also become involved in the management of the insolvent estate. On 24 February, the widow of Joost Brest transferred fl. 2365 – 19 – 8 to the account of the Desolate Boedelskamer in the Amsterdam Bank of Exchange after having bought a share in the WIC (Dutch West India Company) from the estate of Jan Beuningh.[30] Three weeks later, another share with the same nominal value of fl. 3,000 was sold for fl. 2,364 – 9 – 8; of which fl. 35 – 0 – 8 had to be subtracted as auction costs. This is interesting evidence for shifting prices on the stock exchange, as well as for the fact that an execution sale at times necessitated liquidating assets at an inconvenient moment, below their nominal value.[31] On 7 March, Mr. Hendrick Kaldekercke ordered fl. 739 – 2 to be transferred to the commissioners in favour of the estate of Jan Beuningh. These were further proceeds of the execution sale that had been organized after potential buyers had been notified by means of placards. It was also noted that a further fl. 36 had been withheld to cover the costs of the auction, as proven by two receipts written by one of the secretaries.[32] On 11 March, the curators received permission to convert certain proceeds obtained from the sale of commercial goods from Jan Beuningh's estate into bank guilders.[33] In general, these entries indicate very well

27 Municipal Archives Amsterdam, DB, 1, fol. 57r.
28 Municipal Archives Amsterdam, DB, 1, fol. 95v–96r.
29 Municipal Archives Amsterdam, DB, 1, fol. 96v. On *seureté de corps*, see: Den Hollander, *Court, Credit, and Capital*, 126–131.
30 Municipal Archives Amsterdam, DB, 1, fol. 67v.
31 Municipal Archives Amsterdam, DB, 1, fol. 94v.
32 Municipal Archives Amsterdam, DB, 1, fol. 87v.
33 Municipal Archives Amsterdam, DB, 1, fol. 89r. On the advantages of using the Bank of Exchange for transactions, see: P. Dehing, *Geld in Amsterdam. Wisselbank en wisselkoersen, 1650–1725*, Hilversum, 2012.

how the commissioners and their supporting officials made optimal use of Amsterdam's commercial and financial infrastructure for the management and execution of insolvent estates.

Finally, on Saturday, 19 March 1644, eighteen of Beuningh's creditors – among whom we find the three curators – came together in the Desolate Boedelskamer to engage in negotiations about the accord described above. The commissioners aided this process by providing a transparent overview of the condition of the insolvent estate and by mediating the parties.[34] The definitive composition was presented to the commissioners on 23 March 1644, to be signed by Beuningh and his creditors.[35] Attached to the duplicate copy of the accord, we find a notarial attestation drawn up by Frans Bruijningh (who was also employed as the secretary of the Desolate Boedelskamer) on 13 June 1645. Jacques van Poelwijck appeared in the Desolate Boedelskamer together with Pieter Regenmorter, a Haarlem citizen, as witness, to confirm that he had received the money that was due to him from the estate of Jan Beuningh on account of a bill of exchange, *pro rata* with the other creditors, after signing the accord. The fact that such transactions still took place more than a year after the curatele had ended highlights the value of an institution such as the Desolate Boedelskamer for (foreign) creditors. Even if they could not immediately collect their claims – for instance, due to being out of the country on a commercial expedition – these would still be stored at a trustworthy, public institution, which would keep the proceeds safe until they would be able to collect them.[36]

The conclusion of accords between insolvents and their creditors to wrap up an insolvency – such as the case of Jan Beuningh, or any of the other compositions noted in the second part of the aforementioned register of curatele – was not a new phenomenon. What was new in the 1640s, however, is the intensive involvement of a public institution – the Desolate Boedelskamer – in their conclusion. From the late sixteenth century onwards, we come across these accords in Amsterdam notarial protocols. As I have argued elsewhere, the basic style of such compositions was continuously employed until the end of the ancien régime and developed among a network of notaries surrounding Jan Fransz. Bruijningh. As one of the most important networks, it included his

34 Municipal Archives Amsterdam, DB, 1, fol. 97r–98r.

35 Municipal Archives Amsterdam, DB, 1, fol. 102v–103r.

36 Municipal Archives Amsterdam, DB, 1234. On the advantages of the Desolate Boedelskamer for foreign creditors and hence investors in Amsterdam, see: M. den Hollander and R. Mooi, "Protecting the Foreign Creditor – International Insolvency in Early Modern Amsterdam and Frankfurt Am Main", *TSEG/Low Countries Journal of Social and Economic History* 16/3-4 (2020), 37–57.

son Frans, the first secretary of the Desolate Boedelskamer. The Bruijninghs stood at the core of Amsterdam's maritime commercial economy, producing not just thousands of freight contracts, but also arranging the initial subscriptions to the VOC (United East India Company).[37] The second part of the oldest register of curatele shows how immediately after the establishment of the Desolate Boedelskamer, part of the accords started to be concluded before its commissioners. Likely, this transition was eased by Bruijningh's crucial role in this institution. At the time, however, it was still possible to opt for a public notary to register one's accord.

This arrangement changed in 1647.[38] The original ordinance of the Desolate Boedelskamer did not include specific rules regarding accords. It just stated that they had to be included within six weeks after the curatele began; however, this term could be prolonged at the discretion of the commissioners.[39] In 1647, the burgomasters decreed that henceforth no accords could be concluded between insolvents and their creditors without the involvement of the Desolate Boedelskamer. This regulation ended the practice of concluding accords before notaries, or at least declared it illegal. Closer supervision on the conclusion of such agreements by a public authority will have helped to ensure that the rights of all creditors were respected.[40] At the same time, however, concluding majority compositions was for the first time explicitly allowed. The *ampliatie* to the 1643 ordinance states that when a majority of the creditors representing three fourths of the debts supported an accord, it would enter into effect. Any proceeds were to be handed over to the court, to be distributed *pro rata* to signed and unsigned creditors alike.[41] In 1659, the Desolate Boedelskamer received an entirely revised and expanded ordinance, which also altered the rules for majority compositions. Henceforth, an accord would enter into effect once either three fourths of the creditors holding two thirds of the total debts or two thirds of the creditors holding three fourths of the debts had signed the proposal.[42]

These were radical innovations. Emperor Charles V's ordinances from the 1540s had completely ruled out the possibility of a *remissio* (acquittal of debts)

37 Den Hollander, *"Stay of Execution"*, 140–145.
38 This passage on the introduction of majority compositions is based upon the fifth chapter of my book: Den Hollander, *Court, Credit, and Capital*, 173–215.
39 Rooseboom, *Recueil*, 304–309.
40 On creditors' rights, see Den Hollander and Mooi, "Protecting the Foreign Creditor".
41 Rooseboom, *Recueil*, 310–311.
42 H. Noordkerk, *Handvesten; ofte Privilegien ende octroyen: Mitsgaders willekeuren, costuimen, ordonnantien en handelingen der stad Amstelredam*, dl. 2, Amsterdam, 1748, 687–688.

through majority compositions.[43] Even though in 1596, the States-Provincial of Holland had stated that they would continue to uphold these decrees, from the middle of the seventeenth century onwards it became increasingly common to conclude accords that de facto – though explicitly not de jure – acquitted part of the debt. As indicated by the local ordinances of 1647 and 1659, the Amsterdam Desolate Boedelskamer even made it possible to do so through majority compositions, without all creditors' explicit consent.[44] As I have elaborated upon elsewhere, this example was subsequently followed by many other cities and regions in the Dutch Republic.[45] Even though it is often stated that the States of Zeeland, through an 1649 ordinance, would have been the first to introduce the possibility of majority compositions to the Dutch Republic, as discussed above this case fails to take the crucial Amsterdam innovation of 1647 into account.[46] It is often assumed that scholars would have paved the way for such significant changes. Nevertheless, it appears that the evolution of Amsterdam's insolvency legislation rose out of the needs of individual businessmen, entering into legal doctrine only subsequently, rather than the other way around.

Jan Hendrik Dalhuisen argues that the emperor's reservations regarding majority compositions were still present in the work of Voet and Van Leeuwen. However, this interpretation seems to be incorrect.[47] Voet and Van Leeuwen do not oppose a majority of the creditors binding a minority to accept a *dilatio*, in which the repayment of the full debt is simply postponed, but in fact argue against a *remissio*, in which debts would be discharged. It is important to keep in mind that even when the agreed upon repayment percentages only covered part of the debt, in principle accords concluded in seventeenth-

43 *Recueil des Ordonnances des Pays-Bas. Deuxème Série 1506–1700*, vol. 5, Brussels, 1910, 52–56 (Brussels, 10 May 1544).

44 A.C. Lagerwey, *Het Accoord van den Gefailleerde met zijne Schuldeisers*, Utrecht, 1862, 60; J. Dalhuisen, *Compositions in Bankruptcy. A Comparative Study of the Laws of the E.E.C. Countries, England and the U.S.A.*, Leiden, 1968, 15 and 22.

45 M. den Hollander, "Failliet in de Republiek. Lokale ordonnanties over de omgang met desolate boedels, circa 1643–1713", *Pro Memorie* 24/2 (2022), 190–217.

46 Often citing: Dalhuisen, *Compositions in Bankruptcy*, 22. Note that in other regions, especially Castile, forms of majority compositions had become entrenched in laws such as the *Siete Partidas* from the late medieval period onwards. From the seventeenth century onwards, this idea also gained support in the Holy Roman Empire: W. Forster, *Konkurs als Verfahren: Francisco Salgado de Somoza in der Geschichte des Insolvenzrechts*. Köln: Böhlau, 2009, 212–218.

47 Dalhuisen, *Compositions in Bankruptcy*, 22, referring to: G. Voetius, *Commentarius Ad Pandectas*, dl. 1, Leiden, 1698, lib. II, tit. 14, no. 23 *and following.*; Van Leeuwen, *Rooms-Hollands Regt*, lib. 4, ch. 41, no. 7.

century Amsterdam never truly acquitted an insolvent of his responsibility to pay the remainder. Even though creditors could no longer 'molest' their debtor or start a lawsuit about debts falling under the ratified accord, it always remained an insolvent's moral obligation to repay the creditors if he ever managed to revive his business. Almost every accord included a formula that expressed this principle, as we have also seen in the case of Jan Beuningh.

The diligent and transparent management of insolvent estates such as Beuningh's by the commissioners of the Desolate Boedelskamer was a crucial factor in the growing acceptance of majority compositions. The latter could potentially undermine the trust of investors in the security of their investments in Amsterdam. There was the possibility that they might be forced to accept a composition in case of their debtor's insolvency, even against their personal wishes. In practice, however, the services provided by the Amsterdam courts and the supporting institutional infrastructure in which these were embedded (e.g. the city clerk, or the Bank of Exchange) significantly improved the position of creditors vis-à-vis their insolvent debtors. Before the 1640s, they had to rely on the services of notaries and the good faith of their debtor. Now, the books, papers, and affairs of any insolvent estate were analyzed and managed by a public institution that sought the benefit of all creditors involved, both locals and foreigners.[48] An ordinance issued by the States of Zeeland from 1649, which introduced the possibility of majority compositions for this entire province, explains why this arrangement worked to the advantage of the vast majority of creditors. Usually, those with the smallest claims would "so stubbornly latch onto their full right" that the proceedings were greatly delayed, resulting in losses for "those who would try and save a decent part of the estate, rather than risk losing it in its entirety".[49]

The Amsterdam regents must have followed a reasoning similar to these arguments voiced by the States of Zeeland. Majority compositions that allowed a restructuring of debts and a continuation rather than an execution of insolvent businesses would eventually benefit not just the insolvent, but also the civic community as a whole. By establishing the Desolate Boedelskamer – which subsequently replaced the public notaries as supervisors over the conclusion of all accords – the equal treatment of all parties involved could be guaranteed to the extent that it allowed for the involuntary restructuring of

48 On the role of the *Desolate Boedelskamer* in the restoring of trust, see M. den Hollander, "Restoring Trust and Credit through Innovative Governance in 17th-Century Amsterdam", *Tijdschrift voor Rechtsgeschiedenis* 89 (2021), 481–499.

49 C. Cau, *Groot-placaetboek, vervattende de placaten, ordonnantien ende edicten van de Staten Generaal der Verenigde Nederlanden*, vol. 1, The Hague, 1655, 407–410. See also: Den Hollander, "Failliet in de Republiek."

property rights of the unwilling minority of creditors, which was an unescapable feature of such majority compositions. This situation marks the greatest discontinuity in Amsterdam insolvency legislation and legal practice before and after the Desolate Boedelskamer, which will most likely have contributed to the city's continuing flourishing economy in the second half of the seventeenth century.

4 Conclusion

The introduction of majority compositions in case of insolvency is a powerful indication of the continued institutional flexibility of the Amsterdam regents well into the 1650s. As the analysis of the first preserved register of curatele has revealed, there were important continuities in the work of the aldermen and the commissioners of the *Desolate Boedelskamer*, before and after 1643, respectively. What did change, however, was the increasingly professional management of insolvent estates, as well as a shift of focus from privately contracted notaries to this new public institution. This important change was enabled by the enlarged staff of this dedicated court, which also allowed a much more intensified supervision of curators and an increasingly equal treatment of all creditors involved. Crucial innovations, such as the introduction of majority compositions between 1647 and 1659, were rooted in legal and commercial practice rather than in pre-existing black-letter law or the doctrine of legal scholars such as Van Leeuwen or Voet. The bottom-up evolution of the legal and institutional arrangements surrounding debt adjustment schemes in seventeenth-century Amsterdam are a clear example of law functioning as a resource for economic growth. Through professionalization and, if needed, a top-down restructuring of specific private property rights, the Desolate Boedelskamer could maintain a level social and economic playing field. This situation proved to be a stable and secure environment for continued economic growth and prosperity.

CHAPTER 5

Amsterdam as an International Exchange Centre (Late Seventeenth Century): Legal Aspects of Transnational Practices in the *Cambium* System

Victor Le Breton-Blon

> Midday school every day / on the stroke of twelve / an uncommon wonder [is seen] / a thousand souls or more together, / great and small, low and high / men of great wealth / ships' masters, merchants and factors / Russians and Moors, / Scots and English, Spaniards, Frenchmen / small traders, great Hanseatics / farmers and citizens, pensioners / brokers and moneychangers, / goods worth tons [hundreds of thousands] for sale / money to be had on bills of exchange, money to be had at interest. / a great market heaped high / where these goods are sold / where great trade is done / both in oil and olives, / mace, sugar, spices and rice.[1]

This is how the Dutch Catholic playwright Jan Harmenszoon Krul (1601–1646) described the Amsterdam stock exchange in his 1639 emblem book *Minnespiegel ter Deughden*: a palace filled with precious commodities and people from all over the world. It was then the perfect reflection of the economic attractiveness of the Venice of the North.

1 Introductory Remarks: Global Dynamic, Transnational Practices, and Bills of Exchange in Amsterdam

Amsterdam became one of the main economic centres of the old continent during the early modern period. Its commercial dynamism virtually spread to all parts of the world since the end of the sixteenth century. The city grew from a regional warehouse to one of the largest markets under the influence of European and transatlantic trade.[2] This phenomenon was mainly the result

1 Quoted by Cl. Lesger, *The Rise of the Amsterdam Market and Information Exchange: Merchants, Commercial Expansion and Change in the Spatial Economy of the Low Countries, c. 1550–1630*, Aldershot, 2006, 223.

2 "One of the commonplaces of early modern economic history is the dominance of Amsterdam over European international commerce in the seventeenth century. Amsterdam was

© 2026 THE AUTHOR(S) | HTTPS://DOI.ORG/10.1163/9789004761537-007

of an advanced and very profitable freight activity, a competitive shipbuilding industry; and a strategic position between the Hanseatic area, Southern Europe and the overseas colonies.

Amsterdam took on in that context the function of an international economic gateway: an exchange centre bringing together buyers and sellers, lenders and borrowers, or port workers and shipowners, over long distances. It was conceived all at once as a major financial market, a hub for information flow and a merchant warehouse. The city was in consequence a centralizing location where goods, money and people circulated to foster a wide range of international ventures. This situation contributes to explain why it was, at that time, one of the most influential places of Europe and the symbol of the Dutch Golden Age.[3]

These introductory remarks outline a global economic framework in Amsterdam. The latter was indeed marked by the coexistence of far-flung connections and entangled transactions from and to various territories. It was fully integrated with a broader background, forged by the mobility of wealth, thanks to the combined effect of its geographical situation, the diversity of its mercantile activities and its openness to the outside.[4] These aspects were not underestimated by Jan Harmenszoon Krul in his description of the stock market, particularly by mentioning bills of exchange.

Bills of exchange were indeed a driving force in the general expansion of long-distance trade during the early modern period. These private instruments were created between the thirteenth and the fourteenth centuries in

---

the apex of several different regional hierarchies of trade and finance": S. Woodruff, "The Function of Commercial Centres in the Modernization of European Capitalism: Amsterdam as an Information Exchange in the Seventeenth Century", *The Journal of Economic History* 44/4 (1984), 985–1005, here 985.

3 See further: V. Barbour, *Capitalism in Amsterdam in the Seventeenth Century*, Ann Arbor, 1963; F. Delleaux, *Histoire économique de l'Europe moderne: XVe-XVIIIe siècle*, Paris, 2015, 96–107; Cl. Lesger, "Intraregional Trade and the Port System in Holland, 1400–1700" in K. Davids and L. Noordegraaf (eds.), *The Dutch Economy in the Golden Age*, Amsterdam, 1993, 185–217; E. Pieter, "The Rise and Decline of the Dutch Atlantic, 1600–1800" in G. Oostindie and J. Roitman (eds.), *Dutch Atlantic Connections, 1680–1800. Linking Empires, Bridging Borders*, Leiden, 2014, 339–354; J.G. van Dillen, "Amsterdam's role in Seventeenth-Century Dutch Politics and its Economic Background" in J. Selwyn Bromley and E. Kossman (eds.), *Britain and the Netherlands*, vol. 2, Groningen, 1964, 133–147.

4 These elements emphasize the specific global environment of a city within a more general global framework linked to international trade during the early modern period, F. Trivellato, *The Familiarity of Strangers: The Sephardic Diaspora, Livorno, and Cross-Cultural Trade in the Early Modern Period*, New Haven, 2009, 710. They are also part of a global perspective in legal history, Th. Duve, "What is Global Legal History", *Comparative Legal History* 8/2 (2020), 88–96.

Italy. They were gradually used to ensure the transfer of capital without any physical movement of cash across Europe. The *cambium* transaction allowed more precisely one person to pay a sum of money at maturity to another, via a third party, between two locations. This system functioned in that regard as a payment and credit method for cashless transactions, but also as a medium for speculating on the value of currencies over time and space.[5]

Between the sixteenth and the seventeenth centuries, the development of the indorsement (from Italian *in dorso*, and French *en dos*, meaning 'on the back') represents a major turning point by renewing the importance of the *cambium* instrument for the circulation of money on a wide scale. The technique was a simplified transfer of claims and debts with a brief, handwritten indorsement on the back of the bill. It played a decisive role in the expansion of global trade – especially towards Northern European markets, including Amsterdam[6] – by creating chains of payments, credits and speculations on a short term, with no cash disbursement and across more than two places, using only one commercial paper.[7]

Bills of exchange were closely connected to the development of business law across territories. They were conceived as a tool for cooperation amongst individuals acting towards the same economic purpose, yet from distant locations. This dynamic involved in consequence a unique legal framework. The physical support of the act, a simple and short letter, allowed merchants to

5 The historiography on the bill of exchange is very rich. For a general overview, from the end of the medieval period to the early modern era, see J. Bolton and F. Guidi Bruscoli, "'Your Flexible Friend': The Bill of Exchange in Theory and Practice in the Fifteenth Century", *Economic History Review* 74/4 (2021), 873–891; Fl. Garnier, *Histoires du droit commercial*, Paris, 2020, 337–339; M. Denzel, *Handbook of World Exchange Rates, 1590–1914*, Abingdon, 2016, 1944; V. Santarosa, "Financing Long-Distance Trade: The Joint Liability Rule and Bills of Exchange in Eighteenth-Century France", *The Journal of Economic History* 75/3 (2015), 690–719; C. Wilder, "The Rigor of the Law of Exchange: How People Changed Commercial Law and Commercial Law changed People (Hesse-Cassel, 1654–1776)", *Zeitschrift für Historische Forschung* 42/4 (2015), 629–659.

6 See the following pages for more development on the influence of Amsterdam regarding the evolution of the *cambium* system during the first part of the early modern period.

7 L.-F. Li, "International Credit Market Integration in Northwestern Europe in the 1670s", *Financial History Review* 26/2 (2019), 127–145; D. Lucena-Piquero, O. Accominotti and S. Ugolini, "The Origination and Distribution of Money Market Instruments: Sterling Bills of Exchange during the First Globalisation", *The Economic History Review* 74/4 (2021), 892–921; N. Matringe, "The Meandering Trajectories of Financial Innovations: Commercial Paper and its Uses in Sixteenth-Century Lyon's Trading Networks", *Financial History Review* 30/2 (2023), 198–230; J. Munro, "The Medieval Origins of the Financial Revolution: Usury, Rentes and Negociability", *International History Review* 25 (2003), 502–562.

develop homogenous legal terms, principles and terminologies throughout Europe.[8]

These practices were essential to avoid conflict in a system connecting multiple actors, places, currencies, temporalities and services. They contributed to create special spaces where bills were drawn and paid to support trade across sovereign territories. This phenomenon could even encourage the creation of self-directed structures, with their own legal and economic rules approved by local or national authorities, such as the great international exchange fairs of Lyon.[9]

This is a clear indication that bills of exchange facilitated global trade in Europe[10] because, from their inception, they were of a transnational nature. This perspective concerned more precisely legal rules traveling independently across sovereign spaces through economic connections between individuals from various geographical areas, though also, in a broader sense, from different cultural, ethnic or religious backgrounds.[11]

It is therefore not surprising that Amsterdam became a nodal point for the circulation of commercial papers during the seventeenth century. The city was indeed a decisive centre for international finance. It was a particularly safe and lucrative environment to hedge the risks of currency fluctuations,

8 J. Bottin, "Signature, marque, souscription. Validation et identification des documents commerciaux (fin du Moyen Âge-première époque moderne)", *Hypothèses* 9/1 (2006), 350–353; L. Brunori, "La représentation devient droit: la lettre de change (XVIe–XVe siècle)" in N. Goedert and N. Maillard (eds.), *Le droit en représentation(s)*, Paris, 2017, 233–244; V. Le Breton-Blon, "La pratique européenne du change pendant la seconde modernité. L'exemple de l'activité cambiaire de Bordeaux (fin XVIIe–XVIIIe siècle)" in A. Mages (ed.), *Les fondements historiques du droit européen des affaires*, Toulouse, 2020, 83–112.

9 For some general elements on the international exchange fairs, see A. Tiran, *Le royaume de Naples (1580–1620). Économie, monnaie et finance à l'époque d'Antonio Serra*, Paris, 2020, 349–375; Cl. Marsilio, "'Four Times a Year for So Many Years'. The Italian Exchange Fairs During the 16th-17th Century: Comparing Financial Institutions", *Bankhistorisches Archiv. Banking and Finance in historical perspective* 36/2 (2010), 151–165; R. De Roover, *L'évolution de la lettre de change (XIVe–XVIIIe siècle)*, Paris, 1953, 74–83.

10 The *cambium* system was mostly limited to European territories, as other parts of the world had no corresponding banking or monetary system.

11 On the legal rules contributing to the global framework on a transnational level, see Duve, "What is Global Legal History?", 96. On the economic connections participating to the same global framework, see A. Belem Fernández Castro, "A Transnational Empire Built on Law: The Case of the Commercial Jurisprudence of the House of Trade of Seville (1583–1598)" in Th. Duve (ed.), *Entanglements in Legal History: Conceptual Approaches*, Frankfurt, 2014, 192–193; B. Yun-Casalilla, "Localism, Global History and Transnational History. A Reflection from the Historian of Early Modern Europe", *Historisk Tidskrift* 127/4 (2007), 88–98.

unsecured deposits or scattered information.[12] The massive influx of goods led to a reciprocal movement in the supply and demand for money, while the concentration of news facilitated speculative manoeuvres.[13] It was in consequence a very strategic location for banking companies to create a multilateral payment system by connecting mercantile networks, while *kassiers* were able to offer low and competitive interest rates for monetary conversion.[14]

This situation was strongly favoured by the municipal government, which was particularly concerned by commercial issues. Many of the burgomasters and the aldermen at the city council were former merchants, bankers and shipmasters, or rich investors from other professions.[15] They played an active role in protecting local business interests, by monitoring the Dutch East India Company and the Dutch West India Company, for example, or by creating the Chamber of Insurance in 1589, the *Wisselbank* in 1609 (Figure 5.1) and the new stock exchange building in 1611.[16]

Urban authorities even took commercial law into their own hands, especially from the seventeenth century onwards, to keep pace with the economic expansion of the city. They promoted a growing number of commercial customs through *turben* (testimonies on law). They also issued new ordinances – regularly at the instigation of petitions by merchants – to solve emerging problems, reform old regulations or enact practices that had previously been accepted in courts, to the detriment of the direct application of external rules, such as the Antwerp *costuymen*.[17]

---

12 Denzel, *Handbook of World Exchange Rates*, 262–271; O. Gelderblom and J. Jonker, "Completing a Financial Revolution: The Finance of the Dutch East India Trade and the Rise of the Amsterdam Capital Market, 1595–1612", *The Journal of Economic History* 64/3 (2004), 641–672; S. Quinn and W. Roberds, "The Bank of Amsterdam and the Leap to Central Bank Money", *American Economy Review* 97/2 (2007), 262–265; Ch. van Bochove and H. Kole, "Uncovering Private Credit Markets: Amsterdam, 1660–1809", *Tijdschrift voor Sociale en Economische Geschiedenis* 11/3 (2014), 39–72.

13 Lesger, *The Rise of the Amsterdam Market*, 9.

14 Delleaux, *Histoire économique de l'Europe moderne*, 98–101; P. Jeannin, *Marchands d'Europe. Pratiques et savoirs à l'époque moderne*, Paris, 2002, 123, 155 and 156; P. Jeannin, *Marchands du Nord. Espaces et trafics à l'époque moderne*, Paris, 1996, 110–111.

15 "Merchants had an overriding impact upon state policies, at least up to the 1650s or 1660s when regents with fewer direct interests in commerce would take over their position", M. 'T Hart, "Cities and Statemaking in the Dutch Republic, 1580–1680", *Theory and Society* 18/5 (1989), 663–687, at 679. See also Lesger, *The Rise of the Amsterdam Market*, 143.

16 For an example, see S. Go, "The Amsterdam Chamber of Insurance and Average: A New Phase in Formal Contract Enforcement (Late Sixteenth and Seventeenth Centuries)", *Enterprise & Society* 14/3 (2013), 511–543.

17 De ruysscher, "Antwerp commercial legislation in Amsterdam". For more insights on the governance of trade and the development of commercial law in Dutch cities, see

FIGURE 5.1 Old city hall of Amsterdam, in which the Exchange Bank (*Wisselbank*) was located in 1609–1651, by Jan Abrahamsz. Beerstraten – Amsterdam Museum, 38005

This phenomenon highlights the close links between the global development of trade and the transformation of public governance in the making of law. Bills of exchange were heavily affected by this situation because of their importance for the city's commercial prosperity. For example, a *turbe* of 1601 recognized the acceptance of a bill (i.e. the debtor's commitment) on behalf of a third party, while an official ordinance of 1660 subsequently regulated the formalism of the acceptance to simplify dispute resolution.

The *cambium* system was in that regard the beating heart of international trade in Amsterdam. Commercial papers were used daily to clear claims, as well as to give or find financial resources for external operations. Their distribution was guaranteed by the presence of banking institutions with extensive

---

O. Gelderblom, *Cities of Commerce. The Institutional Foundation of International Trade in the Low Countries, 1250–1650*, Princeton, 2013, 19–168.

networks, as well as cross-border communities formed by personal and professional ties.[18]

Amsterdam was more precisely the scene of financial innovations, promoted by the municipal power, especially after the economic decline of Antwerp. For example, the *Wisselbank*, monitored by the local government, organized an advanced multilateral and bilateral clearing system and promoted the early introduction of the negotiability principle with order notes based on the *assegno in banco* formula. The municipal government itself joined this dynamic by explicitly accepting the validity of the indorsement mechanism, along with its consequences, whereas it was still prohibited in certain Italian cities or was not mentioned in the legislation of the kingdom of France or that of German-speaking territories.[19]

In consequence, the transnational dimension of the bills of exchange was particularly well suited to the global economic development of Amsterdam since the seventeenth century. This situation nevertheless raises specific and overlooked relations between commercial practices, urban life and legal features.[20] It interrogates more precisely the emergence of a privileged ecosystem for the development of financial law between mercantile actors crossing territories and a city as well as its public authorities or structures.[21] The circulation of norms and practices appears moreover as a central element to be explored

18 M. Lindemann, *The Merchant Republics. Amsterdam, Antwerp and Hamburg, 1648–1790*, New York, 2014; Cl. Marsilio, "The Genoese Exchange Fair and the Bank of Amsterdam: Comparing Two Financial Institutions of the 17th Century", *História Econômica & História de Empresas* 18/1 (2015), 39–59; Jeannin, *Marchands du Nord*, 110 and 275–277.

19 D. De ruysscher, "Innovating Financial Law in the Early Modern Netherlands and Europe: Transfers of Commercial Paper and Resource Liability in legislation and *Ius Commune* (Sixteenth-Eighteenth Centuries)", *European Review of Law* 5 (2011), 505–518; H. Van Der Wee, "Les innovations de la technique financière à Bruges, Anvers et Amsterdam (XIIIe–XVIIIe siècle)", *Revue belge de philologie et d'histoire* 89/2 (2011), 867–870.

20 This is inspired by the main historiographic teachings on the great international exchange fairs of the sixteenth and seventeenth centuries. See for example J.G. da Silva and R. Ruggerio, "L'histoire des changes: les foires de "Bisenzone" de 1600 à 1650", *Annales. Économies, Sociétés, Civilisation* 17 (1962), 715–721; P. Stabel, "Italian merchants and the fairs in the Low Countries (12th-16th centuries)" in P. Lanaro (ed.), *La pratica dello scambio. Sistemi di fiere, mercanti e città in Europa (1400–1700)*, Venice, 2003, 131–159.

21 On the idea of a specific ecosystem, which is related to the European history of business law and economy, see L. Brunori, "History of Business Law: A European History?" *Glossae. European Journal of Legal History* 15 (2018), 62–79; Th. Duve, "Global Legal History. Setting Europe in Perspective" in M. Dubber, M. Godfrey and H. Pihlajamäki (eds.), *The Oxford Handbook of European Legal History*, Oxford, 2018, 116–140.

in that context, insofar as it could have contributed to manage international relationships and regulate the interweaving of diverse interests in a convergent space.[22]

The aim of this chapter is thus to analyze local legislation with a transnational dynamic and a global perspective. Amsterdam can be seen as a global designer, as well as an ideal normative vessel for an external framework forged by transnational practices. This aspect leads us to reconsider the communication spaces that can transform legal acts through interaction with local or more broader environments. It will clarify the normative power of businessmen with a complementary view on public governance of commercial issues regarding the influence of local authorities, especially the aldermen of the city council and their influence on commercial regulation.

To deal with this subject, it is necessary to see the law in action by consulting bills of exchange circulating between Amsterdam and various parts of Europe. This approach requires the use of sources from the eighteenth century, in line with the legal and economic context of the seventeenth century, because the previous period does not provide a sufficiently consistent corpus of documents from multiple locations.

Two complementary groups of sources will be used to reconstitute the economic and legal environment of a global city like Amsterdam.[23] The first concerns the archives of Thierry Daniel de Marolles, a notary from Amsterdam who worked mainly for numerous international traders,[24] with 95 bills transcribed in notarial deeds.[25] The second comes from a representative sample of merchants, bankers and shipowners in Bordeaux. It includes 98 bills that were

---

22 These elements reflect recent studies on the making of commercial law, especially on the idea of norms on the move. See, for example, A. Cordes, S. Dauchy, D. De ruysscher, S. Gialdroni and H. Pihlajamäki (eds.), *Migrating Words, Migrating Merchants, Migrating Law. Trading Routes and the Development of Commercial Law*, Leiden, 2020, 19; D. De ruysscher, "Antwerp Commercial Law in the Sixteenth Century: A Product of the Renaissance? The Legal Facilitating, Appropriating and Improving of Mercantile Practices" in J. Puttevils and B. Blondé (eds.), *Antwerp in the Renaissance*, Turnhout, 2020, 55–88.

23 The differences between the two groups of sources are intended to reconstitute the legal and economic diversity of a large-scale study. A few letters from merchants will be added for illustrative purposes. I am very grateful to Guido Rossi for his suggestion on the meaning of some formulas on bills of exchange written in Italian.

24 T. de Boer, "*"Ma coustume ne soit de m'addresser aux villes*"; Early Modern Amsterdam's Dealings in City Diplomacy", *Diplomatica* 3 (2021), 173 and 176.

25 The bills, drawn or indorsed to Amsterdam, are dated between 1737 and 1738. They provide an internal perspective of the global city and are based on the first half of a notarial register for a coherent and quantitatively appropriate corpus. See Municipal Archives Amsterdam, Notaries (inv. 5075), 11243.

part of solid partnerships between the French and the Dutch city, with the inclusion of other intermediary locations.[26]

This total of 193 acts covers a specific dynamic made up of transnational practices profoundly connected to Amsterdam's expansion. The situation reveals more precisely the formation of intertwined networks to fit in a globalized market. This phenomenon has facilitated the spread of a homogenous legal model forged by old customs, well known by traders and sometimes promoted by the municipal authority.

2 Intertwined Networks in a Globalized Market

Amsterdam's economic expansion was heavily dependent on the multiplication of networks based on hierarchical and durable structures, whether formal or informal, through which people sought to increase their profits or intensify control of their activities over long distances.[27]

Bills of exchange were one of the preferred means for establishing such links to support international exchanges. They allowed merchants to create circular movements of money across territories thanks to personal and professional connections.[28] The mobility of bills is therefore a point of entry into these transnational spaces, along with the human partnerships, all of which contributed to make Amsterdam a global city of trade and a welcoming legal environment.

26 The bills, drawn or indorsed from or to Amsterdam, are dated between 1735 and 1775. They provide an external perspective of the global city and are mainly based on Franco-Dutch collaborations. See Archives départementales de la Gironde, 7 B: 1131, 1188, 1345, 1346, 1622, 2147, 2148, 2165; 37 J 37.

27 On this definition of business networks during the early modern period, see D. Coulon, "Introduction" in D. Coulon (ed.), *Réseaux marchands et réseaux de commerce. Concepts récents, réalités historiques du Moyen Âge au XIXe siècle*, Strasbourg, 2010, 12–13; A.S. Ribeiro, *Early Modern Trading Networks in Europe: Cooperation and the case of Simon Ruiz*, London, 2017, 18.

28 See, for example, A. Bartolomei, "Paiements commerciaux et profits bancaires: les usages de la lettre de change (1780–1820)", *Rives méditerranéennes* 54/1 (2007), 109–127; Bolton and Guidi Bruscoli, "'Your Flexible Friend': The Bill of Exchange", 873–891; Santarosa, "Financing Long Distance Trade", 690–719.

2.1 The Transnational Spaces of the *Cambium* System in Amsterdam

The corpus of 193 acts contains valuable information on the contribution of the *cambium* system to the commercial success of Amsterdam.[29] Places of issuance (where the money was sent by the drawer), payment (where the money was given to the creditor by the drawee), and indorsement (where the new beneficiary was located) reveal more precisely the main economic and legal motivations behind these operations. Each drawing city reflects more precisely the remittance of money to obtain the drawer's order (the bill) to give the equivalent sum elsewhere to settle a debt. The payment city refers to the delivery of the promised cash to a creditor which can be changed by an indorsement to support a new transaction.[30]

The first group of 95 documents reflects an international dynamic covering a large diversity of locations.[31] The bills in this corpus are copies transcribed in protest claims, which are notarized deeds drawn up at the place of payment to declare the debtor's default. They are therefore all payable in Amsterdam, but they nevertheless come from 26 towns in nine different countries, and made for the drawer-payer partnership to remit the money to the primary creditor. The situation is similar for the indorsements, despite some methodological difficulties. Details of the operations are indeed sometimes incomplete, as the formalism for this technique could vary.[32] However, some examples among the 184 *endos*[33] contain the name and residence of the new beneficiary to whom the money was transferred. This feature shows how some bills circulated, after their creation, through as many as 27 cities in eight different countries.

---

29 The two groups of sources will be studied separately, with a few exceptions, to ensure methodological consistency regarding their proper characteristics.

30 On this methodological approach, see Ch. Carrière, M. Courdurié, M. Gutsatz and R. Squarzoni, *Banque et capitalisme commercial: la lettre de change au XVIIIe siècle*, Marseille, 1976, 56; K. Fukasawa, "Les lettres de change et le commerce du Levant au XVIIIe siècle" in H. Bonin and S. Marzgalli (eds.), *Négoce, ports et océans, XVIe-XXe siècle: mélanges offerts à Paul Butel*, Bordeaux, 2000, 76.

31 Municipal Archives Amsterdam, Notaries (inv. 5075), 11243. The reference to modern or general names of territories, or 'countries', aims to facilitate the identification of the places without ignoring the geographical, political and social realities of the time.

32 The writing of an indorsement, on the back of the bill, did not always comply with a very strict formalism. It might or might not mention the place where the value was received, or was supposed to be remitted, and the town where the new beneficiary lived. Even if it did, this information did not always reflect where the money was supposed to go. On this difficulty, see Fukasawa, "Les lettres de change et le commerce du Levant", 64.

33 One bill can include several indorsements, which explains the excessive number of indorsements compared to the bills.

These observations confirm the European attractiveness and centrality of Amsterdam for exchange operations. The places of issuance and indorsement involved regular contacts between the Amstel city and French (97), Italian (56) or German (32) localities. In addition, they entailed more sporadic co-operation with Great Britain (11), the Iberian Peninsula (6), other Dutch places (6) and Swiss towns (6).

The other collection of 98 acts demonstrates a much narrower perspective according to the sources derived from merchants working mainly between Amsterdam and Bordeaux.[34] The issuance and payment imply, respectively, three different countries with eleven cities, while the indorsements include two distinct countries with seven localities for 91 *endos*.

This setting reflects closer and less diversified channels. The issuance, payment and indorsement places show more specifically a durable and reciprocal cooperation between Amsterdam and the kingdom of France (153), with the incidental interposition of German (13) and other Dutch cities (4). The European dimension is thus still present despite a more restrictive scope.

The role of Amsterdam in this schematic overview can be clarified. The circulation of the bills between places of issuance, payment and indorsement reveals two complementary patterns in a global trading environment.

The first group of 95 bills refers to converging flows of transactions from various places to organize payments in Amsterdam.[35] The greatest diversity of drawing locations comes from fifteen different cities, each of which appear only once, including Bayonne (France), Frankfurt (Germany) or Lisbon (Iberian Peninsula). The most recurrent networks, between two and eleven incidences, but the least varied, involve ten issuance localities such as Bordeaux (France) and Genoa (Italy). One city (Lyon) stands out with seventeen mentions. It is the most frequent individual place, but it remains isolated from the other two dynamics due to the unique role of its annual foreign exchange fairs. The indorsements present a similar situation with a diversity of places occurring regularly or more sporadically. This observation supports, as seen above,

---

34 Archives départementales de la Gironde, 7 B: 1131, 1188, 1345, 1346, 1622, 2147, 2148, 2165; 37 J 37.

35 Places of issuance: Alicante (1); Bayonne (1); Berbice (1); Bergerac (3); Berlin (1); Bordeaux (9); Cádiz (1); Danzig (11); Dunkirk (1); Florence (2); Frankfurt (1); Geneva (2); Genoa (10); Königsberg (4); La Rochelle (1); Île de Ré (1); Lisbon (1); London (8); Lyon (17); Madrid (1); Montpellier (1); Paris (6); Rome (4); Seville (1); Troyes (1); Venice (5). Places of indorsement: Agen (1); Alicante (1); Amsterdam (1); Bergamo (4); Bergerac (4); Berlin (4); Bordeaux (10); Danzig (6); Dunkirk (1); Florence (1); Geneva (1); Königsberg (1); La Providence (1); La Rochelle (3); Leiden (4); Leipzig (3); Livorno (4); London (3); Lyon (14); Milan (12); Nuremberg (1); Paris (20); Rome (5); St. Gallen (2); Seville (1); Venice (9); Zurich (4).

both the idea of converging transactions from numerous international channels as well as the presence of close, reciprocal and less diversified partnerships with Amsterdam.[36]

The second sample of 98 bills corresponds to back-and-forth movements showing a dominant reticular structure centred on Amsterdam.[37] Bordeaux and Amsterdam represent almost all issues and payments with approximatively 94 percent of the transactions. This primary Franco-Dutch network was accessorily connected to Hamburg, which is the third most recurrent drawing location, with only thirteen incidences. The indorsements show the same situation for Bordeaux and Amsterdam, which are the main locations where the papers were negotiated to new beneficiaries (around 76 percent). The nearly exclusive presence of the same places where bills of exchange were sent or received perfectly demonstrates the idea of reciprocal and reticular transactions.

All these configurations reflect the role of a dominant capitalist city. Amsterdam was a decisive centre for sending or receiving money as part of consistent or infrequent partnerships with other locations in Europe. This role was partly due to the existence of attractive structures for the manipulation of values, such as currencies with bills of exchange, in long-distance trade.

One can mention in that regard the presence of prosperous private banking compagnies or public institutions such as the *Wisselbank*, the Bank of Loans and the Chamber of the East India Company. These structures provided a centralized, regulated and innovative securities market, which helped to ensure a high degree of price stability, a solidity of deposits and cash withdrawals, as well as an attraction for speculative manoeuvres in various mercantile activities.[38]

This dynamic was also associated with the relation between a shipping location and a warehouse of redistribution – in other words, the role of Amsterdam as an international staple market. Indeed, the drawing, payment

36 Ten places appear only once, like Seville (Iberian Peninsula), Florence (Italy) or Geneva (Switzerland). Sixteen others occur between two and fourteen times each with Bordeaux (France), London (Great Britain) or Leipzig (Germany), while one individual location totals twenty bills (Paris).

37 Places of issuance: Amsterdam (28); Bergerac (1); Bordeaux (51); Cleirac (1); Hamburg (13); Morlaix (1); Périgueux (1); Rotterdam (2). Places of payment: Amsterdam (55); Bayonne (2) Bordeaux (30); La Rochelle (1); Paris (9); Rotterdam (1). Place of indorsement: Abbeville (1); Amsterdam (30); Bergerac (1); Bordeaux (40); Paris (1); Rotterdam (1); Sainte-Foy (1).

38 't Hart, "Cities and Statemaking in the Dutch Republic", 677–679. For an illustration, see O. Gelderblom, J. Jonker and Cl. Kool, "Direct Finance in the Dutch Golden Age", *Economic History Review* 69/4 (2016), 1178–1198.

and indorsement site could reflect the circulation of goods from a purchase point to a selling site, or from the location where an order to buy or sell was given to the one where it was supposed to be executed.[39]

In this context, the bills studied demonstrate a significant flow of payment and credit facilities in and out to satisfy import and export activities. This situation was part of the transformation of Amsterdam, during the seventeenth century, into a buffer stock to regulate supply and demand, for various products like silk, rye, cotton, tobacco, alcohol or spices, especially thanks to its leading position in transatlantic trade.[40]

The convergent and reciprocal circulation of bills specifies the idea of a global environment in an economic gateway. Amsterdam was at the heart of multilateral connections between localities from distinct sovereign territories. Most of the time, these transnational spaces were interconnected, because of the continuous movement of goods, people and money, especially with the indorsement technique making it possible to re-claim a bill from one economic venture to another by transferring it to a new creditor.

That phenomenon was of great importance in Amsterdam. It encouraged the meeting of different legal systems through the reception, translation, adaptation or rejection of rules, practices and traditions from various geographical origins where the bills were circulating from or to the Dutch city.[41] This setting was also linked to the economic actors themselves, in addition to their respective socio-professional backgrounds, within personal and connected networks that need to be clarified to understand fully the global dynamic in action.

---

39 For a few examples on that dynamic, see Bartolomei, "Paiements commerciaux et profits bancaires", 113–117; J. Bottin, "En quête de profits. La pratique des changes à Rouen et en Europe de l'Ouest (1580–1640)", *Revue d'histoire moderne et contemporaine* 63/1 (2016), 69–82; O. Uwe Janzen, "A Scottish Venture in the Newfoundland Fish Trade, 1726–1727" in O. Uwe Janzen (ed.), *Merchant Organization and Maritime Trade in the North Atlantic, 1660–1815*, St. John's, 1998, 133–153, at 141; K. Samuelsson, "International payments and credit movements by the Swedish merchant houses, 1730–1815", *Scandinavian Economic History Review* 3/2 (1955), 163–202, at 70, 173–174 and 177; N. Zahedieh, "Credit, Risk and Reputation in Late Seventeenth-Century Colonial Trade" in Janzen (ed.), *Merchant Organization and Maritime Trade in the North Atlantic, 1660–1815*, Liverpool, 2017, 53–74, at 57.

40 Lesger, *The Rise of the Amsterdam Market*, 183–184.

41 Duve, "What is Global Legal History?", 97–100.

2.2 Personal Relationships in a Connected Market

Since the early seventeenth century, Amsterdam has been strongly connected to Europe's main financial markets and, because of its centrality for the circulation of money and goods, it became a very flexible intermediary for finding bills to be remitted or cashed.[42] This dynamic encouraged long-distance partnerships with Hamburg, Danzig and Frankfurt in the Hanseatic area, as well as Paris, Bordeaux, Venice and Lisbon further south, or even London and beyond the North Sea[43] – all places that appear regularly on our bills of exchange.

It is then not surprising that merchants directed their bills towards Amsterdam for a wide diversity of activities. Gabriel Da Silva, a Portuguese Jewish banker established in Bordeaux, offers a relevant example of how bills of exchange were used to connect various markets in the Dutch city. He appears on 26 documents, drawn or indorsed from or to Amsterdam, in the role of the remitter, the payee, the drawee, and the indorsee, along with 48 different partners.[44]

Da Silva's main activity was to organize a large flow of money for merchants who imported and exported colonial – mostly spices, sugar and cotton – and European – mostly wine, spirits and lumber – products via the Dutch city. He was more precisely an international financier who granted loans or found payers with bills of exchange.[45]

He worked in that context with a few regular collaborators directly in Amsterdam. Pierre Dutilh, a Franco-Dutch Protestant, was one of the most important. He acted as an intermediary who could be either the beneficiary, the drawer, the drawee, the indorser or the indorsee in exchange operations.[46] His role was even more flexible through communicating economic news and executing diverse orders as a true commission agent. In this way, Dutilh acted

42 Denzel, *Handbook of World Exchange Rates*, 267–269; Lesger, *The Rise of the Amsterdam Market*, 62–72.

43 Denzel, *Handbook of World Exchange Rates*, 267. See, as an illustration, the study of Lindemann, *The Merchant Republics*.

44 Archives départementales de la Gironde, 7 B: 2147, 2148, 2165.

45 He is one "of the five most taxed Jewish merchants in Bordeaux" whose "names were well known in international trade", S. Marzagalli, "Atlantic Trade and Sephardim Merchants in Eighteenth-Century France: The Case of Bordeaux" in P. Bernardini and N. Fiering (eds.), *The Jews and the Expansion of Europe to the West, 1493 to 1800*, Providence, 2001, 268–286, at 272.

46 Archives départementales de la Gironde, 7 B: 2147, 2148.

more broadly as a local contact who provided access to his own networks or dealt with his partner's customer base.[47]

This partnership is perfectly illustrated in a letter dated 18 March 1737. Dutilh informed Da Silva of the bills he had received, accepted or paid, and of those he would be negotiating for Da Silva and his clients. He added a few words on the activity of the East India Company and the quotation prices to examine the local options for speculation.[48]

The distribution of exchange rates confirms how vast the market was in that regard, underlining the importance of a reliable association with a local agent. Dutilh's letters – not uncommonly – can contain up to seventeen prices for an important range of places regularly mentioned in these bills, such as Bordeaux, Paris, Hamburg, Lisbon, Madrid, Genoa, Livorno or Venice. This aspect was also linked to Amsterdam's key position as a nexus of news. The city was indeed very active in the distribution of printed information in many languages,[49] while private letters had circulated – sometimes only to communicate on the economic context outside any commercial venture – at an increasing rate since the seventeenth century.[50]

This overall situation reflects faithfully the global dimension of early modern trade in an international exchange centre. It shows the convergence of economic forces – people, money, information and goods – in long-distance and multicultural partnerships related to the circulation of bills.

This aspect was crucial for the economic development of Amsterdam.[51] Close connections between locals and foreigners – combining skills within professional, in addition to familial and religious ties – were a decisive factor for the attractiveness and centrality of the city. The *cambium* system was undoubtedly the perfect tool to connect cities and individuals in a truly cosmo-

47 Commission agents played an important role in the development of long-distance trade since the sixteenth century, see for example A. Wegener Sleeswijk, "La relation problématique entre principal et agent dans la commission: l'exemple de l'exportation des vins vers les Provinces Unies au XVIIIe siècle" in Bonin and Marzagalli, *Négoce, ports et océans*, 29–45.

48 Archives départementales de la Gironde, 7 B: 2023.

49 Lesger, *The Rise of the Amsterdam Market*, 215–218 and 225–229; C. Gravesteijn and J. McCusker, *The Beginnings of Commercial and Financial Journalism: The Commodity Price Currents, Exchange Rate Currents and Money Currents of Early Modern Europe*, Amsterdam, 1991, 48.

50 Woodruff, "The Function of Commercial Centres", 991–992.

51 Lesger, *The Rise of the Amsterdam Market*, 218.

politan environment in view of its European origins.[52] The flexible legal mechanism of the bill, an acknowledgment of debt from the drawer to the remitter, and an order to pay from the drawer to the payee – to ensure the immaterial transfer of capital by a simple private letter – contributed more precisely to creating small transnational partnerships connected by the financial and trading influence of Amsterdam.

As their case suggests, the relationship between Gabriel Da Silva and Pierre Dutilh was not unique. André Pels, from a French Protestant family, worked in Amsterdam as a shipowner, banker and wine merchant.[53] He appears on eleven titles from our corpus with the Portuguese Jew David Lindo (Bordeaux), members of the Sephardic Vernazobre family (Amsterdam), the French Protestant Balgueries (Bordeaux), and more isolated German merchants (Hamburg). Pels was in this context a drawer, payee, indorser or indorsee, in accordance with his purchase and sale of goods, particularly wine, to the Baltic or Great Britain via the Dutch city.[54]

This illustration shows the close relationships between multiple trading houses and the interweaving of networks based on the need for money in granting payment and repayment involving multiple markets.[55] The situation clarifies furthermore the influence of diasporas on the multicultural or cosmopolitan environment mentioned above.[56]

Amsterdam was indeed a privileged space for the inclusion of newcomers – especially for economic purposes – under the influence of the municipal government. Foreigners were allowed to live or work in the city and to be in close contact with the locals, despite a few restrictions.[57] This phenomenon encouraged large waves of commercial migration from other Dutch and European places, mostly since the demise of Antwerp's commercial and financial lead-

---

52 Some studies even mention a "republic of bills of exchange"; in that regard, A. Bartolomei, "Mobilité et cosmopolitisme marchands. Les enseignements de la colonie française de Cadix (XVIIIe–XIXe siècles)", *Cahiers de la Méditerranée* 84 (2012), 93.

53 H. Lüthy, *La Banque Protestante en France*, vol. 1, Paris, 1959, 121; Trivellato, *The Familiarity of Strangers*, 254.

54 Municipal Archives Amsterdam, Notaries (inv. 5075), 11243; Archives départementales de la Gironde, 7 B: 1622, 3028, 2148.

55 Bolton and Guidi Bruscoli, "'Your Flexible Friend': The Bill of Exchange", 885.

56 On the methodological issues about the cross-cultural and the diaspora aspects, see Trivellato, *The Familiarity of Strangers*, 12.

57 See, for example, E. Kuijpers, *Migrantenstad: immigratie en sociale verhoudingen in 17e-eeuws Amsterdam*, Hilversum, 2005, especially 121–206.

ership at the end of the sixteenth century, with the dissolution of the Habsburg empire.[58]

Amsterdam quickly became a new home for external residents or visitors from diverse socioeconomic communities. This phenomenon contributed to the international network connections in the city, but most of all to the formation of substantial capital resources coming from the outsiders,[59] which favoured the extensive traffic in bills of exchange.

Foreign religious communities were particularly well integrated as permanent inhabitants. The Sephardim had been one of Amsterdam's largest since the seventeenth century, following a massive exodus from the Iberian Peninsula. They enjoyed relative freedom and played an active role in Amsterdam's commercial success.[60] This phenomenon explains part of the circulation of our bills. Jewish diasporas, alongside other groups, have greatly amplified the formation of transnational networks across Europe for mercantile activities.[61]

In that context, the Sephardim Vernazobre family exemplifies the contribution of religious, familial and commercial affinities in creating a global environment with bills of exchange.[62] The Vernazobres appear on 22 acts among many traders from various places, but they regularly mobilized their relatives, so as to connect their respective networks in the direction of Amsterdam. For example, Daniel and Pierre operated as drawers, from London and Danzig, with Abraham as a drawee in Amsterdam. The latter, identified as a banker,

58 O. Gelderblom, "From Antwerp to Amsterdam: The Contribution of Merchants from the Southern Netherlands to the Commercial Expansion of Amsterdam (c. 1540–1609)", *Review (Fernand Braudel Center)* 26/3 (2003), 247–282, here 248 and 259.

59 Gelderblom, "From Antwerp to Amsterdam", 262–264 and 276; Lesger, *The Rise of the Amsterdam Market*, 171.

60 H. Blom, H. Berg, B. Wallet and D. Wertheim, *Geschiedenis van de Joden in Nederland*, Amsterdam, 2017; M. Bodian, *Hebrews of the Portuguese Nation; Conversos and Community in Early Modern Amsterdam*, Bloomington, 1997. For a more synthetic presentation, see N. Eliasar, *The Jewish communities of Amsterdam. A separate collective existence*, PhD dissertation VU University Amsterdam, 2018, 1325 and 3541.

61 On Jewish networks in general, see D. Studnicki-Gizbert, "La 'nation' portugaise. Réseaux marchands dans l'espace atlantique à l'époque moderne", *Annales. Histoire, Sciences Sociales* 58/3 (2003), 645–646; Trivellato, *The Familiarity of Strangers*, 10–20. In relation with bills of exchange and crosscultural trade, see B. Arbel, "Mediterranean Jewish Diasporas and the Bill of Exchange: Coping with a Foreign Financial Instrument (14th-17th centuries)" in A. Beihammer, S. Burkhardt, G. Christ, J. Morche, W. Kaiser and R. Zaugg (eds.), *Union in Separation. Diasporic Groups and Identities in the Eastern Mediterranean (1100–1800)*, Rome, 2015, 527–542, here 540–541; C. Aust, "Transfer of Credit, Mercantile Mobility, and Language among Jewish Merchants in Seventeenth and Eighteenth Century Central and East Central Europe" in Cordes, Dauchy, De ruysscher, Gialdroni and Pihlajamäki (eds.) *Migrating Words*, 232–259, at 232.

62 Municipal Archives Amsterdam, Notaries (inv. 5075), 11243.

was able to pay the bills thanks to his own exchange activity in Berlin, Lyon or Paris, acting as a drawer or a payee to provide money in the Dutch city.

The elements mentioned clarify the entanglements that have contributed to making Amsterdam an international financial exchange centre and, by extension, a global city of trade. Bills of exchange were polyvalent tools to connect people, money and goods, over long distances. They responded well to the position of Amsterdam as an economic gateway – an international warehouse and financial centre – to forge sites for communication in the form of multilateral and cross-border linkages.

Nevertheless, this dynamic challenges the circulation of rules, models or practices via economic relationships. The convergence and reciprocal transactions with the *cambium* system raise the question of an appropriate legal environment to facilitate interactions between local and foreign traders, but also between those foreigners themselves.[63] Amsterdam was, in that regard, a normative vessel for the use of homogenous or even uniform laws by the influence of private – insiders as well as outsiders – and public actors.

3 Limiting Particularities in a Globalized Market: A Legal Preference for Old Models

The circulation of bills of exchange naturally posed the problem of drafting and receiving the legal terms it contained. The use of a simple private letter involved such mobility of people and money with words that formalism had become the linchpin of the *cambium* system since medieval times.[64] How did this imperative work in Amsterdam during the early modern period, given the massive circulation of commercial documents?

This question can be resolved by studying the clauses of the instruments, considering that commercial practice followed a very identifiable pattern. Indeed, the acts contain several texts of varying importance and significance on a legal perspective. Some of them were associated with the creation and the justification of the payment, credit or speculative mechanism. They were therefore considered mandatory by practitioners, scholars and sometimes public authorities. Others were more incidental, because their main purpose

63 For general remarks on the legal influence of a global environment, see for example Duve, "Global Legal History", 29.

64 This singular formalism is highlighted by Bottin, "Signature, marque, souscription", 350–353; Brunori, "La representation devient droit", 233–244; E. Kadens, "The Myth of the Customary Law Merchant", *Texas Law Review* 90 (2012), 1153–1206, here 1160 and 1174.

was simply to add instructions to assist the parties on their obligations. They were in consequence often seen as secondary or optional.[65]

This organization embodied the legal regime of the exchange system. Each term was the expression of an economic need and could evolve according to the situation. It was of great importance because it reflected the nature of the bill of exchange. The act was both the physical medium of a claim and the claim itself, that is, the sole and sufficient title to enforce and prove the rights of the holder.[66]

The general drafting process and the significance of the main clauses are therefore conducive to understanding the adaptation of the regulation of bills to the global economic environment of Amsterdam.

3.1 The General Drafting Process

The first observation that emerges from the 193 bills is the presence of a homogenous writing process.[67] On the main body (recto), corresponding to the relation between the drawing and payment places, 169 acts were drawn up in French, 24 in Italian and only two in English. As a result, the range of languages was singularly limited, despite the diversity of economic channels.[68]

The rise of French as an international language of trade since the end of the sixteenth century, to the detriment of Italian, may explain this situation.[69] French became more precisely the language of business education in Amster-

65 Le Breton-Blon, "La pratique européenne du change", 83–112; O. Descamps and R. Szramkiewicz, *Histoire du droit des affaires*, Paris, 2019, 111–114 and 227–233.

66 On the legal nature of the bill, see De Roover, *L'évolution de la lettre de change*, 29–43. For a more recent and specific study, see G. Rossi, "La ricezione della lettera di cambio nella *common law* tra Cinque e Seicento", *Annali del seminario giuridico* 65 (2022), 208–222.

67 The two groups of bills will be studied together here for a more synthetic view.

68 This common language dynamic was not observable in every economic channel in Europe during the early modern period, see for example M. Hope, "Commercial Networks, Maritime Law, and Translation in a Spanish Insurance Claim on Trial in France, 1783–1791" in Ph. Hellwege and G. Rossi (eds.), *Maritime Risk Management*, Berlin, 2020, 210–247, here 238–239.

69 This question raises many more issues, which we cannot develop here, about the influence of colonial trade, public governance, networking, cultural identities, the use of commissioners or familial and religious connections. For example, see Jeannin, *Marchands d'Europe*, 324.

dam,[70] especially through printed handbooks.[71] This dominant language appears of course for bills drawn or paid with the kingdom of France,[72] but also with Danzig, Frankfurt, London, Cádiz, Königsberg or Madrid, even without traders identifiable as French.[73]

Italian was used, on the contrary, in a narrower perspective for bills drawn from Genoa and Rome to Amsterdam. This situation is more the expression of smaller networks between agents who could make use of a less widespread language.[74] The titles implied indeed a very strict pattern with the recurring – nearly exclusive – presence of Gerolamo Belloni (payee), Giacomo and Antonio Meyraldi (payee), Antonio Cambiaso (drawer) and Salomon di Moseh Franco (drawee) for Genoa; and Giuseppe Cica (drawer) as well as Abraham Vernazobre (drawee) for Rome.[75]

The indorsements present a similar dynamic. French was the dominant language, with the exception of seventeen bills drawn from Lyon to Amsterdam.[76] These were mostly written in French, but some of them contain numerous Italian *endos*. This unevenness corresponds to the influence of the great international exchange fairs of Lyon, which had been dominated, since the sixteenth century, by Italian merchant-bankers.[77]

This general writing process was therefore conducive to the use of standardized legal terms. Seven clauses, out of a total of seventeen formulas appearing on the front of the bills studied, were used systematically with a high degree of homogeneity. Some of these terms give only general information that could not be customized: the parties, the localities, the date of issuance and the price.

Others, on the contrary, are more interesting because they could vary in expressing the mechanism of payment, credit or speculation according to economic circumstances or personal preferences: the maturity date, the value

70 W. Frijhoff, "La formation des négociants de la République hollandaise" in F. Angiolino and D. Roche (eds.), *Cultures et formations négociantes dans l'Europe moderne*, Paris, 1995, 185–186; Lesger, *The Rise of the Amsterdam Market*, 231–235.

71 The best example is the French translation of Johannes Phoonsen's famous *Wisselstyl tot Amsterdam*: J. Phoonsen, *Les lois et les coutumes du change*, Amsterdam, 1715.

72 Archives départementales de la Gironde 7 B: 1131, 1188, 1345, 1346, 1622, 2147, 2148, 2165; 37 J 37.

73 Municipal Archives Amsterdam, Notaries (inv. 5075), 11243.

74 On this question, see the recent study by M. Draper, *Italian merchants in Amsterdam: ca 1650–1700*, PhD dissertation European University Institute, 2021.

75 Municipal Archives Amsterdam, Notaries (inv. 5075), 11243.

76 Ibid.

77 For a general overview on this subject, see A. Orlandi, *Le Grand Parti. Fiorentini a Lione e il debito pubblico francese nel XVI secolo*, Florence, 2002.

provided to the drawer and the number of copies. In that second category, the maturity (payment term or deadline) and the value (otherwise called the cause) clearly indicates the influence of a global environment to reduce legal diversity in Amsterdam.

3.2 Determining the Payment Period

The 193 bills studied present a limited diversity of five dates of payment with one of them totalling around 93 percent of the operations: usance or *usanza* (160); X *jour(s)* or *semaine(s) de date* (21); X *de* Y *prochain* (5); *à vue* (4); X *jours de vue* (3).[78]

The dominant occurrence of the practice *usance* reflects a medieval tradition forged by transnational practices. This formula was indeed used to indicate the existence of a local custom, at the place of payment, to determine the due date of the bill.[79] That duration could vary – for example, from thirty days in Paris to ninety days in London – without the possibility of changing the usance dedicated to one location.[80]

The usance represented in consequence a standard to avoid the multiplication of other terms that may or may not been known or utilized by all participants of an exchange operation. It was an important tool for creating a homogenous legal framework in long-distance trade and, by extension, in a global economic environment. It represented a homogenous modality of expressing the due date of a bill across Europe, while remaining adaptable to the specificities of the payment locations.[81]

This mechanism explains why usance became very popular from the sixteenth century onwards with the development of international money markets or foreign exchange fairs. It turned out to be one of the most widespread trading customs and was gradually used to facilitate the fixation of quotation

78 The formulas can be translated as follows: usance (160); payment by a certain number of days or weeks of the present month (21); payment on a given day of a specific month (5); payment on sight (4); payment after a few days on sight (3).

79 The term *usance* literally means custom. It is derived from the Italian *uzansa* and the French *usage*.

80 Descamps and Szramkiewicz, *Histoire du droit des affaires*, 224; Kadens, "The Myth of the Customary Law Merchant", 1178; S. Moshenskyi, *History of the weksel*, Bloomington, 2008, 196.

81 On this question, see E. Kadens, "Order within Law, Variety within Custom: The Character of the Medieval Merchant Law", *Chicago Journal of International Law* 5/1 (2004), 39–65, here 62–63.

prices, the calculation of profit on monetary values, and the circulation of claims through a clearing process.[82]

Amsterdam undoubtedly benefited from these advantages because of its position as an international exchange centre. The domination of one specific method of expressing the payment date was more appropriate for reciprocal, reticular and multilateral operations, especially to avoid the confrontation of customs, habits or written rules from various origins.

The 160 bills at usance covered in this way the most important variety of markets linked to the Amstel city. It is a recurring and sometimes exclusive feature with the kingdom of France (Bordeaux, Paris and Lyon), the Iberian Peninsula (Lisbon and Madrid), as well as Italian (Rome, Venice and Genoa) and German (Hamburg) localities, and Great Britain (London).[83]

Variations in the estimated duration of the deadline could nevertheless give rise to disputes.[84] However, merchants' handbooks multiplied during the early modern period and distributed lists of usances to instruct traders. This literary production was particularly active in Amsterdam as shown by Johannes Phoonsen's *Wisselstyl tot Amsterdam* first published in 1676. This work shows how relevant usance was in embracing a global economic environment in the Dutch city. The manual recorded 23 different duration for exchange operations between Amsterdam and other European places. This situation covers more than 28 locations regularly mentioned in our bills.[85]

It is however difficult to know whether merchants favoured this medieval custom for their own interests, or whether they were compelled by default because it was the most common way to act in international markets.[86] The activity of Gabriel Da Silva and Pierre Dutilh (Bordeaux-Amsterdam) testifies on a few occasions to the unsuitable nature of the usance,[87] because the diver-

82 Bolton and Guidi Bruscoli, "'Your Flexible Friend': The Bill of Exchange", 886.

83 This estimation includes bills drawn or indorsed from and to Amsterdam. See Archives départementales de la Gironde 7 B: 1131, 1188, 1345, 1346, 1622, 2147, 2148, 2165; 37 J 37; Municipal Archives Amsterdam, Notaries (inv. 5075), 11243.

84 Kadens, "The Myth of the Customary Law Merchant", 1178.

85 J. Phoonsen, *Wisselstyl tot Amsterdam*, Amsterdam, 1976, 120–122. See also the French and updated version, Phoonsen, *Les lois et les coutumes du change*, 57–58.

86 This question is very hard to resolve outside of a dedicated study. It depends on many factors, such as the knowledge of traders and the presence of commissioners or correspondents who were well informed about local practices.

87 For example, a letter dated 3 Jan. 1735 from Dutilh to Da Silva expresses the impossibility of finding a buyer for bills payable at four and a half usances, because the market was too unstable for such a long maturity; see Archives départementales de la Gironde, 7 B: 2023.

sification of the term for payment debts was an important key in the credit mechanism.[88]

It is also difficult to determine the legal contribution of the Dutch city in this context. The bills show no preference for the use of the custom according to the place of drawing, payment or indorsement, reflecting the European origin of a reciprocally accepted practice.[89]

Furthermore, while the local customs of Amsterdam mentioned the usance and its duration, no specific written rules enacted by the aldermen have been found on the subject.[90] This omission was remarkable given that many written regulations in Europe – such as the French ordinance of 1673 or the Augsburg *Wechselordnung* – regulated the practice in order to limit errors made by foreign traders unfamiliar with local rules.

This silence is probably related to how commercial law was made in Amsterdam. The creation of ordinances by the aldermen was foremost directed by the interactions with business communities, by *turbe* inquests, for example, or petitions to solve a dispute.[91] One can imagine that the usance was sufficiently well known and integrated into daily practice to avoid any intervention of the legislator.

However, the situation illustrates the influence of transnational practices in a global economic environment. Amsterdam shows its specificity on this issue compared to smaller markets dictated by specific needs and narrower networks. The use of various payment dates was indeed more frequent in the last case, which significantly reduced the importance of the usance.[92]

The Dutch city appears in consequence as a favourable ecosystem of trade for the diffusion of homogenous customs forged by transnational practices. The reciprocal, reticular and multilateral circulation of bills – in an inter-

88 J. Villain, "Terms of payment in retaining: a tool for fostering customer loyalty or a form of managerial constraint? A few observations based on accounting from Lorraine in the eighteenth century" in P. Gervais, Y. Lemarchand and D. Margairaz (eds.), *Merchants and Profit in the Age of Commerce, 1680–1830*, London, 2014, 5373.

89 For bills drawn from Amsterdam, the usance appears 90 times versus one other mention. For bills drawn on Amsterdam, the usance appears 131 times versus twenty-four other clauses. For bills circulating in Amsterdam by indorsements, the usance appears fifteen times versus two formulas.

90 See the second part of Phoonsen, *Wisselstyl tot Amsterdam*, especially 1–23, 45–57, and 173–192. Also Phoonsen, *Les lois et les coutumes du change*, 177–183, 199–203, and 218–229.

91 De ruysscher, "Antwerp commercial legislation", 471.

92 The example of Bordeaux, including bills in international markets or for smaller inland connections, is quite relevant in this regard, see V. Le Breton-Blon, *La lettre de change pendant la seconde modernité (1673–1789). Pratique bordelaise, règlementations, discours*, PhD dissertation Université de Bordeaux, 2021, 105–143.

national exchange centre characterized by cosmopolitan merchant communities – was more legally suitable for the use of one homogenous date of payment.

3.3 Determining the Form of Remittances

The maturity of bills of exchange is not the only remarkable legal clause regarding the influence of Amsterdam as a global environment of trade. The fact that all 193 bills contain the indication of the value given to the drawer – meaning the cause for the operation – is also of major importance. This aspect was indeed a medieval condition of validity linked to the primary function of the *cambium* system. It was used to express the immaterial transfer of money from one place to another with a monetary conversion.[93]

More precisely, the value clause was a proof of the money provided in exchange for the delivery of the equivalent amount in a different location. It was an important requirement for merchants to avoid the prohibition of usury by justifying the profit made by manipulating currencies.[94] This situation was furthermore related to the medieval conception of the bill, which was conceived as an enforceable instrument of a contract between a person (the remitter) giving a value to another (the drawer) who was committed to provide the same capital, depending on exchange rates, through a third person.[95]

However, since the end of the fifteenth century, the evolution of the bill of exchange towards a more diversified form of cashless payment and credit had gradually moved away from this contractual origin in business practice.[96] The development of the indorsement since the sixteenth century has extended this development by providing the character of auxiliary paper money with a more abstract legal nature,[97] as "commercial paper was juristically deemed to be the embodiment of a claim rather than the reflection of a contract".[98]

---

93 Denzel, *Handbook of World Exchange Rates*, 19–30; J. Steven Rogers, *The Early History of the Law of Bills and Notes*, Cambridge, 1995, 32–43.

94 Munro, "The Medieval Origins of the Financial Revolution", 502–562; R. De Roover, "The Scholastics, Usury and Foreign Exchange", *Business History Review* 41 (1967), 257–271.

95 B. Geva, *The Payment Order of Antiquity and the Middle Ages: A Legal History*, Oxford, 2011, 392–393; De Roover, *L'évolution de la lettre de change*, 92–94.

96 See for example Bolton and Guidi Bruscoli, "'Your flexible friend': the bill of exchange", 873–891.

97 On the most synthetic and recent studies on this question, see J. Puttevils, "Tweaking financial instruments: bills obligatory in sixteenth-century Antwerp", *Financial History Review* 22/3 (2015), 337–361; De ruysscher, "Innovating Financial Law", 505–518.

98 De ruysscher, "Innovating Financial Law", 507.

This practice has not been received simultaneously and uniformly across Europe, especially in written laws. For example, the French ordinance of 1673[99] and the decree of the Genoa Council of 1636[100] retained a contractual approach by requiring the value to be a formal and substantive condition of validity. In contrast, the *Leipziger Wechselordnung* of 1682 allowed merchants to choose between using or avoiding the clause, which was more open to an abstract conception by removing the written requirement.[101]

Amsterdam was in a special position in that regard. The centrality of its financial market and international merchant entrepot exerted a major attraction for bills from various origins, as mentioned above. The reciprocal, reticular, and multilateral exchange operations encouraged more precisely the convergence of diverse legal frameworks in the Dutch city. This situation was therefore conducive to an appropriate regulation for avoiding conflicts related to the European disparity on the value clause.

However, the Amsterdam legislation made no mention of the value cause, despite its recurrent intervention on conflictual rules in the *cambium* system, such as the acceptance mechanism to enshrine the drawee's commitment.[102] More precisely, the ordinances of the aldermen did not regulate at all the formalism of bills. Instead, they focused on dispute resolution – in particular the right to payment – and on concrete or new topics rather than old medieval customs.[103]

This dynamic, either intentional or not, regarding the tendency of the city council to seek commercial advice from locals and foreigners alike,[104] offered great flexibility in using a specific model adapted to various economic and legal imperatives. Indeed, the fact that Amsterdam laws did not place restrictions on the value clause was not negative. On the contrary, it had a positive influence on the systematic inclusion of the medieval value clause, which was still required in some places. It gave merchants freedom to draw, pay or indorse bills without having to deal with opposite written norms. It was in consequence an important factor in securing international transactions. This phenomenon is another illustration of the centrality or globality of the Dutch

99 See the text in Isambert, *Recueil général des anciennes lois* vol. 19, Paris, 1829, 97–102.

100 Phoonsen, *Wisselstyl tot Amsterdam*, 102–103.

101 L. Dabin, *Fondements du droit cambiaire allemand*, Liège, 1959, 27–29.

102 De ruysscher, "Antwerp commercial legislation", 472.

103 See the second part of Phoonsen, *Wisselstyl tot Amsterdam*, 110. On this normative dynamic, which was not unique to Amsterdam, see Kadens, "The Myth of the Customary Law Merchant", 1198.

104 Lesger, *The Rise of the Amsterdam Market*, 163.

city, favouring homogeneity over particularities for the legal regime of bills of exchange.

To round out this observation, the 193 bills show that the value was also limited to seven distinct formulas with only two of them accounting for 92 percent of the acts:[105] *valeur reçue comptant, valeur reçue de* and *valuata dal medemo* (186);[106] *valeur reçue en compte* or *valuata dal medemo contini* (45); *valeur en nousmêmes* (7); *valeur en moimême* (4); *valeur pour solde* (1); *valeur en quittance* (1).[107]

Not only did merchants prefer an old clause, but they also used a classic method to express it. The *valeur reçue comptant*, along with its derived expressions, means that the value was received in cash. This was the main way during medieval times to stipulate the cause, as it reflected the primary legal relationships between the remitter and the drawer based on the function of transferring and converting coins from one place to another.[108]

The dominance of this stipulation in Amsterdam is quite interesting given the low number of the account value. Double-entry bookkeeping became one of the most effective methods of mobilizing claims, extinguishing debts, and granting credit during the early modern period, especially in international markets. Traders can be expected to have opted for accounting manipulations to avoid spending cash to draw bills.[109]

The influence of import and export can explain this situation. Amsterdam was a central, international market for purchasing and reselling goods from various customers. This situation normally involved a significant movement of cash, which could be invested in bills in the same place because of Amsterdam's complementary financial attractiveness.[110]

Despite this hypothesis, we must also bear in mind the idea of fictitious writings in order to comply with written laws, without any concrete reality. The freedom offered by Amsterdam laws on bills' formalism was particularly suitable for using the value received in cash as a standard legal clause. The main advantage was then to avoid dispute related to the diversity of economic

---

105 Archives départementales de la Gironde 7 B: 1131, 1188, 1345, 1346, 1622, 2147, 2148, 2165; 37 J 37; Municipal Archives Amsterdam, Notaries (inv. 5075), 11243.

106 These three expressions mean the reception of the value in cash either by expressing it clearly (*valeur reçue comptant*) or by signifying that the value was received by default, according to the price on the bill (*valeur reçue de* and *valuata dal medemo*)

107 One handwritten indorsement was impossible to read because of the poor preservation of the source.

108 De Roover, *L'évolution de la lettre de change*, 42–43.

109 Jeannin, *Marchands d'Europe*, 294.

110 Bartolomei, "Paiements commerciaux et profits bancaires", 112.

and legal frameworks connected to the Dutch city, as the formula had been the most traditional way to draw a bill since medieval times in Europe.

The influence of the French ordinance of 1673 illustrates perfectly that point.[111] The text maintained the formal requirement of the cause and even mentioned the classic "*valeur reçue comptant*". The importance of French cities on the Amsterdam foreign exchange market may have promoted the value received in cash, in accordance with the legislation of King Louis XIV. It can be seen as a safety measure to preserve all transactions, passing via the Dutch city, linked to French merchants and the kingdom of France.

This overall situation emphasizes the preference for a medieval custom as a standardized model well suited to a global environment. This hypothesis is reinforced if we consider – apart from the idea of complying with specific written rules – that the clause had the economic advantage of facilitating the traceability of transactions, through the main obligatory relationship (remitter-drawer), for bills that circulated in multiple networks.[112] In both cases, the value clause was like a default rule favoured by transnational practices and the silence of Amsterdam legislation.[113]

These remarks highlight once more the presence of a homogenous legal space for the *cambium* system. Diversity was not totally rejected, especially with secondary legal terms, but bills relied heavily on a consistent archetype that could fit in a wide diversity of frameworks. Amsterdam was then the nexus for a legal process of rationalization in long-distance trade.[114]

The same conclusion applies largely to the indorsements. This technique had been regularly used in Europe since the end of the sixteenth century, but it was not consecrated at the same pace in all written laws. Amsterdam – with Antwerp as a precursor, followed by Hamburg and the kingdom of France – gradually accepted the mechanism between 1630 and 1673, despite legal uncertainties. On the other hand, Frankfurt and cities of southern Italy prohibited the transfer of a bill with a simple *endos* during the first half of the seventeenth century.[115]

---

111 Moshenskyi, *History of the weksel*, 125.

112 Studies on early modern trading networks show that the logistical, financial and organizational complexity of long-distance trade increased the need for precise monitoring of business relationships. See for example Ribeiro, *Early Modern Trading Networks in Europe*.

113 For a complementary point of view on this idea, see D. De ruysscher, "From Usages of Merchants to Default Rules: Practices of Trade, *Ius Commune* and Urban Law in Early Modern Antwerp", *The Journal of Legal History* 33/1 (2012), 3–29.

114 This process involves the imitation of the most accepted practices across time and space through the idea of a legal and economic model, Jeannin, *Marchands d'Europe*, 335–336.

115 De ruysscher, "Innovating Financial Law", 508–515.

The 275 indorsements collected show that traders applied in this context a strong formalism with the inscription of the date, the value received by the indorsee and the place of the remittance, in addition to the name of the new creditor.[116] This approach was coherent with most doctrinal opinions, which analyzed the indorsement as a new exchange contract with formal requirements to mimic the first agreement between the remitter and the drawer.[117]

This practice was generally translated into written laws like the French ordinance of 1673.[118] Yet the rules imposed by the aldermen of Amsterdam neglected this aspect in order to focus on the right of the new beneficiary.[119] As a result, the formalism observed displays the same dynamic as that of the bills themselves, reflecting the use of an old model in Amsterdam to manage a European disparity of regulations.

4 Conclusion: Global Framework, Transnational Practices and Financial Law – A Dynamic of Slowness in Amsterdam?

In late seventeenth-century Amsterdam, foreign exchange transactions revive in a specific way the idea that merchants were latent brokers.[120] Traders had common tools at their disposal, sometimes consecrated in written laws, to merge deeds into a form that was as standardized as possible at the expense of particularities. This situation reflects the still active debate on the medieval *lex mercatoria*, that is, the existence of a homogenous or uniform merchants' law on a European scale.[121]

It is certain that links between merchants from different origins, especially through cosmopolitan networks, helped the application of similar rules.[122] Amsterdam was at the heart of a vast international market, which allowed a high degree of porosity between business communities. Networks played an

---

116 As follows: inscription of the date (196); inscription of the value received by the indorsee (267); inscription of the place of the remittance (196). One difference, regarding our previous observations, is the dominance of the value in account over the value in cash.

117 De ruysscher, "Innovating Financial Law", 508–517; De Roover, *L'évolution de la lettre de change*, 116.

118 Isambert, *Recueil général des anciennes lois*, 97–102.

119 See the second part of Phoonsen, *Wisselstyl tot Amsterdam*, 110.

120 S. Gialdroni, "*Propter Conversationem Diversarum Gentium*: Migrating Words and Merchants in Medieval Pisa" in Cordes, Dauchy, De ruysscher, Gialdroni and Pihlajamäki (eds.) *Migrating Words*, 28–53, here 47–49; Trivellato, *The Familiarity of Strangers*, 120.

121 Kadens, "The Myth of the Customary Law Merchant", 1153–1206; A. Cordes, "The Search for a Medieval *Lex mercatoria*" in V. Piergiovanni (ed.), *From lex mercatoria to commercial law*, Berlin, 2005, 53–68.

122 De ruysscher, "Innovating Financial Law", 512–513.

important role in that regard. They were sometimes directed by a few groups of specific traders, but they were always connected in an entanglement of various and extended economic relationships.

This phenomenon strongly influenced the legal regime of the bills used to trade in the Dutch city. The combination of several factors such as nonrestrictive regulations, the acceptance of foreigners and religious diversity, as well as the function of economic gateway with a central financial position and the role of an international warehouse of goods, surely channelled forces to make an old legal model for bills effective.

This conclusion suggests that the predominance of a medieval tradition of *cambium* law was part of the expansion of international trade during the early modern period. It shows the inclusion of a slow normative process[123] – sacrificing personal preferences, disparity in written rules, or new techniques – in a more unified system, at a time when the Venice of the North was also considered a place of major financial innovation.[124] This normative process recalls in that respect the origin stories for bills of exchange since medieval times:

> The regulation of bills of exchange impelled a great deal of similar legislation. The preambles of numerous seventeenth-century statutes across Europe relate that the rules were made because "the merchants of this town ... requested that we establish some ordinances concerning exchange, for the advancement of commerce and to prevent disorders, disputes, and costly suits, which arise too often".[125]

123 This observation offers a complementary view to the conclusion made by Puttevils, "Tweaking financial instruments", 339.

124 De ruysscher, "Innovating Financial Law", 508–510; Van Der Wee, "Les innovations de la technique financière", 867–869.

125 Kadens, "The Myth of the Customary Law Merchant", 1198.

CHAPTER 6

Innovating Market Exchange: The Amsterdam Bourse as a Blueprint for Modern Derivative Markets

Johannes W. Flume

> It is in this trading-house that virtually the whole world is negotiated. Besides German merchants from upper and lower Germany, one might find Poles, Hungarians, Walloons, French [...] and, indeed, occasionally even Indians, and all manner of other foreign peoples. Here, one speaks of the purchase and value of goods, of exchanging merchant goods, of loading and unloading of ships, and of changing and counter-changing. Indeed, here one experiences the status of all kingdoms and countries of the world and, no less, what is most remarkable in these [countries]. (Filips von Zesen, *Beschreibung der Stadt Amsterdam*, Amsterdam, 1664, 301)

1 Right in the Heart of the City[1]

The Amsterdam Exchange rises majestically above the Amstel, right in the heart of the city. From the south, through the *Beurssluis*, smaller vessels with lowered masts were able to pass beneath the building via the *Damsluis*, before reaching the *Damrak* and the Fish Market on Dam Square located to the north.[2] The *Oude Beurs* was not located directly on the Dam but was somewhat

1 Unless otherwise stated, all translations are by the author.

2 According to Johannes C. Breen, ships were not permitted to berth in front of the *Beurssluis* either during the day or at night without permission from the lock keeper (J.C. Breen, "Topografische geschiedenis van den Dam te Amsterdam", *Jaarboek van het Genootschap Amstelodamum* 7 (1909), 99–196, here 148). The passage is later said to have been barred by a beam, both during trading hours as well as at night, after an arson attack on the city centre was thwarted in 1622. The stonemason's apprentice Balthazar Paul, from a village near Namur, was bribed by the Spanish general Ambrogio Spinola (1569–1630) to carry out an arson attack on central buildings in the centre of Amsterdam – including the old city hall and the East India House – after the end of the twelve-year armistice (*Twaalfjarig Stand of Treves* [1609–1621]). Scheltema assumes that the attack must also have been aimed at the Exchange (P. Scheltema, *De Beurs van Amsterdam*, Amsterdam, 1846, 36). Tradition has it that the attempted attack was detected by an orphan boy, which resulted in the government

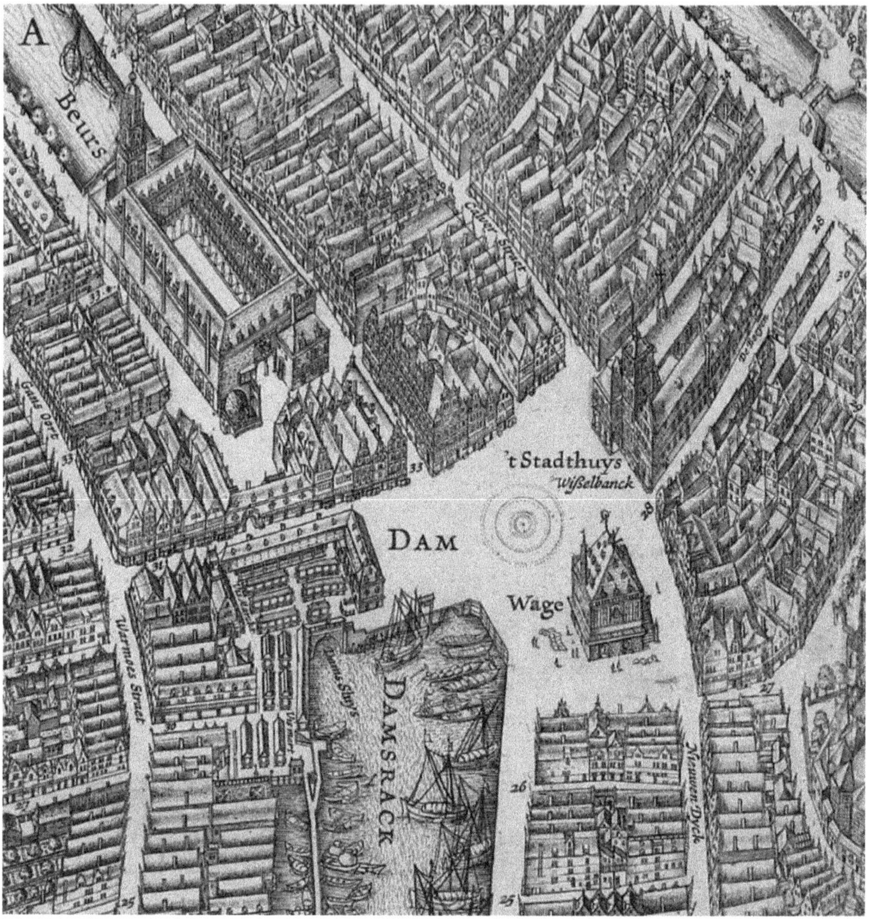

FIGURE 6.1 Map of Amsterdam (centre page) [detail] (1625), Balthasar Florisz van Berckenrode (1591/2–1645) – Rijksmuseum Amsterdam, RP-P-1892-A-17491D

concealed by a row of houses. One gained access, by way of the *Beurs Steeg* – later renamed *Beurs Straat* – to the two entrances located to the north and south, from which one then entered the Bourse's inner courtyard (Figure 6.1).

---

granting the children permission to play drums at the Beurs during the first week of the fair, which takes place in September. This practice of drumming at the Exchange (*Beurstrommelen*) has survived to this day. Balthazar was sentenced to death by strangulation on the scaffold in front of the city hall; two small bags of gunpowder were hung around his chest and ignited so as to obliterate his features (see Scheltema, *De Beurs van Amsterdam*, 35, note 2, quoting the text of the judgement). By 1675, the *Beurssluis* is said to have been permanently closed (Breen, "Topografische geschiedenis", 148)

With the exception of the bell tower – to the shape and sound of which Filips von Zesen (1619–1689)[3] gave particular attention – the Bourse viewed from the outside had a functional, indeed somewhat plain exterior, displaying little decorative embellishment.[4] That said, it doubtless left a splendid impression on the observer; thanks to its unique construction, it appeared as if enthroned above the water and adjacent buildings.

The building was opened for trade on 1 August 1611, following the laying of the foundation stone on 29 May 1608.[5] It was cast in the style of the Dutch

3 F. von Zesen, *Beschreibung der Stadt Amsterdam*, Amsterdam, 1664, 320 "Above the same alley / indeed, right above the lower gate towards the Rokin / there is a fine tower / with four clocks / and a bell / which tolls every full and half hour / as well as above / towards the top / fitted with three rows of musical bells / which rise into the air. These chimes / cast by the French bell ringer above / make such a lovely and graceful sound / that passers-by are moved to remain silent / and to listen to these charming artistic chimes / with almost enraptured senses"; according to Georg Galland, the tower is said to have been 43 meters high (*Geschichte der Holländischen Baukunst und Bildnerei im Zeitalter der Renaissance, der nationalen Blüte und des Klassicismus*, Frankfurt am Main, 1890, 184).

4 For a detailed architectural history of the Amsterdam Bourse, see Breen, "Topografische geschiedenis", 131–217; H. Engel and E. Gramsbergen, "Het eerste beursgebouw en de vorming van het centrum van Amsterdam", *Over Holland* 3 (2006), 57–88; E. Neurdenburg, *Hendrick De Keyser: Beeldhouwer en bouwmeester van Amsterdam*, Amsterdam, 1930, 68–70.

5 One riddle that has yet to be fully resolved is the date on which the exchange was officially first opened for trading. The initial details appear to be fairly clear; over the centuries, popular accounts of the city of Amsterdam make reference to an inscription on a black marble slab in gold lettering in the former inner courtyard. The presumably original marble slab is still on display today in the *Beurs van Berlage*, in what is known as the *Keurzaal* of the Corn exchange. The text states:

"*Door Godes zeegen is tot gerief der Coopluyden dese Borze gestigt an CIƆIƆVIII den XXIX Meye den Isten steen geleyt ende den ersten Aug CIƆIƆXIII de Iste vergaderinge geweest* [By God's grace, this exchange was erected for the benefit of the merchants, the first stone was laid on 29 May 1608, and the first meeting convened on 1 August 1613.]"

Doubts arise as to the dating when we consider what is probably the first text by Johannes Pontanus (1571–1639) *Rerum et urbis Amstelodamensium historia*, completed in August 1611. There Pontanus explains: "*Ad umbilicum et eum, quo nunc conspicitur modum deductum anno, dum haec commentaremur, CIƆIƆXI*" (See J. Pontanus, *Rerum et urbis Amstelodamensium historia*, Amsterdam, 1611, 229; see also the Dutch version by Petrus Montanus, *Historische beschrijvinghe der seer wijt beroemde coopstadt*, Amsterdam, 1614, 270 of the same year. The exchange was thus already completed in 1611, by the time Pontanus finalized in August of the same year the manuscript for the book. Why did the Bourse only go into operation in 1613? Johannes Christiaan Breen (1865–1927) was thus the first to argue that the dates of the inscription must be false (Breen, "Topografische geschiedenis", 211 and following). This is owing to the fact that the ordinances had already been issued to regulate public trading on the exchange. Furthermore, the facilities in the exchange were allegedly rented out as early as 1611. Lastly, he refers to an interesting archival find. According to the notes of Lambert Cornelisz Opsy (1583–1637), construction should have been completed in 1611 and the first exchange or meeting of merchants held there on 1 August 1611 (Breen,

Renaissance, as a so-called *Galerijbeurs* or *Hofhallebörsen*,[6] closely modelled on the Antwerp Bourse, built by Dominicus van Waghemakere (1460–1542) in 1531, and on London's Royal Exchange I of 1566.

Architecturally, its genealogy may be established simply by referencing architects and master builders. For the London Stock Exchange was built in direct imitation of the Antwerp Exchange by its builder Sir Thomas Gresham,[7] long-serving financial agent to the English Crown in Antwerp, and the Flemish architect Hans Hendrik van Paesschen (*c.* 1510–1582), who had been commissioned for the work in London. Furthermore, Hendrick de Keyser (1565–1621) and Cornelis Danckerts (1561–1634) had undertaken advance research visits to London in 1607 as part of their preparations for the projected Amsterdam Exchange.[8] The former – widely regarded in literature on the topic as the Bourse's chief planner and architect – is thus cited on the engraved plaque of 1609 (see Figure 6.2).[9]

"Topografische geschiedenis", 213). The riddle surrounding the precise date of the inauguration of the Bourse cannot be fully explained. However, it may also be contained in Pontanus's work. Boëtius Adams Bolswert (1585–1633) created the first engraving of the exchange that has come down to us in 1609 – i.e. after the start of construction on 29 May 1608 (Pontanus mentions 28 May) and before the completion of construction (see illustration 14). Curiously, Bolswert placed the tower on the wrong side. In the 1611 edition of Pontanus's book (after page 228), this "mistake" is corrected. However, in the inscription in the bottom left-hand margin, the year 1613 appears for the first time. Is the date 1613 the result of a lapse by the engraver, erroneously included in the aforementioned inscription? Or was the Exchange used only provisionally from 1611 to 1613 before its scheduled official inauguration in 1613? Be that as it may, besides Bolswert's illustrations, we also have several depictions of the Exchange by Claes Janszoon Visscher (1587–1652), produced in 1611 and 1612, showing lively activity in and around the Exchange. These may, of course, have also been fabricated, as was Bolswert's depiction. But more convincing is the assumption that trading on the exchange commenced in 1611.

6 See on the architectural history of the exchange, S.A. Meseure, *Die Architektur der Antwerpener Börse und der europäische Börsenbau im 19. Jahrhundert*, Munich, 1987; N. Pevsner, *A History of Building Types*, Princeton, 1976, 193–195; K.H. Schreyl, *Zur Geschichte der Baugattung Börse*, Berlin, 1963.

7 An impressive painting of Gresham by Anthonis Mor is on exhibition at the Rijksmuseum, http://hdl.handle.net/10934/RM0001.COLLECT.4638.

8 Neurdenburg, *Hendrick De Keyser*, 68.

9 The following inscription is cited illustration by Boëtius Adamsz. Bolswert (illustration 15), in the bottom-left corner:

"Benignis. Benevolis.Que. MMaecenatiBus.// NoBiLibus. ATQue. CLaris. AMSTERODAMENSIS POPVLI.// MAGISTRIS. COnSuliBus. PATRIBVS. // Hoc. DE. INGENIO. SVO. EXSCVLPTVM. INGENIVM // Vltro. ATQue. Libere .// Dedit. Dedi.Cavit.Que // HENRICus. DE. CAISAR // OPERVM. APVT. EOS. MOLITIONVMQue. ICONOGNOSTES .// CIVISQue. GRATVS. AC. PERPETVVS."

FIGURE 6.2 This remarkable curiosity is the oldest surviving depiction of the Amsterdam Bourse. It was produced by Boëtius Adamsz. Bolswert (1585–1633) shortly after construction began on 29 May 1608, but prior to completion in 1609; the tower is positioned on the wrong side. In the 1611 edition of Johannes Pontanus, *Rerum et urbis Amstelodamensium historia*, Amsterdam, 1611 (added after page 228), this 'error' is rectified.

1.1 The Three Levels

The aforementioned, column-supported edifice, constructed over the water, facilitated a uniquely functional design across three levels. Situated at the lowermost level and adjacent to the wharves there were ten retail stalls along

---

"In Honour of the Benevolent and Gracious Patrons,// The Noble and Illustrious Magistrates, Mayors and Elders of the People of Amsterdam,// Bestowed, dedicated and inspired of his own talent // His own accord and of his own free will // Hendrick de Keyser,// Draughtsman of these buildings and fortifications // and eternally indebted citizen."

(The transcription and translation into German was kindly undertaken by Gottfried Eugen Kreuzer (Salzburg)).

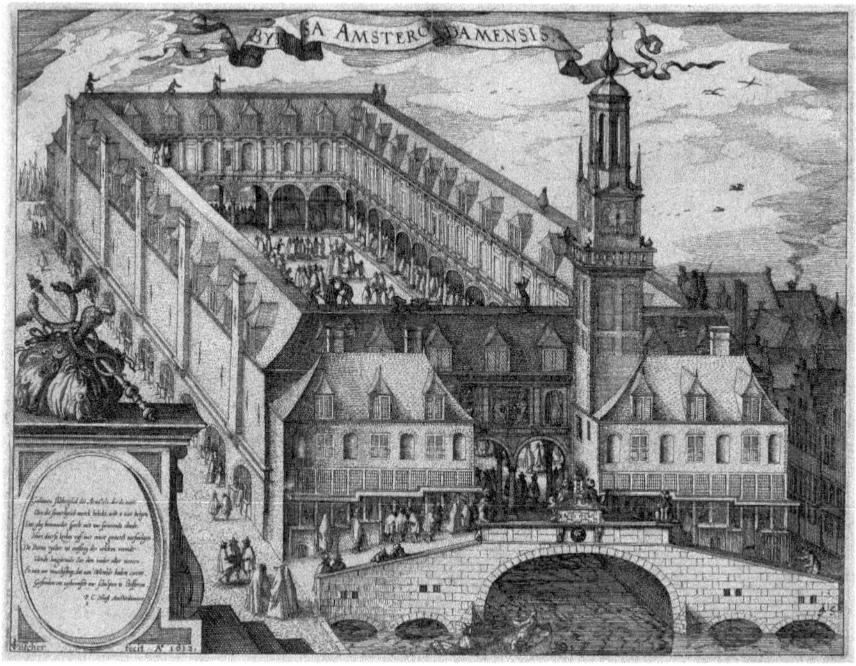

FIGURE 6.3 Byrsa Amsterodamensis (1612) by Claes Janszoon Visscher (1587–1652)

each of the lengthy eastern and western walls (Figure 6.2), together with a total of six additional stalls located on the gable ends of the building.[10]

Exposed to the open air, the Bourse's inner courtyard was located on the intermediate principal level; elevated several metres above the quays, its design took in considerably more decorative embellishments.[11] The building's rectangular atrium, unroofed and surrounded by an open arcade, rested on forty Doric columns. That section of the courtyard, exposed to the arcade, encompassed two elevated squares in the northern section, the vantage point of which afforded a superior overview of the activity below. The upper level, embellished with decorative, Ionic-inspired pilasters, alternated with blind recesses, which – in contrast to London's Royal Exchange – were free of sculptural adornments. The stonework was throughout rendered in blue Arduin, while the walls were finished in red brick. A flight of steps running adjacent to the bell tower led to the third level, housing some one-hundred commercial

10 Pontanus, *Amstelodamensium historia,* 229; O. Dapper, *Historische Beschryving der Stadt Amsterdam,* Amsterdam, 1663, 453, and Breen,"Topografische geschiedenis", 148.

11 See also Galland, *Geschichte der Holländischen Baukunst,* 187.

cassen (stalls), which some consider the prototype of the shopping 'arcade' or mall.[12]

1.2 Minor Expansions

As Henk Engel and Esther Gramsbergen[13] have shown, in terms of urban planning, the construction of the Amsterdam Bourse of 1611 marks a decisive step in the urbanization and transformation of Amsterdam's city centre at the onset of the seventeenth century. The period beginning some fifty years prior to the erection of the city hall on Dam Square witnessed the emergence of a central trading hub, which remained in operation for over two centuries between 1611 and 1838, before being demolished in 1838 due to deterioration. Objections to the modest size of the Bourse were voiced from the outset, however, and in 1668, three years after the Stadhuis was completed, plans were drawn up for its expansion.[14] The scale of the original building, dating from 1611, comprised a surface area of 200 by 124 feet (61 × 38 metres) and included a total of 42 columns.[15] The building's length was subsequently extended towards the south by 230 feet or 70 metres, whilst the arcade was extended by a total of 46 columns.[16] This expansion entailed the dismantling of the bell tower, since the upper part of the old tower – the spire – was secured to a plateau fastened directly atop the pediment of the new roof.[17] The newly erected southern end

---

12 On the *cassen*, see Cl. Lesger, *Shopping Spaces and the Urban Landscape in Early Modern Amsterdam, 1550–1850* Amsterdam, 2020. The first floor of the Antwerp Exchange was the site of the so-called *Schilderspand* from 1540, a collection of over one-hundred sales galleries where the first modern European art market was established (see F. Vermeylen, "Marketing Paintings in the Sixteenth-Century Antwerp: Demand for Art and the Role of the Panden" in P. Stabel e.a. (eds.), *International Trade in the Low Countries (14th-16th Centuries): Merchants, Organisations, Infrastructure*, Leuven, 2000, 193–213; L. Guicciardini, *Descrittione di tutti i Paesi Bassi*, Antwerp, 1567, 99, speaks of "*Panto delle dipinture*"). On the galleries of the Royal Exchange London, see K. Morrison, *English Shops and Shopping: An Architectural History*, New Haven, 2004, 32 and following. On the idea of the passage: J.F. Geist, *Passagen: Ein Bautyp des 19. Jahrhunderts*, Munich, 1996.

13 H. Engel and E. Gramsbergen, "Het eerste beursgebouw", *Over Holland* 3 (2006), 73 and following.

14 Scheltema, *De Beurs van Amsterdam*, 40.

15 Breen, "Topografische geschiedenis", 148; Pontanus, *Amstelodamensium historia*, 229 makes reference to 40 pillars.

16 Scheltema, *De Beurs van Amsterdam*, 41; Zesen, *Beschreibung der Stadt Amsterdam*, 300.

17 Galland, *Geschichte der Holländischen Baukunst*, 472 and following.

FIGURE 6.4 Frederick de Wit, De binnenplaats van de beurs te Amsterdam (c. 1690) (after the renovation work of 1668)

now featured the city's coat of arms and a statue of Mercury by Bartholomeus Eggers (1637–1692) (Figure 6.4).[18]

The sources from which Eggers drew inspiration for the sculpture remains a matter of conjecture. Though purely speculative, he may well have read Joost van den Vondel's (1587–1679) thought-provoking lines, penned in 1655 to mark the inauguration of the city hall.[19] Lines 435 and following of the 1,377-verse

18 On Eggers, see Galland, *Geschichte der Holländischen Baukunst*, 357 and following; an illustrative depiction of the sculpture also appears in Scheltema, *De Beurs van Amsterdam*, after page 42.

19 For more on this subject S. Bussels e.a., "'Far more to wonder, than to fathom completely': one hundred poems devoted to the town hall" in S. Bussels e.a. (eds.), *The Amsterdam Town Hall in Words and Images: Constructing Wonders*, London, 2022; S. Bussels, "The Wondrous Town Hall of Amsterdam: Laudatory Poems on the Impact of Art and Architecture" in G. Alexander e.a. (eds.), *The Places of Early Modern Criticism*, Oxford, 2021, 158 and following.

poem *Inwydinge van't Stadhuis t'Amsterdam* (Inauguration of the city hall in Amsterdam) also touch on the exchange and trading.[20]

> The Bourse, where the Amstel discharges from five stone arches, shoots its water arrows, which are fired with full force when the water recedes, and catches its breath in the IJ. The neighbourhood receives the sounds from either side. And all the foreigners, having come from all quarters and now assembled there at noon, infuse the whole place with life.
>
> This is where Mercury, feted and adulated, baton-sticked and wing-heeled is worshipped. Here the merchant's mind fumes and toils, choked full with freights, hulls, opportunities to meet a bill, coinage, and with the Bourse's clamour of profit and loss. All grab what they may, insuring his cash and his packages against shipwreck and damages; arranging goods, possessions and person on masts, and on wrecks. While fickle Fortuna, unblinking, casts into the melee all the riches of the world.[21]

In the immediate vicinity of the Dam is also the "*wandelstreeck*" along which the "*Amsterdamsche Heeren*" (Amsterdam gentlemen), "*Wethouderen en Raet*" (Mayor and Members of the Council), concerned about the government, engage in lofty discussion.[22] Meanwhile, merchants exchange intelligence while reports come in on various vessels:

> Here the merchant harkens to the rumours from the sea, draws forth documents, grasps the purport of letters dispatched from all quarters. One moment the market slumps, before recovering in the next. Here, one ship is stranded, while some distance away, another is docked following a battle with Turkey that torched the Corsair vessels, or ventured to far-off Tunis.[23]

20 A poem has also come down to us: "Aen de Beurs van Amsterdam", also by Vondel and published in 1643, with illustrations by Salomon Jacobsz Savery (1594–1683). However, the lines in the *Inwydinghe* provide a more instructive account of everyday trading life.

21 J. van den Vondel, "Inwydinge Van Het Stadthuis t'Amsterdam" in L. Simons e.a. (eds.), *De werken van Vondel, Deel 5, 1645–1656*, https://www.dbnl.org/tekst/vond001dewe05_01/vond001dewe05_01_0208.php, lines 437–453.

22 Vondel, "Inwydinge", line 489.

23 Vondel, "Inwydinge", lines 489–495.

1.3 Financial Innovation

So far, this discussion has turned solely on the central incorporation of the Bourse within the urban hub of Amsterdam and less on its prominence as an institution in the economic life of the Netherlands and Europe. That Amsterdam stands out as *the* central European market of the seventeenth century is well known and well documented. The meteoric rise of the city and the Netherlands as a whole was concomitant with the Dutch Revolt of 1568. The religious wars fought between the Catholic South and the Protestant North led to the exodus of Protestant merchants from Antwerp, and to their relocation north to Amsterdam, circumstances that set in motion the development which eventually saw the former's economic decline.[24] Favourably located as a shipping centre, Amsterdam firmly established itself as Europe's central commodities, financial and capital market.[25] It was here, at the Amsterdam Exchange, that the modern liquid commodity and stock market was first established and referred to as such,[26] and is, to be sure, considered the birthplace of European futures and options trading.[27] The prices of 350 goods were listed weekly, each

---

24 O.C. Gelderblom, *Cities of Commerce, The Institutional Foundations of International Trade in the Low Countries, 1250–1650*, Princeton, 2013, 32–41; Id., "From Antwerp to Amsterdam: The Contribution of Merchants from the Southern Netherlands to the Commercial Expansion of Amsterdam (c. 1540–1609)", *Review* (*Fernand Braudel Center*) 26/3 (2003), 247–282.

25 See V. Barbour, *Capitalism in Amsterdam in the Seventeenth Century*, Ann Arbor, 1950, 11 and following, and 18 and following; Ch. Wilson, *Anglo-Dutch Commerce & Finance in the Eighteenth Century*, Cambridge, 1941, 3 and following; J.I. Israel, *Dutch Primacy in World Trade, 1585–1740*, Oxford, 1989; M. North, *Das goldene Zeitalter: Kunst und Kommerz in der niederländischen Malerei des 17. Jahrhunderts*, Cologne, 2001, 19 and following.

26 Among the extensive literature on the subject, see Barbour, *Capitalism in Amsterdam*, 74 and following; S.G. Binnerts, "Amsterdamer Effektenbörse" in M. Palyi and P. Quittner (eds.), *Handwörterbuch des Bankwesens*, Berlin, 1933, 37–40; R. Ehrenberg, "Die Amsterdamer Aktienspekulation im 17. Jahrhundert", *Jahrbuch für Nationalökonomie und Statistik* 58 (1892), 809–826; J.I. Israel, "The Amsterdam Stock Exchange and the English Revolution of 1688", *Tijdschrift voor Geschiedenis* 103 (1990), 412–440; Lesger, *The Rise of the Amsterdam Market and Information Exchange*; L. Petram, *The World's First Stock Exchange*, New York, 2014; Wilson, *Anglo-Dutch Commerce*, 79 and following; L. Samuel, *Die Effektenspekulation im 17. und 18. Jahrhundert*, Berlin, 1924; M.F.J. Smith, *Tyd-affaires in Effecten aan de Amsterdamsche Beurs*, The Hague, 1919.

27 See Gelderblom and Jonker, "Amsterdam as the Cradle"; E.P. Stringham, "The extralegal development of securities trading in seventeenth-century Amsterdam", *The Quarterly Review of Economics and Finance* 43/2 (2003), 321–344; exceptionally informative on this subject is E.L. Jacobson, *Termijnhandel in Goederen*, Rotterdam, 1889 (a German translation was published by F. Stapff, *Terminhandel in Waaren*, Rotterdam, 1889).

of which was translated into Italian, French and English.[28] The *Vereenigde Oost-Indische Compagnie* (VOC), the *Geoctroyeerde Westindische Compagnie* (WIC), along with the tulip mania or bubble of the 1630s, are well known and much discussed.[29] Similarly, the first accounts of the functionality of exchange trading date from this period, such as Joseph de la Vega's famous *Confusion des confusions* (1688), which presents exchange trading in dialogue form, along with a remarkably detailed portrait of the merchant Jean-Pierre Ricard in *Le Negoce d'Amsterdam* (1722) and, finally, Isaac de Pinto's (1717–1787) *Traité de la Circulation et du Crédit* of 1771.

However, to assume that the character and function of the Amsterdam Exchange bears any resemblance to our present-day conception of it would be misleading: it was not a 'stock exchange' and was certainly not 'the world's first stock exchange'. Financial transactions on the Antwerp Exchange were already conducted as early as 1531, as well as on the London Exchange (1566), although to date sources on the subject remain few and far between.[30] At the time, specialization in securities and commodities exchange were unknown, having only later emerged over the course of the nineteenth century.[31] In short, the Amsterdam Bourse was a *Beurs*, namely, a general exchange through which commodity and financial securities were traded in the inner courtyard.

1.4 Market Design and the Revolutionizing of Contract Performance

That said, the Amsterdam exchange remains an important research locus for economic and legal history. A comparative glance at various other prominent trading places across the Mediterranean region, above all, the *fondachi* – not infrequently mistakenly regarded as precursors of exchanges – gives a clear

28 For a more detailed account, see Lesger, *The Rise of the Amsterdam Market*, Ch. 6 (= 214 and following.) (For price listings, see p. 232 and following); J.J. McCusker and C. Gravensteijn. *The Beginnings of Commercial and Financial Journalism: The Commodity Price Currents, Exchange Rate Currents, and Money Currents of Early Modern Europe*, Amsterdam, 1991, 43 and following.

29 On the VOC and WIC, see Israel, *Dutch Primacy*; on the tulip trade, R. Stammler, *Deutsches Rechtsleben im Alten Reich: Lehrreiche Rechtsfälle. I. Band*, Charlottenburg, 1928, Ch. *Die Harlemer Tulpenmanie (1634–1637)* (= p. 211 and following.); A. Goldgar, *Tulipmania: Money, Honor and Knowledge in the Dutch Golden Age*, Chicago, 2007.

30 But see J. Denucé, "De Beurs van Antwerpen", *Antwerpsche Archievenblad* 6 (1931), 81–145; De ruysscher, "Antwerp commercial law in the sixteenth century: a product of the Renaissance?; De ruysscher, "From Usages of Merchants to Default Rules".

31 J.W. Flume, "Constructing the Stock Exchange. On the Rise and Fall of an Iconic Place of Capitalism", *Rechtsgeschichte – Legal History* 29 (2021), 412–430.

illustration as to why the emergence of exchanges in Northern Europe during the sixteenth and seventeenth centuries brought about a new type of trading venue (see 2.). At the same time, contract law was revolutionized within the exchange through *termijnhandel* (futures trading). The future was unlocked by contract law. Now, not only were trading partners able to negotiate spot contracts (*marché au comptant, Baarkauf; Handgeschäft*) for the immediate trade of goods for money, but they were also able to conclude futures contracts (*Termin- und Zeitgeschäft, marché à terme, time contracts*).[32] Exchange relationships among sellers and buyers ceased to be static; the future could be priced and fluctuations in market prices hedged.

Futures – bilateral sales contracts for standardized goods for future delivery – were concluded by way of *makelaars* (brokers) commissioned by merchants in the courtyard. Here, one peculiar aspect stands out, which, to the 'normal' understanding of private law, is bound to seem downright outrageous: insofar as the process of concluding contracts is handled globally through the so-called *rescontre* system, the fate of all contracts within a certain trading period on the exchange are correlated. At the *rescontredag* (settling date or *Liquidationstag*), the *makelaars* would meet to clear all contracts. A merchant would be obliged to deliver or receive goods, or simply pay cash. Connecting all contracts in a market via the *rescontre* system, however, had a staggering effect: by agreeing to participate in the *rescontre*-clearing, the parties either accepted performing, or receiving performance, by any member of the futures market. Mutual claims were canceled out. If a merchant bought and sold commodities or shares during the same campaign, he would be able to neutralize specific performance by way of cash settlement. Today, this activity is called: closing out a position.

Existing (economic history) literature on the subject accords secondary, inessential importance to the *rescontre* mechanism.[33] Yet there is far more to it than meets the eye, for it constitutes the legal foundation of all derivatives

---

32 It was only over the course of the twentieth century that the term "futures" became established as a global *terminus technicus* of commodity and financial markets. In the nineteenth century, *Börsentermingeschäfte* (futures) were frequently termed "*Differenzgeschäfte*" in German-speaking countries (on this see J.W. Flume, *Marktaustausch: Grundlegung einer juristisch-ökonomischen Theorie des Austauschverkehrs*, Tübingen, 2019, 231–245). J. Aroni, *Futures*, New Orleans, 1882, is recognized as one of the first English-language works to employ the term 'futures'; cf. also H.C. Emery, *Speculation on the Stock and Produce Exchange of the United States*, New York, 1896, 32 and following.

33 See for instance Gelderblom and Jonker, "Amsterdam as the Cradle of Modern Futures", 189, 191; G. Poitras, "From Antwerp to Chicago: The History of Exchange Traded Derivative Security Contracts", *Revue d'Histoire des Sciences Humaines* 20/1 (2009), 11–50, here 27.

markets. The *rescontre* system, introduced to the Amsterdam Exchange during the seventeenth and eighteenth centuries, is the blueprint for the construction of any modern derivatives market. It also helps us get to the core of one of the greatest myths in economic legal history, namely, the gambling stigma: contrary to the classic notion, one can clearly show that futures contracts are not breeding grounds for illegitimate betting, but for innovating contract performances.

Finally, one caveat is pertinent. Exchange trading, and futures trading in particular, is often portrayed in terms of bans, restrictions and litigation. This approach is justified and provides some interesting insights, but it always runs the risk of presenting a distorted picture of how derivative trading works, since it only describes the 'malignant' cases. The focus of the present analysis, however, is to show how exchange trading was legally constructed and operated.

2 Visiting Two (Historical) Marketplaces

We start by visiting two very different seventeenth-century marketplaces, the *Fondaco dei Tedeschi* at Venice and the Amsterdam Bourses, as well as their predecessors at the Antwerp and London Exchanges. As we shall see, both types of venue represent fundamentally different concepts in the organization of trade.

2.1 The *Fondaco Dei Tedeschi* in Venice

Our first site, the *Fondaco dei Tedeschi* in Venice located next to the Rialto Bridge, may still be admired today. Figure 6.5 shows an engraving dating from 1616. Produced by Augsburg draughtsman and engraver *Raphael Custodis*, it gives a fair idea of the stately dimensions of the building, which underwent complete reconstruction by the Republic of Venice following a fire in 1505. The *fondaco* was doubtless an overwhelmingly splendid edifice: The exterior walls were embellished with frescoes by Giorgione and Titian, while the first floor comprised a winter hall furnished with a magnificent fireplace and a summer hall, which housed, among other things, various works by Titian, Palma Veccio, Paolo Veronese, and others.[34]

34 For a comprehensive account, see Ph. Braunstein, *Les Allemands á Venise (1380–1520)*, Rome, 2016; W. Heyd, "Das Haus der deutschen Kaufleute in Venedig", *Historische Zeitschrift* 32 (1874), 193–220; S.P. Oakes, "'Hieronymo Thodesco' and the Fondaco dei Tedeschi: A Reappraisal of the Documents and Sources Relating to a German Architect in Early Sixteenth-Century Venice", *Zeitschrift für Kunstgeschichte* 72/4 (2009), 479–496;

FIGURE 6.5 Raphael Custos, *Domvs Germanorvm emporica*, 1616 – Germanisches Nationalmuseum Nuremberg, *Graphische Sammlung*, HB 2300, 1228 (published in: *German History Intersections*, https://germanhistory-intersections.org/en/migration/ghis:image-151 (last consulted 13 June 2025)).

As far as the operation of this unique building complex is concerned, it is worth starting with the etymology of the word *fondaco*, as it shows us that what we are dealing with here is an institution of commercial law deeply rooted in the historical and cultural roots of the Mediterranean region. The common Latin word *fondaco* derives from the Arabic word فندق (*funduq* [lodging]), itself an adaption of the Greek πανδοχεῖον (pandocheion [hostel]).[35] As is well known,

J. Schulz, "Titian at the Fondaco dei Tedeschi", *The Burlington Magazine* 143/ 1182 (2001), 567–569; H. Simonsfeld, *Der Fondaco dei Tedeschi in Venedig und die deutsch-venetianischen Handelsbeziehungen: Eine historische Skizze*, Stuttgart, 1887; extensively E. Concina, *Fondaci: Architettura, arte e mercatura tra Levante, Venezia e Alemagna*, Venezia, 1997.

35 O.R. Constable, "Reconsidering the Origin of the Funduq", *Studia Islamica* 92 (2001), 195–196; L. Goldschmidt, "Ursprünge des Mäklerrechts. Insbesondere: Senal", *Zeitschrift für das Gesamte Handels- und Wirtschaftsrecht* 28 (1882), 115–130, at 124; W. Heyd,

'Tedeschi' denotes the 'Germans'; while merchants from across Central Europe were also granted admission, the Upper German merchants from Regensburg, Nuremberg and Augsburg were said to have been predominant in most of what took place there.[36] The *Fondaco dei Tedeschi* thus served as living quarters or hostel for the Germans, or, as it was often referred to in the nineteenth century, the "German purchasing and storage house".[37]

As institutions of medieval commercial law located throughout Italy, the *fondachi* were buildings designed to channel and control trade coming in from the East.[38] The basic design consisted for the most part of a rectangular compound of buildings set around an inner courtyard, complete with adjoining storage facilities, and accessed via a large gate. In Venice, merchandise was transported by way of barge across the Rio Grande to the *fondaco* landing station on the canal, where it was weighed and registered before being stored in the inner courtyard.[39] The inner courtyard housed twenty-five vaulted storage facilities (*volte*), miscellaneous function rooms, some eighty guest rooms, as well as a wine tavern and chapel.[40] There were also twenty-two shops outside the building that were rented out to Venetians by the government of the city-state.[41] Unlike the *fondachi* of the Arab region,[42] – or, indeed, the London seat of the Hanseatic League in the steelyard[43] – the Germans' trading and warehousing was not self-administered by foreign merchants, but instead supervised by the Venetian *visdomini*, who also monitored the levying of cus-

Geschichte des Levantehandels im Mittelalter, Zweiter Band, Stuttgart, 1879, 430, note 6; W. Heyd, "Ueber Funda und Fondaco. Zu Diez' etymol. Wörterbuch der roman. Sprachen. 4. Aufl. 1878", *Sitzungsberichte der philosophisch-philologischen und historischen Classe der k. b. Akademie der Wissenschaften zu München* (1880), 617–627; U. Israel,"Fondaco" in A. Cordes e.a. (eds.), *Handwörterbuch zur deutschen Rechtsgeschichte, Band 1*, Berlin, 2008, col. 1614; H. Kellenbenz, "Fondaco" in R. Autty (ed.), *Lexikon des Mittelalters, Teilband 4*, Munich, 1989, col. 617.

36 Kellenbenz, "Fondaco", col. 617; Simonsfeld, *Der Fondaco dei Tedeschi*, 41, 167.

37 Thus, e.g., L. Goldschmidt, *Vermischte Schriften, Band 2*, H.V. Simon (ed.), Berlin, 1901, Ch. Handelsrecht (geschichtliche Entwicklung) (1892) 43 ("Kauf- und Lagerhaus der Deutschen").

38 See D. Calabi, *The Market and the City, Square, Street and Architecture in Early Modern Europe*, Aldershot, 2004, 187 and following; O.R. Constable, *Housing the Stranger in the Mediterranean World: Lodging, Trade, and Travel in Late Antiquity and the Middle Ages*, Cambridge, 2004; for a concise and informative account: H. Kellenbenz, "Fondaco", col. 617 and U. Israel, "Fondaco", col. 1614.

39 Constable, *Housing the Stranger*, 323.

40 See, in reference to the seventeenth century, Simonsfeld, *Der Fondaco dei Tedeschi*, 111 f.

41 Simonsfeld, *Der Fondaco dei Tedeschi*, 111.

42 See Constable, *Housing the Stranger*, 323.

43 On this, A. d'Haenens, *Die Welt der Hanse*, Antwerp, 1984, Ch. Der Stalhof oder Steelyard in London, 189 and following.

toms duties.[44] The merchants, moreover, were authorized to enter into contracts with Venetian citizens for those commodities[45] stored in the *fondaco* only through the agency of brokers, the so-called *sensali* (or *Unterkäufel*), who, in some cases, also doubled as interpreters.[46] As Levin Goldschmidt trenchantly pointed out in his *Universalgeschichte des Handelsrechts,* "[t]he state-appointed broker [...] tended to be a mandatory intermediary in foreign trade."[47] It is worth noting that during this period Venetians were forbidden to trade with German merchants outside the city and were barred from travelling north to trade in German cities.[48]

2.2 The *Beursen* at Antwerp (1531), London (1566) and Amsterdam (1611)

Whereas German merchants came and went at the *fondaco*, where merchandise was loaded and unloaded, in the North – as the result of the economic history of the 'cities of commerce' (Bruges, Antwerp and Amsterdam)[49] – the Low Countries witnessed the emergence of a new, centralized type of trading venue, namely, the exchange.[50] We first learn of what an exchange building is – namely, a new, independent type of building and trading venue – in the first half of the sixteenth century. Thus, inaugurated in 1531 under the aegis of Charles V, the *Nieuwe Beurs Antwerpen* (New Antwerp Exchange) (Figure 6.6.) was to set the standard for subsequent centuries.

The name adopted for this new trading place was *boers, beurs, byrse*, as was familiar from Bruges. Contrary to a common misunderstanding, it did not refer to an exchange building, but simply to the name of a particular exchange

44 Constable, *Housing the Stranger,* 322 and following; Heyd, "Das Haus der deutschen Kaufleute in Venedig", 210 and following.

45 For traded goods, see Constable, *Housing the Stranger,* 319 and following; Simonsfeld, *Der Fondaco dei Tedeschi,* 103 and following.

46 On the historical origins of brokerage law (*Maklerrecht*), see Goldschmidt, "Ursprünge des Mäklerrechts"; Simonsfeld, *Der Fondaco dei Tedeschi,* 23 and following.

47 L. Goldschmidt, *Handbuch des Handelsrechts, Erster Band, Geschichtlich-literarische Einleitung und die Grundlehren, Erste Abteilung, Universalgeschichte des Handelsrechts,* 3rd ed., Stuttgart, 1891, 22 (with detailed sources in footnote 18).

48 See Constable, *Housing the Stranger,* 319.

49 Thus, the title of the seminal work by Oscar Gelderblom on the economic history of international trade in the Low Countries from the thirteenth to the seventeenth centuries (*Cities of Commerce: The Institutional Foundations of International Trade in the Low Countries, 1250–1650*, Princeton, 2013).

50 For a detailed account see Flume, Constructing the Stock Exchange", 412 and following.; Id., *Marktaustausch,* 21 and following.

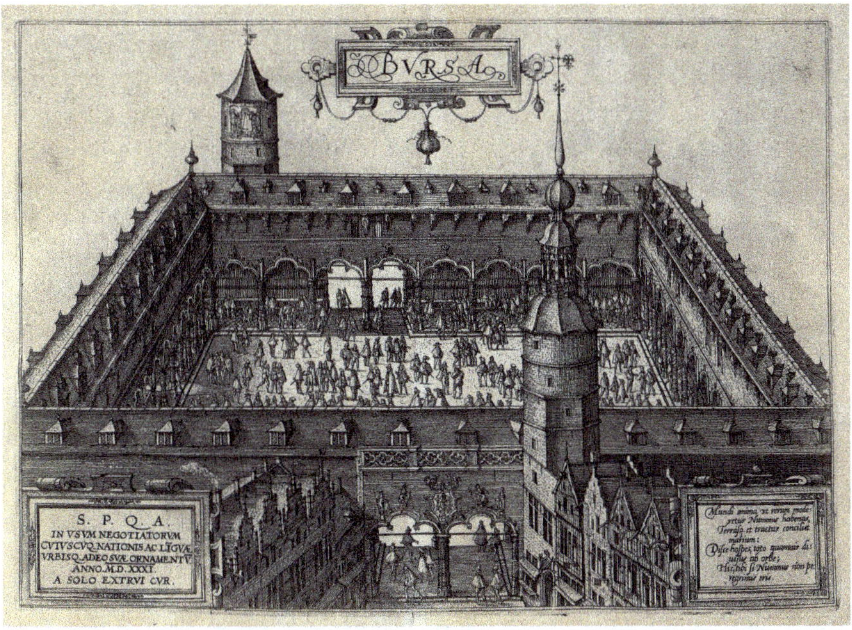

FIGURE 6.6 Lodovico Guicciardini, *Descrittione di tutti i Paesi Bassi*, Antwerp, 1567, 100 and following

square. It was located, namely, where the "van der Beurze" family operated three hostels from the thirteenth through to the fifteenth centuries, which can still be seen today.[51] Together with London's Royal Exchange I (1566), and the Amsterdam Exchange of 1611, this new, revolutionary exchange in Antwerp, is above all noticeable – especially when contrasted with the *Fondaco* – by two striking, highly significant and, at first glance, easily overlooked details that best characterize the building's function.

The first is that the squares are 'empty', that is, absent of goods. In contrast to the *fondachi* or the later Gothic trading halls of Flanders, the Bourse was an enclosed space serving not the on-site purchase or inspection of goods, but the exchange of information and the initiation and conclusion of contracts. The unique structure of this trading area was vividly detailed in Jacques Accarias de Sérionne's *La Richesse de la Hollande* (1778):

> Trade requires activity, and no institution was more effective in the provision of such than a public forum at which merchants and brokers meet daily at a prearranged hour. It is here that the most numerous of contracts are negotiated

51 Flume, "Constructing the Stock Exchange", 413 and following.

> and concluded each day, and where the greatest commercial operations are carried out in the blink of an eye; without meetings, such transactions would proceed only very slowly. Here, at an hour heralded by the peal of bells, the *macklers* receive engagements from merchants, whose word, once given to these *macklers* is irrevocably binding, for whomsoever it may be. The exchanges of Amsterdam and Rotterdam are two large marketplaces to which no merchandise is conveyed, but only where bids and requests for the merchandise in the merchants' warehouses are tendered, and at which only credit and commercial acumen have a place. And it is here, too, where all merchants gather especially useful knowledge for directing the operations of their *comptoir*, for expanding their reputation, for fortifying their credit, for shaping, revising and further expanding their speculations. These are things that draw the merchants to the exchange each day, even if they have no other particular business to transact there. Here is where the rates for bills of exchange for all European countries are adjusted daily, depending on whether a greater or lesser number of bills are requested for each place: this is a commercial operation barely feasible elsewhere, or not without greatest inconvenience, something which, if attempted, would only result in a great deal of delay in trade itself.[52]

The second essential piece of information in the engraved depictions of the exchanges may be gleaned by looking at the wide variety of garments and headgear – hats, turbans and the like – worn by the merchants gathered in the courtyard (Figure 6.7).

The Bourse was a place instituted for general trading – not imposed by individual groups – where merchants of all nations and origins were able to assemble at specific trading times. The motto of the Antwerp Exchange was entirely in this spirit: *in usum negotiatorum cujuscunque nationis ac linguae* (dedicated to the merchants of all peoples and to all languages). According to the *Ordonnantien van de Beurs* of 1592, amended in 1611, during trading hours – 11 a.m. to 12 a.m. and 6.30 p.m. to 7.30 p.m., access was free, except for children, beggars and those likely to cause a disturbance, who were barred entry during assembly hours.[53] The organization of the market within the exchange, how-

52 The translation is based on Jacques Accarias de Sérionne, *Der Reichthum von Holland, oder Untersuchungen über den Ursprung des Handels und der Macht der Holländer; den allmähligen Anwachs ihres Handels und ihrer Schiffahrt, die Ursachen ihrer Fortschritte und ihres Verfalls, und die Mittel, sie wieder empor zu bringen. Erster Band. Aus dem Französichen*, Leipzig, 1778, 590.

53 Scheltema, *De Beurs van Amsterdam*, 45–47. For the discussion on access restrictions to the exchanges during the nineteenth century, see A. Engel and J.W. Flume, "Bullen, Bären – und Lämmer? Auseinandersetzungen um die Börsenfreiheit und die Termin-

FIGURE 6.7 Boëtius Adamsz. Bolswert, *Byrsa Amsterdamensis* (1609), detail of figure 6.2.

ever, did not end here: Within the inner courtyard of the exchange, market organization or market separation was affected by allocating specific places to the various products, but also to traders from different nations. Thus, a plan for the Amsterdam Exchange has been preserved in which the 46 columns dating from the 1668 reconstruction were numbered consecutively, such that each number was assigned to a type of commodity, occupational class or group of people (Figure 6.8.).[54]

De koophandel van Amsterdam (1753) – the merchant's handbook by Isaac le Long – provides an informative impression of the traded goods and objects and also details the market's physical divisions.[55] It also explains

spekulation des 'unberufenen Publikums' im 19. Jahrhundert", *Rechtsgeschichte – Legal History* 28 (2020), 164–181.

54 Similar plans have been preserved for the Royal Exchange II in London (1761) and the Neue Börse Hamburg (1841).

55 Isaac le Long, *De Koophandel Van Amsterdam: Naar Alle Gewesten Des Werelds*, Rotterdam, 1753, 49–51: "Yet, thanks to the good order, orientation is easy, despite all the hustle and bustle. Indeed, the 46 columns that form so many arcades leading up to the perimeter wall are all marked with numbers, from N°. 1 to 46, to denote the kind of negotiators who are to be found at each pillar. When approaching from the lock side of the Exchange, in the narrow lane, between and around pillars N°. 2. and 3 one first finds where the noble Jewish people are who trade and exchange all manner of gold and silver 'minted' and 'unminted'. Between N°. 4 and 5 can be found the tobacco merchants. And at N°. 6 and 7 the sub-dealers of Suriname, Curaçao, and other places from the West Indies and Sweden. Somewhere around N°s. 8, 9, 10, 11 and 12 there are the merchants and mariners who trade with Spain, Italy, Egypt and the Mediterranean, Turkey and the Canary Islands. Roughly at N°s. 13, 14, 15 we see the manufacturers of silk fabrics and silk merchants, Greeks, Armenians and Persians. At N°s. 16, 17, 18 some brokers (*maakelaars*) trading in hard commodities, and some of the renowned banquiers who deal in bills of exchange, as well as merchants in Bilbao, Biscay and Portugal. At pillar N°s. 19 and 20 when approaching from the tower side, to the left one finds spice merchants. At the same time, near pillar N°s. 28, 29 and 30, the goldsmiths and bond dealers, etc. At N°s. 31, 32 there are some more merchants of hard commodities (stationary merchandise), &c. N

how the exchange acted as a "knowledge hub" for disseminating information.[56]

°s. 33, 34, 35 are home to the leather merchants, oil merchants, soap boilers, and cashiers. While at N°s. 36, 37, 38 we see the wool and cloth merchants, and others who deal with the Spanish Netherlands. At and around N°s. 39 and 40 we find the Muscovite and Oriental merchants, the mariners and grain traders. At N°s. 41, 42, 43 the resin and train-oil [whale oil] merchants. At N°s. 44, 45 and 46 the merchants and mariners, who trade with Denmark, Norway, etc., along with the timber merchants; among these are the several Zardammer (Zaandam) merchants every Monday, Wednesday and Friday. Then, at the centre of the Beurse, when entering via the lock side, at N°. 1 there are: First, the wine merchants and then the French merchants and mariners. A little further along there are the Bremen and Hamburg merchants and merchants, as well as the bargemen (*Schuytevoerders*). Somewhat beyond these are the paint merchants and druggists followed by the English merchants and mariners, the cotton merchants, linen, cloth and paper traders. And, lastly, we find the confectioners, stockbrokers and Portuguese Jews."

56 Ibid., 51–54: "Public auctions of wine and sales of all other goods are announced on the majority of pillars, as are the ships loaded in various regions of the world, along with other things, as may be read from the advertisements displayed on them. On some of the pillars can be read the following text, which one ought to look out for there: N°. 1: Wines sales. N°. 6: Sweden. N°. 9: Spain. N° 10: Auctioning of ships. N°. 12: Italy. N°. 13: Auctioning of chemicals and paint products. N°. 15: Bay of Biscay. N°. 18: Portugal. N°. 35: Auctioning of chemicals and paint products. N° 39: Gdansk. N° 40: Coninxbergen (*Königsberg*). N° 41: Denmark and the Baltic Sea. N° 42: Auctioning of ships. N° 43: Renting of warehouses, attics and cellars. N° 44: Bergen, Trondheim and the whole of Norway. N° 45: France. Beneath the arches and along the wall, there are various black, inscribed wooden panels all around, with white letters that read: Between N°s. 4 and 5: Tobacco. At N°. 7: West Indies, Suriname and Curaçao. Between N°s 9 and 10: Departure of ships to Cádiz, the entire Mediterranean and Canary Islands. Between N°s 12 and 13: Auction of silks and manufactories. Between N°s. 15 and 16: Sales of stationary goods. Between N°s. 32 and 33: Sales of stationary goods. Between N°s 33 and 34: Auctioning of skins. Between N°s 35 and 36: Soap boilers and oil storage. Between N°s 37 and 38: Auctioning of wool and cloth. At N° 39: Moscow, Archangelsk and Russia. Between N° 41 and 42: Greenland. At N° 42: Riga, Reval, Lübeck, Gdansk and Courland. At N° 43: Auctioning of wood products. Displayed on every pillar, accordingly numbered, throughout and beneath the arches, and on the walls, are countless slips of paper, each according to the above inscription; containing the auctioning of houses and other immovable goods, ships and all manner of merchandise; as well as notices of the ships currently being loaded, their departure times, their anchorages, the brokers, agents, etc., from whom may be obtained additional information. With the numbers on which only countries and cities are listed, there are, as a rule, those merchants and mariners who trade or sail to those destinations. On both sides of the gallery, one also finds along the wall a great number of noticeboards of persons tendering their services for the provision of clerks for comptoir- and shopkeepers, bookkeepers, housekeepers, maids, gardeners, and all manner of other salaried servants. Since the number of these service suppliers

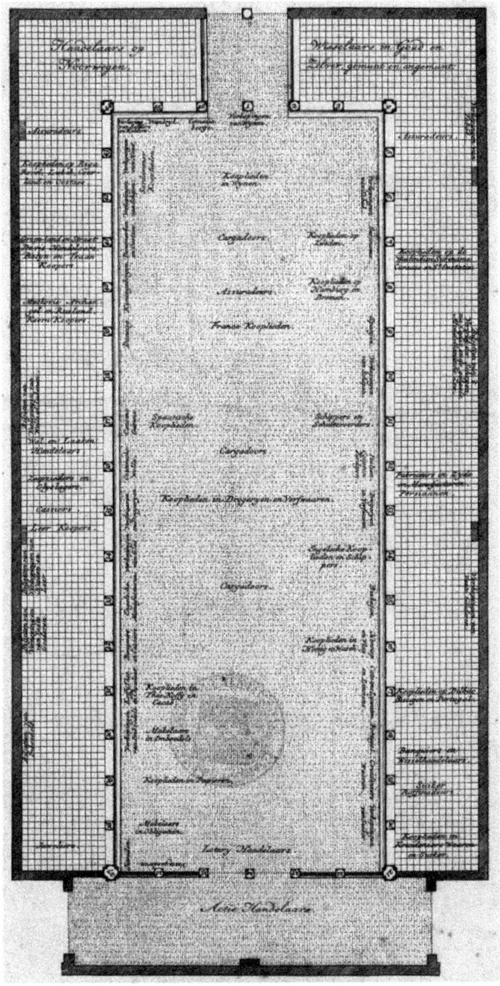

FIGURE 6.8

Anonymous, *Plattegrond van de Beurs van Hendrick de Keyser in Amsterdam* (1801) – Municipal Archives Amsterdam, *Tekeningen en prenten* (inv. 10097), 2627

3 Markets and Market Design

The two distinct types of trading places – Venice, then Antwerp, London and Amsterdam – are not only impressive as sites for observing economic life, but their juxtaposition reveals just how fundamental trading practices within the exchange had an impact on the evolution of private and commercial law.

(*Besteeders*) is continually on the rise, one may clearly infer the increase of commerce in this famous city.

3.1 Weekly Markets and Bazaars

The institutional provision of "*Markt- und Handelspolizei*"[57] (market and trade police) – which, among other things, were deployed to audit units of measurement and weight, the quality of commodities as well as price control – has been in place since antiquity. Hence the *agoranomoi* (ἀγορανόμοι) in the Athenian *Agora*, as well as the *aediles curules* in Rome, which, according to Theodor Mommsen[58] were based on the Greek model, oversaw activities in the market.[59] These represented fascinating early attempts to regulate the market. Nevertheless, from a private law perspective, a weekly market, bazaar or *fondaco* are little short of primitive. In these markets, goods were traded on the spot and cash sales, *Handgeschäfte, Barkäufe, Handgeschäfte* or *marché a comptant* were executed. Goods are exchanged for nominal cash or other means of payment. Presumably, according to ancient Greek law, ancient common law and the Germanic legal traditions, sales contracts were not understood as consensual, but as real contracts (*Realverträge*).[60] As Reinhard Zimmermann summarizes: "In all the ancient laws, sale was essentially a market transaction. It was concluded inter praesentes, and where conclusion of the contract and execution of the mutual performance (i.e. the transfer of the object of sale and payment of the purchase price) coincided."[61] Neither party was ever contractually obliged to render performance or to effect payment. The relationship stood or fell on the basis of the actual exchange.

---

57 The expression employed by Goldschmidt, *Universalgeschichte des Handelsrechts*, 70.

58 Th. Mommsen, *Römisches Staatsrecht, 2. Band, 1. Abtheilung*, 3rd ed., Leipzig, 1887, 497 and following.

59 On the *agoranomoi* and trade on the Agora: A. Bresson, *The Making of the Ancient Greek Economy: Institutions, Markets, and Growth in the City-States*, trans. Steven Randall, Princeton, 2016, 234 and following; E. Jakab, *Praedicere und cavere beim Barkauf: Sachmängel im griechischen und römischen Recht*, Munich, 1997; see also links between *agoranomos* and Islamic *muḥtasib:* B.R. Foster, "Agoranomos and Muhtasib", *Journal of the Economic and Social History of the Orient* 13/2 (1970), 128–144.

60 W.W. Buckland, A.D. McNair and F.H. Lawson, *Roman Law and Common Law*, 2nd ed., Cambridge, 1952, 282; A. Heusler, *Institutionen des Deutschen Privatrechts, Zweiter Band*, Leipzig, 1886, 253; F. Pringsheim, *The Greek Law of Sale*, Weimar, 1950, 86 and following; R. Zimmermann, *The Law of Obligations, Roman Foundations of the Civilian Tradition*, Cape Town, 1990, 237. On the origin of the Roman legal idea of consensual contracts, see F. Pringsheim, "L'origine des contrats consensuels" in *Gesammelte Abhandlungen*, vol. 2, Heidelberg, 1961, 175–193, at 179 and following (also published in *Revue historique de droit français et étranger* 31 (1954) 475–495).

61 Zimmermann, *The Law of Obligations*, 237.

3.2 Exchanges

The exchange is a completely different place. Stripped of the atmosphere evoked by the feel, the aromas, the colours and the merchandise of the bazaars and market halls, it is far more abstract. At first glance, one is faced with the chaotic hustle and bustle of all manner of people from far and wide. A second glance, however, reveals a remarkably organized market structure, which, as epitomized by Max Weber in his economic history of 1919/1920, facilitates the "emancipation of economic action from the momentary situation" ("[*die*] *Emazipation des wirtschaftlichen Handelns von der Augenblickslage*").[62] Here, one may negotiate both the immediate exchange of goods for money and "speculate on future market situations".[63] In the exchange, in contrast to the regular weekly market or bazaar, contracts may be concluded on two different markets: on the spot market and on the forward respectively futures market. Wheat or whale baleen, for instance, may be purchased directly, or contracts may be concluded for delivery in one, two or even six months.

3.2.1 Fundamentals of Spot and Futures Markets

Traders know only the current market price or spot price of a commodity. The future, on the other hand, is impossible for anyone to predict, and natural disasters, wars and epidemics – all issues we are unfortunately facing again today – are apt to lead to price volatility and uncertainty with respect to price trends. Now, however, the risk of market price fluctuations may be addressed and price risk hedged by way of a simple over-the-counter forward market as well as a standardized and exchange-driven futures market. In these markets, the future has a 'price tag'. Now, commodities no longer have a spot market price only, but also a forward and futures price.

3.2.2 Trading Baleen in the Courtyard of the Exchange

The implications of this crucial financial innovation are best exemplified by way of a straightforward scenario. For the sake of clarity, we shall consider a purely fictional case in which a merchant acquires baleen from the upper jaw of a whale in January 1612; he sells the baleen to manufacturers who then

62 M. Weber, *Wirtschaftsgeschichte, Abriss der universalen Sozial- und Wirtschaftsgeschichte*, Munich, 1924, 5.

63 Weber, *Wirtschaftsgeschichte*, 5.

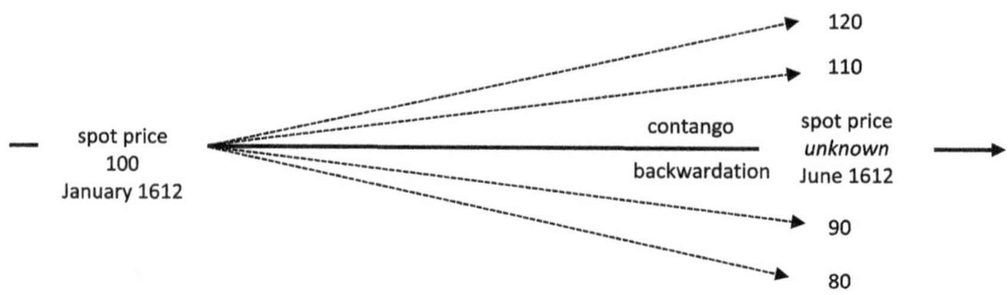

FIGURE 6.9 Example of *rescontre*

process the baleen into luxury goods such as hats, parasols and so on. Now, let us suppose that the spot price for the immediate purchase of whale baleen in January is 100, whereby, the future spot price for baleen in June 1612 is, of course, given that nobody can predict the future, unknown in January. At the same time, baleen is offered at 110 for delivery in June. There may be very different causes for this pricing: Perhaps traders are well aware that during the summer months ever fewer catchers land in Amsterdam. Prices reflect implicit information as to how the market assesses price developments. Forward or futures prices exceeding or falling below market prices are referred to as *contango* or *backwardation* respectively. Further details should not concern us here.

Let us now further assume that the parties agree on 110 in January for delivery in June. The months go by and show fluctuations in the price for whale baleen. In June, finally, the spot market price for whale baleen is at 120. For our two traders, this means that the baleen must be delivered for 110, even if the market price is 120. In this case, the buyer is protected from any price increase above the purchase price of 100 – he is *hedged.*

Hedging is regularly discussed as a feature of sophisticated financial market instruments. It is also sometimes claimed that hedging requires the combination of two transactions, namely, that a spot-market transaction must be combined with an opposite transaction on the futures market.[64] But things are much easier. A 'simple' hedge requires neither a combination of a large number of transactions nor complex financial instruments. Rather, the sales contract itself is the archetype, the mother of all hedges. Generally speaking,

64 The matter in which it is perpetually stated is misleading: for offsetting price risk (i.e. hedging), one needs to take an opposite position in *another* asset or market, see, for example, Ch. O. Hardy and L.S. Lyon, "The Theory of Hedging", *Journal of Political Economy* 31/2 (1923), 276–287. It needs no other opposite position in *another* contract to effectuate hedging, because every contract itself addresses the problem of price risk.

every sales contract has an *inbuilt hedge effect*.[65] While this important effect is hardly ever dealt with in contract law,[66] it is described, by default, in the context of forwards and (exchange-traded) futures in the economics literature on derivatives.[67] However, from a contract law perspective, a forward contract is nothing other than a simple sales contract – a contract in which the price is already fixed in the present, but whose execution is postponed to the future. The one feature distinguishing a forward and futures contract from a spot contract is only that in the latter instance, the performance interval is extremely short, albeit that the risk structure remains the same.

3.2.3 The Futures Market of the Amsterdam Exchange during the Seventeenth and Eighteenth Centuries

How did futures trading work on the Amsterdam Exchange, and what provisions were taken to safeguard its functioning? One of the clearest and most remarkable accounts – almost completely overlooked in previous research – was given by Jean-Pierre Ricard in *Le Négoce d'Amsterdam* at the beginning of the eighteenth century. His first, general characterization of futures trading is as follows:

> Trades such as these are usually based on vague, fanciful manifestations rather than on realities; generally, very dangerous, they have invariably ruined and reduced many people: the peculiarity of this trade is such that it so jinxes and enthrals the minds of those who indulge in it, that they are unable to escape it without having first utterly wrecked themselves. This always arises when war is announced against some country, or when the impending harvest of some commodity in one or the other country has failed; or even when an obstacle prevents the trader from being able to export the goods from the country whence they originate; and, finally, when certain people contrive to think that a certain commodity is set to increase substantially in price by a certain date, and that, accord-

65 Flume, *Marktaustausch*, 121 and following; 257.

66 For one of the very few detailed analyses from a law and economics perspective, see John H. Barton, "The Economic Basis of Damages for Breach of Contract", *The Journal of Legal Studies* 1/2 (1972), 277–304. See also Cl.P. Gillette and S.D. Walt, *Sales Law, Domestic and International*, 3rd ed., New York, 2016, 418 (acknowledging that parties of fixed price contracts care about the allocation of market price fluctuations).

67 See, e.g., R.E. Bailey, *The Economics of Financial Markets*, Cambridge, 2005, 4 and following; J.C. Hull, *Options, futures and other derivatives*, 10th ed., New York, 2017, 25.

ingly, they purchase large quantities thereof with a view to reselling the same only at great profit.[68]

In addition to the shares of the Dutch East India and West India Companies – those of the British East India Company are said to have been excluded from trading – pepper, saltpetre, coffee, cocoa, cochineals, brandy, grain, whale baleen and whale oil were traded as futures (*à terme*).[69]

The contract was concluded by a broker (*makelaar*) who would fill out two pre-printed contract forms, which the parties would then countersign and exchange with each other.[70]

> After trade is concluded, the broker fills out two contracts, one of which he has countersigned by the seller and the other by the buyer; he then he exchanges them by returning the one signed by the seller to the buyer and the one signed by the buyer to the seller; such pre-printed contracts are available from booksellers, and brokers simply have to fill in the names of the buyer and the seller and the list of names, quantities and prices of commodities, and delivery date.[71]

---

68 J.-P. Ricard, *Le Négoce d'Amsterdam* […], Amsterdam, 1722, 54: "*Ces sortes de marchez sont plus souvent sur des apparences vagues & chimeriques que sur des realitez, ils sont en géneral très-dangereux & ont de tems ruiné & fait manquer beaucoup de monde: ce Commerce a cela de particulier, qu'il enchante & enforcele presque tellement l'Esprit de ceux qui s'y adonnent, qu'ils n'en reviennent que lors qu'ils s'y sont entierement ruinez. Il se fait presque toujours lors qu'il y a des apparences d'une guerre prochaine avec quelque Pays; ou lors que la recolte de quelque marchandise a manqué dans quelque Pays; ou bien lors qu'il y a quelque obstacle qui empêche de pouvoir tirer à droiteure des marchandises du Pays d'où elles viennent; ou bien enfin lors que quelques uns se mettent en tête, que quelque marchandise augmentera considerablement dans certain tems, & qu'ils en achetent de grosses parties, dans le dessein de ne les revendre qu'à un gros profit.*"

69 Ricard, *Le Négoce d'Amsterdam*, 62; see also J.G. van Dillen, "Termijnhandel te Amsterdam in de 16de en 17de eeuw", *De Economist* 76 (1927), 503–523.

70 For the precise wording of such forms, see Ricard, *Le Négoce d'Amsterdam*, 55 and following.

71 Ricard, *Le Négoce d'Amsterdam*, 55: "*Le Marché etant conclu, le Courtier en écrit deux Contracts dont il fait signer l'un au Vendeur & l'autre à l'Acheteur, qu'il échange ensuite en donnant celui que le Vendeur a signé, à l'Acheteur, & celui que l'Acheteur a signé, au Vendeur; ces Contracts se trouvent imprimez chez les Libraires, & les Courtiers n'ont qu'à remplir les vuides du nom de l'Acheteur ou du Vendeur, & du nom, de la quantité & du prix de la marchandise & du tems de la livraison, voici la marchandise dont ils se font.*"

At the account settlement date or *Rescontredag,*[72] liquidation was effected by the brokers.[73] The usual settlement dates for trading in coffee, according to Ricard, were the first of January, May, July and October.[74] For such settlements, each broker maintained a *rescontre* book detailing the quantities sold and bought by his client and from whom,[75] whereby obligations to deliver and to purchase may have resulted.[76] The lion's share of such transactions, however, was settled by paying the difference. "A great number of parties settle accounts once business has been transacted, one by paying out a surplus to the other: something known as *rescontres ou rencontre les parties*."[77]

The coordination as to how much was to be paid by and to whom for what commodity (delivery, acceptance or paying the difference) was settled by the brokers among themselves. This procedure is outlined in Isaac de Pinto's book, published some fifty years later:

> Those concerned with settlement gather around a large table in a hall during one day of the settlement month. Each broker can take on the task of settlement for up to ten to twelve persons, and everything (*Skontrobogen?*) [accounts ledgers] is lined like music paper. – The procedure is thus: Whosoever is entrusted with the settlement declares that someone has sold 1000 pounds to someone else who is ordered to pay for it. The person charged with settling the buyer's transactions issues confirmation of this. Once the buyer himself takes delivery of the securities, everything is settled [...] but since the first buyer may have resold his lot to another, and, in turn, the new buyer to another, and so on in cascade fashion until the buyer or seller locates a closing operation, i.e., an effective or artificially induced acceptance. In settlement, this transfer is called

72 In literature on nineteenth-century stock exchanges, this date is referred to as the *Liquidationstermin, settling day, account day* or *fin*, cf. C.S. Grünhut, "Die Börsengeschäfte" in W. Endemann (ed.), *Handbuch des deutschen Handels- See- und Wechselrechts, Dritter Band*, Leipzig, 1885, § 279 (= p. 12).

73 Smith, *Tyd-affaires*, 6; see also the brief notes by Gelderblom and Jonker, "Amsterdam as the Cradle of Modern Futures", 202.

74 Ricard, *Le Négoce d'Amsterdam*, 56; see also Isaac de Pinto, *Traité de la circulation et du crédit*, Amsterdam, 1771, 261 and following; Ch. Wilson, *Anglo-Dutch Commerce & Finance in the Eighteenth Century*, Cambridge, 1941, 14.

75 According to Ehrenberg, "Die Amsterdamer Aktienspekulation", 819, there were traders "called '*rescontrantes*', as they assumed as far as possible the task of balancing the parties against one another, and for collecting and paying out the differences (*surpluses*)."

76 For an exemplary calculation, see Ricard, *Le Negoce d'Amsterdam*, 58 and following.

77 Ricard, *Le Négoce d'Amsterdam*, 57 (emphasis as in the original): "*il se fait un nombre incroyable de parties, qui s'amortissent au bout du terme en se payant le surplus les uns aux autres: on appelle cella rescontrer ou rencontrer les parties.*"

marrying seller to buyer in the last instance. Settlement, therefore, runs back and forth like a weaver's shuttle or is a true cycle.[78]

In addition to the highly advanced *rescontre* procedure, settlement between the contracting parties in the trade in spirits is believed to have been effected by the handing over of a note from party to party, known in Dutch as an "*Overwysing*"[79] (or *Overwijzing*).

As Ricard clarifies towards the end of his remarks, all the details of futures trading described above serve to make comprehensible one of the basic ideas of exchange-based futures trading:

> I was somewhat more explicit on this kind of market, for many among those who heard of it seem incapable of grasping how any man dares undertake to buy or sell ten times more than he disposes over, [...] about which he is well aware that he is not in a position either to take delivery of, or to supply; [...].[80]

3.2.4 The Legal Anatomy of Futures Trading

This final remark by Ricard touches the core functionality of futures markets: Having sold whale baleen ten times over, is not a trader obliged to actually deliver whale baleen ten times? How is it possible for a trader, having sold baleen ten times and purchased it ten times over the course of a trading period, to collect his profit or pay a loss on the *rescontredag*, and not actually deliver or take delivery of the goods? Bearing in mind that sales contracts are types of contracts aimed at the actual exchange of goods for money, doesn't all this look somewhat dubious? The answer to all these questions can be found in the ultimate advancement of sales law: All sales agreements transacted at the exchange over a trading period and of the same class of commodity or financial instrument, are linked by the *rescontre* procedure – or, as it was later called, by way of *Skontration* or the *vivrement de partie*.[81] *Skontration* or

78 Pinto, *Traité de la circulation*, 305 and following; the English translation in the main text of this article is based on the German translation by O. Pringsheim, *Die Verwirrung der Verwirrungen: Vier Dialoge über die Börse in Amsterdam*, Breslau, 1919, XVII; see Wilson, *Anglo-Dutch Commerce*, 83.

79 Jacobson, *Terminhandel in Waaren*, 23 and following; Ricard, *Le Negoce d'Amsterdam*, 59.

80 Ricard, *Le Négoce d'Amsterdam*, 59: "*Je me suis peu étendu sur ces sortes de marchez, parce que beaucoup de gens, qui en ont souvent entendu parler, m'ont paru ne pas pouvoir comprendre comment un homme ose s'engager d'acheter ou de vendre pour 10 fois plus qu'il n'a vaillant,* [...], *qu'il fait bien qu'il n'est pas en état de recevoir ni de livrer.*"

81 Among fundamental works in German literature on the subject, see Grünhut, "Die Börsengeschäfte", § 279 (= p. 12 and following); and prior to this, by the same author, "Das

rescontre amounts to an exchange clearing procedure devised at the Champagne trade fairs during the twelfth and thirteenth centuries.[82] The objective here is to offset a large number of contracts by reducing the *gross balance* of all outstanding claims and debts to a *net balance*. This amounts to legal practice, facilitating what is today referred to as *close out* or *Glattstellen*. A trader on the exchange may terminate trading by way of a profit or a loss, namely, through offsetting a position. He is no longer bound to actually deliver or accept the object of trade. Where necessary, he must only pay the difference, or else collect a profit.

To better grasp the effects of *Skontration* or the *rescontre* system and the possibility of closing out positions, we should first briefly review the nature of contracts concluded at the Bourse. According to a common characterization in economics literature on the subject, almost all derivatives may be classified as variants of two basic types of contracts: forwards and futures, on the one hand, options on the other.[83] This dichotomous classification was already introduced by Jean-Pierre Ricard and Isaac de Pinto, who distinguished the *marché fermé* (time contracts, *Termin- oder Zeitgeschäft*) from the *marché à option* (options).[84] This distinction also signaled the point of departure for Louis Bachelier's and Vinzenz Bronzin's pioneering work in financial mathematics at the beginning of the twentieth century, who similarly distinguished "*opérations fermes*" or "*feste Geschäfte*" from "*opérations à prime*" or "*Prämiengeschäfte*".[85] *Marchés fermés* are fixed or unconditional insofar as the mutual contractual obligations are binding and not subject to the exercise

Börsen- und Mäklerrecht und seine Neugestaltung in Oesterreich", *Zeitschrift für das Privat- und öffentliche Recht der Gegenwart* 2 (1875), 535–613, at 590 and following; K. Cosack, *Lehrbuch des Handelsrechts*, 3rd ed., Stuttgart, 1895, § 63 10. (= p. 402 and following); C. Malß, "Ueber Kompensationscourse, Klagbarkeit der s. g. Differenzgeschäfte und rechtliche Natur der Börsenabrechnung", *Zeitschrift für das Gesamte Handels- und Wirtschaftsrecht* 4 (1861), 1–12.

82 L. Börner and J.W. Hatfield, "The Design of Debt-Clearing Markets: Clearinghouse Mechanisms in Preindustrial Europe", *Journal of Political Economy* 125/6 (2017), 1991–2037, prior Leopold Ladenburg, "Die Börsengeschäfte", *Zeitschrift für das Gesamte Handels- und Wirtschaftsrecht* 3 (1860), 439 and following; G. Cohn, "Die Zahlungsgeschäfte" in W. Endemann (ed.), *Handbuch des deutschen Handels- See und Wechselrechts, Dritter Band*, Leipzig, 1885, § 448 (= p. 1056 and following); G. Neuhaus, *Die Skontration, ihre historische Entwicklung, juristische Natur und volkswirtschaftliche Bedeutung*, Dar-es-Salaam, 1892, 5 and following.

83 Bailey, *The Economics of Financial Markets*, 4 and following; Hull, *Options, futures and other derivatives*, 6 and following.

84 Pinto, *Traité de la circulation*, 292 and following; Ricard, *Le Négoce d'Amsterdam*, 52.

85 L. Bachelier, "Théorie de la Spéculation", *Annales scientifiques de l'École Normale Supérieure* 17, 3e série (1900), 22 = M. Davis and A. Etheridge, *Louis Bachelier's Theory of*

of an option. As we have already noted, they also have a symmetrical risk profile (see 3.2.2. above), since the risk of price volatility is shared between buyer and seller.

Forwards and futures are commonly defined as agreements to buy and sell an asset at a certain future date and price. The difference is that forwards are traded over the counter (OTC), while futures are traded on an exchange. This distinction, today, means that a forward is contracted bilaterally; while futures are concluded on the exchange in a star-shaped structure via so-called central clearing parties (CCPs) – the counterparty risk is addressed via margin accounts – whereby contracts are executed via a technically sophisticated system of clearing and settlement.[86] From a contract law perspective – despite the many refinements in the legal architecture of the financial market, particularly since the nineteenth century – one core idea remains essential: spot, forward and futures are sales contracts. The threefold distinction made in economics literature on the subject, amounts to economic variants of one and the same type of contract, that is, a sales contract. What differs is the time of execution. In a spot transaction, the exchange occurs almost immediately, whereas in the case of forwards and futures, the actual exchange is deferred to the future.

Yet how was it even possible to distinguish between a forward and a futures contract in the Amsterdam Exchange? With respect to content, futures and forwards were indistinguishable. Each variant was aimed at the delivery of goods or financial instruments at a point in the future, and were bilaterally negotiated between the traders in the inner courtyard of the exchange. The primary difference between forwards and exchange-traded futures, however, consisted in whether they were included into the clearing process and were executed at a specifically fixed settlement date, *rescontredag* or *Liquidationstag*.

The main objective of this procedure was to shorten the settlement of all contracts concluded in a given futures market over a trading period by netting the entirety of obligations by all trading participants. We know of two procedures on the Amsterdam Exchange.[87] The first was a tender or ticket process conducted by the exchange participants themselves (i). This model corresponded to the trading of spirits on the Amsterdam exchange by means

---

Speculation, Princeton, 118: "*Il y a deux sortes d'opérations à terme: Les opérations fermes; Les operations à prime*"; V. Bronzin, *Theorie der Prämiengeschäfte*, Leipzig, 1908, 1.

86 See Flume, *Marktaustausch*, 216 and following; P. Norman, *The Risk Controllers, Central Counterparty Clearing in Globalised Financial Markets*, Chichester, 2011.

87 See also Flume, *Marktaustausch*, 212 and following.

of tender notes ("*Overwijzing*"), as mentioned by Ricard. The liquidation system used by many exchanges was also organized according to this simple procedure and was operative through to the mid-twentieth century. However, futures were also processed by a central office that utilized a far more elaborate accounts-based clearing system (ii). This process was in keeping with the much higher complexity of the *rescontre* procedure, operated by brokers on the Amsterdam Exchange since the seventeenth century (or, later, for instance during the nineteenth century), by so-called liquidation associations (*Liquidationsvereine*) on the Berlin and Vienna Exchanges.[88]

By way of illustrating the significance of clearing and the way the two different procedures work on the exchanges, let us take one further, deliberately simple, example in which four traders (A, B, C and D) trade in whale baleen. All sales contracts are concluded for delivery of baleen at a certain future time X. A sells baleen to B for 100 (contract No. 1). Later, B successfully sells baleen to C for 105 (contract No. 2). The market price subsequently falls, for instance due to the news of good catches – and C determines to sell baleen to D for 98 to obviate his losses that have increased yet further (contract No. 3). D enters into no further transactions. Hence, we have a total of 3 contracts:

A–B to 100 (contract No. 1)
B–C to 105 (contract No. 2)
C–D to 98 (contract No. 3)

Now let's see how our exemplary mini-futures market is liquidated by the two procedures.

(i) Tendering and Ticketing Procedures

The tendering or ticketing process effects the direct supply of baleen from the first link in the chain (A) to the last link (D).[89] The system, of which there are different variants, rests on the underlying premise that a tender note (also known as a *filière, declaration of tender, Kündigungszettel* or *Overwijzing*) is issued at the top of the chain, namely, by the trader (i.e. A) who intends to deliver, before then being passed on from one trader to the next (i.e. from B to

88 Flume, *Marktaustausch*, 216.

89 For further details, see Jacobson, *Terminhandel in Waaren,* 22 and following; C.J. Fuchs, "Der Waren-Terminhandel, seine Technik und volkswirtschaftliche Bedeutung", *Schmollers Jahrbuch* 15 (1891), 61 and following; P. Gramse, *Warentermingeschäfte, Andienung und Andienungsschein*, Marburg, 1921, 104 and following; H. Trumpler, "Börsenwesen" in J. Kohler (ed.), *Enzyklopädie der Rechtswissenschaften, Band III*, Berlin, 1913, 215 and following.

TABLE 6.1 Tender or ticket procedure (without liquidation rates)

A	100	B	105	C	98	D
−5		5				
7				−7		
98						−98
= 100		= +5		= −7		baleen

C and from C to D) and before reaching person (D) desiring to receive the goods.[90] D then requests A to deliver, whereby effective delivery and acceptance results between A and D.

The technical implementation of paying the purchase price and paying the difference is more involved. Initially, it is conceivable that purchase prices are paid in full between the separate links of chain (D 98 → C; C 105 → B; B 100 → A).[91] The disadvantage here is that the total purchase price must be paid by each buyer in the chain, despite the fact that, economically, all that matters to the intermediate links is the settling of profit and loss.

Yet it is also feasible for a commitment to be made whereby, with each indorsement of the tender note, the respective purchasers (B and C) settle their profits or losses with the initial purchaser in the chain (A).[92] This process is illustrated in the Table 6.1.

The first in the chain (A) must thus settle the difference with all chain members (B and C) who do not intend to purchase. Thus, A must pay B 5 and receives 7 from C. The final member of the chain intending to purchase (D) then pays the (full) purchase price he promised (98) to the supplier and first buyer in the chain (A).

This procedure is complicated, susceptible to error and generally problematic since all market participants are informed of the contract prices of the other transactions; the first in the chain, furthermore, is burdened with settling the difference with each contracting party in the chain. Again, Ricard explains the trade in brandy: “For I have heard a thousand times over how brandy merchants swear not to know when or to whom they should deliver

90 Conversely, the procedure can also be initiated by the last buyer, see Trumpler, “Börsenwesen”, 215.

91 See Fuchs, “Der Waren-Terminhandel”, 62.

92 Thus, the procedure for spirits trading in Ricard, *Le Négoce d’Amsterdam*, 59.

the liquor they have thus sold; indeed, I have witnessed as many as 36 indorsements for a consignment of 25 units of liquor."[93]

To tackle these problems, during the second half of the nineteenth century until late into the twentieth century, the exchanges in Austria and Germany used a so-called liquidation price (*Liquidationskurs, Kündigungskurs* or *Kündigungspreis*).[94] Each contractual relationship is then adjusted according to a centrally specified, so-called liquidation rate by calculating the balance. The value of the liquidation rate is determined such that the total settlement amounts payable are kept as low as possible.

(ii) Clearing of Accounts by a Central Body

Account settlement is the most effective form of liquidation on the exchange: In comparison to the other procedures, the *gross stock* of all claims and debts incurred on the futures market, is reduced to the smallest conceivable *net stock*. By the settlement date, all contractual rights and obligations are registered and balanced, for example, by applying the model accounts-based list illustrated below in Table 6.2.[95]

The combined total of all delivery and purchase obligations (each with a value of -1 and +1 respectively), together with payments obligations and receipts must amount to zero: in our sample futures market, the 'total liquidity' of the market resulting from the three transactions is 303 (100 + 105 + 98), for three delivery and three purchase obligations – namely, the above-mentioned *gross balance*.

Thus, in our model futures market we have an effective total of only one quantity of baleen to deliver and a total of 105 (98 through D and 7 through C) to be deposited by two parties, whereby there is no requirement to spend a total of 303 in the chain, namely, the net stock. The distribution of the deposited money (100 to A as well as 5 to B) and the allocation of the performance

---

93 See Ricard, *Le Négoce d'Amsterdam*, 59: ("*car j'ay vu pester mille fois des Marchands d'Eau de Vie, pour ne pas savoir quand, ni à qui ils livroient l'Eau e Vie, qu'ils avoient ainsi venduë, & j'ai vu jusques à 36 endossemens pour une même partie de 25 Pieces d'Eau de Vie.*"); on the interest in confidentiality, see Fuchs, "Der Waren-Terminhandel", 63 and following.

94 See, for example, A. Bayerdörffer, "Der Kaffee-Terminhandel: Ein Beitrag zur Geschichte der neueren Entwickelung der Börsengeschäfte in Waren", *Jahrbücher für Nationalökonomie und Statistik* 56 (1891), 641–874, at 646 and following; Fuchs, "Der Waren-Terminhandel", 64; H. Göppert, *Über das Börsentermingeschäft in Wertpapieren, Erster Band*, Berlin, 1914, 43 and following; O. Pisko, *Lehrbuch des österreichischen Handelsrechts*, Vienna, 1923, § 63 II. (= p. 242 and following).

95 For an example calculation, see Ricard, *Le Négoce d'Amsterdam*, 58 and following. For further illustration, see F. Schmidt, *Liquidation und Prolongation im Effektenhandel: Eine systematische Darstellung ihrer Technik*, Leipzig, 1912, 20 and following.

TABLE 6.2 Basic model of account-based exchange liquidation

A	Delivery	Acceptance	Receipt	Payment
Contract No. 1	−1		+100	
Net total:	−1		+100	
B	Delivery	Acceptance	Receipt	Payment
Contract No. 1		+1		−100
Contract No. 2	−1		+105	
Net total	0		+5	
C	Delivery	Acceptance	Receipt	Payment
Contract No. 2		+1		−105
Contract No. 3	−1		+98	
Net total	0		−7	
D	Delivery	Acceptance	Receipt	Payment
Contract No. 3		+1		−98
Net total	+1		−98	
Overall Balance	3−3=0		303−303=0	

pair (A to D) is then effected by way of *makelaars* or *rescontrantes*, namely, by brokers.

3.2.5 Gambling?

Let us briefly outline the functioning of the Amsterdam futures market: the mandatory incorporation of all futures into the clearing and settlement at the end of the term facilitates the so-called closing-out of positions at the futures exchange. A trader, for example, who purchases a baleen futures contract assumes a so-called long position; should he then sell the same commodity, he assumes a so-called short position, and may thus settle his exposure on the futures market. The trader is not required to purchase and supply a quantity of whale baleen; only the profit or loss between the two transactions is recorded. This mandatory linkage and clearing of all futures contracts establishes the basis for the crucial functioning of futures markets: *the contract itself becomes the object of trading*, in other words, futures can be traded. Insofar as there is a possibility of closing a position, a trader may then end his exposure economically by way of profit or loss and then transfer the price risk to the next trader entering the market. In such a case, the trader remains – in accordance with the structure of exchange trading through to the beginning of the twentieth century – a contracting party to two futures contracts, which are settled only on *Rescontredag*. His economic commitment, however, is concluded and quantifiable.

The option to close out a position also serves as an explanation as to why very diverse types of players are willing to participate in the market: *hedgers*, aiming to hedge price risks; *speculators*, who seek to maximize profits on the market; and finally *arbitrageurs*, seeking to realize profits without risk by exploiting price differences in different markets. As a whole, all market participants create market liquidity. The vast majority of contracts concluded during the term of a futures contract are settled by calculating a difference as a result of closing out.[96]

In part due to political agitation, in part from sheer misunderstanding and, in part, as a defence tactic in court, one sought from the outset to shed disliked investments, as well as discredit futures markets as the site of gambling bets. For this purpose, it is not possible to retrace the history of interventions and prohibitions against various types of forward and futures trading, which have been known at least since the sixteenth century.[97] However, it seems helpful to refer to a discussion on German law: the nineteenth-century German legal literature on the subject – yet also in the controversy over the moral policy pertaining to the function and justification of futures speculation – reveals repeated attempts to characterize future markets transactions as so-called *Differenzgeschäfte* (contracts for difference).[98] The widely held perception was

96 See J.C. Hull, *Options, futures and other derivatives*, 25: "The vast majority of futures contracts do not lead to delivery"; see also, prior to this and as early as nineteenth century: Grünhut, "Die Börsengeschäfte", § 279 (= p. 14): "The rule is that sales are paralysed by purchases and, conversely, purchases are paralysed by sales; the delivery of the object of purchase and the payment of the purchase price are only an exception."

97 See for example Dillen, "Termijnhandel", 506 and following.

98 See A. Engel, "'Ist nämlich der ganze Spekulationsverkehr erst einmal in einen krankhaft erregten Zustand hineingerathen...': Pathologien der Börse im späten 19. Jahrhundert", *Jahrbuch für Wirtschaftsgeschichte / Economic History Yearbook* 57/2 (2016), 333–365; Flume, *Marktaustausch*, 230 and following; U. Wolter, *Termingeschäftsfähigkeit kraft Information: Eine rechtshistorische, rechtsdogmatische und rechtspolitische Studie über die stillschweigende Entfunktionalisierung des § 764 BGB durch die Börsengesetz-Novelle 1989*, Paderborn, 1991, 21. For France, A. Stanziani, *Rules of Exchange: French Capitalism in*

that only *Differenz- und Börsenspiele* took place on futures markets, which, as a gambling or betting activity, gave rise to no liabilities and from which the general public was to be excluded.[99] In short, it was the misconception of the legality of paying the difference at the futures markets that led to one of the greatest myths in legal history, namely, to the stigma of gambling.

Prevailing assumptions as to the alleged legal character of futures contracts as contracts of differences, namely, as gambling, stem from a fundamental misunderstanding of how the futures market works. In an organized futures market, as on the Amsterdam exchange, no contracts for difference were entered into, but only sales contracts, all of which were tied by the *rescontre* system or *Börsenliquidation*. In a series of essays on the results of the German Exchange Enquiry Commission of 1896, Max Weber elucidated the correlations in no uncertain terms:

> The lamentable fact is that in the field of futures trading one still encounters the most primitive notions as to its nature. Those groups who imagine futures trading to be a wager between two persons on the price of a certain security on a certain day in the future are still widespread. The party betting on a price rise beyond a certain level (*à la hausse*) appears as the buyer, while the party betting on a decline below this level (*à la baisse*) appears as the seller of a certain quantity at that price on the respective date. According to the default of price development, the party who bets wrongly, that is, either – in the case of a fall – the 'buyer', or – in the case of a rise – the 'seller' pays the difference of the contract price on which the bet is based, and the actual price on the date of contract. To claim that such [difference] bets are mere figments of the imagination and do not exist at all would be rash. Rather, they have existed from time immemorial: in the same way that people bet on the life of the Pope, etc., so also do they bet on the course of prices at the beginning of the formation of prices on the exchange. And they still exist today. Yet – and this is crucial, insofar as they do exist – *they do not exist on the exchange*. Futures trading on the exchange – that legal literature on the subject still all-too frequently employs the absolutely non-technical expression "*Differenzgeschäft*" ["transaction for dif-

---

Comparative Perspective, Eighteenth to Early Twentieth Centuries, Cambridge, 2012, 247 and following; for the USA: J. Levy, *Freaks of Fortune: The Emerging World of Capitalism and Risk in America,* Cambridge, 2012, 231 and following; R. Kreitner, *Calculating Promises: The Emergence of Modern American Contract Doctrine*, Stanford, 2006, 105 and following; A. Engel, *Risikoökonomie, Ein Geschichte des Börsenterminhandels*, 2021.

99 M. Weber, *Max Weber Gesamtausgabe, Abteilung I Schriften und Reden, Band 5, 1. Halbband, Börsenwesen, Schriften und Reden 1893–1898,* K. Borchardt (ed.), Tübingen, 1999, 25 and following, with further references.

ferences"] is unacceptable – is structured such that it differs considerably from primitive forms of such bets for differences.[100]

The opinion that *Differenzgeschäfte* ought to be combatted is, for the most part, a deep-rooted aversion to settling contracts by way of pecuniary interest and in acknowledging only the natural exchange of services to be the legitimate form of the exchange of goods. Accordingly, the exchange of contracts is to be carried out in actual or effective terms by means of the exchange of goods for money: settlement by the calculation of a sum of money is suspect and, in case of doubt, is to be regarded as gambling and betting. Such a primacy of physical exchange does not however exist. The calculation of the differences establishes a new type of contract performance. Contracts can be calculated either on the basis of the actual physical trade of goods for money or by calculating the difference between market and purchase prices. With the latter, the *monetary value of a contract* is calculated. This concept was established both in legal theory and in the early days of financial mathematics in the late nineteenth and early twentieth centuries as the market-price-rule, whereby the relationship between purchase price and market price is determined and thus the risk structure of a sales contract is depicted.[101] Its range of application is almost universal: it can be applied not only to the calculation of damages in lieu of pecuniary damages arising from straightforward (bilateral) sales contracts, but also to the entire settlement of futures trading on exchanges, namely, by ascertaining the pecuniary interest of each individual trading transaction in automated (now computerized) calculation operations.[102]

4 The World's First Futures Market?

When were the first futures markets established? Recent American literature on the subject cites the Dojima rice futures market in eighteenth-century Osaka, Japan, while other authors allude to the Amsterdam Exchange at the beginning of the seventeenth century.[103] Identifying the emergence and on-

---

100 M. Weber, "Die Ergebnisse der deutschen Börsenenquoten", *Zeitschrift für das Gesamte Handels- und Wirtschaftsrecht* 45 (1896), 100–102 (also in *Max Weber Gesamtausgabe*, vol. 1/5, 494–496 (emphasized as in the original)). See also Idem, "Die Börse II", *Göttinger Arbeiterbibliothek* 2 (1896), 67, 70 (also in *Max Weber Gesamtausgabe*, vol. 1/5, 639, 643).

101 Flume, *Marktaustausch*, 114 and following.

102 Flume, *Marktaustausch* 197 and following, 260 and following.

103 O. Gelderblom and J. Jonker, "Amsterdam as the Cradle of Modern Futures Trading and Options Trading, 1550–1650" in W.N. Goetzmann and K.G. Rouwenhorst (eds.), *The*

going evolution of futures markets can only be meaningfully clarified insofar as it is possible to legally determine the way in which 'simple' market transactions by means of sales contracts differ from those of (organized) futures trading. Answering this question in terms of legal history is somewhat difficult: all forwards and futures were entered into bilaterally – each on the trading floor – and were practically indistinguishable with regard to content. And yet one striking difference turns on the question as to whether or not the sales contracts were included in the *rescontre* procedure on *Rescontredag*, *Liquidationstag,* or settling day. Futures trading is feasible only if all contracts concluded in a special futures market are necessarily linked. As one gleans from Ricard's remarks, traders on the Amsterdam exchange from the seventeenth century onwards were perfectly aware of the distinctions; no trader would have otherwise agreed to "purchase or sell ten times in excess of the amount at his disposal [...] which, as he is perfectly well aware, he is neither in a position to purchase nor to deliver."[104] They were only able to do this insofar as they were confident that all contracts would be settled on *Rescontredag*.

The *rescontre* mechanism forms the legal core of futures markets and thus of today's modern derivatives markets, without which these markets would be inconceivable. The fact that purchase contracts were concluded and cleared by means of *rescontre* or *Skontration* by the first half of the seventeenth century, at the latest, proves that a futures market has existed since then.[105]

As a result of the development of futures trading and the constant refinement of market structures, the exchanges functioned as legal innovators. Futures markets have, from the outset, been based on the idea that a large number of the sales contracts concluded in them are fulfilled quasi-automatically by calculating pecuniary interest. If a position is closed out, the pecuniary interest of the party exiting the market is calculated, and the price risk is transferred to the new party entering the market. The development on current futures markets has advanced one step further insofar as futures are now also traded by *cash settlement*, such that all contracts are settled from the outset by calculating pecuniary interest.[106]

Origins of Value. The Financial Innovations that Created Modern Capital Markets, Oxford, 2005, 189, 191; M.D. West, "Private Ordering at the World's First Futures Exchange", *Michigan Law Review* 98/8 (2000), 2574–2615.

104 Ricard, *Le Négoce d'Amsterdam*, 59.

105 See also Dillen, "Termijnhandel", 519; M.F.J. Smith, *Tyd-affaires in Effecten aan de Amsterdamsche Beurs*, 6, footnote 1; Wilson, *Anglo-Dutch Commerce*, 14.

106 See also Flume, *Marktaustausch*, 263.

5 Conclusion

Amsterdam stands out as the central European market of the seventeenth century. Centrally located to the south of the city's Dam Square, the *Byrsa Amsterdamensis*, built in 1611, was where the various threads of this commercial metropolis came together. By examining the architectural history of the building along with the economic and legal functioning of this place, one can show why the Amsterdam Exchange can rightly be called the first modern liquid commodity and stock market, how it differed from other prominent trading places of the time, and how the exchange acted as a legal innovator. A closer look at the operation of the exchange, in particular futures trading (*termijnhandel*), reveals how fundamental trading practices within the exchange revolutionized private and commercial law. Now, not only were trading partners able to negotiate spot contracts for the immediate trade of goods for money, but they were also able to conclude futures contracts. In short, the future was unlocked by contract law. This development, in turn, helps us dispel one of the greatest myths in economic legal history, namely, the gambling stigma. Contrary to such classic common notions of exchange trading, one can argue that futures are not breeding grounds for illegitimate betting, but instead innovate contract performances.

CHAPTER 7

The Involvement of Amsterdam's Aldermen in Shaping the Law of Secured Credit in the Seventeenth Century

Vincent J.M. van Hoof

1 Introduction

Amsterdam was the dominant commercial centre of the Dutch Republic. Its trade was a catalyst for the Dutch Republic's wealth in the seventeenth century. Recent studies have shown that well-functioning private credit markets contributed to the success of this trade.[1] Amsterdam was keen to attract merchants in competition with other early modern cities of commerce, such as Antwerp, by providing a favourable institutional framework for credit.[2] Recent studies have shown that this aim led to innovation or imitation of institutional credit frameworks of regional rivals. For example, the introduction of the specially instituted division of the Amsterdam court – the *Desolate Boedelskamer* of Amsterdam that facilitated debt renegotiations[3] between debtors and creditors – was in line with innovations in other early modern commercial cities.[4]

1 J. Zuijderduijn, *Medieval Capital Markets. Markets for Renten, State Formation and Private Investment in Holland (1300–1550)*, Boston, 2009, 246–247; Ch. Van Bochove and H. Kole, "Uncovering Private Credit Markets: Amsterdam, 1660–1809", *TSEG* 11/3 (2014), 39–72; O. Gelderblom, *Cities of Commerce. The Institutional Foundation of International Trade in the Low Countries, 1250–1650*, Princeton, 2013; O. Gelderblom, J. Jonker and Cl. Kool, "Direct finance in the Dutch Golden Age", *The Economic History Review* 69/4 (2016), 1178–1198.

2 Gelderblom, *Cities of Commerce*, 137.

3 M. Roestoff, *'N kritiese evaluasie van skuldverligtingsmaatreëls vir individue in die Suid-Afrikaanse*, PhD dissertation University of Pretoria, 2002, 47 and following; M. Lindemann, The Merchant Republics. Amsterdam, Antwerp and Hamburg, 1648–1790, New York, 2014, 273 and following.

4 D. De ruysscher, "Antwerp Commercial Legislation in Amsterdam in the 17th Century: Legal Transplant or Jumping Board?", *Tijdschrift voor Rechtsgeschiedenis* 77 (2009), 459–479, here 473–474; De ruysscher, "The Struggle for Voluntary Bankruptcy and Debt Adjustment in Antwerp (c. 1520–c. 1550)" in A. Cordes and M. Schulte Beerbühl (eds.), *Dealing with Economic Failure: Between Norm and Practice (15th to 21st Century)*, Frankfurt, 2016, 77–95. For Augsburg: M. Häberlein, "Merchant's Bankruptcies, Economic Development and Social Relations in German Cities During the Long Sixteenth Century" in Th. M. Safley (ed.), *The*

Creditors profited from lending money by means of various debt instruments.[5] Many loans were evidenced by private contracts, but some were formalized by the city's aldermen (*schepenen*) or notaries.[6] The formalization of a loan was often necessary to create security rights, such as the right of hypothec (*onderzetting*), a creditor's limited property right in the debtor's assets (*ius in re aliena*) to secure the performance of an obligation.[7] In the event of a debtor's default, the secured creditor could enforce his right of hypothec by having the charged assets sold at a public auction and using the proceeds to satisfy the secured debt.

Unlike the institutional framework regarding credit, the law of secured credit in Amsterdam was quite conservative compared to other cities in the county of Holland. Recent research has suggested that the city's officials opposed innovation with regard to security rights. For example, the city applied the priority rule (*prior tempore potior iure*) to determine the priority of secured creditors,[8] whereas all other cities in Holland awarded priority to later rights of

---

History of Bankruptcy: Economic, Social and Cultural Implications in Early Modern Europe, Abingdon, 2013, 19–34.

5 Gelderblom, Jonker and Kool, "Direct finance". Employees of the VOC frequently sold bearer bonds (issued by the VOC) for their future salary claim at a discount to get money instantly. See: Ch. Van Bochove and T. Van Velzen, "Loans to salaried employees: the case of the Dutch East India Company, 1602–1794", *European Review of Economic History* 18/1 (2014), 19–38, here 21. This practice is remarkably similar to the present-day legal practice of "reverse factoring". See T. Peshkova and H. Veerbeek, "A financiers' perspective on financing the supply chain" in G. Bergervoet, e.a. (eds.), *Financiering van de productieketen*, Deventer, 2019, 7–42.

6 See O. Gelderblom, M. Hup and J. Jonker, "Public Functions, Private Markets: Credit Registration by Aldermen and Notaries in the Low Countries, 1500–1800" in M. Lorenzini, C. Lorandini and D'Maris Coffman (eds.), *Financing in Europe*, London, 2018, 161–192.

7 H. de Groot, *Inleiding tot de Hollandsche Rechts-geleertheyd*, The Hague, 1631, 2.48.1, p. 103. In this paper, the term 'pledge' will be used as the generic term for a possessory or non-possessory security right, that is, a limited property right, not an ownership right, in the debtor's assets. The term 'hypothec' will be used specifically for non-possessory pledges. The grantor of a right of pledge to secure its own obligation will mostly be referred to as 'debtor'. It will be stated expressly if the grantor created a right of pledge to secure the obligation of another person. The person who had a right of hypothec will mostly be referred to as '(secured) creditor'. Encumbering, pledging, hypothecating and charging will be employed interchangeably.

8 V. Van Hoof, *Generale zekerheidsrechten in rechtshistorisch perspectief*, Deventer, 2015, § 4.4.2.2 and § 4.6.1; D. De ruysscher and I. Kotlyar, "Local traditions v. academic law: collateral rights on movables in Holland (c. 1300–c. 1700)", *Tijdschrift voor Rechtsgeschiedenis* 86/2 (2018), 365–403, here 388.

hypothec (in immovables) over earlier general rights of hypothec.[9] Another example is the city's reluctance to accept debt acknowledgement forms that were not acknowledged by or passed in the presence of the aldermen, when notarial deeds of hypothec of movables were recognized in other parts of Holland.[10]

In both instances, it has been suggested that these policies were aimed at protecting merchants.[11] To attract merchants in competition with other early modern cities of commerce, perhaps the city of Amsterdam adapted not only its institutional framework but also its substantive law regarding secured credit. In this chapter, some explanations for the conservative character of the law of secured credit in Amsterdam are put forward. In order to ascertain the conservative level of the law of secured credit in Amsterdam, this contribution will analyze how the Amsterdam approach compared to the approach taken by other commercial competitor-cities, such as Antwerp, and other cities in the county of Holland. The focus is on three aspects of security rights: the formal requirements for creating security rights, the rules that determined the priority between competing rights of hypothec in the same encumbered asset, and the right to pursue (or trace) encumbered assets in the hands of third parties.[12]

This analysis paints a picture of how the city's aldermen opposed innovation regarding the substantive law of secured credit. Their attempts may have been aimed at protecting the interests of merchants but certainly resulted in the preservation of their own involvement in and control over the creation of security rights.

---

9 Section 35 of the *Politieke Ordonnantie van de Staten van Holland van 1580* in: A.S. De Blécourt and N. Japikse, *Klein Plakkaatboek van Nederland: verzameling van ordonnantiën en plakkaten betreffende regeeringsvorm, kerk en rechtspraak (14e eeuw tot 1749)*, Groningen, 1919, 132. See also Van Hoof, *Generale zekerheidsrechten*, § 4.6.1.

10 See § 4.

11 On the reluctance to accept notarial hypothec deeds: J. Loenius and T. Boel, *Decisien en observatien*, Amsterdam, 1745, XXVI, 220–221; A. Pos, *Bezitloos pandrecht: Enkele rechtshistorische en rechtsvergelijkende beschouwingen*, Deventer, 1970, 161. On the *prior tempore*-rule: Octroy of 18 March 1594 in *Hantvesten priuilegien*, 95.

12 See *Amsterdamsche secretarye, bestaande in formulieren van scheepenen-kennissen, quytscheldingen, schatbrieven en ander die gewoonlyk daar gebruikt worden*, Amsterdam, 1737, 4: "*Schepenen-kennissen, wettelyk gepasseert, geregistreert, en den 40sten. penning daar van betaalt zynde, hebben ten verschyndage parate executie tegens Debiteuren binnen deze Stad en hare Jurisdictie woonende.*" (Aldermen's deeds, duly registered and for which the 40th penny was paid, can be enforced directly on their due date). The topic of summary execution was recently discussed by Van Hoof, De ruysscher and Kotlyar. See Van Hoof, *Generale zekerheidsrechten*, 90–91; De ruysscher and Kotlyar, "Local traditions v. academic law", 365–403.

First, a short overview of security rights in the county of Holland will be presented, followed by a discussion of the city's aldermen involvement in the creation of security rights in a debtor's assets in the seventeenth century. Subsequently, the comparatively limited role of notaries in this process is examined. The fifth section will delve a little bit deeper into the past by discussing the ways in which the city's aldermen shaped the substantive law of secured credit at the end of the sixteenth century. This examination will include an analysis of their approach to resolving priority competitions between secured creditors and the enforcement of security rights, including the right to follow (or trace) encumbered assets in the hands of third parties. Within its thematic structure, the chapter navigates through different themes rather than a linear chronology. Embedded within these thematic discussions is an exploration of security rights' 'lifespan', encompassing their creation, ensuing rights, and termination.

2 Dutch Rights of Pledge and Hypothec in General

In the seventeenth century, the Dutch Republic's private law was an amalgamation of Roman law and (indigenous) customary law. From the fifteenth century onwards, the revival in the study and application of Roman law (*ius commune*) across Europe strongly influenced Dutch private law. Because of this mixed character, the law of Holland is often referred to as Roman-Dutch law (*Rooms-Hollands recht*),[13] the law of Friesland as Roman-Frisian law,[14] and so on.[15] The law of secured credit was not exempt from the reception of Roman law.

Creditors frequently required their debtors to provide security for the (re) payment of the extended credit.[16] The right of pledge (*pand*) was recognized as a creditor's limited property right in the debtor's assets (*ius in re aliena*) to

13 S. Van Leeuwen, *Het Rooms-Hollands-Regt*, Leiden, 1664. See also R. Lee, *Introduction to Roman-Dutch Law*, Oxford, 1953, 2–7; R. Zimmermann, *Das römisch-holländische Recht in Südafrika: Einführung in die Grundlagen und usus hodiernus*, Darmstadt, 1983.

14 J. Lokin, N. Jansen, and Fr. Brandsma, *Roman-Frisian law of the 17th and eighteenth century*, Berlin, 2003.

15 For example: R. Verhagen and I. Haazen, "De cessie naar Rooms-Gelders recht", *Groninger Opmerkingen en Mededelingen* 19 (2002), 97–114.

16 See for the frequency of secured loans recorded by aldermen and notaries between 1500–1780: Gelderblom, Hup, and Jonker, "Public Functions, Private Markets", 174.

secure the performance of an obligation.[17] If the debtor defaulted, the secured creditor could have the encumbered assets sold and use the proceeds to satisfy their secured claim. A secured creditor had priority over other creditors in the distribution of the proceeds.

'Pledge' (*pand*) was used as the generic term for a possessory or non-possessory security right, referring to a security interest where the creditor had control over the collateral and one where the debtor retained control while granting the creditor a security interest in the asset. The term 'hypothec' (*hypotheek, onderzetting*) was used specifically for non-possessory right of pledges. The debtor remained in possession of the asset encumbered by the hypothec (for example, a shipmaster made use of the ship that was collateral for the loan that had financed the purchasing of the ship).[18]

Roman-Dutch law distinguished between special and general rights of pledge based on the description of the encumbered assets, as Roman law did.[19] For example, a debtor created a general right of hypothec by referring to "all of his property, movable and immovable, claims and credits, present and future, without any excluded."[20] As this example illustrates, the general right of hypothec affected, among other things, movable property, claims and immovable property. The general right of hypothec was known by different names, such as *generaal pandrecht* or *generale hypotheek, algemene onderzet-*

---

17 De Groot, *Inleiding tot de Hollandsche Rechts-geleertheyd*, 2.48.1, 136r; S. Groenewegen van der Made, *Tractatus de legibus abrogatis et inusitatis in Hollandia vicinisque regionibus*, Amsterdam, 1669, ad D. 20,1,1; D. Van der Keessel, *Voorlesinge oor die hedendaagse reg na aanleiding van De Groot se 'Inleiding tot de Hollandse rechtsgeleerdheyd'* (translation of: Praelectiones juris hodierni ad Hugonis Grotii introductionem ad jurisprudentiam Hollandicam), vol. 3, Amsterdam, 1964, ad De Groot, *Inleiding* 2.48, 407; J. Voet, *Commentarius ad Pandectas*, vol. 1, Leiden, 1698, ad D. 20,1,1, 854; Van Leeuwen, *Het Rooms-Hollands-Regt*, 4.13.24, 325. In this paper, the grantor of a right of hypothec to secure his own obligation will mostly be referred to as "debtor". It will be stated expressly if the grantor created a right of hypothec to secure the obligation of another person. The person who had a right of pledge will mostly be referred to as "(secured) creditor". See for a discussion of the concept of *iura in re aliena* in Roman-Dutch law: A.Fl. Mollema, *Het beperkte recht: een analyse van zijn theoretische constructie, zijn plaats in het systeem van het vermogensrecht en zijn mogelijke inhoud*, PhD dissertation Leiden University, 2013, 62–65.

18 By contrast, a pawn is a possessory pledge: the item that is given as collateral for a debt is handed over to the creditor.

19 V. Van Hoof, "'The 'generalis hypotheca' and the sale of pledged assets in Roman law", *Tijdschrift voor Rechtsgeschiedenis* 85/3-4 (2017), 474–491, here 476–478.

20 "*alle zijn goederen roerende en onroerende Actien en Crediten tegenwoordige en toekomende geen dien uitgezondert*" in: J. Naeranus, *Consultatien, advysen en advertissementen, gegeven en geschreven by verscheiden treffelyke rechtsgeleerden in Holland en elders*, Rotterdam, 1645–1685, vol. 5, 49, 181.

ting or *algemeen verband*.[21] It was common practice to combine a special right of hypothec with a general right of hypothec by specifying one or more assets and indicating the rest of the debtor's assets as also pledged.[22]

If the debtor defaulted, the secured creditor could have the encumbered assets sold at a public auction by means of a court-supervised procedure and use the proceeds to satisfy their secured claim.[23] A conditional sale of the encumbered asset by the debtor to the creditor for its market value, triggered by an event of default, was valid. Such a sale, however, did not nullify other existing rights of hypothec in the sold asset.[24]

The basic rule was that the chronological order of creation of rights of hypothec determined the priority between competing rights of hypothec in the same encumbered asset(s). This rule was expressed in the famous legal maxim *prior tempore, potior iure* (i.e. earlier in time, stronger in right; hereinafter: the *prior tempore* rule).[25] It meant that the first secured creditor could use the proceeds from a sale of the encumbered assets to satisfy the secured obligation before lower-ranking secured creditors.

21 See for an elaborate analysis of the development of the general hypothec in the Netherlands: Van Hoof, *Generale zekerheidsrechten*.

22 Gelderblom, Hup and Jonker, "Public Functions, Private Markets", 174; Van der Keessel, *Voorlesinge oor die hedendaagse reg*, vol. 3, ad De Groot, *Inleiding* 2.48.32, 455; Van Leeuwen, *Het Rooms-Hollands-Regt*, 4.12,4, 313; Voet, *Commentarius ad Pandectas*, vol. 1, ad D. 20,1,10, 858.

23 See on the out-of-court enforcement of rights of pledge: De Groot, *Inleiding tot de Hollandsche Rechts-geleertheyd*, 2.48.41, 136v; Groenewegen van der Made, *Tractatus de legibus abrogatis*, ad I. 2,8,1, ad D. 13,7,8. ad D. 13,7,13, and ad C. 8,27(28); Naeranus, *Consultatien*, vol. 1, 183, 307; Van Leeuwen, *Het Rooms-Hollands-Regt*, 4.13.24, 325; Voet, *Commentarius ad Pandectas*, vol. 1, ad D. 20,5,3, 911; Van der Keessel, *Voorlesinge oor die hedendaagse reg*, vol. 3, ad De Groot, *Inleiding* 2.48.41, 475. See also De ruysscher and Kotlyar, "Local traditions v. academic law", 371–378.

24 Naeranus, *Consultatien*, vol. 1, 281, 454; Voet, *Commentarius ad Pandectas*, vol. 1, ad D. 20,5,10, 913.

25 Derived from C. 8,17,3 (Imp. Car.): "[…] *sicut prior es tempore, ita potior iure*". See also: Van der Keessel, *Voorlesinge oor die hedendaagse reg*, vol. 3, ad De Groot, *Inleiding* 2.48.35, 463; Van Leeuwen, *Het Rooms-Hollands-Regt*, 4.13.17, 322.

3 The Role of the Amsterdam Aldermen in the Creation of Security Rights

3.1 The Execution of the Deed before a Local Court

The involvement of the local aldermen (*schepenen*) was required for the creation of a hypothec in a debtor's *immovable* assets located in that jurisdiction. The parties frequently made a debt acknowledgement form containing the right of hypothec in the presence of the aldermen, a so-called *schepenkennis*.[26] In 1529, Emperor Charles V provided that general or special rights of hypothec (*hypothecatien* of *hypotheecqueringe*) not created before a local court were null and void (*nul*).[27] According to the emperor, purchasers were often deceived by sellers who deliberately withheld information on existing encumbrances ("*gecircumvenieerd ende bedrogen, omdat de lasten verzwegen werden*"). The creation of rights of hypothec before the local court only encumbered the immovable assets that were located within the jurisdiction of that court.[28] The emperor wanted to protect third-party purchasers of immovable property.

Legal practice in Holland, however, decided that a general right of hypothec could be created before any local court in Holland and still encumber all

26 *Amsterdamsche secretary*, 1: "*Schepenen-kennissen zyn in 't generaal alle Actem, die voor Schepenen verleden en gepasseert worden; maar gemeenlyk verstaat men daar door zodanige Schuld-kennisse, die, ter zake van geleende en verstrekte penningen, ten overstaan van Schepenen, gepasseert zyn; de andere hebben byzondere namen, als van Quytscheldingen. Kustingbrieven. Rentebrieven, enz. Schepenen-kennissen, in 't byzonder en by uitnementheid alzo ogenaamt, (om dat Schepenen kennisse dragen van de Schuldbelydenisse) zyn Obligatien of Schuld-brieven, die by Debiteuren, ten behoeve van hunne Crediteuren, wegens geleend geld en verstrekte penningen, ten overstaan twee Regeerdende Schepenen, werden verleden, die dezelve den Comparant, of Comparanten voorlezen, en vervolgens ondertekenen.*" ("*Schepenkennissen* are in general all acts passed before the aldermen, but in particular they are acknowledgments of debt handed out for lent sums that are passed before the aldermen; others have specific names such as letters of acquittal, *kustingbrieven*, letters of annuity, etc. In particular the term refers to bills obligatory or letters of debt which are handed out by debtors to their creditors for reason of borrowed money, and they are passed before two aldermen who read the letter and then have it signed by them"). See also P. Nève, *Schets van een geschiedenis van het notarisambt in het huidige België tot aan de Franse wetgeving*, Nijmegen, 1995, 5 and following; Van der Keessel, *Voorlesinge oor die hedendaagse reg*, vol. 3, ad De Groot, *Inleiding* 2.48.40, 471–473.

27 Notice of 10 May 1529 in Cau, *Groot placaet-boeck, vervattende de placaten, ordonnantien ende edicten vande Staten Generael der Vereenighde Nederlanden, ende vande Staten van Hollandt ende West-Vrieslandt, midtsgaders vande Staten van Zeelandt*, vol. 1, The Hague, 1658, 373–374.

28 Naeranus, *Consultatien*, vol. 2, 123, 248.

of the debtor's immovable assets located elsewhere in Holland.[29] The States-Provincial of Holland confirmed this deviation from the imperial legislation in the *Politieke Ordonnantie* of 1580 (Art. 35 *juncto* art. 37).[30] In Amsterdam, however, assets which were situated in Amsterdam were only encumbered if the deed was executed before the court of Amsterdam.[31]

3.2 Registration

Deeds of hypothec had been recorded in the local court's registers for a long time when, in 1560, the Spanish King Phillip II required all hypothec deeds regarding immovable assets to be registered there.[32] Phillip II noted that abuse and inconveniences occurred with regard to the sale or encumbrances because of a lack of adequate registration.[33] The required registration meant that a secretary of the court transcribed (a part of) the contents of the deed of

29 Ibid., vol. 2, 130, 261.

30 "[...] *dan sal de voorsz. constitutie van generale hypoteque voor gerechte gedaen, plaetse hebben ende effect sorteren jegens dengheenen die gelijcke constitutie ofte verbandt hebben, onder denwelcken de oudtste constitutie de jonger sullen worden geprefereert, sonder dat in dien gevalle onderscheyt gemaeckt ofte reguard genomen sal worden voor wat rechters in de voorschreve landen de generale constitutie van hypoteecque sal wesen gedaen.*" ("Then shall the aforementioned creation of a general hypothec have place and exert effect against those who have a similar creation or hypothec, among whom the oldest creation (of a hypothec) shall be preferred over the younger, without any distinction being made or regard taken in that case before which judges in the aforementioned lands the general creation of hypothec shall have been made") in: De Blécourt and Japikse, *Kleint Plakkaatboek van Nederland*, 132.

31 De Groot, *Inleiding tot de Hollandsche Rechts-geleertheyd*, 2.48.38-9, 105v; Van der Keessel, *Voorlesinge oor die hedendaagse reg*, vol. 3, ad De Groot, *Inleiding* 2.48.23, 437, ad De Groot, *Inleiding* 2.48.30, 451, and ad De Groot, *Inleiding* 2.48.39, 469; Van Leeuwen, *Het Rooms-Hollands-Regt*, 4.12.4, 313; Voet, *Commentarius ad Pandectas*, vol. 1, ad 20,1,10, 858.

32 E. Ketelaar, "Van pertinent register en ordentelijk protocol. Overdracht van onroerend goed in de tijd van de Republiek" in J. Lokin, E. Ketelaar and J. de Groot (eds.), *De levering van onroerend goed. Vijf opstellen over de overdracht van onroerend goed vanaf het Romeins Recht tot het Nieuw Burgerlijk Wetboek*, Deventer, 1985, 42–43; Ch. Van Bochove, H. Deneweth, and J. Zuijderduijn, "Real estate and mortgage finance in England and the Low Countries, 1300–1800", *Continuity and Change* 30/1 (2015), 9–38, here 14.

33 *Placaat* of 9 May 1560, in: Cau, *Groot placaet-boeck*, vol. 2, 1401–1402: "*ter cause vande verkoopingen ofte belastingen van goeden veele abuysen, inconvenienten ende questien gebeuren endoe voort ghestelt worden, uyt dien dat vande selve verkoopingen en belastingen geen behoorlijck registre gehouden wort*". ("because of the sales or encumbrances of assets many abuses, incoveniences and problems happen and have to be settled, due to the fact that of the same sales and encumbrances no ledger is kept").

hypothec in a register or record.[34] The States of Holland maintained these rules on registration in the *Politieke Ordonnantie* of 1580.[35]

Parties that wanted to create a right of hypothec in all of the debtor's immovable assets needed to register their deed of hypothec at every local court where the immovable assets were situated. They could not replace local registration with a single registration at the Court of Holland (*Hof van Holland*).[36]

In Amsterdam, deeds of hypothec were registered in different publicly accessible registers, such as the register for *schepenkennissen*[37] and the register for census contracts and (life and hereditary) annuities.[38] These registers had an index on the basis of the (first) name of the debtor but were not connected to cadastral registries.[39] Publicity enabled prospective buyers to estab-

---

34 See also P. Konings, *De openbare registers ten hypotheekkantore*, Deventer, 1990, 15.

35 Art. 37: "[…] *dat een yegelick,* […] *die eenige constitutie van generale oft speciale hypoteecque op eenige onroerende goederen in den voorsz. landen ende graefschappen van Hollandt ende Vrieslant hebben ofte pretenderen willen, binnen een jaer nae de publicatie van desen, deselve aenbrengen sullen den gerechte van de plaetse daer de goederen, ten hypoteecque gestelt, zijn ghelegen, omme aldaer volgende d'instructie die by de voorsz Staten daertoe sal worden ghemaeckt, aengheteeckent te worden,* […]." ("That each and every one […] who has or wishes to claim any creation of a general or specific hypothec on any immovable goods in the aforementioned lands and counties of Holland and Friesland, within one year from the publication of this, shall bring the same to the court of the place where the goods put up for hypothecation are situated, in order to be recorded there according to the instructions that will be made for this purpose by the aforementioned States […]"). The text can be found in: De Blécourt and Japikse, *Klein Plakkaatboek van Nederland*, 132. A small fee (*halve stuiver*) had to be paid to the Secretary. See for registration fees: Van Bochove, Deneweth and Zuijderduijn, "Real estate and mortgage finance", 15–16.

36 Voet, *Commentarius ad Pandectas*, vol. 1, ad 20,1,10, 858. Registration was not required for tacit rights of pledge. See Voet, *Commentarius ad Pandectas*, vol. 1, ad D. 20,1,11, 859 and D. 20,2,17, 876.

37 *Amsterdamsche secretary*, 3: "*Schepenen-kennissen moeten, binnen acht dagen, naar zy gepasseert zyn, ter Secretary werden geregistreert; omdat, by faute van dien, de houders der Schepenen-kennissen geen regt van Hypotheek, en vervolgens ook geen preferentie op de goederen van den Debiteur zouden hebben*". ("Aldermen's deedsare required to be registered within eight days after their agreement; because, if it is not done, the holders of the aldermen's deeds have no right of hypothec, and consequently also no preference in the goods of the debtor"). See also: Municipal Archives Amsterdam, *Archief van de Schepenen* (inv. 5063).

38 Municipal Archives Amsterdam, *Archief van de Schepenen* (inv. 5065).

39 See for example art. 17 of the (concept) *Ordonnantie voor de Secretarij en voor de Secretarissen*: Municipal Archives Amsterdam, *Archief van de Burgemeesters* (inv. 5031), 111. See Ketelaar, "Van pertinent register", 405. In Leiden, however, a new register was established that was connected to a cadastral land register. This so-called *Register Vetus* was

lish a person's entitlement to the immovable assets and credit providers to assess a person's creditworthiness.[40] Interested parties had to look in multiple registers to establish whether or not assets were encumbered. However, they could also make use of the (paid) services offered by the city's secretary to look up any encumbrances.[41] Recent research suggests that the registers were consulted frequently.[42]

3.3 Taxation

Registration not only provided publicity of security rights to the public at large but also enabled tax collection. In 1529, Emperor Charles V had expressly mentioned that a lack of publicity prevented magistrates from assessing their citizens' wealth and imposing taxes.[43] The requirement of registration enabled magistrates to identify a tax base. Ironically, the States of Holland used the registration introduced by Charles V to levy taxes to fund the Dutch Revolt against Charles V's son, Philip II of Spain. From 1598 onwards, a tax was levied on the transfer of ownership of immovable assets, the so-called fortieth tax (*veertigste penning*), or 2.5 percent of the worth of the transferred immov-

---

later replaced by new registers, but the cadastral connection was maintained to provide publicity to third parties.

40 *Amsterdamsche secretary*, 3: "*En op dat, by exhibitie van de Origineele Schepenen-kennisse, van de Registratie zoude mogen blyken, zo word in margine of onder aan dezelve genoteert, in welk Register, op wat folio, end ag van't jaar, dat ze geregistreert is; en deze Registratie is noodzakelyk, op dat een ieder daar aan gelegen zynde, ten alen tyden zoude konnen laten opzoeken, en vernemen, of en hoe veel de goederen van de gene, die geld op Schepenen-kennisse willen opnemen, belast zyn.*" ("Because at the showing of an original *schepenkennis* it must be checked whether they were registered, it is mentioned in the margin of the document, or below the text, in which register it was written, which allows consulting at any moment to what extent the property on which money is raised using the *schepenkennis* is burdened"). This is one of the reasons why notaries did not evolve into credit intermediaries in the way Parisian notaries did. See: Gelderblom, Hup and Jonker, "Public Functions, Private Markets", 183.

41 *Amsterdamsche secretary*, 316. See also *Ordonnantie voor de Secretarij en voor de Secretarissen*, art. 16 in Municipal Archives Amsterdam, *Archief van de Burgemeesters* (inv. 5031), 111.

42 Van Bochove, Deneweth and Zuijderduijn, "Real estate and mortgage finance", 15–20.

43 *Placaat* of 10 May 1529, in: Cau, *Groot placaet-boeck*, vol. 1, 373–374. "*de voorschreve Officieren ende Rechters den rijckdom van heuren Poorters, Buyren ende Ingesetenen niet en konnen geweten, omme daer nae heur settinge ende ommeslagen, ende anders te maecken nae grootheyt van elcks goet*". ("because the officers and judges mentioned could not know the wealth of their citizens, neighbours and residents, in order to determine their taxes and otherwise according to the value of each one's assets").

ables.[44] From 1612 onwards, the same tax was levied on the creation of special rights of hypothec in immovables.[45] This meant that the parties had to pay 2.5 percent tax over the secured claim.[46] The creation of general rights of hypothec was similarly taxed from 1632 onwards.[47] If a secured creditor assigned the secured claim to a third party, the assignment was taxed too.[48]

Rights of hypothec could secure existing and future claims. If the value of the future claim was uncertain at the moment of registration, the parties needed to provide an estimate for taxation purposes.[49] If a secured creditor enforced his right of hypothec and the secured claim was not entirely satisfied, the secured creditor could ask for a tax return for 2.5 percent of the unsatisfied part of the secured claim.[50]

The payment of the tax was required under penalty of nullity of the right of pledge.[51] Amsterdam, however, initially only levied taxes on the creation of special rights of pledge. The States of Holland provided in 1665 that secured

---

44 *Placaat* of 22 Dec. 1598, in: Cau, *Groot placaet-boeck*, vol. 1, 1954 and 1961.

45 *Placaat* of 22 Dec. 1598, in: Cau, *Groot placaet-boeck*, vol. 1, 1954. See also C. Van Bijnkershoek, *Observationes tumultuariae*, vol. 1, Haarlem, 1926, 68, 23 (14 Jan. 1705). It should be noted that the preamble to the *plakkaat* of 4 March 1599 states: "*Van schepenen kennissen ofte obligatien verleeden met speciale hypothèque van sekere sommen van penninghen te betalen op daghen, wordt verstaen dat den impost meede sal worden betaelt*". ("Aldermen's deeds and bills obligatory containing a general hypothec and which were agreed for a specific date of payment shall pay taxes as well"). See *Verklaring* of 4 March 1599, *Hollandts placcaet-boeck*, Amsterdam, 1645, 253 and in: Cau, *Groot placaet-boeck*, vol. 1, 1963. This suggests that the fortieth penning was levied from 1599 onwards for the creation of general rights of pledge. It is conceivable that this statement was changed when the notice of 1612 came into force, but this change is not evidenced by the notice ledgers (*plakkaatboeken*). No tax was levied when a transferor of an asset reserved a right of pledge at the moment of the transfer. See for this reservation of a right of pledge: Voet, *Commentarius ad Pandectas*, vol. 1, ad 20,1,11, 859.

46 Art 1 of *Placaat* of 17 July 1632, in: *Hollandts placcaet*-boeck, 237; Voet, *Commentarius ad Pandectas*, vol. 1, ad D. 20,1,9, 858. "*van alsulcke penningen, als sij bij preferentie tegen andere crediteuren* [...] *sullen komen te ghenieten*" ("of those sums which they will receive in preference over other creditors").

47 Art 1 of *Placaat* of 17 July 1632, in: *Hollandts placcaet-boeck*, 237; Loenius and Boel, *Decisien en observatien*, vol. 17, 118; Voet, *Commentarius ad Pandectas*, vol. 1, ad D. 20,1,9, 858.

48 Groenewegen van der Made, *Tractatus de legibus abrogatis*, ad D. 13,7,18; Van Bijnkershoek, *Observationes tumultuariae*, vol. 2, Haarlem, 1932, 1881 (27 Oct. 1722).

49 Voet, *Commentarius ad Pandectas*, vol. 1, ad 20,4,30, 905.

50 Legal opinion by Ioan de Witte, Cloeck, W. Cats, Hercules Roch and Francoys Roskam of 5 May 1635 in Naeranus, *Consultatien*, vol. 3, 71, 219.

51 *Placcaat* of 22 Dec. 1598, in: Cau, *Groot placaet-boeck*, vol. 1, 1957. See also Groenewegen van der Made, *Tractatus de legibus abrogatis*, ad I. 3,23,3.

creditors had no priority over other creditors if they had not paid the 2.5 percent tax over the value of the secured claim.[52]

4 The Limited Involvement of Notaries in the Creation of Security Rights

4.1 The Reluctance to Accept Notarial Deeds of Pledge

From the sixteenth century onwards, notarial deeds gained popularity as debt instruments.[53] Historically, local courts were reluctant to accept debt acknowledgement forms that were not acknowledged by or made in the presence of the aldermen.[54] It should be noted that a registered *schepenbrief* or *schepenkennis* automatically awarded priority to the creditor over unsecured and subsequent secured creditors with regard to the proceeds of all of a debtor's assets, immovable and movable.[55] Gradually, however, the creation of rights of hypothec by means of notarial deeds was recognized in many parts of Holland.[56]

---

52 See Van der Keessel, *Voorlesinge oor die hedendaagse reg*, vol. 3, ad. De Groot, *Inleiding* 2.48.23, 433, ad De Groot, *Inleiding* 2.48.28, 445, and ad De Groot, *Inleiding* 2.48.40, 473; Voet, *Commentarius ad Pandectas*, vol. 1, ad D. 20,1,11, 859.

53 De ruysscher and Kotlyar, "Local traditions v. academic law", 374. See for a historical development of the role of notaries in the low countries in the early modern period: A. Gehlen, *Het notariaat in het tweeherig Maastricht*, Assen, 1981, 39 and following; A. Gehlen, "Benelux: Le notariat aux Pays-Bas: perspective historique" in E. van der Marck (ed.), *Atlas du notariat: Le notariat dans le monde*, Deventer, 1989, 127–142; Nève, *Geschiedenis van het notarisambt*, 51 et seq.

54 De ruysscher and Kotlyar, "Local traditions v. academic law", 372–374.

55 See H. Van Waesberge and P. Schouten, *Handvesten; ofte privilegien ende octroyen; mitsgaders willekeuren, costuimen, ordonnantien en handelingen der stad Amstelredam*, vol. 2, Amsterdam, 1748, 530; Van Bijnkershoek, *Observationes tumultuariae*, vol. 2, 1879 (16 Oct. 1722); Van der Keessel, *Voorlesinge oor die hedendaagse reg*, vol. 3, ad De Groot, *Inleiding* 2.48.21, 431.

56 Bosch and Moors stated that notarial deeds awarded no priority over other creditors in their legal opinion of 7 July 1640 in Naeranus, *Consultatien*, vol. 1, 241, 395. Van Berendrecht, Vermeeren and Van Veen, however, recognized that notarial deeds awarded priority over unsecured creditors in their legal opinion of 19 April 1641, in Naeranus, *Consultatien*, vol. 4, 190, 344. Ockers argued that a notarial deed also conferred priority over unsecured creditors with regard to the proceeds of immovable assets: H. Gall, *Regtsgeleerde decisien: Aan de raadsheer Ockers toegeschreven aantekeningen betreffende uitspraken van het Hof (1656–1669) en de Hoge Raad (1669–1678) van Holland, Zeeland en West-Friesland*, Amsterdam, 2002, vol. 1, 5, dec. 18, 126 (between 1656–1669).

Again, this development was probably the result of the reception of Roman law. In 472 CE, the (Eastern) Roman Emperor Leo I (r. 457–474) had awarded rights of hypothec created by means of public deeds priority over rights of hypothec created by other means.[57] In Roman law, public deeds were prepared by a notary (*tabellio*) and sealed in the presence of witnesses.[58] A written agreement signed by three respectable witnesses was put on par with public deeds by Emperor Leo. The *prior tempore* rule determined the priority between competing rights of hypothec in the same encumbered asset(s).

In the city of Amsterdam, the reluctance to recognize deeds of hypothec that were not acknowledged by or made in the presence of the aldermen persisted.[59] On 5 and 6 April 1622, a hearing of expert witnesses (a so-called *turbe*) took place to establish the customary law of Amsterdam with regard to deeds made in the presence of the Amsterdam aldermen. The question of whether notarial deeds of hypothec awarded priority to creditors was put before a group of lawyers (*Procureurs postulerende voor den Gerechte*) and aldermen.[60] The lawyers stated that they had knowledge of court rulings where creditors whose claims were evidenced by notarial deeds were preferred (*geprefereert*) with regard to the proceeds of the debtor's movables.[61] The aldermen declared they knew of no priority for creditors whose claims

57 (C. 8,17,11,1). See Nov. 73,1.

58 For a historical development of the role of Roman notaries, see H. Ankum, "Les tabellions romains, ancêtres directs des notaires modernes" in E. van der Marck (ed.), *Atlas du notariat: Le notariat dans le monde*, 5–44, Deventer, 1989, 5–44.

59 The above-mentioned *turbe* of 1562 implied that deeds passed in the presence of the aldermen awarded priority to the secured creditor over *all* other creditors. See Van Waesberge and Schouten, *Handvesten*, vol. 2, 530.

60 "*Of henluyden oock bekent is dat gedurende hunne bedieninge hier ter Stede by Vonnisse vanden Gerechte uyt sake van een notariale acte voor Notaris ende twee getuygen gepasseert, inhoudende generael verbant van goederen, imant is geprefereert geworden in meuble goederen, penningen, actien of crediten van den genen die de voorschreven acten hebben gepasseert?*". ("Whether it is known to them that during their service here in the city judgements were issued on a notarial deed passed before a notary and two witnesses, containing a general hypothec, which was considered as granting priority in movables, sums, claims or credits of those having signed the deed?"). See Van Waesberge and Schouten, *Handvesten*, vol. 2, 535. See also A.G. Pos, *Hypotheek op roerend goed (bezitloos pandrecht). Enkele rechtshistorische en rechtsvergelijkende beschouwingen*, Deventer, 1970, 161.

61 "*Verklaren alle gelijckelijck den inhouden van dit tegenstaende Articul waer te wesen, ende sulcx geduerende hare bedieninge, hebben sien practiseren ende observeren*". ("All declare in the same manner the content of this article to be valid, and that they saw it applied and observed during their service"). See: Van Waesberge and Schouten, *Handvesten*, vol. 2, 535–536. See Van der Keessel, *Voorlesinge oor die hedendaagse reg*, vol. 3, ad De Groot, *Inleiding* 2.48.28, 447.

were evidenced by notarial deeds and remarked that such creditors were treated as unsecured creditors.[62] According to Loenius, the Amsterdam customary law was aimed at protecting merchants.[63] It did not award priority over unsecured creditors to creditors whose claims were evidenced by notarial deeds, because merchants lacked the time to have their debt forms notarized.[64] On 17 April 1625, the Burgomasters (*Burgermeesteren*) of Amsterdam requested the States of Holland to approve (*Approbatie*) the customary rule that notarial deeds awarded no priority over other creditors.[65]

4.2 Fiduciary Transfer of Ownership Instead of Pledge

In addition to rights of pledge, the law of Amsterdam recognized the transfer of ownership as a security right in movable assets, a concept also known in (classical) Roman law as *fiducia cum creditore*.[66] It entailed that the debtor transferred ownership of an asset to the creditor to secure the performance of an obligation. If the creditor's claim was satisfied, the creditor was under the obligation to transfer the asset back to the debtor. The well-known collection of legal opinions – entitled the *Consultatien, Advysen en Advertissementen gegeven ende geschreven by verscheijden Treffelijke Rechtsgeleerden in Hollant*

62 "*Verclaren eendrachtelijck sulcx niet te weten; maer wel ter contrarie kennisse te hebben, dat ten tyde als zyluyden respective hebben gedient in 't voorszegde Schepenampt, die acten Notariael niet anders of verder in Judicio zijn aengenomen geweest, als voor personele actien omme nevens andere deughdelijcke schulden te komen in concurrentie vande Debiteuren*". ("Declare united to not know this, but they know of a contrary example when they were in the office of aldermen that notarial deeds were not considered as anything more than claims *in personam* which competed with other claims"). According to one legal opinion by Bosch and Moors, the same applied in The Hague. Bosch and Moors stated that notarial deeds awarded no priority over other creditors in their legal opinion of 7 July 1640 in Naeranus, *Consultatien*, vol. 1, 241, 395. Van Berendrecht, Vermeeren, and Van Veen, however, recognized that notarial deeds awarded priority over unsecured creditors in their legal opinion of 19 April 1641, in Naeranus, *Consultatien*, vol. 4, 190, 344. Ockers argued that a notarial deed also conferred priority over unsecured creditors with regard to the proceeds of immovable assets: Gall, *Regtsgeleerde decisien*, vol. 1, 5, dec. 18, 126.

63 Loenius and Boel, *Decisien en observatien*, vol. 26, 221. See also Pos, *Hypotheek op roerend goed*, 161.

64 Loenius and Boel, *Decisien en observatien*, vol. 26, 221. See also Pos, *Hypotheek op roerend goed*, 161.

65 Van der Keessel, *Voorlesinge oor die hedendaagse reg*, vol. 3, ad De Groot, *Inleiding* 2.48.28, 447. See also Pos, *Hypotheek op roerend goed*, 161.

66 The Institutes of Gaius II, 60.

en elders (commonly known as the *Hollandsche Consultatien*)[67] – provides several examples of this practice.

In a case of 1632, the debtor was a guardian (*voogd*), whose assets were encumbered with a right of hypothec in favour of orphans (*weeskinderen*).[68] This right of hypothec was created by operation of law and secured the orphans' claims on the tutor regarding the management of the pupils' estate. Subsequently, the guardian transferred ownership of his movables to his creditor, a wealthy businessman called Bartolotti.[69] The transfer was evidenced by a notarial deed. The assets were delivered by means of constructive delivery, which means that the guardian kept direct physical control (*detentio*) over the assets. According to Bartolotti, the assets were no longer encumbered by the pupils' right of pledge, since movables could not be traced into the hands of third parties (*mobilia non habent sequelam/ roerend goed heeft geen gevolg van hypotheek*). When asked for a legal opinion on this matter, Grotius remarked that the legal maxim that *meuble geen vervolg van hypotheecq en geeft* (hypothecs in movables goods cannot be traced), did not apply, since the debtor still had physical control over the transferred assets. The constructive delivery where the debtor granted possession by mere contract was insufficient to trigger the maxim. De Groot even remarked that he considered the practice of fiduciary transfer of ownership with a constructive delivery suspect of simulation and collusion.[70] In a different case of 1642, however, Joannes Corvinus (1582–1650)[71] considered the fiduciary transfer of ownership as a valid transfer and effective in a debtor's insolvency.[72] Title transfer as a security right was also recognized by the High Court of Holland and Zeeland.[73]

It should be noted that these two documented legal opinions by Grotius (in 1632) and Corvinus (in 1642) coincided with the period of Amsterdam's reluc-

---

67 For a short history of these works, see W. Druwé, *Loans and Credit in Consilia and Decisiones in the Low Countries* (*c. 1500–1680*), Leiden, 2020, 106–115.

68 In Naeranus, *Consultatien*, vol. 3, 174, 466–70 (26 Febr. 1632). See also V. Van Hoof, "Waakzaamheid en artikel 3:90 lid 2 BW", *WPNR* 6896 (2011), 633–640.

69 Also known as Willem van den Heuvel tot Beichlingen, the first owner of the so-called Huis Bartolotti, situated on the Herengracht 170–172 in Amsterdam.

70 "*suspect van simulatie en collusie*".

71 Druwé, *Loans and Credit*, 112.

72 Naeranus, *Consultatien*, vol. 2, 315, 630.

73 Van Bijnkershoek, *Observationes tumultuariae*, vol. 3, Haarlem, 1946, 2823 (17 Febr. 1734). See also J. Lokin, "De spagaat van de Hoge Raad: Eigendom en zekerheid" In D. Faber, C. Jansen and N. Vermunt (eds.), *Fiduciaire verhoudingen,* Deventer, 2007, 137–155, at 151–153; A. Pos, "The Hoge Raad of Holland and Zeeland in the eighteenth century and chattel mortgages (transfer of ownership as security for debt)" in J. Pikkemaat (ed.), *The Old Library of the Supreme Court of the Netherlands*, Hilversum, 2008, 83–102.

tance to accept notarial deeds of pledge. This suggests that legal practice dealt with the inability to use notarial hypothec deeds to create non-possessory rights of hypothec in movables by looking for alternative ways to create non-possessory security interests in movables. Fiduciary transfer of ownership must have been one of those alternatives.

4.3 The Recognition and Registration of Notarial Hypothec Deeds and Fiduciary Transfers

Eventually, however, notarial deeds were recognized as a means to create security rights in movable assets. In 1644, the Burgomasters and Court (*Burgermeesteren ende Gerechten*) of Amsterdam provided that notarial deeds of hypothec needed to be registered in a special register of the local court if the rights of hypothec secured prior claims (*vorige schulden of lasten*).[74] Registration was required within eight days after the deed was passed under penalty of nullity of the right of pledge.[75] Registration was not required if the encumbered assets were handed over to the secured creditor (possessory security right).[76] The fiduciary transfer of ownership of movables also needed to be registered if the movables were delivered by means of constructive delivery (*constitutum possessorium*). The registers that were used to record the notarial deeds can (partially) be found in ledger no. 8 of archival fund 5064 (*Archief van de Schepenen: register van verbonden goederen en van transporten*) of the Amsterdam Municipal Archives.

Registration of these notarial bonds was introduced to prevent fraudulent transfers and encumbrances.[77] The preamble to the new provisions implied that it was common practice for debtors to give movables in payment or to create security rights in movables for previous debts (*'t sy tot betalinge of versekeringe van vorige schulden*) just before they were declared insolvent.[78] Art-

74 Art. 1 in *Handvesten, privilegien, octroyen*, 3.1.11 (*Vande Desolate Boedels*) 4, 259: "[...] *voor ende al eer de selve transporten, cessien, verpandingen of andere acten sullen wesen geregistreert ter secretarie alhier in seker register daer toe bij de E. Heeren van de Geregte specialijck gedestineert*". ("Before the same transports, cessions, pledges and other acts will be registered at the Secretary, they will be written into a special register destined thereto by Our Lords of the Court"). This provision was also mentioned in Van Bijnkershoek, *Observationes tumultuariae*, vol. 4, Haarlem, 1962, 3112 (20 Dec. 1738) and W. Pauw, *Observationes tumultuariae novae*, vol. 1, Leiden, 1964, 187.

75 Art. 2 in: *Handvesten, privilegien, octroyen*, 3.1.11 (*Vande Desolate Boedels*) 4, 259.

76 Art. 4 in: *Handvesten, privilegien, octroyen*, 3.1.11 (*Vande Desolate Boedels*) 4, 259–260.

77 *Amsterdamsche secretary*, 50.

78 *Handvesten, privilegien, octroyen*, 3.1.11 (*Vande Desolate Boedels*) 4, 259. The article was later amended by article 12 of the Ordonnance of 19 July 1777, see J. Farret, *Tweede Vervolg*

icle 8 of the new provisions declared such transfers or encumbrances null and void if the debtor was declared bankrupt within four weeks after the notarial deed had been registered. In other words, the requirement of registration facilitated the application of the *actio Pauliana*, the legal remedy used to challenge legal acts of the debtor that were detrimental to one or more creditors.[79] If a debtor could have encumbered his movable assets in favour of one creditor shortly before insolvency (four weeks prior), other creditors would have been deprived of their share of the proceeds. Registration, or recordation of notarial deeds aimed to prevent antedating a transfer or encumbrance.[80]

Despite the fact that the records were publicly accessible,[81] registration only led to a limited level of publicity of security rights.[82] Firstly, only rights of hypothec for previous debts were subject to registration and not rights of hypothec for new debts or credit.[83] Secondly, information about the encumbrances of a debtor's assets was scattered over multiple registers. Interested parties could, however, also make use of the services offered by the city's secretary to look up any encumbrances.[84]

In a way, the requirement of registration of notarial deeds of hypothec was innovative, since Amsterdam was one of the first cities in the county of Holland to introduce such a requirement. Similar provisions on the registration of notarial bonds (to prevent fraudulent transfers and encumbrances) were later adopted in the cities of Leiden, Haarlem, Delft and Gouda.[85]

However, the registration of notarial deeds was as conservative as it was innovative. By subjecting the notarial hypothec deeds (or fiduciary transfers) to registration, the city's aldermen ensured their own involvement in the cre-

---

van de Handvesten ofte Privilegien ende Octroyen mitsgaders Willekeuren, Costuimen, Ordonnantien en Handelingen der stad Amstelredam: voortgezet tot in het Jaar 1777, Amsterdam, 1778, 104.

79 See H. Ankum, *De geschiedenis der "actio Pauliana"*, Zwolle, 1962, 370–373.

80 Gelderblom, Hup and Jonker have illustrated that a pledge of movables was regarded as less secure than a general right of pledge. Gelderblom, Hup and Jonker, "Public Functions, Private Markets", 188. Perhaps notarial deeds of pledge of movables were still used in cases where the debtor was in financial difficulties, as it would explain a higher interest rate.

81 Art. 6 in: *Handvesten, privilegien, octroyen*, 3.1.11 (*Vande Desolate Boedels*) 4, 260.

82 See B. Arruñada, *Institutional foundations of impersonal exchange: theory and policy of contractual registries*, Chicago, 2012, 55 and 173 on conveyancing under recordation of deeds in general.

83 Van der Keessel, *Voorlesinge oor die hedendaagse reg*, vol. 3, ad De Groot, *Inleiding* 2.48.27, 441.

84 *Amsterdamsche secretary*, 316; Van Bochove, Deneweth and Zuijderduijn, "Real estate and mortgage finance", 15.

85 Van Leeuwen, *Het Rooms-Hollands-Regt*, 2.7.8, 109–10.

ation of security rights. This way, notarial deeds of hypothec did not put a secured creditor in a more favourable position than *schepenkennissen*. Notarial deeds only encumbered movable assets, whereas *schepenkennissen* covered all of a debtor's assets. Both debt instruments were subject to registration. Moreover, from 1665 onwards, the creation of a right of hypothec by means of a notarial deed was equally subject to the payment of the 2.5 percent tax over the value of the secured claim.[86]

Furthermore, parties could not circumvent the restrictions on rights of hypothec by opting for a fiduciary transfer of ownership. The fiduciary transfer was regarded as a security interest in several different ways. Firstly, the *veertigste penning* – the tax for the creation of security rights amounting to 2.5 percent of the value of the secured claim – was levied.[87] Secondly, from 1644 onwards, the (notarial) deed evidencing the fiduciary transfer needed to be publicly registered at the aldermen court, just like notarial hypothec deeds. Thirdly, if the debtor became insolvent, the value of the fiduciary transferred movables recovered by the secured creditor could not exceed the value of the secured claim.[88] Despite this treatment, and even when notarial hypothec deeds were recognized, fiduciary transfers of ownership were still being used as a means to create security interests.[89] One of the advantages of *fiducia* over non-possessory hypothecs was that movables that were transferred to a creditor could be traced, unlike movables encumbered by a (non-possessory) right of pledge.[90]

The enduring involvement of the city's aldermen in the creation of security rights is also apparent in Bruges and Antwerp, Amsterdam's predecessors in commercial primacy in the Low Countries.[91] The involvement of the aldermen in Bruges and Antwerp was required for pledging a debtor's immovable and

86 Cau, *Groot placaet-boeck*, vol. 3, 1006; See *Amsterdamsche secretary*, 52; Voet, *Commentarius ad Pandectas*, vol. 1, ad D. 20,1,12, 859. See also Pos, "The Hoge Raad", 85.

87 Naeranus, *Consultatien*, vol. 3, 147, 426; Van Bijnkershoek, *Observationes tumultuariae*, vol. 2, 1485 (27 Oct. 1718). See also Pos, "The Hoge Raad", 86.

88 Van Bijnkershoek, *Observationes tumultuariae*, vol. 2, 1485 (27 Oct. 1718).

89 Van Leeuwen remarked that fiduciary transfers of ownership in order to satisfy or secure debts were known all over Holland. See: Van Leeuwen, *Het Rooms-Hollands-Regt*, 2.7.8, 109–110.

90 That does not mean, however, that an owner could always recover his assets from a possessor. For example, if a possessor had purchased the asset on a public market, the owner was required to reimburse the possessor for the purchase price. See Pos, *Hypotheek op roerend goed*, 183; De ruysscher and Kotlyar, "Local traditions v. academic law", 394.

91 Gelderblom, *Cities of Commerce*, 20–33.

movable assets.[92] The published custom of Bruges of 1619 shows that all encumbrances (including rights of pledge) and transfers of movable assets without handing over control over the movable assets had to be made before the city's aldermen and had to be registered.[93] The city of Antwerp chose a different approach by recognizing a weak non-possessory right of hypothec in movables.[94] If parties tried to encumber movables without handing over control over the movables, the creditor only had the (contractual) right to acquire control over the assets.[95] The creditor's right was not enforceable against third-party purchasers or creditors with subsequent possessory security rights.[96] It was also unenforceable if the debtor became insolvent.[97] In short, non-possessory security in movables provided little security and secured transactions were either based on possessory security rights in movables or a special right of hypothec (*hypotheek*) in immovables. Overall, both Bruges and Antwerp kept notaries at bay with regard to the creation of (non-possessory) security rights.[98]

In 1653, King Philip IV of Spain bypassed notaries in the Spanish Netherlands by harmonizing the formal requirements for the creation of non-possessory security rights in movables. All transfers or encumbrances of movables where no control had been handed over were null and void, unless a deed was made before the aldermen of the city where the transferor or debtor lived. The king noted that "collusion, abuse, fraud, and simulation" occurred on a daily

---

92 Van Bochove, Deneweth and Zuijderduijn, "Real estate and mortgage finance", 23.

93 Title 28 of the Customs of Bruges of 1619, in *Costvmen Brvgghe 1619*, 80. The custom of the Brugse Vrije (the castellany around Bruges) of 1542 required parties to announce the transfer of movables without factual delivery at the local church (*kerkgebod*). See: Art. 173 of the *Costume van de Vrije van Brugge*, Cahiers de 1542, in: L. Gilliodts-van Severen, *Coutume des Pays et Comté de Flandre, Coutume du Franc de Bruges*, Brussels, 1879, vol. 1, 726.

94 Art. 10 and 11, paragraph 2, of title 12 of part 4 of the *Compilatae* of 1608: "*Generaele verbintenissen van hem selven ende alle sijne goeden, ruerende ende onruerende, tegenwoordige ende toecommende, en geven geen recht van pantschap, noch verplichten de goeden nijet, al waeren alsucke generaele verbintenissen voor schepenen deser stadt, oft oock in den reade van Brabant verleden*". ("General obligations of the debtor and on his properties, either movable or immovable, present and future, do not yield a right of pledge, and do not bind the assets, even when such general obligations were registered before the aldermen of this city or in the Council of Brabant"). See Ph. Godding, *Le droit privé dans les Pays-Bas méridionaux du 12e au 18e siècle*, Brussels, 1987, *no.* 374; F. Stevens, *Revolutie en notariaat: Antwerpen 1794–1814*, Assen, 1994, 289.

95 Art. 31, paragraph 2 of title 12 of part 4 of the *Compilatae* 1608.

96 Art. 32, paragraph 2 of title 12 of part 4 of the *Compilatae* 1608.

97 Art. 33, paragraph 2 of title 12 of part 4 of the *Compilatae* 1608.

98 See Gelderblom, *Cities of Commerce*, 91; Van Bochove, Deneweth and Zuijderduijn, "Real estate and mortgage finance", 23.

basis because of transfers and encumbrances without control having been handed over.[99] Even though general pledges were still mentioned in notarized contracts, the mention should be regarded as a stylistic habit.[100]

4.4 Secured Transactions without the Involvement of Notaries

By the 1660s, various jurists recognized the priority of rights of hypothec that were evidenced by notarial deeds.[101] The *prior tempore* rule determined the priority between competing rights of hypothec in the same encumbered movable asset(s), regardless of whether they were evidenced by notarial deeds of hypothec or schepenkennissen.

However, notarized loans only comprised a tiny part of the overall credit market in Amsterdam.[102] Unlike in Paris,[103] Amsterdam notaries lacked an information advantage because of the city's public registration of secured debts. The above-mentioned development of the legal effects of notarial deeds of hypothec in Amsterdam also shows a reluctance by the city's aldermen to accept notarial deeds as a full-fledged alternative to *schepenkennissen*. Loenius remarked that the local custom aimed to protect merchants who did not have the time to have their debts formalized.[104] However, the aldermen's treatment of notarial deeds also suggests that the aldermen were not willing to give up their institutional hegemony regarding the creation of security rights. Many of the services provided by the notaries were in competition with those provided by the city's aldermen and secretaries.[105]

---

99 *Placcaet 's Konincx, rakende de solemniteyten gherequireert tot het vertransporteren ende oppignoreren van Catheylen, Vruchten ende andere mobiliare Goederen, vanden 29. Julij 1653*, in: *Derden placcaet-boeck van Vlaenderen*, Ghent, 1685, 428–430.

100 Stevens, *Revolutie en notariaat*, 289. See J.-B.-J. Huygens, "De generale verbintenisse die men in de contracten ordinaris stelt onder deze ofte diergelijke clausule: Verbindende tot diën alle zijne goederen, haeffelijk en erffelijke present, en toekomende, en affecteert niet" in *Notarius Belgicus*, Brussels, 1745, cap. 24, 36. See for other restrictions on notarial involvement in civil matters: Nève, *Geschiedenis van het notarisambt*, 66. Nève remarks that notaries in the Southern Low Countries sometimes lacked expertise and were regarded as second-rate officials. See Nève, *Geschiedenis van het notarisambt*, 143.

101 Van Leeuwen, *Het Rooms-Hollands-Regt*, 4.13.20, 323; Van Strijen, Nein, Dassonville, Pothoven, Kloek, Poot, and Hop in: Naeranus, *Consultatien*, vol. 5, 70, 237 (5 May 1660). Zwanenburg in: Naeranus, *Consultatien*, vol. 5, 85, 308 (15 Oct. 1625); Gall, *Regtsgeleerde decisien*, vol. 1, 5, dec. 18, 126.

102 Gelderblom, Jonker and Kool, "Direct finance", 1183.

103 Ph. Hoffman, G. Postel-Vinay and J.-L. Rosenthal, *Priceless Markets, the political economy of credit in Paris, 1660–1870*. Chicago, 2000, 117.

104 Loenius and Boel, *Decisien en observatien*, vol. 26, 221.

105 Gehlen, "Benelux. Le notariat aux Pays-Bas", 139.

The limited role of notaries in the creation of security rights can also be explained by the wide availability of pre-printed loan contracts in Amsterdam. The emergence of standardized, pre-printed forms made the involvement of notaries superfluous for many transactions.[106] Standardized forms included secured transactions where the debtor provided shares in the VOC or bonds as collateral.[107] Kole and Van Bochove remarked: "Loan forms were cheap, could be purchased in well over a hundred bookshops across the city, and were used in all segments of society and the credit market."[108] These pre-printed contracts were the result of a stamp duty introduced by the States of Holland on 13 August 1624. The *middel van't kleyne Zegel* was a tax to fund the defence against an invasion by the Spanish army.[109] The ordinance stated that all official documents (e.g. contracts, wills, court rulings) created by magistrates or notaries had to be written or printed on paper bearing the *kleyne Zegel* and signed by a local official (*Secretaris*). The rate for the stamp duty was first set at four *stuivers* for claims with a value from 200 to 600 guilders and eight *stuivers* for claims with a higher value and was raised throughout the years.[110] The ordonnance also provided that contracts and other official documents that were not written or printed on the taxed paper were inadmissible in court proceedings.[111]

Most loans were not formalized and merchants may have preferred direct, private dealings with friends, relatives and business associates.[112] Pre-printed loan contracts which were not recorded in a public register were quite common, as were bills of exchange.[113] Only when "they were unfamiliar with a particular type of contract, uncertain about its outcome, unsure about their counterparty, or when they wanted legal advice" would they have turned to notaries or the city's aldermen to have their contracts formalized, thus requiring the creation of security rights.[114] In 1620, only 52 loan contracts were

106 Van Bochove and Kole, "Uncovering Private Credit Markets", 71.

107 O. Gelderblom and J. Jonker, "Completing a Financial Revolution: The Finance of the Dutch East India Trade and the Rise of the Amsterdam Capital Market, 1595–1612", *The Journal of Economic History* 64/3 (2004), 641–672, here 659–661; Van Bochove and Kole, "Uncovering Private Credit Markets", 56–57 and 60.

108 Van Bochove and Kole, "Uncovering Private Credit Markets", 42.

109 Cau, *Groot placaet-boeck*, vol. 1, 1995–1997.

110 Ibid., vol. 1, 1995–2017. See Van Bochove and Kole, "Uncovering Private Credit Markets", 43–44.

111 Ibid., vol. 1, 1996–1997.

112 Gelderblom, Hup, and Jonker, "Public Functions, Private Markets", 183.

113 Gelderblom, Jonker and Kool, "Direct finance", 1182; Van Bochove and Kole, "Uncovering Private Credit Markets", 44.

114 Gelderblom, Hup, and Jonker, "Public Functions, Private Markets", 183.

recorded by Amsterdam notaries, compared to a total of 1,149 *schepenkennissen* and *rentebrieven*.[115] By 1660, the number of registered notarial loans had increased to 354.[116]

4.5 Explanations for the Limited Role of Notaries

Amsterdam was innovative in the sense that it may have been one of the first cities in the county of Holland or the Spanish Netherlands to recognize notarial deeds of pledge. However, by requiring the public registration of these notarial deeds the city's aldermen effectively limited the involvement of notaries in creating non-possessory security rights. This situation meant that the city's aldermen ensured their own involvement, since *schepenkennissen* put a secured creditor in a more favourable position than notarial hypothec deeds.

The position of the city's aldermen suggests that the aldermen were unwilling to give up their control over the creation of security rights. Perhaps they had their own interests at heart, since the creation of security rights generated an income and enabled tax collection. This result would not have been the first time the city's political elite passed "bylaws and regulations from which it profited".[117] The consequences of public registration of hypothec deeds for the market, however, were also favourable. The public registration of hypothec deeds prevented fraud by means of antedating. The records provided a certain date that was essential for determining the priority between competing rights of hypothec in the same encumbered asset (*prior tempore* rule). The registration and taxation of hypothec deeds also facilitated a well-considered choice in determining the most suitable security right for a transaction. Parties could either choose to have their hypothec deed registered and pay fees and tax, or opt for possessory security rights in movables (and only pay stamp duty). If a debtor only had movable assets to provide as collateral, the transaction costs (time, fees and tax) for the creation of non-possessory security rights in movables must have made it an unappealing option. Parties would probably opt for one of the possessory security rights in movables, unless the debtor absolutely needed the availability of the movables for his ordinary course of business.

---

115 Gelderblom, Jonker and Kool, "Direct finance", 1182.

116 Ibid., 1182.

117 Cl. Lesger, *The Rise of the Amsterdam Market and Information Exchange: Merchants, Commercial Expansion and Change in the Spatial Economy of the Low Countries, c. 1550–1630*, Aldershot, 2006, 174.

Loenius implied that registration of notarial hypothec deeds aimed to protect merchants who lacked the time to have their deeds formalized.[118] Merchants could still rely on possessory security rights in movables without having to have their deeds formalized or having to pay taxes. Even if they were unsecured and the debtor became insolvent, they at least knew that they had to share the proceeds of the debtor's assets with other unsecured creditors. Only a creditor who had his hypothec deed registered and had paid a tax had priority over other creditors. For many merchants, this priority probably did not outweigh the transaction costs involved, and they avoided having their deeds formalized before the aldermen or having the city's secretary look up any encumbrances.[119]

The continuing involvement of the city's aldermen in the creation of security rights is also apparent in Bruges and Antwerp, Amsterdam's predecessors in commercial primacy in the low countries.[120] In the Spanish Netherlands, notarial hypothec deeds awarded no priority at all, and the aldermen's involvement was (also) required to create (non-possessory) security rights in movables. In other words, the limited involvement of notaries in the creation of security rights is another example of institutional convergence between commercial cities.[121]

5 The Involvement of the Aldermen in Shaping the Substantive Law of Secured Credit

5.1 The Preservation of the *Prior Tempore* Rule in the Late Sixteenth Century

Amsterdam recognized the rule that hypothec rights were ranked according to their date of creation, which determined the priority between competing hypothec rights in the same encumbered asset(s). This acknowledgement meant that the first secured creditor could use the proceeds from a sale of the encumbered assets to satisfy the secured obligation before lower-ranking secured creditors. This rule is expressed in the ubiquitous legal maxim *prior tempore, potior iure* (earlier in time, stronger in right: hereinafter: the *prior*

118 Loenius and Boel, *Decisien en observatien*, vol. 26, 221.

119 Merchants also avoided legal proceedings to resolve business disputes and relied either on personal pressure, arbitration, and mediation, or took their losses. See: Gelderblom, *Cities of Commerce*, 139.

120 Gelderblom, *Cities of Commerce*, 20–33.

121 Ibid., 204.

tempore rule).[122] At first sight, it is hard to see how this rule is connected to the position of the city's aldermen, since it is matter between secured creditors. The aldermen, however, successfully tried to preserve this rule at the end of the sixteenth century.

In 1580, the States of Holland decreed that later conventional special rights of hypothec in immovables awarded priority over earlier conventional general rights of pledge.[123] This exception to the *prior tempore* rule is usually referred to as "*bijzonder gaat voor algemeen*" or "special precedes general".[124] The special right of hypothec only provided priority over general rights of hypothec with regard to immovables. The priority rule still applied to rights of hypothec regarding the distribution of the proceeds of *movables*.[125]

The main objective of the rule "special precedes general" was the protection of the debtor.[126] A debtor who created a general right of hypothec could still confer a higher-ranking security right to a subsequent creditor by creating a special right of hypothec in an immovable. This possibility enabled the debtor to negotiate more advantageous terms in a loan agreement than if he only had been able to offer a lower ranking right of pledge. The States of Holland implied that the prior creditor with a general right of hypothec had more security than necessary and would still have enough after a subsequent creditor got a higher-ranking right of hypothec in a specific immovable.

According to the burgomaster, aldermen, and council of Amsterdam. the introduction of the rule "special precedes general" led to "various disputes, legal proceedings and misunderstanding" in the city of Amsterdam.[127] They argued that the *prior tempore* rule was beneficial to trade and they successfully asked the States of Holland permission *not* to apply the rule "special precedes general" in Amsterdam.[128] The city's officials suggested that they placed the

---

122 Derived from C. 8,17,3 (Imp. Car.): "[...] *sicut prior es tempore, ita potior iure*".

123 Section 35 of the Politieke Ordonnantie van de Staten van Holland van 1580 in: De Blécourt and Japikse, *Kleint Plakkaatboek van Nederland*, 132.

124 De Groot, *Inleiding tot de Hollandsche Rechts-geleertheyd*, 2.48.34, 105 recto; Van der Keessel, *Voorlesinge oor die hedendaagse reg*, vol. 3, ad. De Groot, *Inleiding* 2.48.24, 439, and ad De Groot, *Inleiding* 2.48.34, 459; Van Leeuwen, *Het Rooms-Hollands-Regt*, 4.13.18, 322.

125 See Van Hoof, *Generale zekerheidsrechten*, § 4.6.2.

126 See Van der Keessel, *Voorlesinge oor die hedendaagse reg*, vol. 3, ad De Groot, *Inleiding* 2.48.24, 439 and ad De Groot, *Inleiding* 2.48.24, 459. In my dissertation, I discuss several other explanations for the rule. See: Van Hoof, *Generale zekerheidsrechten*, § 4.6.1.

127 "*verscheyden questien, processen ende misverstant*" ("several cases, lawsuits and confusion"), in: *Octroy* of 18 March 1594 in *Hantvesten priuilegien*, 95.

128 Placaat of 8 May 1594, in: Cau, *Groot placaet-boeck*, vol. 2, 2211. See Groenewegen van der Made, *Tractatus de legibus abrogatis*, ad C. 4,10,14,3; Van der Keessel, *Voorlesinge oor die*

interests of the prior secured creditor up front. Subsequent creditors could only get lower-ranking rights of hypothec but had access to information regarding prior rights of hypothec. Priority only ensued from rights of hypothec if the hypothec deed was registered in public registers of the town where the charged immovables were situated.[129] It enabled later creditors to make an exposure assessment and to contact creditors with prior rights of hypothec in order to negotiate the terms for a contractual change in priority.

The city's officials' request suggests they had the interests of secured creditors at heart. As noted above, registered *schepenkennisen* were, by their nature, all-encompassing and automatically awarded priority to the creditor above all other creditors with regard to the proceeds from all of a debtor's assets, immovable and movable.[130] At first glance, it would have made no difference to the aldermen whether the *prior tempore* rule or the "special precedes general" rule applied, as they would also be involved in the creation of special rights of hypothec in immovables. However, by awarding special rights of hypothec in immovables priority over earlier *schepenkennissen*, *schepenkennissen* would lose their appeal as a way to create security. A creditor whose claim was evidenced by a *schepenkennis* could not know if a general right of hypothec would offer him security in the future, if subsequent special rights of hypothec had priority over older *schepenkennissen*. In other words, the legal effects of *schepenkennissen* were well known and valued by legal practice, and the aldermen had no interest in tampering with these legal effects. Perhaps they were also afraid legal practice would try to circumvent the effects of the "special precedes general" rule. A creditor whose claim was evidenced by a *schepenkennis* could compel his debtor to specify as many of the debtor's assets as he deemed necessary, if he wanted to mitigate the risk that a subsequent special right of hypothec had priority over his general right of pledge. In other words, maintaining the status quo may have been a motive for the aldermen to preserve the *prior tempore* rule.

Amsterdam was not the only city in the Dutch Republic that tried to preserve the *prior tempore* rule. According to one of the parties in a case before the High Court of Holland and Zeeland in 1705, the rule still applied in determining the priority between a general right of hypothec and a special right of

---

hedendaagse reg, vol. 3, ad De Groot, *Inleiding* 2.48.24, 439, ad De Groot, *Inleiding* 2.48.38, 467, and ad De Groot, *Inleiding* 2.48.40, 469–471; Van Leeuwen, *Het Rooms-Hollands-Regt*, 4.13.18, 322.

129 Art. 37 of the *Politieke Ordonnantie van de Staten van Holland* (1580) in: De Blécourt and Japikse, *Kleint Plakkaatboek van Nederland*, 132.

130 See Van Waesberge and Schouten, *Handvesten*, vol. 2, 530.

hypothec in immovables in Zierikzee.[131] In Zutphen, the *prior tempore* rule applied, since subsequent creditors were able to consult the public records to establish previous encumbrances.[132] The *prior tempore* rule also applied in Friesland.[133] In the Spanish Netherlands (and the north of France, the so-called *pays de nantissement*), however, the rule "special precedes general" was often applied.[134] The Belgian jurist Patou wrote that the city of Lille refrained from applying the rule "special precedes general" in order to prevent debtors from creating all-encompassing security by means of special security.[135] Without actual obstacles, a creditor could insist on his debtor's specifying as much collateral as the creditor deemed necessary. By doing so, the debtor lost the opportunity to confer a higher-ranking right of hypothec in specific property to subsequent creditors.

5.2 The Right to Trace Encumbered Immovable Assets in the Hands of Third Parties

Rights of hypothec were a limited property right in the debtor's immovable assets (*ius in re aliena*), as the debtor had ownership of the assets which was encumbered by the right of pledge. By creating a right of hypothec, the debtor no longer had the power to transfer unencumbered ownership, which meant that the assets remained encumbered when the debtor transferred the assets to a third party. The secured creditor could recover hypothecated immovable assets which were transferred to a third party, if the debtor defaulted on the secured claim.[136]

---

131 Van Bijnkershoek, *Observationes tumultuariae*, vol. 1, 77 (3 March 1705). Unfortunately, the High Court did not comment on this statement and ruled that first the question of whether the proceeds were sufficient to satisfy all creditors had to be answered.

132 J. Schomaker, *Selecta Consilia et Responsa Juris*, Zutphen, 1765, vol. 3, 73–75 (cons. 7, nos. 53–62).

133 U. Huber, *Heedendaegse rechtsgeleertheyt.* Soo elders, als in Frieslandt gebruikelyk, vol. 2, Leeuwarden, 1686, 391 (L, no. 10.

134 Godding, *Le droit privé*, no. 374. For France: P. Ourliac and J. De Malafosse, *Droit romain et ancien droit, les obligations*, Paris, 1957, 338, 351–352; P.-Cl. Timbal, *Les obligations contractuelles d'après la jurisprudence du parlement (XIIIe–XIVe siècles)*, vol. 2, Paris, 1977, 502.

135 F. Patou, *Commentaire sur les coutumes de la ville de Lille et de sa châtellenie, et conférences de ces coutumes avec celles voisines et le droit commun*, vol. 2, Lille, 1788, 187 (gl. 5 ad ch. 8, art. 1).

136 See De Groot, *Inleiding tot de Hollandsche Rechts-geleertheyd*, 2.48.40; Groenewegen van der Made, *Tractatus de legibus abrogatis*, ad C. 4,10,14,3; Voet, *Commentarius ad Pandectas*, vol. 1, ad D. 20,1,14, 861.

The right to follow (or trace) encumbered assets in the hands of third parties deviated from the law of secured credit in the rest of Holland. In the rest of Holland, the right to pursue ended when the debtor transferred generally hypothecated immovables for value (*om baat*).[137] The right to follow endured if the asset was transferred without compensation. A special right of hypothec in immovables awarded the right to pursue in either situation.[138] The absence of the right to follow generally charged assets was foremost aimed at protecting third-party purchasers. Various different scholars, including Voet and Grotius, argued that someone who paid a purchase price for an asset should not be confronted by a seller's creditor whose claim was secured with a general right of pledge.[139] The purchaser was protected because he provided a purchase price that replaced the transferred immovable asset.[140] The seller could use the purchase price to satisfy his creditors. A third party who did not pay for the acquisition was not protected against secured creditors because he was enriched at the expense of the (secured) creditors.[141]

In 1594, Amsterdam's officials requested the permission of the States of Holland to deviate from the above-mentioned *Politieke Ordonnantie* of 1580.[142] The States provided that "charges and other deeds made in the presence of the city's aldermen will, from now on, have complete effect over all goods located within the city's jurisdiction belonging to the creator (debtor) at the time of the creation or the charge and over those (goods) that he were to acquire afterwards, so that those who have a charge, either general or special, will always have priority."[143] Groenewegen van der Made remarked that this

---

137 De Groot, *Inleiding tot de Hollandsche Rechts-geleertheyd*, 2.48.24; Gall, *Regtsgeleerde decisien*, I,5, dec. 19, 126–127; Groenewegen van der Made, *Tractatus de legibus abrogatis*, ad C. 4,10,14,2; Naeranus, *Consultatien*, vol. 4, 319, 578 (6 July 1656); Van Leeuwen, *Het Rooms-Hollands-Regt*, 4.13.19, 322–323; Van Bijnkershoek, *Observationes tumultuariae*, vol. 2, 1276 (28 Sept. 1716); Van der Keessel, *Voorlesinge oor die hedendaagse reg*, vol. 3, ad De Groot, *Inleiding* 2.48.24, 439, and ad De Groot, *Inleiding* 2.28.32, 455; Voet, *Commentarius ad Pandectas*, vol. 1, ad D. 20,1,14, 861.

138 See Van der Keessel, *Voorlesinge oor die hedendaagse reg*, vol. 3, ad De Groot, *Inleiding* 2.28.32, 454; Voet, *Commentarius ad Pandectas*, vol. 1, ad D. 20,1,13, 860.

139 De Groot, *Inleiding tot de Hollandsche Rechts-geleertheyd*, 2.48.24, 104v; Groenewegen van der Made, *Tractatus de legibus abrogatis*, ad C. 4,10,14,2; Van Assendelft in Naeranus, *Consultatien*, vol. 4, 319, 578 (6 July 1656); Voet, *Commentarius ad Pandectas*, vol. 1, ad D. 20,1,1, 854.

140 Voet, *Commentarius ad Pandectas*, vol. 1, ad D. 20,1,14, 861.

141 Ibid., 861.

142 *Octroy* of 18 March 1594, in *Hantvesten priuilegien*, 95 and Placaat of 8 May 1594, Cau, *Groot placaet-boeck*, vol. 2, 2211.

143 "[...] *verbande ende andere acten voor ofte by Schepenen der voorsz. Stede ghepasseert, voortaen volcomen effect sorteren sal over alle de goederen onder de Jurisdictie der selver*

meant that a general right of hypothec still encumbered immovable assets which were transferred to a third party for value.[144] Van Bijnkershoek later stated: "I believe that the people of Amsterdam, who wanted that special rights of hypothec be awarded no priority over general (rights of pledge), have returned to Roman law, since in precisely that law the general right of charged was not nullified by a transfer".[145]

Amsterdam may have been an exception within the county of Holland but not within the Dutch Republic. In cities such as Utrecht,[146] Middelburg[147] and 's-Hertogenbosch[148] a general right of hypothec also awarded the right to follow encumbered assets in the hands of third parties. In Paris, every notarial hypothec deed entailed a general right of hypothec in the debtor's immovable assets, and encumbered assets could be traced in the hands of third parties.[149]

At the beginning of the eighteenth century, there was some scepticism as to Amsterdam's deviation from the rest of Holland. One of Van Bijnkershoek's fellow justices remarked that "the consequences would be great, if assets, even immovables, that he once encumbered by means of a deed in the presence of

---

gheleghen toebehoorenede den constituanten ten tijde vanden constitutie ofte verbande ende die hy naemaels vercrijghen mochte sulcx dat inde selve goederen altijdts ghegpreferеert sullen zijn die ghene die onder recht van verbant t'sy generael ofte speciael sal hebben vercreghen." *Octroy* of 18 March 1594, in *Hantvesten priuilegien*, 95 and Placaat of 8 May 1594, Cau, *Groot placaet-boeck*, vol. 2, 2211.

144 Groenewegen van der Made, *Tractatus de legibus abrogatis*, ad C. 4,10,14,3.

145 Van Bijnkershoek, *Observationes tumultuariae*, vol. 2, 1879 (16 Oct. 1722): "*Ego putem, Amsterdammenses, qui voluerunt speciales hypothecas non plus valere quam generales, ad jus Romanum recurisse, eo autem jure generalis hypotheca alienatione non solvitur* [...]".

146 Voet, *Commentarius ad Pandectas*, vol.1, ad D. 20,1,14, 861.

147 Art. 12 van de Costumen van Middelburg, in: Cau, *Groot placaet-boeck*, vol. 4, 1015. "*In sulcken manieren, dat hebbende soodanige generale hypothecque van ouder date, wordt geprefereert op alle de goeden van den debiteur, die hij ten tijde van de constitutie gehadt, en namaels verkregen heeft, alwaer 't oock sulcks dat deselve goederen, of eenige van dien naderhandt specialijck gehypothequeert en verbonden ware, of oock veralieneert aen particuliere of universele successeurs.*" ("In such ways, that a general hypothec of older date receives priority over all assets of the debtor which he had at the time of the hypothec's constitution, as well as those received later, even if these assets, or some of them afterwards, were burdened with a special hypothec, or were transferred onto special or universal heirs").

148 J.-B. Christyn, *Brabandts Recht dat is generale costumen vanden lande ende hertoghdomme van Brabandt*, Antwerp, 1682, vol. 2, 895.

149 On the right to follow, see: art. 164 en 165 of the *Coutumes de Paris*. See also Ourliac and De Malafosse, *Droit romain*, 340, 354; Timbal, *Les obligations contractuelles*, vol. 2, 472: "*Cette évolution était inévitable et on peut penser que l'insertion dans les contrats d'une clause d' «obligation spéciale de tous les biens» a constitué un important jalon.*"

aldermen, would be encumbered forever, and that he could invoke the right *in rem* against purchasers and other third parties".[150] The *Amsterdamsche Secretary* called the exception "a bit dark and dubious".[151] Willem Pauw (1712–1787), president of the Dutch High Court, questioned the validity of the Amsterdam exception. According to Pauw, said permission only allowed Amsterdam to deviate from the rule "special precedes general". Despite the fact that Pauw expressed a minority view, he believed that neither the city of Amsterdam requested permission to award the right to follow encumbered assets in the hands of third parties, nor did the States grant permission to do so.[152]

As with the application of the *prior tempore* rule, the right to follow encumbered assets in the hands of third parties had benefits for the city's aldermen. On the one hand, it made *schepenkennissen* a very appealing instrument to create maxim security in immovable assets since a secured creditor knew he could take recourse against all of the debtor's immovable assets, regardless of whether the assets were subsequently transferred (or hypothecated to a different creditor). On the other hand, the right to follow encumbered assets in the hands of third parties also provided the aldermen with the opportunity to offer their extensive services to potential purchasers of immovables. The aldermen were willing to help purchasers – for a fee – to acquire immovable assets without any encumbrances.

5.3 The Involvement of the Aldermen in Terminating Rights of Pledge

A purchaser of an immovable was exposed to the seller's secured creditors, because they could recover the sold immovable from the purchaser for the seller's debts. The purchaser could request the secured creditors to waive

150 Van Bijnkershoek, *Observationes tumultuariae*, vol. 2, 1879 (16 Oct. 1722): "'*magnae* [...] *fore consequentiae, si bona, etiam immobilia, ejus, qui semel apud scabinos instrumentum confecisset, semper manerent obligata, et jure in re agi posset adversus emptores, et quosvis tertios possessores*".

151 *Amsterdamsche secretary*, 7: "*wat duyster en twyffelachtig*".

152 Pauw, *Observationes tumultuariae novae*, vol. 2, 574 (29 Jan. 1756): "*Ut vero in tantum apud se valeret pignus generale, ut aeque ac speciale, alienatum licet, oneri subnoxium maneret, nec petierant Amsterdamenses nec privilegio isto largiti sunt Ordines; neque adeo video, qui ex speciali ista concessione possit effici in omnibus et per omnia in hoc argumento ad jus Romanum recurrisse Amsterdamenses* [...]." ("In order that the general pledge might be valid with them to such an extent that the general pledge, though alienated, should remain subject to the burden, neither did the people of Amsterdam ask for it, nor were the Orders bestowed with this privilege; nor do I see that it is possible, from this special concession, that the people of Amsterdam resorted to the Roman law in all and through all things on this subject.")

their rights of pledge. The purchaser would have needed to consult the public records to determine whether any of the previous owners of the immovable asset had ever encumbered the asset. Even if he could retrace all encumbrances, the secured creditors may have been unwilling to waive their security rights.

The Court of Holland (*Hof van Holland*) and Amsterdam's aldermen provided protection to purchasers by drawing inspiration from the way in which immovable assets were sold and transferred in execution proceedings. If a creditor enforced his claim by means of a forced public sale other interested parties were invited. The court would then award ownership of the immovable to the highest bidder by means of unvoluntary decree (*onwillig decreet*). The purchaser was certain of his acquisition and could "not be confronted by someone claiming to have any encumbrances, charges or rights of pledge, other than those that were mentioned and specified in the decree."[153] In other words, the immovable asset was cleared of unreported encumbrances, and the purchase price was distributed between the secured creditors according to their rank.[154]

The Court of Holland (*Hof van Holland*) and Amsterdam's aldermen adopted this way of terminating rights of hypothec in non-contentious situations.[155] Firstly, all interested parties, such as secured creditors, were invited. If no secured creditors appeared, the aldermen would clear the immovable asset of all real encumbrances ("*van alle zakelijke lasten*").[156] A secured creditor who wanted to preserve his right of hypothec could oppose the unencumbered transfer. In that case, ownership would transfer with the said encumbrance ("*met de genoemde lasten*").[157] The aldermen would deliver the asset by

153 Ph. Wielant, *Practyke civile*, Rotterdam, 1642, X,VI,3: "*van zijnen coope ende en mach van dan voor(r/s)t niemant hem yet heesschen van eenigen lasten, verbande oft hypotheken dan vanden genen die int decreet gestelt ende gespecificeert staen*".

154 Wielant, *Practycke civile*, X,VII,4.

155 Van Leeuwen, *Het Rooms-Hollands-Regt*, 4.18.5, 340; J.W. Verburgt, *Levering van onroerende zaken te Leiden*, Leiden, 1930, 78; W. Van Iterson, *Willig decreet in Holland en Utrecht*, Haarlem, 1939, 17; E. Ketelaar, "Jan van Houts "Registratuer"" in C. van de Kieft e.a. (eds.), *Scrinium et scriptura: Opstellen betreffende de Nederlandse geschiedenis aangeboden aan professor dr. J.L. van der Gouw bij zijn afscheid als buitengewoon hoogleraar in de archiefwetenschappen en in de paleografie van de veertiende tot de zeventiende eeuw aan de Universiteit van Amsterdam*, Groningen, 1980, 400–412. See for a more detailed illustration of this procedure: M.-C. Le Bailly, *Hof van Holland, Zeeland en West-Friesland: de hoofdlijnen van het procederen in civiele zaken voor het Hof van Holland, Zeeland en West-Friesland zowel in eerste instantie als in hoger beroep*. Hilversum, 2008, 112.

156 Van Iterson, *Willig decreet in Holland*, 21; Verburgt, *Levering onroerende zaken Leiden*, 79.

157 Verburgt, *Levering onroerende zaken Leiden*, 104.

means of voluntary decree ("*willig decreet*").[158] This procedure was described in Leiden as follows:

> At the proposed day the aldermen, if no intervention has been made, decree the measure of "decreeing, entitling and securing" the buyer in what was bought and "expropriating, disinheriting and divesting" the seller from what was bought, and imposing upon everyone an eternal silence of their right to the sold plot of land, except for right of preference on the promised buying price.[159]

A secured creditor who had not come forward lost his right on the asset but could still have recourse against the purchase price. This condition meant, however, that the secured creditor was subject to the debtor's behaviour. The secured creditor could end up empty-handed if his debtor spent the proceeds or used them to satisfy other (unsecured) creditors. That is why the debtor had to keep the proceeds available to secured creditors. In 1608, the aldermen of Amsterdam obtained the States' permission to require the debtor to provide sufficient security ("*suffisante cautie*") in the presence of the city's aldermen by means of two guarantors for when a secured creditor came forward afterwards.[160]

The transfer by means of voluntary decree was not unique to Amsterdam or Holland. Voluntary decrees were also used in the kingdom of France and the Spanish Netherlands.[161] In Paris, every notarial hypothec deed entailed a general right of hypothec in the debtor's immovable assets, and encumbered

158 Van Leeuwen, *Het Rooms-Hollands-Regt*, 4.18.5, 340.

159 Verburgt, *Levering onroerende zaken Leiden*, 101: "*Ten voorgestelden dage zullen schepenen, als er geen verhindering is voorgekomen, het decreet interponeeren, den kooper in het verkochte 'decreteren, erven ende vestigen', den verkooper en alle anderen daarvan 'onteigenen, onterven ende ontvestigen' en een ieder een eeuwig zwijgen van zijn recht op het verkochte perceel opleggen, behoudens een ieder zijn recht van preferentie op de beloofde koopppeningen.*"

160 Cau, *Groot placaet-boeck*, vol. 2, 3006; Naeranus, *Consultatien*, vol. 6, 21, 39 (3 Dec. 1623): "*penningen weder te brengen ter Secretarye aldaer, omme tusschen hen ende de geenen die tot wat tyde dat het zy pretendeert daer op beter recht, 't zy van voorganck of ander te hebben, opte preferentie van dien bij schepenen voorfz. ghedisponeert te worden* [...]." ("to bring the coins to the Secretary, in order to distribute them and those that will pretend at any time a better right, either of priority or otherwise, on the priority of which will be decided by the aldermen [...]"; Voet, *Commentarius ad Pandectas*, vol. 2, ad D. 42,5,2, 829; Van der Keessel, *Voorlesinge oor die hedendaagse reg*, vol. 3, ad De Groot, *Inleiding* 2.48.38, 467–9.

161 For France: Fr. Bourjon, *Le droit commun de la France, et la coutume de Paris réduits en principes*, Paris, 1775, II,6,3,2,XVII, 546; Ph. Merlin, *Répertoire universel et raisonné de jurisprudence*, Brussels, 1826, vol. 13, 462; Ourliac and De Malafosse, *Droit romain*, 340,

assets in the hands of third parties could be followed. Bourjon remarked: "A voluntary decree is a fiction that produces the same effect as the reality of a forced decree: it was introduced for the protection of commerce and protects the acquirer against the rights of hypothec on account of his seller […]."[162]

The Amsterdam aldermen's involvement in preserving a secured creditor's right to follow encumbered assets, the way in which to terminate rights of pledge, and the requirement to provide security for the proceeds of the sale clearly show that the aldermen tried to balance the interests of secured creditors, the debtor, and purchasers of immovables. At the same time, the aldermen also ensured their ongoing (fee-based) involvement in and control over these matters.

6 Conclusion

In several different ways, the city of Amsterdam was conservative in its approach to the law of secured credit compared to other cities in Holland. Not only was the city reluctant to accept notarial deeds of hypothec or to levy taxes on the creation of general rights of hypothec, but it also maintained the *prior tempore* rule and the right to follow generally hypothecated immovables in the hands of third parties.

Even when the Amsterdam aldermen eventually recognized notarial deeds of hypothec, they effectively limited the involvement of notaries in the creation of non-possessory security rights. By subjecting the notarial hypothec deeds (or fiduciary transfers) to registration, the city's aldermen ensured their own involvement in the creation of security rights. This way, notarial deeds of hypothec did not put a secured creditor in a more favourable position than *schepenkennissen*. Notarial deeds only encumbered movable assets, whereas *schepenkennissen* covered all of a debtor's assets.

354; Timbal, *Les obligations contractuelles*, vol. 2, 197. For the Spanish Netherlands: Godding, *Le droit privé*, no. 390.

162 Bourjon, *Le droit commun France*, II,8,8,1,I, 748: "*Le décret volontaire est une fiction qui produit le même effet que la réalité d'un décret forcé; elle a été introduite pour la sûreté du commerce, & mettre un acquéreur à couvert des hypotheques du chef de son vendeur* […]". According to Loyseau, however, the procedure of the voluntary decree was far from perfect, as it took a lot of time and money, invaded the privacy of the seller, and barred the secured creditors from taking recourse against the proceeds until the procedure was finished. See Ch. Loyseau, *Traicté du deguerpissement deguerpissement et delaissement par hypotheque*, Paris, 1606, 3.1.19, 57r.

The continuing involvement of the city's aldermen in the creation of security rights also occurred in Bruges and Antwerp, Amsterdam's predecessors in commercial primacy in the Low Countries.[163] In the Spanish Netherlands, notarial hypothec deeds awarded no priority at all, and the aldermen's involvement was (also) required to create (non-possessory) security rights in movables.

Perhaps the city's aldermen had their own interests at heart, since the creation of security rights generated an income and enabled tax collection. The consequences for the market, however, were also favourable. The public registration of hypothec deeds prevented fraud by means of antedating. The records provided a certain date that was essential for determining the priority between competing rights of hypothec in the same encumbered asset (*prior tempore*-rule). The registration and taxation of hypothec deeds also facilitated a well-considered choice in determining the most suitable security right for a transaction. Parties could either choose to have their hypothec deed registered and pay fees and tax, or opt for possessory security rights in movables (and only pay stamp duty).

Amsterdam's eminence as the primary commercial hub within the Dutch Republic in the seventeenth century may have enabled its aldermen to shape the law of secured credit in a way they deemed fit, sometimes by diverging from legal norms observed in other cities within the county. In Amsterdam, a secured creditor could recover generally hypothecated immovable assets which were transferred to a third party if the debtor defaulted on the secured claim. This process was in accordance with other cities such as Paris and Utrecht, but it deviated from other cities in Holland where the right to follow (or trace) encumbered assets in the hands of third parties ended when the debtor transferred generally hypothecated immovables for value (*om baat*).

The Amsterdam aldermen's involvement in preserving a secured creditors' right to follow encumbered assets shows how the aldermen tried to balance the interests of secured creditors, the debtor and purchasers of immovables. At the same time, the aldermen also ensured their ongoing (fee-based) involvement in and control over these matters, since the right to follow encumbered assets in the hands of third parties had benefits for the city's aldermen. On the one hand, it made *schepenkennissen* a very appealing instrument to create maxim security in immovable assets, since a secured creditor knew he could take recourse against all of the debtor's immovable assets, regardless of whether the assets were subsequently transferred (or hypothecated to a different

163 Gelderblom, *Cities of Commerce*, 20–33.

creditor). On the other hand, the right to follow encumbered assets in the hands of third parties also provided the aldermen with the opportunity to offer their extensive services to potential purchasers of immovables. The aldermen were willing to help purchasers – for a fee – to acquire immovable assets without any encumbrances.

CHAPTER 8

Regulating Religious Diversity: Amsterdam's Legal Regulations for Jews (1616)

Marc de Wilde

1 Introduction

On 8 November 1616, the burgomasters of Amsterdam issued a set of legal regulations (a *keur* or *willekeur*) for Jews residing in the city.[1] The regulations of 1616 were the first official document to recognize the presence of a "*Joodsche Natie*" (Jewish Nation) in Amsterdam and to determine its legal status.[2] The regulations were meant to be provisional until the States-Provincial of Holland and West-Friesland enacted a provincial statute for the Jews. However, in 1619, amidst religious turmoil, the States decided to leave the issue to the municipalities; hence, the Amsterdam regulations became a permanent law that remained on the books until the emancipation of the Jews in 1795. As its preamble suggested, complaints about Jewish men having sexual relations with Christian women had led the burgomasters to adopt the regulations. The Jews were thus warned "not to have any carnal relations, whether in or out of wedlock, with Christian women or girls, not even those of ill repute."[3] In addition, they were instructed not to speak or to write anything that tended to the disparagement of the Christian religion, nor to seduce any Christian person away from the Christian religion or to circumcise one. In mentioning restrictions only, the Amsterdam regulations differed from the Jewish charters of other Dutch cities, such as Alkmaar, Haarlem and Rotterdam, as well as from the proposal for a provincial statute drafted by Hugo Grotius. More specifically, the Amsterdam regulations did not mention any religious rights for

1 *Keur* of 8 Nov. 1616, Municipal Archives Amsterdam, *Archief van de burgemeesters, privilegeboeken en keurboeken* (inv. 5020), 12 (*Willekeuren*), boek J (I), fol. 107r-108r. The *keur* was published in H. Noordkerk, *Handvesten, ofte Privilegien ende Octroyen, mitsgaders Willekeuren, Costumen, Ordonnantien en Handelingen der Stad Amstelredam*, Amsterdam, 1748, vol. 2, 472.

2 This chapter analyzes developments until 1619; the subsequent history of the Jewish nation(s) in Amsterdam is detailed in the next chapter, by Bart Wallet.

3 *Keur* of 8 Nov. 1616, fol. 107v (also in Noordkerk, *Handvesten*, vol. 2, 472).

the Jews, and, in sharp contrast to the charters of Haarlem and Rotterdam, prohibited the construction of a public synagogue.

However, in spite of their negative tone, the Amsterdam regulations do not seem to have prevented the growth and prosperity of the city's Jewish community. As Rena Fuks-Mansfeld has pointed out, the lack of a more extensive Jewish charter was favourable for the Jews, as it left important aspects of their social and economic life unregulated.[4] Arend Huussen explains that, in spite of their focus on restrictions, the Amsterdam regulations implied that the Jews would "in fact be tolerated", as no mention was made of any intention to limit their numbers.[5] In a similar vein, Miriam Bodian observes that the regulations testified to a lack of interest in controlling the Jewish population, which was "unknown in contemporary Europe, where the trend was, if anything, toward stricter regulation."[6] Moreover, as Daniel Swetschinski notes, the Amsterdam regulations were rarely enforced in practice, and both the use of (private) synagogues and sexual relations between Jews and Christians were generally tolerated.[7] This contribution seeks to analyze and evaluate the significance of the Amsterdam regulations. It addresses three questions: first, how did these regulations relate to existing legal documents, such as the Jewish charters of Alkmaar, Haarlem and Rotterdam, as well as to the proposal for a provincial statute that had been drafted by Grotius? Second, how can it be explained that the regulations were rarely enforced in practice? What does this tell us about their function and significance? And, third, to what extent did the Amsterdam regulations contribute to, or prevent, the acceptance of Jews among the Christian population?

2 Regulating Jewish Settlement in the Dutch Cities

In the early 1590s, Sephardi Jews from Spain and Portugal started to settle in Amsterdam.[8] They included many "new Christians", whose families had been

4 R. Fuks-Mansfeld, *De Sefardim in Amsterdam tot 1795: Aspecten van een joodse minderheid in een Hollandse Stad*, Hilversum, 1989, 57–58.

5 A. Huussen, "Legislation on the Position of the Jews in the Dutch Republic, c. 1590–1796", *Tijdschrift voor Rechtsgeschiedenis* 69 (2001), 43–56, at 49.

6 M. Bodian, *Hebrews of the Portuguese Nation: Conversos and Community in Early Modern Amsterdam*. Bloomington, 1997, 61.

7 D. Swetschinski, *Reluctant Cosmopolitans: The Portuguese Jews of Seventeenth-Century Amsterdam*, London, 2000, 12 and 14.

8 E. Koen, "The Earliest Sources Relating to the Portuguese Jews in the Municipal Archives of Amsterdam up to 1620", *Studia Rosenthaliana* 4/1 (1970), 25–42, at 39.

forced to convert to Christianity generations ago, but who had maintained the stigma of being Jewish.[9] When the Portuguese Inquisition was established in 1536, it focused on interrogating these new Christians, who were suspected of adhering to their ancestral belief in secret.[10] Many of them took refuge in the Southern Netherlands, in particular in Antwerp, which was part of the Habsburg empire.[11] However, Emperor Charles V and his governor in the Low Countries, Mary of Burgundy, regarded the new Christians as enemies of the Catholic faith. In the 1540s and 1550s, they issued a series of edicts revoking the privileges that had been granted to the new Christians and commanding them to leave the Low Countries.[12] These edicts led to new persecutions: the records of those investigated for heresy in Antwerp include many new Christians and Jews as both alleged and convicted persons.[13] When the Dutch provinces started to revolt against Spain in the late 1560s, many of them emigrated to other cities, including Frankfurt, Emden, Bremen, Cologne and London. The Spanish conquest of Antwerp in 1585 and the subsequent sea blockade by Dutch rebels ended the city's economic predominance: although a small Portuguese community remained in Antwerp, it had lost much of its previous importance.[14]

After the fall of Antwerp, the Dutch States General (representing the seven Northern provinces that had declared themselves independent from Spain in 1581), actively encouraged the Portuguese merchants to settle in the Dutch cities. In 1588, and again in 1592, they granted the request of the Portuguese merchants for a *sauvegarde*, allowing them to freely enter and leave the Dutch territories with their families, servants and possessions (on the condition that they did not maintain any correspondence with the king of Spain or other enemies of the Dutch Republic). However, they also instructed the burgomasters of the cities, where the Portuguese intended to settle, to keep them

9 Fuks-Mansfeld, *Sefardim*, 22–23, 26; Swetschinski, *Reluctant Cosmopolitans*, 4.

10 Swetschinski, *Reluctant Cosmopolitans*, 4. Although the jurisdiction of the Church was limited to those who were baptized, the new Christians, who had been forcibly baptized, fell under its jurisdiction.

11 As early as 1488, there had been a small colony of Portuguese merchants in Antwerp, which included several new Christians. In 1526, the Portuguese King John III had given a laissez-passer to New Christians who wanted to settle in Antwerp. Fuks-Mansfeld, *Sefardim*, 21.

12 Sixteenth-century copies of these edicts can be found in the the Ets Haim library of the Portuguese Synagogue in Amsterdam: Imperial edicts against the new Christians of 1549 and 1550, Ets Haim, MS EH 48 A 05, fol. 38r–41r and 46r–48r. On these edicts see also: Huussen, "Legislation", 48.

13 Huussen, "Legislation", 46.

14 Fuks-Mansfeld, *Sefardim*, 22.

under close supervision and prevent them from disturbing the public peace.[15] Initially, the States General's attempt to promote Portuguese settlement in the Dutch Republic remained without effect, with the exception of small groups of Portuguese merchants who settled in the cities of Zeeland.[16] However, around 1592, the first Portuguese merchants started to arrive and settle in Amsterdam. They were apparently attracted by the economic opportunities Amsterdam had to offer, as it had come to replace Antwerp as the main centre of colonial trade in Northern Europe. Also, the Portuguese merchants may have been attracted by the city's religious diversity and relatively tolerant climate. Although Amsterdam had officially become a Protestant city in 1578, its burgomasters conducted a policy of toleration in accordance with the Union of Utrecht.[17] Religious minorities, including Catholics, were thus allowed to exercise their religion, provided that they did not do so publicly, but in *schuilkerken*, clandestine churches that could not be seen from the street.[18]

On 31 March 1596, Emanuel Rodrigues Vega, an importer of sugar and spices born in Antwerp, became the first Portuguese *poorter* (citizen) of Amsterdam.[19] Soon other Portuguese merchants followed his example and requested to buy the *poorterrecht* (municipal citizenship). In response the burgomasters adopted a resolution on 4 September 1598 prescribing that "the Portuguese merchants living in this city and requesting to buy the *poorterrecht* shall be told that the Burgomasters (trusting that they are Christians and that they will live here as good burghers) are willing to grant them citizenship, but that they shall be admonished before taking the oath that no other exercise of religion will be allowed here in the city than the one that is publicly exercised here in the churches."[20] Apparently, the burgomasters were willing to accept at face value the claim of the Portuguese merchants that they were (new) Christians.

---

15 States General, resolutions of 11 Febr. 1588 and 30 July 1592, in N. Japikse (ed.), *Resolutiën der Staten-Generaal*, vol. 6 (1588), 276–277 and vol. 7 (1592), 722. See also Huusen, "Legislation", 47; Fuks-Mansfeld, *Sefardim*, 37; I. Prins, *De vestiging der Marranen in Noord-Nederland in de zestiende eeuw*, Amsterdam, 1927, 87.

16 Bodian, *Hebrews*, 28.

17 Art. 13 of the Union of Utrecht prescribed that "every private person shall be allowed to remain free in his religion and no one shall be seized or examined because of his religion."

18 On the *schuilkerken*, see, for example, B. Kaplan, *Divided by Faith: Religious Conflict and the Practice of Toleration in Early Modern Europe*, Cambridge (MA), 2007, 178–183.

19 Fuks-Mansfeld, *Sefardim*, 39; Bodian, *Hebrews*, 28; Swetschinski, *Reluctant Cosmopolitans*, 10; Prins, *Vestiging*, 162, 176 and following; J. Zwarts, *De eerste rabbijnen en synagogen van Amsterdam, naar archivalische bronnen*, Amsterdam, 1929, 7.

20 H. Bontemantel, *Civiele en judicieele aanteekeningen*. Municipal Archives Amsterdam, Manuscripts (inv. 5059), 35, vol. 4, fol. 88r. Quoted by Fuks-Mansfeld, *Sefardim*, 39–40.

They would thus be granted the *poorterrecht* on the condition that they were Christians who lived an honest life as good burghers. Moreover, in the second part of the resolution, the burgomasters implicitly distinguished between public and private exercise of religion, restricting the former (in the sense that only the Protestant religion could be publicly practised in churches), but allowing the latter (in the sense that private worship of religious minorities would not be interfered with).[21] As Fuks-Mansfeld suggests, the reference to publicly exercised religion was probably added to prevent protest from the Reformed Church Council. However, it did not prevent the Portuguese from practising their religion in private.[22]

The fact that the Portuguese were not allowed to practise their religion in public led them to explore possibilities for settling in other cities. By negotiating with the magistrates of Alkmaar in 1604, Haarlem in 1605 and Rotterdam in 1610, they succeeded in obtaining more favourable settlement conditions.[23] In Alkmaar, they obtained the freedom of (private) worship, but not the right to a (public) synagogue.[24] However, in Haarlem, their request for a synagogue was granted. Initially, the city council had denied their request, as it feared offending the Catholic population, which was forced to worship in clandestine churches. However, after the Portuguese merchants had made it clear that they did not intend to leave Amsterdam without the right to a synagogue, the council granted their request.[25] In the Haarlem charter, the Portuguese were instructed not to insult Christ or the Christian religion, and they were not allowed to marry or have "carnal" relations with Christians. Moreover, the right to a synagogue was made dependent on the condition that at least 50 families would settle in Haarlem.[26] Offering even more favourable settlement

21 Swetschinski, *Reluctant Cosmopolitans*, 11.

22 Fuks-Mansfeld, *Sefardim*, 40.

23 For a more extensive analysis of the Jewish charters of these cities, see A. Huussen, "The Legal Position of Sephardi Jews in Holland, *circa* 1600" in J. Michman (ed.), *Dutch Jewish History*, vol. 3, Assen, 1993, 19–41, here 22–26, and M. de Wilde, "Offering Hospitality to Strangers: Hugo Grotius's Draft Regulations for the Jews", *Tijdschrift voor rechtsgeschiedenis* 85 (2017), 391–433, at 400–406.

24 For the text of the Alkmaar Charter, see Huussen, "Legal Position", 22.

25 The relevant resolutions of the council, as well as the report of secretary Michiel van Woerden describing the negotiations, have been published in A. Huussen, "De toelating van Sefardische joden in Haarlem in 1605", *Haerlem Jaarboek* 1991, 48–62, at 55–62.

26 Resolution of the City Council of Haarlem, 14 May 1605, Provincial Archive North-Holland, City Administration Record Haarlem 1573–1813, Resolutions of the City Council 1602–1609, inv. 3993, 325, fol. 162v-166r (Dutch text) and fol. 166v-169v (French text). Transcriptions of the Dutch text can be found in M. Wolff, *De geschiedenis der joden te Haarlem, 1600–1815*, Haarlem, 1917, 57–63; and in De Groot, *Remonstrantie nopende de ordre dije in de landen van Hollandt ende Westvrieslandt dijent gestelt op de joden*,

conditions, the magistrates of Rotterdam granted the Portuguese request for a public synagogue on the condition that at least 30 families settled in the city and they did not attempt to convert Christians.[27] In addition, the Portuguese obtained the right to elect "two or more consuls" to govern their internal affairs and to decide civil and religious disputes. They were also allowed the same economic freedoms as other inhabitants, and they were exempted from particular taxes. As the Rotterdam magistrates frankly admitted, they had offered these extensive privileges to the Jews "to promote traffic and trade in the city."[28] However, on 14 September 1612, the Rotterdam charter was terminated, because less than 30 families had moved to the city.[29]

The charters of Alkmaar, Haarlem and Rotterdam were relatively favourable for the Jews, because they had been made at the request of the Portuguese merchants themselves. Rather than being unilaterally imposed, they were the result of negotiations between the city magistrates and representatives of the Portuguese community.[30] The charters show how strong the negotiating position of the Portuguese was, as the magistrates proved keen on attracting these prosperous merchants with their valuable trading contacts. The Haarlem magistrates thus decided to grant the request for a synagogue after the Portuguese had made it clear that they would not settle in Haarlem without it. In doing so, the magistrates took the risk of provoking discontent among the elders of the Reformed Church, who defended its status as the only officially recognized *public* church, and among Catholic inhabitants, who were denied the right to publicly practise their religion. As I have explained elsewhere, in their attempt to attract the Portuguese merchants, the city governments even seem to have competed with each other.[31] While Alkmaar had offered the Portuguese the freedom of worship, Haarlem went further by offering not only freedom of *private* worship, but also the right to a *public* synagogue, provided that 50 families settled in the city. However, they were outbid by Rotterdam, which lowered the number to 30 families and exempted the Portuguese from particular taxes. Despite these favourable settlement conditions, the

J. Meijer (ed.), Amsterdam, 1949, 40–43. The French text has been published by Huussen, "Legal Position", 30–35.

27 City Record Office Rotterdam (GAR), *Oud Archief Stad*, 18 (Resolutions of the city council 1608–1621); inventaris Boom and Woelderink, 1976), 52 (reference mentioned in Huussen, "Legal Position", 40, note 17). The text of the Rotterdam charter can be found in De Groot, *Remonstrantie*, ed. Meijer, 45–46.

28 Rotterdam charter, in De Groot, *Remonstrantie*, ed. Meijer, 45.

29 Huussen, "Legal Position", 25.

30 Ibid., 25.

31 De Wilde, "Offering Hospitality to Strangers", 403.

Portuguese decided to stay in Amsterdam. Their decision suggests that the very reason for exploring possibilities for settling in other cities had been to improve their negotiating position in Amsterdam regarding their request for a public synagogue.[32]

However, on 8 May 1612, the Amsterdam burgomasters prohibited the construction of a synagogue.[33] Zwarts has described the background of the burgomasters' decision. In January of 1612, representatives of the Portuguese community – including Belchior and Francisco Mendes, who had negotiated with the Haarlem magistrates in 1605 – had hired a carpenter to build a large house at the Houtburgwal, apparently to be used as synagogue (the carpenter was instructed not to work after sunset on Friday).[34] As the intended function of the building became clear, the elders of the Reformed Church filed a complaint with the burgomasters. On 8 May 1612, the burgomasters decided that "no one of the [Portuguese] nation may live in that building and that no gatherings may be convened or ceremonies of their religion practised, under penalty of demolition, to the ground, of that house or building and the prohibition to practise their religion in any other places within the city and its jurisdiction."[35] It was thus under pressure of the Reformed elders that the burgomasters prohibited the construction of a synagogue. However, despite this prohibition, construction continued, and by the end of the year, the building was finished and used as a synagogue.[36] In the meantime, a member of the city council, Nicolaes van Campen, had bought the building and rented it out to the Portuguese nation.[37] This move proved to be a practical solution for both the burgomasters and the Portuguese. The transfer of ownership enabled the Portuguese to claim that they did not actually *own* a synagogue and that they

32 See also Huussen, "Toelating", 49.

33 Fuks-Mansfeld has suggested that by doing so, the burgomasters responded to the termination of the Rotterdam charter: as the Rotterdam charter was repealed, there was no need for the Amsterdam burgomasters to make concessions regarding a synagogue, because the Portuguese would stay in Amsterdam anyway. However, in fact, the Rotterdam charter was repealed three months *after* the Amsterdam burgomasters prohibited the building of a synagogue. Fuks-Mansfeld, *Sefardim*, 48.

34 Fuks-Mansfeld, *Sefardim*, 52; Swetschinksi, *Reluctant Cosmopolitans*, 11–12; Zwarts, *Eerste rabbijnen*, 65–70. The relevant documents – including the building contract – can be found in Zwarts, *Eerste rabbijnen*, 116–121, appendices XVII–XIX.

35 The text of the resolution can be found in Zwarts, *Eerste rabbijnen*, 70–71. For the English translation, see Swetschinksi, *Reluctant Cosmopolitans*, 12.

36 Fuks-Mansfeld, *Sefardim*, 52.

37 Van Campen may have been driven by financial motives: if the building was used as a synagogue, he could ask a higher rent. Ibid., 52–53.

were merely practising Judaism in *private*.[38] The burgomasters could now point at their official prohibition whenever they were confronted with new complaints from the Reformed elders. Thus, a pragmatic solution was found in Amsterdam by tacitly allowing the Portuguese to have their synagogue under the pretext that they merely practised their religion in private, which benefitted all parties involved.

Soon, however, another affair caused the question of the legal status of the Jews to be taken up at the provincial level. In September 1614, three persons from the area around Hoorn, a city in West-Friesland, were accused of having converted to Judaism. They were arrested by the *schout* (bailiff) of Hoorn and charged with apostasy.[39] In response to these charges, and in the absence of clear laws, the magistrate of Hoorn appealed to the highest authorities, the States of Holland and West-Friesland. On 4 March 1615, the States commissioned the pensionaries of Rotterdam and Amsterdam, Hugo Grotius and Adriaen Pauw, to draft a "set of regulations with which the Jews (residing in these lands) will have to comply for the prevention of all scandals, annoyances and sanctions."[40] In addition, they authorized the "*Gecommitteerde Raden*, with consent of the burgomasters and governors of Hoorn, to impose such order on the Jews held captive there as they deem fit."[41] The States probably chose Pauw and Grotius to draft the regulations, because Pauw represented the city with the largest Jewish community, while Grotius was a renowned jurist who had already written about the rights of non-Christians, including Jews.[42] Although they probably prepared two drafts – the States' 1619 resolution refers to their "drafts" in the plural – only Grotius's draft has been iden-

38 Swetschinski, *Reluctant Cosmopolitans*, 12.

39 A detailed description of this case can be found in A. Van der Haven, "Conversion on Trial: Toleration of Apostasy and the Trial of Three Converts to Judaism in the Dutch Republic, 1614–1615" in Y. Fox and Y. Yisraeli (eds.), *Contesting Inter-Religious Conversion in the Medieval World*, London, 2016, 41–60. Similar cases of Christians converting to Judaism were reported in Amsterdam in 1614. These cases are described by Zwarts, *Eerste Rabbijnen*, 129.

40 *Register van Holland en Westvriesland van de jaaren 1613–1619*, 127 (4 March 1615).

41 Ibid., 127 (17 March 1615). Although the Gecommitteerde Raden advised the city magistrates to expel the three converts from the province, they do not seem to have followed their advice: at least one of the converts was still living in his hometown a year later. Van der Haven, "Conversion on Trial", 43.

42 D. Burgersdijk, H. Nellen, M. de Wilde (eds.), *Hugo Grotius's On Public Partnership with Unbelievers (De societate publica cum infidelibus): Introduction, Transcription and English Translation*, Leiden, Brill, 2026. On this treatise see: P. Borschberg, "De societate publica cum infidelibus: Ein Frühwerk von Hugo Grotius", *Zeitschrift der Savigny-Stiftung für Rechtsgeschichte: Romanistische Abteilung* 115 (1998), 355–393.

tified with certainty. A second draft of an undated resolution of the States, which was found among Grotius's papers, may have been Pauw's proposal or the result of deliberations in the States about their proposals.[43] This second draft is much shorter than Grotius's, consisting of 6 instead of 49 Articles, and its tone is more negative: unlike Grotius's draft, it contains only prohibitions, and no rights or privileges for the Jews.

In the introduction to his draft, Grotius addressed three questions: "First, whether the Jews ought to be admitted to this country. Second, whether they should be allowed to practise their religion. Third, which means are best suited to prevent their presence and the practice of their religion from causing problems, both with respect to the Christian religion and the public peace" (fol. 1v, 61/ 199).[44] Grotius answered the first question affirmatively: the Jews had to be admitted to the Dutch provinces, because it would contribute to their *voluntary* conversion to Christianity, which was not possible if they were "cut off from the conversation with Christians" (fol. 5v, 77/ 202, trans. modified). Moreover, they would be more inclined to convert to Christianity if they were to live among Protestants, who could teach them about the "true religion", than among Catholics, whose religion was "mixed with idolatry" (fol. 6r, 79/ 202). Grotius also gave a more principled argument: in his view, all nations had a natural duty to offer hospitality to strangers, irrespective of their religion. Therefore, the States had a duty to admit the Jews and their exile was contrary to the law of nature (fol. 6r-7r, 80–83/ 202–203).[45] In response to the second question, Grotius argued that the Jews should be allowed to practice their religion, because the alternatives were simply unacceptable. Forcing the Jews

43 Resolution of the States of Holland and West-Friesland concerning the relations between the Jews and the Christian population (undated), Ets Haim, MS 48 A 05, fol. 25–27. The manuscript can be consulted online at http://etshaimmanuscripts.nl/items/eh-48-a-05/ (last consulted on 17 April 2026). A transcription can be found in De Groot, *Remonstrantie*, ed. Meijer, 135–137. On the debate about Pauw's authorship see Huussen, "Legal Position", 29.

44 Hugo Grotius, *Remonstrantie nopende de ordre dije in de landen van Hollandt ende Westvrieslandt dijent gestelt op de joden*, Ets Haim, Lib. Montezinos, MS EH 48 A 02. The manuscript can be consulted online at http://etshaimmanuscripts.nl/manuscripts/eh-48-a-02/ (last consulted on 17 April 2026). A transcription of the manuscript was published in 1949 by Jaap Meijer. A new edition, including facsimile, transcription and English translation, appeared in 2019 at the initiative of the Morasha Foundation: *Hugo Grotius's Remonstrantie of 1615: Facsimile, Transliteration and Analysis*, D. Kromhout and A. Offenberg (eds.), Leiden, 2019. The page numbers in the main text refer to the 2019 edition with page numbers of the facsimile and transcription preceding those of the English translation.

45 On Grotius's understanding of the natural duty to offer hospitality to strangers see my "Offering Hospitality to Strangers", 410–413.

to convert to Christianity was considered "improper and unlawful by all people with common sense, as religion should not be forced" (fol. 10r, 95/ 204). Moreover, prohibiting the Jews from practicing any religion at all "open[ed] the road to pure godlessness, which [was] far worse than Judaism" (fol. 10r, 95/ 204). Grotius's answer to the third question was that the presence of the Jews and the practice of their religion would not be harmful to the Christian religion and the public peace, provided that their legal status was well regulated in a public order. Whatever was not harmful to the Christian religion and the public peace had to be allowed to the Jews, implying that they should have the same freedoms and privileges as Christians, unless specific restrictions were imposed on them (fol. 11v, 101/205).

Having answered these questions, Grotius proposed a set of 49 articles, specifying the rights and duties of the Jews. Most importantly, they were allowed to settle in the cities of their choice (Art. 4). However, a maximum of 200 families was to be admitted to each city, with the exception of Amsterdam, where 300 families were to be admitted (Art. 5). Moreover, the Jews were to live freely in their places of residence and they would enjoy the same economic "liberties, exemptions and privileges" as other inhabitants, without being subject to special taxation (Art. 6). Crucially, the Jews were allowed the "free exercise of their religion" (Art. 7): they could designate "one, two or three or more" houses per city, where they could gather to perform their religious duties (Art. 8).[46] However, they were strictly prohibited from making blasphemous remarks or insulting Christ or the Christian religion (Art. 14). Nor were they allowed to print, possess or use books containing such remarks, including the Talmud (art. 16). The Jews were also required to listen to Christian clergymen, who came to preach and teach them about the Christian religion in their synagogues (Art. 21). They were strictly forbidden from attempting to convert or circumcise Christians (Art. 25 and 28); from marrying or having sexual relations with Christians (Art. 27 and 38); and from having Christian servants or maids living in their houses (Art. 29), with the exception of midwives and wet nurses for their children (Art. 30 and 31). Nor could Jews be appointed to public functions or admitted to the civic guard (Art. 40 and 42). On the other hand, they were allowed to circumcise their children (Art. 18), to have their own butchers (Art. 19), and to govern their internal affairs: they even had the right to ban from their congregation anyone they found

46 This article did not mean that they had the right to a *public* synagogue. As Grotius explained in a note, "in this country, the understanding has always been that there should only be one public religion, so that it is actually better not to allow the Jews the exercise of their religion in public spaces but in private houses, which is also less noticeable for the people" (note to Art. 8, fol. 23r, 147/210).

guilty of misconduct or erroneous opinions (Art. 20). Moreover, they could not be required to live in ghettos (Art. 23) or to wear a badge or any mark distinguishing them from Christians (Art. 24). Finally, they were permitted to buy one or two plots of land in every city to be used as their burial ground (Art. 48).

Whether Grotius's draft regulations would have improved the legal position of the Jews or not remains a theoretical question.[47] Once Pauw and Grotius had finished their drafts, the question of the legal status of the Jews no longer had priority for the States. Instead, they were now fully occupied with the growing religious and political tensions between Calvinists and Remonstrants. In August 1618, Stadtholder Maurice of Orange seized power in an attempt to curb the influence of the States and its Remonstrant deputies. Maurice had his main political opponents arrested: Van Oldenbarnevelt was executed for high treason and Grotius was imprisoned in Loevenstein Castle. It was only after Van Oldenbarnevelt's execution on 13 May 1619 that the States returned to the question of a Jewish statute. On 8 July 1619, the burgomaster of Amsterdam Reinier Pauw (father of Adriaen) requested the States to take a decision about the proposed regulations for the Jews. As Pauw explained, a decision had become necessary in view of persistent complaints about sexual relations between Jews and Christians. Moreover, the fact that Jews were permitted to have synagogues had caused discontent among the Remonstrants, who after the coup of 1618 were prohibited from practicing their religion in public.[48] On 13 December 1619, the States finally agreed on a resolution: referring to the drafts of Grotius and Pauw along with the municipal regulations and oath of Amsterdam, they decided that each city would be free to make its own regulations for the Jews, provided that they did not require them to wear distinguishing marks on their clothes.[49] Moreover, it was left to the cities to decide

47 Kuhn and Meijer believe that Grotius's draft regulations would have improved the legal position of the Jews, while Michman and Swetschinski argue that Grotius's draft was actually more restrictive than existing regulations. For instance, Swetschinski concludes that Grotius's draft "completely reverse[d] the procedure adopted in Haarlem, Rotterdam and (implicitly) Amsterdam. For in contrast to de Groot's ceiling on the number of Jews allowed to reside in each city, these cities stipulated conditions for a bottom figure of Jewish residents below which Judaism could not be practiced publicly." Swetschinski, *Reluctant Cosmopolitans*, 37. On these debates, see my "Offering Hospitality to Strangers", 393–396.

48 For instance, in 1618, Remonstrants had offered a petition to Stadtholder Maurice, in which they complained about the fact that the Jews as "open enemies and blasphemers" of Christ were allowed to freely exercise their religion, while the Remonstrants were not tolerated. The petition is quoted in G. Brandt, *The History of the Reformation and Other Ecclesiastical Transactions in and about the Low-Countries*, London, 1721, vol. 2, 578.

49 *Register van Holland en Westvrieslandt, 1613–1619*, 1165 (13 Dec. 1619); De Groot, *Remonstrantie*, ed. Meijer, 101; Huussen, "Legal Position," 27–28 and 40, note 25.

whether they would require the Jews to live in closed quarters or dispersed among the Christian population. Thus, the only provision of Grotius's draft that was adopted was the prohibition on the badge (Art. 24), but his proposal for prohibiting ghettos (Art. 23) was rejected. More importantly, the resolution of the States did not address the pressing question of religious worship, which was left to the cities to decide.

3 The Amsterdam Regulations of 1616

On 8 November 1616, while the States had not yet decided about the proposal for provincial regulations, the burgomasters of Amsterdam issued municipal regulations for the Jews.[50] It is possible that the burgomasters wanted to influence the discussion in the States and protect their own prerogative to decide about the issue.[51] However, they also responded to complaints about Jewish men having sexual relations with Christian women. As they stated in their preamble, some among the "Jewish nation" had taken "very great and unbounded license" in "frequenting and conversing with the women and daughters of these lands", which had caused "a lot of annoyance" in the city and its surroundings (fol. 107r). To prevent "these and other excesses", which harmed the "public peace of the city and the constitution of its Christian community", the Jews were warned "not to speak or write anything (and to ensure that nothing be spoken or written) that may, in any way, tend to the disparagement of our Christian religion; not to attempt to seduce any Christian person away from our Christian religion or to circumcise one; and not to have any carnal relations, whether in or out of wedlock, with Christian women or girls, not even those of ill repute" (fol. 107v).[52] The Jews were, moreover, instructed to observe the general legislation of the province and city and, more specifically, the burgomaster's prohibition on the construction of a synagogue of 1612 (fol. 107v). Having declared that any violation of the regulations would be severely punished, the burgomasters prescribed a special oath for the Jews (fol. 108r). They ended by emphasizing the provisional character of the regulations, which remained valid until the States decided about a provincial statute (fol. 108v).

50 Municipal Archives Amsterdam, *Archief van de Burgemeesters, privilegeboeken en keurboeken* (inv. 5020), 12 (*Willekeuren*), boek J (I), fol. 107r-108r; Noordkerk, *Handvesten*, vol. 2, 472.

51 D. Swetschinski, "Vestiging, verdraagzaamheid en vereniging tot 1639" in H. Blom, e.a. (eds.), *Geschiedenis van de joden in Nederland*, Amsterdam, 2017, 79.

52 English translation: Bodian, *Hebrews*, 61.

Apparently, the burgomasters had taken these measures in response to a series of scandals involving Portuguese Jews having "carnal relations" with Christian women. In August 1616, the apothecary Abraham Israel, a Portuguese Jew from Lisbon, had been found guilty of adultery with his Christian maid Maria Grandjean. He was convicted to a fine of 100 guilders and exiled from the province.[53] In that same year, the 23-year-old David Bravo was hoisted up with a weight of 200 pounds on his feet to make him confess that he had slept with a Christian girl named Lysbeth Egmontsdochter, a crime to which he partially confessed.[54] Sexual relations between Jewish men and Christian women, often maids, were regularly reported. Notarial records mention thirteen such cases in the period between 1600 and 1623.[55] They were usually reported if something had gone wrong as, for instance, if a maid had become pregnant and sued her employer for the costs of childbirth or child support.[56] Apparently, it had also happened in the case of Abraham Israel, who had been forced to pay child support to Maria Grandjean after she had given birth to (what she claimed to be) his child.[57] To prevent such "excesses", the Amsterdam regulations prohibited all "carnal relations" between Jewish men and Christian women, including those of "ill repute."[58] However, harsh penalties were rarely imposed for the violation of these sexual norms. For instance, Abraham Israel's punishment was revoked after his wife had requested the authorities to remit her husband's sentence.[59] Israel was thus allowed to return to the city, and his name reappears in the registers of the Portuguese Jewish congregations of Beth Jacob and Neve Shalom.[60]

The Amsterdam regulations' prohibition on "carnal relations" may have been informed by the charter of Haarlem, which strictly prohibited all sexual

---

53 E. Koen, "Notarial Records Relating to the Portuguese Jews in Amsterdam up to 1639", *Studia Rosenthaliana* 10/2 (1976), 212–231, at 213–214 (no. 948) and 214, note 27. See also Fuks-Mansfeld, *Sefardim*, 54 and Huussen, "Legislation", 49.

54 Koen, "Earliest Sources", 34. See also Bodian, *Hebrews*, 182, note 43.

55 Bodian, *Hebrews*, 65.

56 Swetschinski, *Reluctant Cosmopolitans*, 14; Bodian, *Hebrews*, 65.

57 Koen, "Notarial Records", 214, note 27.

58 The reference to women of "ill repute [*oneerlijcken leven*]" may have been added because of the Israel-Grandjean affair: Grandjean is thus reported to have lived in a brothel in the Breestraat in Amsterdam before being employed by Israel. Koen, "Notarial Records", 214 (no. 948). The confessions books of the Amsterdam court contain many references to Portuguese Jews visiting the city's brothels. If they were apprehended during police raids, they were fined, but such raids were apparently not carried out with the specific aim of arresting Jews. Swetschinski, *Reluctant Cosmopolitans*, 14, note 22.

59 Koen, "Notarial Records", 222 (no. 1008).

60 Ibid., 214, note 27.

contact between Jews and Christians. It prescribed the death penalty for mixed marriages and adultery.[61] For sexual relations out of wedlock, a fine of 100 guilders was to be imposed – the same to which Abraham Israel was convicted by the Amsterdam court. Grotius's proposal for provincial regulations as well as the States' undated resolution had included similar provisions: mixed marriages were to be punished with death (Art. 36 and Art. 4) and sexual relations out of wedlock (including adultery) with flogging, banishment and confiscation of goods (Art. 38 and Art. 5). However, in a note, Grotius expressed doubts as to whether the city magistrates had the authority to dissolve *existing* marriages between Jews and Christians (sub Art. 36). In Grotius's view, the magistrate could only dissolve such marriages if one of the spouses abused the other in regard of religion. Strikingly, Grotius referred to the Talmud to defend his proposal for prohibiting sexual relations out of wedlock (sub Art. 38). By doing so, he suggested that the Jews themselves agreed with this provision. Moreover, he rejected the opinion of some (he referred to the city government of Paris) that the death penalty had to be imposed for sexual relations out of wedlock and instead proposed a "more lenient treatment" (sub Art. 38). In view of these discussions, it is striking that the Amsterdam regulations did not specify the punishment for violations of the prohibition on sexual relations between Jews and Christians, whether in or out of wedlock. Instead, the Jews were merely warned that justice would be administered to those who violated the prohibition "in conformity with the civil and written laws as well as the public ordinances and regulations" (fol. 107v).[62] In practice, the Amsterdam magistrates seem to have limited themselves to imposing fines for sexual relations out of wedlock, along with banishment for adultery, as they did in the case of Abraham Israel.[63]

The issue of sexual relations offered an opportunity for the burgomasters to also address other concerns about the Jews, which had been raised in previous years by the Reformed Church Council. In the summer of 1614, the Reformed elders had heard several witnesses, including a hatter and a cobbler, who had confessed that a Jewish blacksmith had attempted to convert them to Judaism

61 Haarlem charter, in De Groot, *Remonstrantie*, ed. Meijer, 43.

62 The expression "civil and written laws" was a standard reference to Roman law, which applied in Holland and West-Friesland if local laws were lacking, incomplete, or unclear. The prohibition on mixed marriages between Jews and Christians could be found in both Roman law and canon law. For Roman law, see the imperial statute in the Justinian Code, C. 1.9.6 (Valentinianus, Theodosius and Arcadius). For canon law, see Gratian's Decretum, C. 28.q.1.c.9 (comment on canon 63 of the Fourth Council of Toledo).

63 Fuks-Mansfeld, *Sefardim*, 54.

and had already enticed the cobbler's wife to do so.[64] Other witnesses had declared that a bottle-maker, a Mennonite who had converted to Judaism, had "claimed that our Lord Jesus Christ is not the true Messiah and has not died for our sins, but for his own, and that another Messiah is to be expected, who will not die, but bring his people into the land of Canaan", and had tried to "implant these errors into others."[65] On 12 June 1614, the Reformed elders decided to bring their concerns to the attention of the burgomasters.[66] Although the burgomasters do not seem to have responded at the time, when they issued the municipal regulations two years later, they included a prohibition on blasphemy as well as on attempts of Jews to convert Christians to Judaism. Similar provisions could be found in the charters of Haarlem[67] and Rotterdam,[68] as well as in Grotius's draft regulations (Art. 14, 25 and 28) and the undated resolution of the States (Art. 1 and 2). In all these documents, the prescribed punishment was the same: banishment from the province and confiscation of goods. In a note, Grotius explained that under the "written laws", the penalty for blasphemy was death, but that a milder punishment should be imposed on the Jews "due to their ignorance" (ad Art. 15). By contrast, the Amsterdam burgomasters did not specify the punishments for these offences.

The burgomasters ended the regulations by presenting a special oath for the Jews. As they explained, the oath could be imposed by judicial decision or taken voluntarily at the request of another party (fol. 107v). The oath was apparently not meant to exclude the Jews. Instead, it enabled them to participate in legal proceedings, as they could not use the Christian oath formula.[69] Fockema Andreae has suggested that the main purpose of the oath was to enable the Jews to serve as witnesses, which was also in the interest of Christians, who needed their testimony.[70] Moreover, the oath served to facilitate legal and notarial transactions between Jews and Christians, including those necessary for commerce and trade.[71] As Fockema Andreae has demonstrated,

64 Extract from Protocol no. 4 (Archive of the Reformed Church), 5 June 1614, fol. 3, quoted in Zwarts, *Eerste rabbijnen*, 121, appendix 20, sub b.

65 Ibid., 121, appendix 20, sub b.

66 Ibid., 122, appendix 20, sub c. Amongst other things, the elders also complained about a Jewish school.

67 Haarlem charter, in De Groot, *Remonstrantie*, ed. Meijer, 42–43.

68 Rotterdam charter, in ibid., 45.

69 Fuks-Mansfeld, *Sefardim*, 55.

70 S. Fockema Andreae, "De eed der joden in Nederland onder de Republiek (1908)" in S. Fockema Andreae (ed.), *Bijdragen tot de Nederlandsche Rechtsgeschiedenis*, Haarlem, 1914, 128–144, at 130.

71 Ibid., 135.

the text of the Amsterdam oath was borrowed from existing oath formulas.[72] The fact that the text was provided not only in Dutch but also in Portuguese suggests that members of the Portuguese community had been consulted.[73] Unlike the Amsterdam regulations, the charters of Alkmaar, Haarlem and Rotterdam along with the undated resolution of the States had not included a special oath for the Jews. Grotius's draft had contained a "declaration of faith", which all Jews over the age of 14 were required to give before the city magistrates (Art. 2), but its text differed from the Amsterdam oath formula. By making legal and notarial transactions between Jews and Christians possible, the Amsterdam oath may in practice have been the most important part of the 1616 regulations. It was copied by other cities in Holland, Utrecht and Gelderland, and it was still applied in the eighteenth century.[74]

4 Evaluating the Amsterdam Regulations

Compared to the Jewish charters of Alkmaar, Haarlem and Rotterdam, in addition to Grotius's draft, the negative tone of the Amsterdam regulations is striking: they mention prohibitions only, but no rights or privileges for the Jews. The Jews were thus prohibited from writing or saying anything that tended to disparage the Christian religion; from attempting to seduce any Christian away from the Christian religion or to circumcise one; and from having "carnal relations" with Christian women, whether in or out of wedlock. As we have seen, the charters of Alkmaar, Haarlem and Rotterdam, and Grotius's draft had contained similar provisions, but in addition, had granted important rights to the Jews, including the freedom of worship and the right to a synagogue. The only legal document that resembled the Amsterdam regulations was the undated resolution of the States (i.e. the second draft found among Grotius's papers). Both documents contained prohibitions on blasphemy, on attempts at converting and circumcising Christians, and on sexual relations between Jews and Christians but, again, no rights or privileges for the Jews. These similarities suggest that the States' undated resolution and the Amsterdam regulations were proposed by the same person, perhaps Adriaen Pauw, who, as pensionary of Amsterdam and commissioner of the States, was involved at both the pro-

---

72 For instance, to prevent perjury, the Amsterdam oath formula referred to the divine punishment of Sodom and Gomorrah, Corah, Dathan and Abiram. These references could also be found in medieval oath formulas. Ibid., 132–133.

73 Ibid., 131.

74 Ibid., 128.

vincial and municipal levels.[75] However, there were also differences between these documents, as the States' undated resolution contained a prohibition for Jews to have Christian domestic servants and maids, which was not included in the Amsterdam regulations, and the Amsterdam regulations prescribed a special oath for the Jews, which was not mentioned in the States' undated resolution. Moreover, the States' resolution prescribed harsh punishments for the violation of its provisions, including the death penalty for mixed marriages, while the Amsterdam regulations did not mention any specific punishments at all.

However, despite their negative tone, the Amsterdam regulations do not seem to have limited the freedom of the Jews in any significant way. Indeed, nowhere else did the Jews enjoy as much religious and economic freedom as in Amsterdam. As Fuks-Mansfeld has suggested, the lack of a more extensive Jewish charter proved beneficial for the Jews, as it left important aspects of their social and economic life unregulated.[76] The absence of legal restrictions on Jewish settlement was unique in Europe, as was the undogmatic approach of the Amsterdam burgomasters.[77] In a similar vein, Bodian observes that the Amsterdam regulations testified to a lack of interest in controlling the Jewish population, which was "unknown in contemporary Europe, where the trend was, if anything, toward stricter regulation."[78] For instance, the Amsterdam regulations did not contain residential restrictions, nor did they impose special taxes or establish supervision of religious affairs. Swetschinski has pointed out that by focusing on issues of religion and sexuality, the Amsterdam regulations did not prevent social and economic interaction between Jews and Christians. He even finds the regulations "notable for their restraint", as they did not, for instance, prohibit the Jews from employing Christian domestic servants and maids.[79] As Swetschinski concludes, the burgomasters were reluctant to impose restrictions on the Jews; they only succumbed to pressure from the outside – for instance, from the Reformed elders or the guilds – to keep the religious peace or to prevent popular challenges to their authority. More importantly, the restrictions they proposed were relatively mild com-

75 In view of these similarities, Van Eysinga believes that it is likely that the States' undated resolution served as a basis for the Amsterdam regulations. However, it is also possible that the Amsterdam regulations served as a basis for the States' undated resolution. W.J.M. Van Eysinga, "De Groots jodenreglement", *Mededelingen der Koninklijke Nederlandse Akademie van Wetenschappen, Afd. Letterkunde, nieuwe reeks* 13/1 (1950), 1–8, at 3.

76 Fuks-Mansfeld, *Sefardim*, 57–58.

77 Ibid., 57.

78 Bodian, *Hebrews*, 61.

79 Swetschinski, *Reluctant Cosmopolitans*, 14–15.

pared to clerical demands: the burgomasters accepted only those demands which conformed to their own sense of propriety, for instance, by prohibiting "carnal relations" between Jews and Christians, but not the hiring of Christian domestic servants.[80]

Perhaps more important than what Amsterdam regulations regulated was what they left unregulated: by imposing *explicit* restrictions on the religious and sexual conduct of the Jews, they *implicitly* left them important freedoms. As Swetschinski explains, this "mixture of explicit restrictions and implicit freedoms" was "unquestionably favourable" for the Jews.[81] For instance, by imposing explicit restrictions on their religious conduct (for example, the prohibition on blasphemy), the regulations implicitly acknowledged their right to live in Amsterdam as Jews. Moreover, unlike Grotius's draft, the Amsterdam regulations did not impose restrictions on the maximum number of families which were permitted to settle in the city. The privilege of buying the *poortersrecht*, which had been granted to the Portuguese merchants in 1598 on the condition that they were Christians, was not revoked now that they had started to publicly present themselves as Jews. Nor did the Amsterdam regulations limit their economic activities in any way.[82] Instead, by prescribing a special oath for the Jews, the 1616 regulations implicitly acknowledged the right of the Jews to engage in legal transactions with Christians, including those necessary for commerce and trade. Although the Jews were *expressly* denied the right to a *public* synagogue, the regulations *implicitly* recognized a right to *private* worship: the existing practice of a private house being used a synagogue was thus tacitly allowed. Crucially, the Jews were left free to do anything which had not been expressly prohibited by the regulations. The principle that Grotius had formulated in his draft thus also applied to the Amsterdam regulations: whatever was not contrary to the Christian religion and the public peace was allowed to the Jews, implying that they had the same rights and freedoms as other inhabitants if no specific restrictions had been imposed on them (fol. 11v).

However, paradoxically, it was not only the lack of legal *restrictions*, but also the lack of officially recognized *rights*, which left the Jews more freedom than they would otherwise have enjoyed. To give an example: Grotius had proposed to grant the Jews the "free exercise of their religion [*vrije exercitie van*

---

80 Ibid., 25.

81 Ibid., 24.

82 This only changed in 1632, when, under pressure of the guilds, the burgomasters passed a by-law that excluded the Jews from *poortersneringen* (i.e. admission to the guilds). Ibid., 21.

haere religie]" as well as the right to designate "one, two or three or more" houses per city to be used as synagogues (Art. 7 and 8). However, once Grotius had granted these rights, he also proposed legal conditions for their exercise. For instance, the Jews were required to register the houses which they intended to use as synagogues (Art. 8), they were not allowed to admit more than one hundred persons (Art. 9), or to gather in other houses or at other times than those registered (Art. 10). Moreover, they were prohibited from uttering blasphemous remarks or profanities against Christ or the Christian religion, and if they did so during their congregation, their synagogue was to be demolished (Art. 15). Most importantly, the Jews were required to listen to Christian clergymen, who came to teach and preach to them about the Christian religion in their synagogues (Art. 21). By contrast, the Amsterdam regulations did not grant the Jews either the right to freely exercise their religion or the right to a synagogue, and, since these rights were not officially recognized, there was no need to impose conditions on their practice. Thus, in contrast to Grotius's proposal, the Amsterdam regulations did not require the Jews to register their synagogues or to listen to Christian clergymen. Nor were their synagogues to be demolished if they uttered blasphemous remarks during their congregations, for *officially* no synagogues existed in Amsterdam. It was thus *the lack of officially recognized rights* which explains why the Jews of Amsterdam were left largely undisturbed in their religious affairs, free to worship in "private houses" without municipal supervision.

Another explanation why the Amsterdam regulations seem to have had little impact on the freedom of the Jews was that their provisions were rarely enforced in practice, and if they were, the magistrates refrained from imposing harsh punishments for their violation. One of the reasons may have been that a clear legal basis for punishment was lacking: as we have seen, the burgomasters had not mentioned any specific punishments in their regulations. It was thus left to the discretion of the *schout* and *schepenen* (the judicial authorities) to determine the proper punishment: in practice, they preferred imposing fines instead of corporal punishment.[83] For instance, if Jewish men were caught during police raids on illegal brothels, in clear violation of the burgomasters' prohibition on "carnal relations" (which applied also to women of "ill

83 A typical example is the case of Jacob Alboa, son of Alphonso Rodrigues Cardosa, a Portuguese Jew from Lisbon. On 2 Oct. 1618, Jacob confessed that he had "carnally conversed" with his father's Christian maid Grietgen Jansz. On 13 Oct. 1618, he was convicted to a fine of two hundred guilders (under the additional penalty of imprisonment if he failed to pay). Municipal Archives Amsterdam, *Archieven van de Schout en Schepenen* (inv. 5061), 292 (*Confessieboeken*), fol. 91 and *Justitieboeken*, 570, fol. 68.

repute"), they were fined (not flogged) and exiled as Grotius had proposed.[84] Moreover, examples of mixed marriages have been recorded in Amsterdam, and they were even officially registered with the city's magistrate.[85] Jewish men could thus obtain permission to marry Christian women simply by declaring their intention to convert to Christianity. For instance, in 1619, Jan de Pontremo, a Jew from Ferrara, declared his intention to convert to Lutheranism to obtain permission for marrying Grietgen Christians. The authorities did not object, provided that he would not "converse" with Grietgen until he had converted.[86] In such cases, Jews may have converted for public purposes only, while maintaining their Jewish identities and beliefs in private. For instance, in 1619, Jacques Franco (alias Jacques Fernandez), who had been married to and become a widower of Anna Jansz, confessed that he had presented himself as a Christian in order to be able to register his marriage. Apparently, he was left undisturbed by the authorities, even though he later had his sons circumcised and his daughter buried at the Jewish cemetery at Ouderkerk.[87] Instead of imposing harsh punishments, the authorities seem to have preferred pragmatic solutions, allowing Jews to present themselves as Christians for public purposes such as marriage.

Crucially, the Amsterdam regulations contained norms that were actually shared by the Portuguese Jews themselves. For instance, the prohibition on mixed marriages was of limited practical importance, as the Portuguese Jews themselves had strong inhibitions against marrying outside their own ranks.[88] More important for them was the prohibition on marriages between uncles and nieces, which was not contained in the Amsterdam regulations, but followed from the general marriage laws of the province.[89] Moreover, aware of

84 Swetschinski, *Reluctant Cosmopolitans*, 14, note 22.

85 Fuks-Mansfeld, *Sefardim*, 54.

86 Koen, "Earliest Sources", 34.

87 Ibid., 34 (Municipal Archives Amsterdam, *Archieven van de Schout en Schepenen* (inv. 5061), 292 (*Confessieboeken*), fol. 132).

88 By contrast, sexual encounters that did not involve marriage or the intent to produce offspring, such as affairs with maids or visits to brothels, were considered less problematic within the Portuguese community, as they were not regarded as a breach of ethnic boundaries. Bodian, *Hebrews*, 65–66.

89 On 1 April 1580, the States of Holland and West-Friesland had issued an ordinance regulating marriage law, which, among other things, prohibited marriages of various degrees of consanguinity, including those between uncles and nieces, which were common among the Portuguese Jews. In 1712, the Jews were granted dispensation from this prohibition, but only for *existing* marriages. L.J. Van Apeldoorn, *Geschiedenis van het Nederlandsche huwelijksrecht vóór de invoering van de Fransche wetgeving*, Amsterdam, 1925, 160; Swetschinski, *Reluctant Cosmopolitans*, 19.

Christian sensitivities, the leadership of the Portuguese Jewish community actively enforced the Amsterdam regulations among its members.[90] As early as 1616, the Portuguese merchants had written a letter to the States, declaring their intention to observe the proposed regulations and to enforce them within their community.[91] In their letter, they explained that the regulations had made them vulnerable to false accusations by their servants and debtors (fol. 202r/ 203v). For instance, their debtors could falsely accuse them of blasphemy in order to force them to remit their debts. Therefore, they requested the States to add a simple provision to the proposed regulations, namely that servants and debtors of the Jews would not be permitted to testify against them (fol. 202v/ 204r). If that provision was added, the leadership of the Portuguese community was prepared to strictly observe the regulations and to enforce them among its members (fol. 202v/ 204r). However, apparently, the States did not grant their request, as the proposed provision was not included in the States' resolution; nor was it included in the Amsterdam regulations. Here, the logic of class may have played a decisive role: Portuguese merchants who could afford to hire Christian servants or to have Christian debtors belonged to the same social class as the Amsterdam magistrates. For that reason, it is doubtful whether the magistrates would have allowed their servants and debtors to testify against them.

What, then, was the function of the Amsterdam regulations if their effect in legal practice was limited? Their function seems to have been largely symbolic. By symbolically marking the boundaries between the Jewish and Christian populations, the regulations were meant to quell some of the anxieties the Christian population had about the presence of Jews in their midst.[92] These anxieties focused on sexual relations between Jews and Christians, as well as on the possibility of Christians converting to Judaism. Therefore, the message conveyed by the regulations was not primarily directed at the Jews,

90 For instance, a communal statute of 1639 prohibited its members from circumcising "anyone not of our Hebrew nation", perhaps reiterating a prohibition contained in earlier statutes which have been lost. Bodian, *Hebrews*, 62 and 70.

91 Anonymous letter to the States of Holland and West-Friesland (undated), Amsterdam University Library, Bibliotheca Rosenthaliana, MS ROS 350/ 1, fol. 202r-204r. The manuscript contains a Portuguese version of the letter (fol. 202r-v) and a Dutch translation (fol. 203r-204v). A transcription of the Dutch text can found in De Groot, *Remonstrantie*, ed. Meijer, 141–143. References in the main text are to the Portuguese original and Dutch translation, preceding the page numbers of Meijer's transcription. The traditional dating of the manuscript (1616) is uncertain: it is based on the author's reference to "those of the Portuguese nation having come in these lands twenty years ago, being today in the city of Amsterdam alone with two hundred families" (fol. 202r/ 203r).

92 Kaplan, *Divided by Faith*, 316–317.

but at the Christian population. More specifically, the regulations were meant to take away the fear of the Reformed elders that the "unity of the Christian religion" and the monopoly of the Reformed Church in the public sphere were threatened. Hence, they not only reconfirmed the prohibition on the construction of a synagogue but also prohibited any attempt at "seducing" Christians away from the Christian religion. The regulations also served to ensure the Catholic minority that the Jews would not have a privileged position compared to other religious minorities. Similar restrictions had been imposed on Catholics, who were not only forced to worship in clandestine churches, but also, for instance, actively discouraged from marrying outside their own community.[93] Finally, the regulations sent a clear message to the Jews themselves: their presence in Amsterdam would be tolerated on the condition that they abstained from sexual or religious conduct that could be considered offensive by the Christian population. The leadership of the Portuguese Jewish community seems to have taken this message to heart and actively enforced the regulations among its members.[94] It was thus by symbolically marking the boundaries between the Jewish and Christian populations that the Amsterdam regulations contributed to making a Jewish presence acceptable to the Christian population.[95]

5 Conclusion

My aim in this contribution has been to analyze and evaluate the 1616 Amsterdam regulations for the Jews. As I have explained, compared to existing legal documents, the Amsterdam regulations stood out in their negative tone: they contained prohibitions only, but no rights or privileges for the Jews. While the charters of Alkmaar, Haarlem and Rotterdam had been made at the request of the Portuguese Jews themselves, the Amsterdam regulations were unilaterally imposed on them. Complaints about Jewish men having "carnal relations" with Christian women had caused the burgomasters to issue the regulations. The burgomasters also responded to concerns raised by the Reformed elders about the religious conduct of the Jews. The Jews were thus warned not speak or write anything that could disparage the Christian religion; not to attempt to "seduce" any Christian person away from the Christian religion or to circumcise one; and not to have any carnal relations, whether in or out of wedlock,

93 Kaplan, *Divided by Faith*, 276–277; Swetschinski, *Reluctant Cosmopolitans*, 14.

94 Anonymous letter to the States of Holland and West-Friesland, 143.

95 See also Kaplan, *Divided by Faith*, 317–318.

with Christian women, including "those of ill repute". Unlike the charters of Alkmaar, Haarlem and Rotterdam, in addition to Grotius's proposal for a provincial statute, the Amsterdam regulations did not contain any religious or economic rights for the Jews. The freedom of worship, which had been central to Grotius's proposal, and the right to a *public* synagogue, which had been granted in Haarlem and Rotterdam, were not mentioned. Instead, the Amsterdam regulations merely reconfirmed the prohibition on the construction of a synagogue. As we have seen, the only legal document similar to the Amsterdam regulations was the undated resolution of the States General: both documents contained restrictions only, yet no rights or privileges for the Jews.

However, despite their emphasis on legal restrictions, the Amsterdam regulations do not seem to have limited the freedom of the Jews in any significant way. As historians have pointed out, the Amsterdam regulations testified to a lack of interest in controlling the Jewish population that was unique in Europe. For instance, the regulations did not contain residential restrictions for the Jews, nor did they impose special taxation. By imposing *explicit* restrictions on their religious and sexual conduct, the regulations *implicitly* left them important freedoms. Although they were denied the right to a public synagogue, the existing practice of a private house being used as a synagogue was tacitly allowed. However, as I explained, it was not only the lack of legal *restrictions*, but also the lack of officially recognized *rights* which left the Jews more freedom than they would otherwise have enjoyed. For instance, Grotius had proposed allowing Jews the freedom of worship and the right to use "one, two, three or more" houses as synagogues, yet he had also imposed conditions on the exercise of these rights, for instance, by demanding that they listened to conversionist sermons. By contrast, no conditions were deemed necessary in Amsterdam, as the freedom of worship and the right to a synagogue had not been officially recognized. It was thus *the lack of officially recognized rights*, which explains why the Jews of Amsterdam were left largely undisturbed, free to worship in private houses without municipal supervision. Moreover, unlike the charters of Haarlem and Rotterdam or Grotius's proposal, the Amsterdam regulations did not mention any specific punishments for the violation of religious and sexual norms, thereby enabling judicial authorities to impose fines instead of corporal punishment. As we have seen, Jewish men were even allowed to marry Christian women, provided that they converted to Christianity and promised not to "carnally converse" until they had converted. If they were found guilty of sexual relations, they were fined, instead of flogged and exiled as Grotius had proposed. Apparently, the authorities preferred such pragmatic solutions, which the regulations made possible due to their lack of specificity.

By imposing restrictions on the Jews, the Amsterdam regulations contributed to making their presence acceptable to the Christian population. The significance of the Amsterdam regulations was thus largely symbolic. By symbolically marking the boundaries between the Jewish and Christian populations, the regulations were meant to take away fears about sexual and religious miscegenation. More particularly, they served to ensure the Reformed elders that the unity of the Christian religion and the monopoly of the Reformed Church were not in danger. Hence, the regulations reconfirmed the prohibition on the construction of a synagogue and strictly prohibited the Jews from attempting to seduce any Christian person away from the Christian religion. In addition, the burgomasters addressed the concerns of Catholics that the Jews might have a privileged position compared to other religious minorities. As the burgomasters made clear, the Jews would not receive a preferential treatment, but they would be forced to worship in private and discouraged from mixing with Reformed Christians just like other religious minorities. Finally, the regulations sent a message to the Jews themselves that their presence in Amsterdam would be tolerated on the condition that they avoided any behaviour that could be considered offensive by the local population. In response, the leadership of the Portuguese Jewish community declared its intention to actively enforce the regulations among its members. They understood that their presence in Amsterdam as well as their religious liberty and economic prosperity depended on their legal position being, at least officially, *unequal*. And they may also have realized that the lack of officially recognized rights allowed them more freedom in practice than they would otherwise have enjoyed.

CHAPTER 9

A Nation Apart: Legal Status and Internal Dynamics of Early Modern Amsterdam Ashkenazim

Bart Wallet

1 Introduction

The history of Amsterdam's Jewish community occupies a unique and significant place in the historiography of both the city and early modern Jewish communities. In the study of early modern Amsterdam, the Jewish community serves as a central case in debates about the philosophy and practice of tolerance. Similarly, within the historiography of early modern Jews, Amsterdam is a key site for understanding the formation of a new Western Sephardic diasporic community, resulting in a primary focus on the Portuguese Jewish nation. However, the emergence of a parallel Ashkenazi community in its shadow has received considerably less scholarly attention. This issue was highlighted by Jonathan Israel and Reinier Salverda in 2002, and little progress has been made since then.[1] The limited research that has been conducted on the Ashkenazi community has largely been filtered through the lens of the more established Portuguese community. This imbalance is partly due to the fact that much of the archive of the seventeenth-century Ashkenazi community was lost during the Second World War, with only fragments remaining.

Through the surviving archives of the Portuguese community, scholars such as Yosef Kaplan and Tirtsah Levie Bernfeld have shed light on key aspects of the interactions between Sephardim and Ashkenazim in Amsterdam.[2] In addition, pre-war research – mainly by amateur historians such as David Mozes

1 J. Israel and R. Salverda (eds.), *Dutch Jewry. Ist History and Secular Culture (1500–2000)*, Leiden, 2002, 5.

2 Y. Kaplan, "The Attitude of the Spanish and Portuguese Jews to the Ashkenazic Jews in Seventeenth-Century Amsterdam" [Hebrew] in S. Almog, I. Bartal and M. Graetz (eds.), *Transition and Change in Modern Jewish History: Essays Presented in Honor of Shmuel Ettinger*, Jerusalem, 1987, 389–412; Y. Kaplan, "The Portuguese community in 17th-century Amsterdam and the Ashkenazi world" in J. Michman (ed.), *Dutch Jewish History*, vol. 2, Assen, 1989, 23–45; T. Levie Bernfeld, *Poverty and Welfare Among the Portuguese Jews in Early Modern Amsterdam*, Oxford, 2012, 117–121, 216–221.

Sluys, Jacques Zwarts and Vaz Dias – provides some insights into the content of the lost Ashkenazi records.[3] However, the development of the Ashkenazi community remains a crucial issue in both Amsterdam's and Jewish history, still in need of further analysis. By the end of the seventeenth century, the Ashkenazi population in Amsterdam had grown rapidly, surpassing the Portuguese community in size. By the eighteenth century, it had become the largest Ashkenazi community in the world, with some 20,000 members. This presence makes the study of Amsterdam's Ashkenazim not only a significant local case, but one of wider translocal significance.[4]

This article focuses on the development of the Ashkenazi community in the seventeenth century, a period in which the community gradually established its independence alongside the Portuguese *Hombres de Nação*. While I have previously explored the dynamics between the Portuguese and Ashkenazi communities,[5] this chapter seeks to answer the question of how the Ashkenazi community organized itself internally and how it interacted with the city and its authorities. Specifically, it examines the development of communal autonomy within the Amsterdam Ashkenazi community, as well as the challenges it faced. The primary sources for this study are approximately 200 notarial deeds from seventeenth-century Amsterdam in which Ashkenazim are mentioned, which have recently become accessible through the digitization of Amsterdam's vast collection of notarial deeds.[6] These documents give the Ashkenazi community of early modern Amsterdam a voice of its own.

2 A Nation of their Own

In the early decades of the seventeenth century, the first Ashkenazi Jews arrived in Amsterdam, often employed by the Portuguese Jewish community

3 See for instance: D.M. Sluys, "Hoogduits-Joods Amsterdam van 1635 tot 1795" in H. Brugmans and A. Frank (eds.), *Geschiedenis der Joden in Nederland*, Amsterdam, 1940, 306–381; A.M. Vaz Dias, "Nieuwe bijdragen tot de geschiedenis der Amsterdamsche Hoogduitsch-Joodsche gemeente", *Bijdragen en Mededeelingen van het Genootschap voor Joodsche Wetenschap in Nederland* 6 (1940) 153–158.

4 B.T. Wallet and I.E. Zwiep, "Locals. Jews in the Early Modern Dutch Republic" in J. Karp and A. Sutcliffe (eds.), *The Cambridge History of Judaism*, vol. 7: *The Early Modern World, 1500–1815*, Cambridge, 2018, 894–922.

5 B. Wallet, "Rembrandt's Other Jews: The Amsterdam Ashkenazim in the Seventeenth Century" in M. Knotter and G. Schwartz (eds.), *Rembrandt Seen Through Jewish Eyes. The Artist's Meaning to Jews from His Time to Ours*, Amsterdam, 2024, 71–88.

6 S.L. Alting van Geusau and E.L. Wouthuysen (eds.), *Alle Amsterdamse akten. Ruzie, rouw en roddels bij de notaris, 1578–1915*, Amsterdam, 2022.

in menial jobs, while others made a living as street traders and hawkers. Although they shared the Jewish faith with the established Portuguese Jews, they differed in ethnic origin, social status and religious practice. Initially, under the terms *Tudescos* and *Polacos*, they were considered part of the wider Portuguese Jewish community, which also included Italian and Black Jews, but without any membership privileges like enjoyed by the Sephardim. They were accepted as fellow Jews, but their participation in the Portuguese community was severely limited.[7] Positions of religious and administrative honour, including seats in synagogues, were reserved exclusively for Portuguese Jews. Non-Portuguese Jews were even buried in a separate section of the Beth Haim cemetery in the town of Ouderkerk aan de Amstel.[8]

The unification of the three different Portuguese synagogues into one community marked a clear institutional boundary with Ashkenazi Jews. In 1639, when the single Portuguese Talmud Torah community was formally established, a separate Ashkenazi community began to take shape.[9] Prior to this, from 1635 onwards, Ashkenazim had begun to hold separate synagogue services, and by 1636 a separate synagogue hall was mentioned. While the formal establishment of an Ashkenazi congregation took place in 1639, it was not until 1641 that the Ashkenazim acquired control over their own ritual slaughter. The final step in their separation came in 1642, when Ashkenazim were no longer allowed to bury their dead at Beth Haim. With financial help from the Portuguese, they bought their own cemetery at Muiderberg.[10]

The formation of a separate Ashkenazi community was thus a gradual process, driven primarily by the Portuguese community's desire to exclude Ashkenazim from its institutional structures. However, the Ashkenazim's desire to preserve their own religious traditions, rooted in the Rhineland and southern German regions – the heartland of Ashkenazic religious practice – was also an important factor. According to *halacha* (Jewish law), the early Ashkenazi settlers established the *minhag ha-makom* (local customs) to which later newcomers were expected to conform.

The establishment of an independent Ashkenazi community alongside the Portuguese marked the division of Amsterdam's Jewish population into two distinct 'nations': the Portuguese and the Ashkenazi. The term 'nation' here

---

7 M. Bodian, *Hebrews of the Portuguese Nation. Conversos and Community in Early Modern Amsterdam*, Bloomington, 1999, 125–131; D.M. Swetschinski, *Reluctant Cosmopolitans: The Portuguese Jews of Seventeenth-Century Amsterdam*, 2nd ed., Oxford, 2004, 188–189.

8 L. Hagoort, *Het Beth Haim in Ouderkerk aan de Amstel. De begraafplaats van de Portugese Joden in Amsterdam 1615–1945*, Hilversum, 2005, 41.

9 Swetschinski, *Reluctant Cosmopolitans*, 186–187.

10 Hagoort, *Beth Haim*, 46–47.

FIGURE 9.1 The High-German Synagogue (end of the seventeenth century) – Municipal Archives Amsterdam, *Tekeningen en prenten* (inv. 10097), 010097014882

referred to a corporate entity within the city, distinct from the wider urban community, with its own administration and responsibility for maintaining order within its ranks. Each Jewish nation was expected to provide for its own needs, including education, social welfare, health care, relief of the poor and care of orphans, thereby avoiding dependence on the city's resources. As a result, the Portuguese and Ashkenazi nations each developed parallel institutions to serve their respective communities.[11]

For a brief period, Amsterdam was home to a third Jewish nation: the Polish nation. Following the Chmielnicki Uprisings of 1648–1649 in the Polish-Lithuanian Commonwealth (which involved widespread persecution of Jews) and the outbreak of the Northern War (1655–1660), several hundred Polish-Lithuanian Jewish refugees fled to Amsterdam.[12] With the support of

11 A.H. Huussen, "The legal position of the Jews in the Dutch Republic c. 1590–1796" in Israel and Salverda, *Dutch Jewry*, 25–41.

12 A. Teller, *Rescue the Surviving Souls: The Great Jewish Refugee Crisis of the Seventeenth Century*, Princeton, 2020, 259–271.

the Portuguese community, these refugees established a separate Polish Jewish nation in 1660, distinct from the Ashkenazi one. By this time, Polish-Jewish rituals and traditions had diverged significantly from mainstream Ashkenazi customs, prompting the Polish Jews to form their own community, complete with a synagogue, ritual bath, kosher slaughterhouse and cemetery. However, protests from the Ashkenazi community and displeasure from the city authorities with the multiplication of Jewish nations, led to the dissolution of the Polish Jewish nation in 1673, when it was forcibly merged with the Ashkenazi Jewish nation.[13]

3 Structuring the Ashkenazi Kehillah

The organizational structure of the Ashkenazi kehillah evolved gradually throughout the seventeenth century, culminating in the formalized regulations of 1711.[14] Prior to this, rules and decrees were recorded in the now-lost *pinkassim* – the community's minute books. Fortunately, pre-war historiography, which had access to these documents, allows us to reconstruct some of the dynamics of the earlier period. In addition, this article presents two sets of ordinances from 1658 and 1672, discovered through research into notarial deeds, which provide further insight into the development of the community.

The structure of the Ashkenazi kehillah was shaped by three main influences. First, the founding members brought with them the administrative models of Ashkenazi communities from German-speaking regions. Second, the large and established Portuguese community served as an important model. The Portuguese *parnasim* (administrators) played a key role in the early formation of the Ashkenazi community, often acting as arbiters in internal conflicts, leading to the adoption of some Portuguese administrative practices. Third, the broader political culture of early modern Amsterdam had a significant impact. The governance and membership policies of the Ashkenazi Jewish nation mirrored many aspects of the city's own organizational structure.[15]

These influences are evident in the kehillah's membership policy. In 1639, the 500 or so Ashkenazi Jews who made up the nascent community enjoyed

13 Sluys, "Hoogduits-Joods Amsterdam", 319–325.

14 *Takkanot ha-kehillah de-kahal Ashkenazim de-K"K Amstilredam*, Amsterdam, 1711.

15 Elisheva Carlebach likewise stresses the extent to which urban governance shaped the structure of Jewish communal leadership: E. Carlebach, "The Early Modern Jewish Community and Its Instititutions" in Karp and Sutcliffe, *The Early Modern World,* 168–198, there 172.

equal status, with both active and passive voting rights, and together they built the community's institutions. However, it was soon decided that newcomers would be subject to restrictions. By 1641, newcomers had to pay a membership fee of three guilders to gain full status. This development created a system of tiered membership: full members who had inherited membership or bought in, and other residents who lacked the means to do so.[16]

This tiered structure closely mirrored that of the Portuguese community and the social stratification of Amsterdam itself. The Portuguese community had developed a policy that divided its members by ethnicity: only fully Sephardic Jews could become *yehidim* (full members), with full political rights and the ability to hold religious honours. Jews of other origins, such as Italians, were called *congregantes*, with limited rights. Until the establishment of the Ashkenazi kehillah in 1639, Ashkenazim were neither *yehidim* nor *congregantes*, but rather "foreigners" on the margins of the community.[17]

The Ashkenazi kehillah adopted a similar membership model, but based it on socio-economic status rather than ethnicity, reflecting the social hierarchy of the city. Amsterdam distinguished between the *poorters* – long-established residents who were entitled to civic benefits – and *ingezetenen* – residents who lived in the city without political rights.[18] In the Ashkenazi community, the *yehidim* (full members) were the founding families and their descendants, while newcomers had to pay increasingly high fees to join. By the end of the eighteenth century, only about 20 percent of Ashkenazim were full members. The second group, the *toshavim* (residents), made up the majority of the community. While they could live in Amsterdam and contribute to the kehillah, they had no political rights, could not rent pews in the synagogue, and were buried in the less prestigious Zeeburg cemetery (from 1714 onwards). The *orehim* (foreigners), who had no rights within the community, were also buried at Zeeburg.[19]

The administrative structure of the Ashkenazi kehillah initially followed the classical Ashkenazi model, which had its roots in the Middle Ages. The leadership consisted of a board of *memunim* (later called *parnasim*) and various religious functionaries. In the early stages, the boundaries between lay and reli-

16 Sluys, "Hoogduits-Joods Amsterdam", 311.

17 Swetschinski, *Reluctant Cosmopolitans*, 188.

18 E. Kuijpers and M. Prak, "Burger, ingezetene, vreemdeling: burgerschap in Amsterdam in de 17e en 18e eeuw" in J. Kloek and K. Tilmans, *Burger. Een geschiedenis van het begrip 'burger' in de Nederlanden van de Middeleeuwen tot de 21ste eeuw*, Amsterdam, 2002, 113–132.

19 B. Wallet, *Zeeburg. Geschiedenis van een joodse begraafplaats 1714–2014*, Hilversum, 2014, 119–122.

gious leadership were fluid, with individuals often holding multiple roles. For example, a *hazzan* (cantor) could also serve as a *parnas*, and some *memunim* acted as rabbis. Over time, however, the distinction between lay and religious leadership became more pronounced. Unlike many other Ashkenazi communities, where rabbis wielded considerable administrative influence and sometimes served as community presidents, the Amsterdam kehillah, following the Portuguese model, separated rabbis from lay leadership.[20] Rabbis were appointed and paid by the board, which increasingly viewed them as employees. Nevertheless, the rabbis retained authority in halachic matters, leading to frequent conflicts with the *parnasim* over jurisdiction, especially with rabbis accustomed to greater administrative influence in other communities.[21]

The election of the *memunim* was initially democratic, in keeping with medieval Ashkenazi tradition. From a pool of 15 candidates, the *yehidim* chose three *memunim*, two *gabba'e tsedakah* (charity treasurers) and two *gabba'e bikkur holim* (health treasurers). Three notables were also chosen to advise the board on complex matters, and in the event of a tie, the rabbi cast the deciding vote. In 1648, however, this democratic system gave way to an electoral college of 25 members chosen by the rabbi, who then chose seven to make the final decision on appointments. By 1656, the rabbi's role in the election was removed, and the system became oligarchic. New *parnasim* were chosen twice a year, at Sukkot and Pesach, from a list of 18 candidates chosen by the community elite, with the final selection made by lot. Only the wealthiest and most prominent members, who were married and had lived in Amsterdam for at least three years, were eligible for leadership positions.[22]

By 1641, the number of *parnasim* had grown from three to five, with a rotating presidency, with one of them serving as '*parnas* of the month'. This system, which was also used in other Ashkenazi communities, mirrored the rotating mayoral system of Amsterdam. Over time, the governance of the kehillah became increasingly oligarchic, mirroring the political system of the city, with a few influential families dominating leadership positions. The appointment procedures for new *parnasim* and burgomasters became strikingly similar.[23]

---

20 J.R. Berkovitz, *Jewish Community, Religion, and Family in Early Modern Metz*, Leiden, 2020, 106–108.

21 Carlebach, "Early Modern Jewish Community", 174–175; D.B. Ruderman, *Early Modern Jewry. A New Cultural History*, Princeton-Oxford, 2010, 57–98.

22 Sluys, "Hoogduits-Joods Amsterdam", 311–312, 318.

23 M. Hell, "De Oude Geuzen en de Opstand. Politiek en lokaal bestuur in tijd van oorlog en expansie 1578–1650" in W. Frijhoff and M. Prak (eds.), *Geschiedenis van Amsterdam. Centrum van de wereld 1578–1650*, Amsterdam, 2004, 241–297, there 242–260.

TABLE 9.1 *Parnasim* of the Amsterdam Ashkenazi community, 1656–1687. (Sources: notarial deeds and Sluys, "Hoogduits-Joods Amsterdam").

1656	1661	1670	1677	1681	1687
Mordechai ben Abraham	Salomon Jacobs	Isaac Cohen	Abraham Isaacs	Isaac Samuel Cohen	Moses Yehuda Kalonymus Cohen
Raphael ben Yehiel Michael de Membroe	Jacob from Emden	Zadok Perelsheim	Edenraed Isaacs	Levy Abrahams	Joseph Ruben Yehuda
R. Joseph ben Abraham Jacob	Maier Chaim	R. Joseph Polak	Abraham Jacobsz Levy Marcus Coppels	Abraham Arons	Menachem Mendel Samuels
David ben Alexander	Asar Asarsz	Alexander Süskind ben Bermen	Joachim Joannes Joseph Cohen	Isaac Pinchas	Abraham Jacob Levy Mantspagh
Isaac ben Jacob	Isaac Benjamin	Naftali Herz Cohen	Joseph Salomons	Jacob Ruben Magnus	

Little is known about the identity of the *parnasim* in the seventeenth-century Ashkenazi community, although some names have been traced through notarial deeds from 1656 to 1687.[24] A few came from places such as Membroe (Mönchberg in Bavaria) and Emden, and most were embedded in translocal Ashkenazi trading networks. Despite growing oligarchic tendencies, the diversity of names suggests that social mobility remained possible in the seventeenth century, unlike the more stratified eighteenth century, when administrative roles became more concentrated in a few powerful families (Table 9.1).[25]

24 Some background on the first generation of *parnasim* is given in: D.M. Sluys, "De wederwaardigheden van de Oudste Parnassijns der Hoogduitsche-Joodsche Gemeente te Amsterdam (1635–1660)" in *Orde van den dienst ter gelegenheid van de plechtige herdenking van het 300-jarig bestaan der Hoogduitsch-Joodse gemeente*, Amsterdam, 1935, 1–21.

25 E. Tal, *Ha-Kehilah ha-Ashkenazit be-Amsṭerdam ba-me'ah ha-18*, Jerusalem, 2010.

4 The Ordinances of 1658 and 1672

Two sets of ordinances relating to the internal governance of the Ashkenazi community and the authority of the *parnasim* are preserved in the notarial deeds. These ordinances begin with an important preamble: "The Parnasim, in agreement with the Congregation, have decided to make ordinances according to the customs observed by all Ashkenazi Jews in Germany and Poland, as is customary in Israel".[26] The phrase "Germany and Poland" (*Ashkenaz u-Polin*, in Hebrew) was commonly used to emphasize the common traditions of Ashkenazi Jews, but in the context of Amsterdam in 1658, it clearly reflects an effort by the *parnasim* to integrate the newly arrived Polish refugees into their community. However, as noted above, this effort was not immediately successful, and a separate Polish community was eventually established.[27]

The ordinances of 2 November 1658 consisted of five articles.[28] The first article dealt with members who had been given a mitzvah (a function of honour) in the synagogue. The custom required them to make a charitable donation after Shabbat to one of the funds established by the congregation. Those who failed to pay would be warned three times, and if they persisted they would be excommunicated. The second article applied the same standard to members who were summoned by the *shammash* (sexton) to appear before the *parnasim*, and who refused to comply after three reminders. The third article concerned the rent for synagogue pews, which was collected twice a year. Again, members who failed to pay after three reminders faced excommunication, except in cases of financial hardship. The fourth article concerned the regulation of ritual slaughter, which the congregation had organized since 1641. Members were forbidden to slaughter or sell meat independently; these activities were permitted only through the congregation's official slaughterhouse. As with the other articles, excommunication followed after three warnings. The final article dealt with disturbances during synagogue services: anyone who caused a disturbance against a *parnas* or any other person and persisted in such behaviour would be excluded from the community. This rule was apparently necessary, as notarial records document numerous public quarrels in the synagogue. In one case, in 1694, Elias Jacobsz is reported to have cursed the *Parnasim* without provocation, calling them

26 Municipal Archives Amsterdam, Notaries (inv. 5075), 4091, notary (not.) Dirck van der Groe, 2 Nov. 1658.

27 For the regulations of the Polish community, see: Y.D. Markon, "The Bylaws of the Polish Jewish Community of Amsterdam of 1672" [Hebrew] in *Tsiyunim. Collected Articles in Memory of Y.N. Simchoni*, Berlin, 1929, 161–167.

28 Ibid.

"evil men, unholy beasts, atheists".[29] The document confirms that these five ordinances were read to the entire congregation and accepted by all members.

On 23 December 1672, a supplementary set of regulations was passed, reaffirming the five articles of 1658 and adding two further provisions.[30] The first stipulated that the proceeds of the kosher meat market were to be used exclusively for the relief of the poor. This decision was crucial, as the continuing influx of impoverished migrants from Central and Eastern Europe had dramatically increased the community's need for charitable support. The kosher meat market provided the administrators of the *Kupat Tsedakah* (Poor Relief Fund) with a vital source of income for these efforts. The second provision elaborated on the third article of 1658: members who failed to pay for their synagogue seats would forfeit them, and the seats would be resold. For many members, pews were a financial asset. Seats were often bequeathed in wills or used as collateral in financial transactions.[31] In one notable case, the mother of Abraham Arons, a former *parnas* in 1681, attempted to sell two men's and one women's pews in 1685, after she was widowed. Although the sale was announced in the synagogue, as was customary, Arons himself intervened to prevent the second announcement and opposed his mother's plan to liquidate the seats.[32]

The ordinances of 1658 and 1672 illustrate the increasing regulation and professionalization of the kehillah under the leadership of the *parnasim*. They also reveal the growing authority of the *parnasim*, which they enforced through sanctions, including the threat of excommunication – their most severe measure.[33] As the ordinances explicitly state, excommunication meant exclusion not only from the Ashkenazi community, but also from the city of Amsterdam itself. This sanction underlines the considerable power wielded by the *parnasim*. As administrators of the High-German Jewish nation, they were given the authority by the city to govern their own community, with the city enforcing the sanctions they imposed.

29 Municipal Archives Amsterdam, Notaries (inv. 5075), 4167, not. Dirck van der Groe, 5 April 1694.

30 Municipal Archives Amsterdam, Notaries (inv. 5075), 4091, not. Dirck van der Groe, 23 Dec. 1672.

31 Municipal Archives Amsterdam, Notaries (inv. 5075), 4243, not. Gerrit van der Groe, 25 Nov. 1691; 4169, not. Dirck van der Groe, 30 Aug. 1694.

32 Municipal Archives Amsterdam, Notaries (inv. 5075), 4117, not. Dirck van der Groe, 24 Oct. 1685.

33 On how the Ashkenazi community used its disciplinary powers in the eighteenth century, see: T. Rädecker, *Schuld en boete in Joods Amsterdam: kerktucht bij de Hoogduitse joodse gemeente 1737–1764*, Amsterdam, 2012.

5 Functioning of Internal Courts

The duties of the *parnasim* were wide-ranging, encompassing the governance of their community and the maintenance of internal order. Their responsibilities included organizing synagogue services, providing kosher food, Jewish education and care for the poor. In addition, they performed a legal function about which little is known.[34] An analysis of notarial records provides insight into aspects of their role as judges in the seventeenth century.

Within the Ashkenazi community, there were three legal channels. First, the *parnasim* acted as lay administrators and judges; second, the rabbis acted as religious judges; and third, individual members could be called upon to mediate in conflicts. For the rabbis, legal decisions were based on *halacha*. The *parnasim*, on the other hand, had more flexibility: they could rely on *halacha*, but also on customary law and common sense. The boundaries between the jurisdictions of the *parnasim* and the rabbinate were fluid, with both seeking to extend their influence. This struggle reflected wider debates within the Ashkenazi world in the early modern period, where many communities saw the influence of the *parnasim* growing at the expense of the rabbinate.[35]

Many cases recorded in notarial documents concern arbitration. In such cases, the two parties could choose to go to the *parnasim*, or they could request that authoritative figures (referred to as "good men") adjudicate. One example is a dispute in 1669 between Philips Levi and Nathaniel Cohen, both of whom served in the synagogue as *levi* and *kohen*, respectively. Having served in this capacity for thirty years, Levi was outraged when Cohen attempted to discredit him within the congregation. Levi proposed that the conflict be resolved by an ad hoc tribunal of impartial men chosen by both parties.[36] Typically, each side would choose one judge and both would agree on a third. Any respected Jewish man with sufficient authority could serve as a judge, and in practice these individuals were often knowledgeable in halachic matters, although they did not have to be rabbis.

An example of an ad hoc arbitration decision dates from 1686, when Elias Salomons and Isaac Abrahams brought a business dispute to Rabbi Moses Juda Cohen and two 'good men', Joseph Ruben and Menachem Samuels.

---

34 One of the most comprehesive analyses of the legal organization of an early modern Ashkenazi kehillah is Berkovitz' study on Metz: Berkovitz, *Law's Dominion.*

35 Berkovitz, *Law's Dominion*, 109–112.

36 Municipal Archives Amsterdam, Notaries (inv. 5075), 2231, not. Adriaen Lock, 14 Oct. 1669.

They ruled that Salomons should pay Abrahams 575 guilders, but Abrahams had to travel to Dunkirk to collect the goods and deliver them to Salomons.[37]

The norm within the Ashkenazi community was that internal disputes should be resolved through these legal channels. However, not all members adhered to this practice. Some sought resolution in the general Dutch courts, creating a degree of 'legal shopping', whereby individuals chose the legal system that seemed most favourable to them. For matters involving the congregation in the general courts, the congregation employed a lawyer, Samuel Palache.[38]

In conflicts between Jews and non-Jews, notarial records show that in some cases both parties submitted to the judgement of the Jewish community. For example, the non-Jewish Gregorius van der Gilt and the Frankfurt Jew Jacob Mathijsz jointly purchased a bale of ginger from David Pinto, which turned out to be of poor quality. When Mathijsz left, Van der Gilt and Pinto took their dispute to the 'good men' in the synagogue. The result was that the ginger was returned to Pinto and the money refunded.[39]

The *parnasim* did not hesitate to meddle in the private lives of Amsterdam Ashkenazim. For instance, they mediated in the marital dispute of Manuel Davids and Belijtje Liefmans Cohen. This arbitration was successful, but to guarantee that in time, it was stipulated that Davids would deposit 1,000 guilders with his wife's uncle. That was the amount of money his wife had contributed at the time of the marriage. The uncle, Isaac Cohen, ensured that money was provided from this sum for Belijtje's upkeep. After a year and a half, the *parnasim* and the rabbi would decide whether the arrangement should be extended, or whether Davids would get the money back. If it did come to a divorce, Davids had to promise to deliver a *get* (letter of divorce).[40]

The Ashkenazi *parnasim* also occasionally summoned Portuguese Jews who had wronged members of their community. One such case involved David de Solis, who was accused of using loaded dice to cause significant financial loss to

37 Municipal Archives Amsterdam, Notaries (inv. 5075), 4121, not. Dirck van der Groe, 31 May 1686.

38 Municipal Archives Amsterdam, Notaries (inv. 5075), 4107, not. Dirck van der Groe, 3 Sept. 1682.

39 Municipal Archives Amsterdam, Notaries (inv. 5075), 2202, not. Adriaen Lock, 24 April 1657.

40 Municipal Archives Amsterdam, Notaries (inv. 5075), 4137, not. Dirck van der Groe, 16 Febr. 1699.

an Ashkenazi Jew. The *parnasim* successfully forced De Solis to confess to his fraudulent actions.[41]

While the *parnasim* wielded authority within their own community, their influence informally extended beyond it. As the Ashkenazi community in Amsterdam grew, it became an important centre of Jewish life, and other Jewish communities looked to the Amsterdam *parnasim* and rabbis for guidance. Smaller Jewish communities around Amsterdam accepted the authority of the *parnasim*. For example, two Jews from Muiden sought their judgement in a dispute over the guardianship of Jewish children. Failure to comply with the *parnasim*'s ruling would result in a fine payable to both the Dutch Reformed Church deaconry and the Ashkenazi poor fund.[42] The Amsterdam *parnasim* also intervened in cases involving Jewish communities throughout the Dutch Republic. In 1687, a serious conflict divided the *parnasim* and the rabbi of the Ashkenazi community in Rotterdam, prompting them to seek a solution in Amsterdam. The Amsterdam *parnasim* took the matter seriously, even sending their sextons to Rotterdam to gather testimony.[43]

In addition to the justice administered by the *parnasim* and 'good men', the Ashkenazi community also had a *beth din*, or rabbinical court. Until 1676, the *beth din* was convened on an ad hoc basis, with the chief rabbi serving as *av beth din* (head of the court) alongside other rabbis or halachically knowledgeable figures. After 1676, the rapid growth of the community necessitated a permanent *beth din*, with the chief rabbi and his assistants presiding over cases.[44] This court dealt with matters that fell within the exclusive jurisdiction of the rabbis, such as divorce. In 1677, for example, the *beth din* granted a divorce to Arent Abrahamsz and Brania Levij after nine years of bitter quarrel. Despite cooling-off periods, the marriage remained irreparable, and the rabbis decided to end it.[45]

While the *beth din* dealt primarily with halachically mandated cases, it also occasionally dealt with economic disputes that could have been overseen by the *parnasim*. In these cases, the choice of legal authority was left to the disputing parties. One example is the commercial dispute between Michiel

41 Municipal Archives Amsterdam, Notaries (inv. 5075), 4075, not. Dirck van der Groe, 29 Dec. 1672.

42 Municipal Archives Amsterdam, Notaries (inv. 5075), 4084, not. Dirck van der Groe, 1 Febr. 1677.

43 Municipal Archives Amsterdam, Notaries (inv. 5075), 4128, not. Dirck van der Groe, 12 Aug. 1687.

44 Sluys, "Hoogduits-Joods Amsterdam", 340.

45 Municipal Archives Amsterdam, Notaries (inv. 5075), 4085, not. Dirck van der Groe, 13 Sept. 1677.

FIGURE 9.2 Carel Frederik Bendorp, *De Hoochduitse synagogue* (c. 1790) – Rijksmuseum Amsterdam, BI-B-FM-116-7

Worms and the Portuguese Jew Abraham de Luna Montalto (also known as Abraham Segenberch), which was brought before the rabbis of the High-German Jewish Nation. Both parties agreed in advance to abide by the court's decision.[46]

6 Challenges to Communal Autonomy

The municipal authorities and the Portuguese *parnasim* played an important role in shaping the Ashkenazi community. This was partly due to the status of the Portuguese community as the de facto parent community of the Ashkenazi community, as well as its stronger links within local political structures. However, as the analysis of notarial deeds shows, municipal interference and Portuguese intervention often arose from internal conflicts within the Ashkenazi community or from the demands of its *parnasim* or dissenting members. This is in line with Jay R. Berkovitz's observations of the Jewish commu-

46 Municipal Archives Amsterdam, Notaries (inv. 5075), 4082, not. Dirck van der Groe, 2 April 1676.

nity in Metz, where governmental involvement also resulted from internal dynamics.[47]

An illustrative case is the conflict between Levi Binge and Levi Wolff – known in Yiddish as "die beide Leiben" – and Eleazar Moses Worms and the *parnasim*. The dispute revolved around the financing of a new synagogue on the Houtgracht and escalated to the point where the city authorities intervened. They referred the matter to the Portuguese *parnasim*, who decided that "die beide Leiben" should stand in the next election, thus ensuring that both factions were represented on the board. In 1654, "die beide Leiben" reminded the incumbent *parnasim* of this arrangement.[48]

The Portuguese *parnasim* were not always allies of their Ashkenazi counterparts. They deliberately undermined the Ashkenazi community by supporting the creation of a separate Polish community.[49] A clear violation of communal autonomy occurred when the Portuguese attempted to bury their dead free of charge at the Ashkenazi cemetery at Muiderberg. They claimed this right on the basis of a loan of 300 guilders made at the time of the purchase of the cemetery. In 1676, when the Portuguese wanted to bury the child of a poor Ashkenazi Jew employed by their community, the Ashkenazim protested. The Portuguese escalated their demands, attempting to recover the loan and claim all of the cemetery's income. But the *parnasim*, led by Zadok Salomons, quickly repaid the loan and firmly reasserted their community's independence.[50]

Challenges to the community's autonomy also came from within. Members of the community often denounced the *parnasim*, although the reasons for such actions were not always clear. In 1682, for example, Conssel van Witmond and Joseph Cohen publicly insulted the *parnas* Abraham Levij in the middle of Dam Square, calling him a "soul-seller" and a thief – accusations that echoed inside the synagogue.[51] Similarly, in 1689, the *parnasim* were accused of pressuring a witness to withhold incriminating testimony, threatening to expel him from the community and ostracize his family if he refused.[52]

47 Berkovitz, *Law's Dominion*, 99–103.

48 Sluys, "Hoogduits-Joods Amsterdam", 317–318; Municipal Archives Amsterdam, Notaries (inv. 5075), 2197, not. Adriaen Lock, 15 Sept. 1654.

49 Sluys, "Hoogduits-Joods Amsterdam", 322.

50 Municipal Archives Amsterdam, Notaries (inv. 5075), 4082, not. Dirck van der Groe, 5 Febr. 1676.

51 Municipal Archives Amsterdam, Notaries (inv. 5075), 4103, not. Dirck van der Groe, 17 Sept. 1682; 4103, not. Dirck van der Groe, 17 Nov. 1682.

52 Municipal Archives Amsterdam, Notaries (inv. 5075), 4749, not. David Staffmaker Varlet, 11 Nov. 1689.

These incidents illustrate the many forces that undermined the authority of the *parnasim*. While the Portuguese *parnasim* sought to maintain control over the Ashkenazi community, internal divisions were the latter's greatest vulnerability. As a result, the authority of the *parnasim* was often challenged from within, with members sometimes appealing to external authorities, including the municipal authorities and the Portuguese *parnasim*, to win their plea.

7 Conclusion

In the seventeenth century, a rapidly expanding Ashkenazi community emerged alongside the established Portuguese community. The organization of this new community represented a synthesis of traditional Ashkenazi, Portuguese and urban models of governance. In the administration of the High-German Jewish Nation and the development of its membership policies, the community increasingly mirrored the urban political culture. The governance structure evolved from a relatively democratic model to a more oligarchic one, adopting an appointment procedure similar to that of the burgomasters of Amsterdam. The influence of the Portuguese community is particularly evident in the positioning of the rabbi, who was kept at a distance from administrative affairs. Over time, the Ashkenazi community in the city grew into an independent 'Nation', characterized by a significant degree of communal autonomy, exemplified by its own legal system. However, this autonomy faced challenges from both external and internal pressures. The seventeenth century thus established the foundational framework for the further expansion of the Ashkenazi community in the eighteenth century, when it became a kehillah with a prominent voice in the broader translocal Jewish world. This study also underscores the importance of examining notarial records to understand the multiple ways in which early modern Jewish communities navigated the legal and social challenges they faced.

Index

Index of Persons

Index of Places

Index of Subjects

www.ingramcontent.com/pod-product-compliance
Lightning Source LLC
LaVergne TN
LVHW011216150926
848065LV00004B/31